OPPOSITION IN WESTERN EUROPE

OPPOSITION IN WESTERN EUROPE

Edited by Eva Kolinsky

ST. MARTIN'S PRESS
New York

© 1987 Eva Kolinsky
All rights reserved. For information, write:
Scholarly & Reference Division,
St. Martin's Press, Inc., 175 Fifth Avenue, New York, NY 10010
First published in the United States of America in 1987
Printed in Great Britain
ISBN 0-312-00472-9

Library of Congress Cataloging in Publication Data

Opposition in Western Europe.

  Bibliography: p.
  Includes index.
  1. Political parties — European economic
  community countries. 3. Opposition (political
  science) — European economic community countries.
  I. Kolinsky, Eva.
  JN94.A979073 1987 324'.094 86-31582
  ISBN 0-312-00472-9

Printed and bound in Great Britain

CONTENTS

Contents

LIST OF CONTRIBUTORS

Grant Amyot is Assistant Professor of Political Science at Queens University, Kingston, Ontario.

Klaus von Beyme is Professor of Political Science at the University of Heidelberg.

David Capitanchik is Senior Lecturer in Politics at Aberdeen University.

Byron Criddle is Senior Lecturer in Politics at Aberdeen University.

David Denver is Lecturer in Politics at the University of Lancaster.

Ken Gladdish is Senior Lecturer in Politics at the University of Reading.

Jean Grugel is a Researcher at the Latin American Bureau in London.

Eva Kolinsky is Senior Lecturer in German and Director of German Studies at Aston University.

William E. Paterson is Reader in German Politics at Warwick University.

Benny Pollack is Lecturer in Southern European and Latin American Politics at the University of Liverpool.

Geoffrey Pridham is Reader in European Politics at Bristol University.

Peter Pulzer is Gladstone Professor of Government and Public Administration at Oxford University.

Gordon Smith is Professor of Government at the London School of Economics and Political Science.

Michalina Vaughan is Professor of Sociology at the University of Lancaster.

Douglas Webber is a Research Fellow in Politics at Sussex University.

PREFACE

I am very glad that the European Centre for Political Studies has been able to provide a framework for the planning, discussion, and publication of Eva Kolinsky's important study of opposition.

The central purpose of the Centre, which has been generously supported by the European Cultural Foundation since 1978, is to study the functioning of democratic political institutions. This has often led the Centre and its collaborators to analyse aspects of the exercise of power: in studying, for instance, the problems of governments based on majority coalitions, or the organisation of policy advice at the top levels of government. The present work invites readers to turn their attention to a rather different, but perhaps even more vital, dimension of the political life of democracies: the role and status of their opposition parties and forces.

As Eva Kolinsky and her co-authors demonstrate, the nature and implications of 'opposition' have changed in many subtle and significant ways in the years since earlier studies of the phenomenon appeared. I should like to offer warm thanks not only to the editor for her enterprise in planning and directing the work, but also to all the colleagues and participants who have contributed to its successful conclusion.

Roger Morgan

ACKNOWLEDGEMENTS

The keen support by the Head of the European Centre for Political Studies, Roger Morgan, has steered this volume from a first idea on charting the neglected territory of opposition to the completed book. The Policy Studies Institute hosted a two-day conference in November 1985 where contributors submitted draft chapters to rigorous discussion, chaired admirably by Peter Pulzer and Roger Morgan. The chapters in this volume have been revised in the light of these discussions, to incorporate common perspectives without following a prescribed focus.

Research grants from the Nuffield Foundation and Aston University, and a conference grant from the Economic and Social Research Council, supported the project financially. Yet it could not have taken shape without the untiring and expert assistance of Amanda Trafford at PSI and Carol Gilbert at Aston University; the editorial skills of Margaret Cornell at PSI; the advice and helpful suggestions by Dennis Ager, Malcolm Anderson, Vernon Bogdanor, Martin Kolinsky and Vincent Wright; and, of course, the goodwill and commitment of all the contributors to the book and the conference on Opposition in Western Europe.

Eva Kolinsky

INTRODUCTION

Eva Kolinsky

Opposition has never been in the limelight of political analysis. Its fate could be compared to that of the loser in a cup final: media attention turns to the victorious team and expects everything for the future from those who proved themselves capable of winning. The real test of strength would be a victory next time round and an ascent from opposition to government.

The study of government, electoral processes and party systems - to name just a few major themes of political research - has contributed to defining the parameters of political authority and decision-making in contemporary democracies. Opposition still begs for recognition as an agent of political change and innovation inside and outside parliaments and parties. As an essential component of political democracy, opposition has, of course, been well recognised. The absence of opposition tends to be seen as proof that a political system is not democratic, and attempts to shackle or outlaw opposition have been the hallmark of repressive or authoritarian regimes.(1) By the same token, the existence of opposition implies the existence of a democratic political order where some or all conflicts of interests and aspirations in society can be articulated. In short, opposition is at the core of party democracy and the study of opposition in the democratic process warrants more than a place in the second division of politics.

It is an elusive topic. Perceptions of opposition differ with the socio-political standpoint and between societies. Opinion polls have frequently found that more people claim to have voted for the government in the most recent

1

election than would tally with the actual result.
People who say they voted for the opposition are
more often dissatisfied with their socio-economic
situation and expect a bleak political future;
those who support the victorious party are more
likely to radiate optimism on both counts. These
perceptions do not appear to be determined by
specific policy issues, expectations or disappoint-
ments.

Across countries, the nature of opposition and
its effect on the political process are no less
contradictory. In the British political tradition,
for instance, opposition enjoys equal legitimacy
with the government as the voice of criticism,
political alternatives and parliamentary control.
A majority of West Germans and Dutch expect opposition to support the government, and not to
challenge the political consensus with contrastive
policies; in France and Spain, opposition has
tended to question the legitimacy of the system
itself - albeit for different reasons - while in
Italy opposition draws on certain social strata and
regions as a source of strength and political
influence.

The ultimate goal for opposition in all
democracies must be to influence mainstream
politics and the policy priorities in a given
country. If the 'site' of opposition is a
political party, such influence would mean becoming
the governing party or entering a coalition government. Duverger has already noted that the step
from opposition to government tends to have a
mellowing effect on partisan policies and programmes.(2) The reverse effect - going into
opposition from a position in government - has been
studied for individual political parties and for
individual countries. Responses to opposition have
varied considerably between countries and parties;
but in all cases, the move into opposition provoked
some innovation and adjustments. In Britain,
France and West Germany, and across the political
spectrum, the transition from government to opposition led to a search for a new leader; conservative
parties in opposition tended to place an often
unprecedented emphasis on party organisation, while
parties of the left have been faced with walking
the tight-rope between interest politics for the
working class or its modern equivalents and
broadening their appeal to attract ideologically
open new middle-class voters.

2

Introduction

When Dahl and his teams of collaborators compared oppositions in Western democracies, some twenty years after World War II, the integration of disparate electorates into mainstream political parties and the parliamentarisation of opposition were the major characteristics of party democracies and the yardsticks of opposition. Since then, two things have changed: firstly, parties which were in government at the time have become opposition, or sometimes again the governing party or a member of a coalition government. Alternations have occurred in Britain, France, Holland, and West Germany, and a change of system from authoritarianism to party democracy in Spain; in Italy, the major opposition party has not yet had a taste of government. The sample of countries for detailed discussion in this volume was designed to include a variety of party democracies with contrasting patterns of opposition and government/opposition alternation in order to evaluate the effects of opposition on policies, parliaments and parties.

The second change since Dahl concerns new 'sites' of opposition outside parliaments. Socio-economic changes in advanced industrial societies and a shift of cleavage lines have reduced the poignancy of partisan politics. As centripetal forces gained ground across Western Europe, opposition parties adopted more consensual positions.(3) At the same time, issues gained salience in society without being articulated in or through established parties. New parties focused on these issues and some were able to attract enough voters to enter parliament and even participate in government after the briefest of gestation periods. The twin effects of partisan de-alignment and issue politics diversified democratic politics, and also opposition. Ecology parties, for instance, emerged in most countries with a dual message of environmental protection and a re-orientation of economic priorities. In Holland and Italy, such parties became parliamentary oppositions; in West Germany, representation in several parliaments and a first coalition at <u>Land</u> level point to a significant new factor of contemporary politics; in France and Britain, the issues have surfaced without gathering much momentum or producing politically viable parties.

The diversity of opposition has become even more apparent in extra-parliamentary movements. Since the student movements of the late 1960s, a

3

number of social movements campaigned as correctives to the policies of government and opposition on nuclear energy, the role of women in society, environmentalism, or the deployment of nuclear missiles in NATO member states, to name some of the more volatile issues. The size of such movements and their linkage with parliamentary opposition vary from country to country. In France and Italy, for instance, existing parties have managed to contain and incorporate the new social movements, although France witnessed an upsurge of extremism on the right. In Holland and West Germany, extra-parliamentary movements emerged as a temporary political force which challenged existing parties into policy adjustments. In West Germany, the movements also activated political forces intent on a transformative change of the political system itself. In Britain, comparable pressures on parliamentary politics emanated from the trade-union sector and Labour-controlled local government at a time when parliamentary opposition seemed emasculated in the face of overwhelming government majority. In Spain, the 'sites' of extra-parliamentary opposition relate to the unsettled process of democratic integration and the parliamentarisation of politics.

While national scenarios differ, extra-parliamentary opposition has introduced a new dynamism into opposition across Western Europe as a catalyst of political innovation and the articulation of new issues at parliamentary level. Opposition in contemporary democracies today means opposition inside and outside parliament, with the linkage of the two levels a significant dimension.

The new diversity of opposition determined the shape of the present volume. Faced with Hobson's choice of covering a larger number of countries - Portugal, the Scandinavian democracies, Switzerland and Austria, for instance, all have distinctive patterns of opposition and distinctive traditions of democratic governemnt - or exploring fewer in more depth, the latter course seemed better suited to give ample attention to the changes in parliamentary opposition since Dahl, and the changing function of opposition outside parliament in national and cross-national perspective.

4

Introduction

The Structure of the Book

The conceptual parameters of analysing opposition
are explored in Part I, which contributes towards a
theory of opposition in contemporary democracies.
In the light of the changed dynamics of parliamentary and extra-parliamentary opposition, Peter
Pulzer reflects on the impact of political change
on the role of opposition and the categories
applied to analyse it (Chapter 1). Klaus von Beyme
traces co-operative tendencies of parliamentary
opposition across Europe, and the overlap of the
government/opposition roles in political environments where federal structures, coalition governments or consensus politics play an important part.
A new flexibility of the political process brought
new and possibly short-lived parties into parliaments (Chapter 2). Gordon Smith examines the
constraints placed upon party democracies by extra-
parliamentary opposition and 'new politics'.
Oscillating between accommodative and transformative goals, extra-parliamentary movements and their
linkage with parliamentary opposition produced new
ambiguities as they altered the balance of
influence between majorities and minorities on
policy articulation in parties, parliaments, and
governments (Chapter 3).
   Part II evaluates the state of opposition in
particular countries. For Britain, David Denver
shows the transition from two-party alternation
towards multi-partism. While voting preferences
point to a range of oppositions, the electoral
system still favours the two-party mode, and
parliamentary practice still assumes that only one
opposition party faces the government. Thus
opposition in Britain is characterised by a
disparity between political orientations in society
and their representation through parliamentary
opposition (Chapter 4). In France and Italy, by
contrast, polarised multi-party systems have begun
to develop consensual and centripetal politics.
Byron Criddle emphasises the integrative function
of the presidency in France and evaluates the
effect on consensual politics of the new juxtaposition of a Socialist President and a parliamentary majority and Prime Minister from the political
Right (Chapter 5). Geoffrey Pridham concentrates
on the modifications in the Italian Communist Party
of anti-system opposition in response to socio-
economic changes. If a government/opposition

5

alternation were at all possible in Italy, it would
build on co-operation and coalition rather than
confrontation (Chapter 7). For West Germany,
William Paterson and Douglas Webber argue that
parliamentary opposition has become more contrastive after government alternations in 1969 and
again in 1982, while substantive opposition had
virtually disappeared in the 1960s. Parliamentary
opposition in West Germany has pursued a dual
strategy. In parliamentary decisions, a high
degree of consensus seemed to prevail although
opposition presented more overt alternatives
through plenary debates, the second chamber, the
Constitutional Court, and in programme formulation
(Chapter 6). In the Netherlands, centre-based
politics and multi-partism go hand in hand. Ken
Gladdish shows how the prospects of entering a
government coalition hold parliamentary opposition
parties to a broad consensus. Although unconventional participation has traditionally been high in
Dutch society, extra-parliamentary movements
developed little independent momentum and have fed
into various parties. Similar to West Germany, the
ability of the centre to incorporate new incentives
and issues has characterised opposition in Holland
(Chapter 8). The focus on Spain is the focus on
the consolidation of party government. Benny
Pollack and Jean Grugel discuss the emergence of
democratic parties, and the role of interest groups
and regionalists as oppositions within and against
the system. The socio-economic and political
modernisation of Spain since the early 1970s has
generated the parliamentarisation of politics and -
increasingly - the parliamentarisation of opposition (Chapter 9).

The case studies of opposition outside parliament in Part III evaluate the significance and the
limitations of such opposition in the context of
mainstream political processes and traditions.
David Capitanchik shows for Britain how oppositional functions shifted to segments of trade
unionism as the balance of forces in Parliament
demotivated a weak parliamentary opposition. New
'sites' may have been suitable to articulate socio-
political tensions at times of economic recession
and force them on to the attention of the government and the official opposition, although British
trade unions have been unable to utilise the scope
for opposition from outside Parliament (Chapter
10). Michalina Vaughan demonstrates how the far

Right in France can draw on established value orientations and facets of the political culture which have been radicalised by Le Pen and right extremism. Although proportional representation created the loophole to gain a parliamentary voice, the reservoir of extra-parliamentary opposition on the right and its cohesion with the established Right is bigger than the electoral score would suggest (Chapter 11). For West Germany, the peace movement serves as an example of issue-based extra-parliamentary movements and their potential role as catalysts of innovation. Eva Kolinsky points to the ambiguities of extra-parliamentary opposition which also served as a platform to advocate trans-formative changes and radicalised political action against the institutional framework of West German politics (Chapter 12). In Italy, where socio-economic modernisation processes in the wake of rapid industrial development would lead one to expect electoral de-alignment and a proliferation of new extra-parliamentary movements, the party/ society linkage has remained largely intact. Grant Amyot's profiles of new social movements show their capacity to articulate specific issues, their appeal to a narrow stratum of 'post-materialist' young, and their inability to remain autonomous from political parties. All have been absorbed or emulated by existing opposition parties in their search to break out of the ivory tower of permanent opposition (Chapter 13).

Notwithstanding the differences in political traditions and the diversity of opposition between countries, the integrative capacity of parliamentary parties and a new flexibility between extra-parliamentary and parliamentary politics are evident across Western Europe. The new diversity of opposition in a climate of de-alignment and receding socio-economic cleavages has tended to reinforce the centripetal forces in Western Euro-pean party democracies without altogether uprooting partisan or even terrorist challenges to the para-meters of politics in some of them.

Notes

1.   R.A. Dahl (ed), Political Oppositions in
     Western Democracies, (Yale UP, New Haven,
     Conn., 1966), p.xviii.
2.   M. Duverger, Political Parties 2nd edn,
     (Methuen, London, 1965) pp.281 ff; 412 ff.
3.   K. von Beyme, Political Parties in Western
     Democracies, (Gower, Aldershot, 1985).

PART I : CONCEPTS OF OPPOSITION

1. IS THERE LIFE AFTER DAHL?

Peter Pulzer

Robert Dahl's seminal compendium, Political Oppositions in Western Democracies, is now twenty years
old. Indeed, the mid-1960s saw a flurry of
interest in opposition as an object of academic
study. The journal Government and Opposition had
been launched a year earlier. Ghita Ionescu's and
Isabel de Madariaga's Opposition(1) appeared in
1968. There were good reasons for the sudden
flurry of interest. By the mid-1960s the post-war
constitutional and party structures of Europe had
stabilised and the time seemed ripe for an evaluation. There was a growth in the comparative study
of party systems, especially from the point of view
of the cultural and sociological pre-conditions for
civilised political life, as exemplified by Almond
and Verba's The Civic Culture, Lipset and Rokkan's
Party Systems and Voter Alignments and Arend Lijphart's classic case-study of consociationalism,
The Politics of Accommodation.(2) All these works
addressed three types of questions: what determines
the cleavage structures in different types of
societies; how enduring are these structures and
why; what effect do the answers to those questions
have on the way political forces co-operate and co-
exist in a society? They were less concerned with
the mechanics of political institutions and organisation: tell me your cleavage structure and I will
tell you the state of your constitution. Though
Dahl himself paid due attention to institutional
factors, what interested him most was the 'role of
oppositions', of 'one of the greatest and most
unexpected social discoveries that man has ever
stumbled onto'.(3)
There was, however, another reason why
academic interest in oppositions burgeoned in the

1960s. Just as it looked as though the post-war world had indeed settled into a stable routine, existing institutions were challenged by the youth revolt. It began in the United States with the 'free speech' revolt at Berkeley and developed into generalised opposition to the Vietnam war. It spread to Europe where, as in America, it quickly became part of a battle of generations on an ever-widening range of issues. In West Germany it became a widespread movement under the name of the ausserparlamentarische Opposition or APO.(4) In France it culminated in the student revolt of May 1968. Here was a new radical form of opposition, which challenged not only existing political institutions but existing notions of oppositional behaviour. It exhilarated some and shocked and frightened others, but unquestionably provided a new agenda for students of opposition.

What, then, has happened to opposition, and to our ideas about it, since the 1960s? I should like to suggest answers under four headings:

  i)   changes in the institutional framework;
 ii)   changes in patterns of opinion cleavage;
iii)   changes in patterns of party competition;
 iv)   changes in the way opinion is organised and channelled.

i) Changes in the Institutional Framework

This includes the introduction of new constitutions; changes in the electoral system; changes in the separation of powers; changes in executive-legislative relations or the organisation of the legislature; and the creation or abolition of sub-national tiers of government.

These changes have not been very numerous. The most important have been the emergence from dictatorship to parliamentary democracy of Greece, Portugal and Spain. All three adopted forms of proportional representation for the national parliament; all three reserve considerable discretionary powers to the head of state, though the prerogatives of the Greek President were curbed in 1985. The Portuguese President is directly elected; in Spain there are direct elections for four regional assemblies - Catalonia, Andalucia, Galicia and the Basque region. Both these non-parliamentary electoral contests have had some

11

effect on patterns of party competition.(5)

In countries with a continuity of parliamentary institutions, there have been even fewer
changes. The only state in which there has been a
major change in the electoral system is France,
where proportional representation was introduced
for the National Assembly elections of 1986 in
place of the two-ballot, single-member constituency
in force since the establishment of the Fifth
Republic. At the time of writing, it looks
probable that France will revert to the traditional
Fifth Republic electoral system for subsequent
elections. Two countries have introduced elected
regional councils - Italy in 1970, France in 1986 -
neither with any discernible effect on the party
system. Regionalisation of a different kind in
Belgium - considered below in Section iv - has,
however, led to a re-alignment of parties. For the
sake of completeness one should also mention the
unsuccessful attempt to provide elected assemblies
for Scotland and Wales in the United Kingdom in
1979 - a response to, rather than a cause of, a
changed pattern of opposition(6) - and the periodic
creation and abolition of elected assemblies, with,
however, minimal legislative powers, in Northern
Ireland. If any region of Europe deserves the
label that Alfred Grosser applied to France in the
Dahl volume, 'nothing but opposition', it is surely
this.

Apart from the establishment of constitutional
government in the three Mediterranean states,
therefore, few of the changes in oppositional
behaviour can be attributed to institutional
changes. How far changes in oppositional behaviour
have affected the workings of institutions remains
to be seen.

ii) Changes in Patterns of Opinion Cleavage

A great deal of scholarly work in the 1950s and
1960s emphasised the historical roots of European
party systems and the continuity, often over many
generations, of party loyalties. Otto Kirchheimer,
for instance, declared in 1957 that 'continental
European parties are the remnants of the intellectual social movements of the nineteenth century.
They have remained glued to the spots where the
ebbing energy of such movements deposited them some
decades ago.'(7) This proposition was expanded by

Is There Life After Dahl?

Lipset and Rokkan in their 'freezing' thesis: 'the party system of the 1960s reflects with few, but significant exceptions, the cleavage structures of the 1920s', which in turn owe their existence to 'the freezing of the major party alternatives in the wake of the extension of the suffrage and the mobilisation of the major sections of the new reservoirs of potential supporters'.(8)

There was much merit in this thesis. It helped to liberate the social sciences from one of their principal vices, their ahistoricism, and it helped to re-emphasise the force of institutions in fashioning opinion, something that was in danger of being ignored under the impact of the behavioural revolution. It turned electoral geography into electoral geology. But we can also now see some of its weaknesses. It somehow implied that there had been few 'critical elections', in V.O. Key's sense of the expression, since the end of World War I. Behind this was an underestimate of the impact of the Depression and, above all, of World War II on party systems. The discredit, in many European countries, of pre-war middle-class parties led to the emergence of mass Christian Democratic parties where these had previously been weak or non-existent and to the enfeeblement or disappearance of some long-established parties, such as the French Radicals, the Italian Liberals and the majority of Peasant Parties. In addition, the Left, and particularly Communist parties, emerged strengthened from the war.

It could be argued that changes in party organisation are not the equivalent of shifts in cleavage structures, and in some cases this is demonstrably so. The West German Christian Democrats, for instance, were able to take over the old Zentrum electorate en bloc. But in many cases the changes of label also made changes of allegiance possible, altering the membership of sub-cultures and shifting the divisions between them. Since the context of this discussion is the nature of political opposition, it can be said that changes in party structure, even when not accompanied by substantial changes in cleavage patterns, can have a considerable impact on the working of the political systems, as instanced by the new Christian Democratic parties after 1945. The behaviour of members of the sub-culture may therefore be affected, even though its composition remains constant. Indeed, it is a reasonable criticism of

13

the Rokkan school of political sociology that it is excessively influenced by Scandinavian experience and that its findings, while eminently applicable to the smaller democracies of North-West Europe, are not as widely valid as the original claims suggested.

A second weakness of the 'freezing' thesis is its implied determinism: once the mass electorates had been mobilised and loyalties institutionalised, there appeared to be no reason why the process should not go on for ever. Yet the great age of Rokkanism, it turned out, was also the threshold of the dissolution of inherited loyalties. No sooner was the ink dry on the Rokkanist scriptures than the process of de-alignment began in most Western European states, a process not so much of a shift in allegiances, but in their diminution; a process that could, but need not necessarily, bring about new movements and new loyalties. It has, in turn, inspired a considerable empirical and theoretical literature.(9)

The first and most obvious consequence of de-alignment is greater electoral volatility. The second and third, which directly affect the effectiveness of oppositional behaviour, arise from this volatility. On the one hand, existing parties, with an apparently secure base and a long history of stable support, may suddenly suffer rapid decline. The collapse of the British Labour Party from 48 per cent in 1966 to 28 per cent in 1983 is one example of this; the collapse of the French Communists from 21 per cent in 1978 to under 10 per cent in 1986 is another. On the other hand, it becomes easier for new parties, or even new types of parties, to establish toe-holds in the system. One example of this are territorial secession parties, like the Scottish National Party and Plaid Cymru in Britain; another are parties of integral nationalism, of which the French <u>Front National</u> is the most significant instance; a third are 'new politics' parties, like the Radicals in Italy and the Greens in West Germany. All these will be considered in greater detail below; they are mentioned now as illustrations of 'unfreezing' which, in so far as it has taken place, has had a direct impact on patterns of opposition.

There is one further element in the cleavage structure of European states that is worth noting, because it also influences the nature of oppositional behaviour. Even where particular voter

14

groups have maintained partisan loyalty, their relative strengths can change drastically. Thus religious observance is still a key indicator of political behaviour in many countries. But the level of observance has been declining, which has one of two consequences. Either the parties that depend on the support of religious voters also decline, as in the Netherlands or Italy, or they succeed in attracting new client groups, as in West Germany.

Similarly, one simple explanation for the stability of the political map lies in economic geography. Steel mills, major ports or dairy farms are where they are for good reasons, and once they are there they tend to stay there. Partisan loyalties were frozen where they were, not only by the coming of universal suffrage, but by the completion of the main phase of industrialisation. It is therefore not surprising that the geography of left-right divisions in Belgium in 1985 is not all that different from what it was in 1900. But in occupational ratios, as in religious observance, change has been quite substantial. The agricultural sector has declined drastically in Europe since World War II and there are now few European states where more than 10 per cent of the population gain their living directly from farming. More recently the older basic industries have also been shedding labour. Those who remain in these sectors may be as faithful as their fathers and grandfathers in their partisan loyalties, but their impact is diminished. Indeed, the diminution is not only quantitative but qualitative; declining numbers and changing occupational patterns have all but disintegrated the cohesive sub-cultures of the first phase of mass politics. They have been replaced by a generation of voters more instrumental in their electoral choice and more conditional in their loyalties. This, too, has affected the relationship between parties and that of parties to the system in which they operate.

iii) Changes in Patterns of Party Competition

In Western Europe since World War II we can note five basic types of party competition:

15

> two-party alternation (the 'Westminster
> model');
> moderate unpolarised pluralism;
> moderate polarised pluralism;
> extreme unpolarised pluralism;
> extreme polarised pluralism.

Readers will recognise here the criteria, though
not the exact categories, popularised by Giovanni
Sartori,(10) i.e. the number of parties, the
distances between them, their readiness to collabo-
rate with each other in government and their
willingness to recognise the legitimacy of their
rivals. However, I have added one criterion that
Sartori does not stress, namely the relationship
between elections and the formation of governments.
The evolution of each type will now be considered
in more detail.

A.   Two-party Alternation

This type, characteristic of much of the history of
Britain since the 1860s, rests on strictly competitive electoral and parliamentary political rules,
strong acceptance of the legitimacy of the constitutional status quo, and an approximate equality of
opportunity of victory. In the period between the
end of World War II and the election of Mrs
Thatcher in 1979, there had been five alternations
of power, each major party had held office for
seventeen years and neither major party had gained
more than 50 per cent of the vote or, except in
1974 and 1979, less than 40 per cent. Though
Anglo-Saxon writers have until recently almost
unquestioningly accepted the Westminster model as
the ideal type of parliamentary government, and
many continental observers have echoed this sentiment, Britain remains the only major European
example of this type.

However, some things have changed since the
1960s. The first is that it is now rather misleading to think of Britain in terms of a two-party
system, at least as far as electoral preferences
are concerned. The major parties, which between
them won 93 per cent of the vote in 1959, were down
to 75 per cent in the two elections of 1974 and 70
per cent in 1983. The possibility that multi-party
politics might establish itself in Britain has led
to considerable speculation on the constitutional
implications of such a development.(11) Since

16

parliamentary representation has not reflected this
electoral evolution, electoral reform has, for the
first time in decades, become part of the political
agenda. If it were to be adopted, the principle of
alternation and 'Opposition with a capital O'(12)
could cease to be the distinguishing characteristic
of British party politics.

The second change is an increase in electoral
alternation in many continental European states,
and a widespread assumption that this is a symptom
of maturity in the political system. Alternation,
or at least the expectation of it, has become
characteristic of Austria, West Germany, France,
Greece, Norway and Sweden. This has not primarily
been achieved by a reduction in the number of
parties, but by a reduction in the number of poles.
The mechanics and implications of this will be
explored further under 'Moderate Polarised
Pluralism'.

B. Moderate Unpolarised Pluralism

This is in many ways the 'standard' continental
European type of a stable party system. It is
characterised by somewhere between four and eight
parties, of which none is big enough to form a
government on its own, but of which most, if not
all, are prepared to participate in government and,
in principle, to enter into coalitions with any
other party. Levels of party support do not
fluctuate wildly from one election to the next and
each party represents a well-defined set of
interests or points of view. Electing a parliament
and forming a government are conceptually and
temporally separate, though the occasional election
may be turned into a referendum on a particular
coalition's achievements or a particular intract-
able issue, such as state aid for church schools.

Under these conditions, opposition is in the
main non-structural. Parties out of power are not
alienated from the system and have an interest in
maintaining its stability. Nor, since government
is generally by coalition, do they envisage
bringing about major shifts in the distribution of
rights or resources. The policy of one coalition
will not differ substantially from that of its
predecessor or successor, certainly not to the
extent that is possible under two-party alternation.

Twenty years ago this group would have been

17

quite sizeable. It would have included all Scandinavia, Switzerland and the Benelux; even the
Netherlands would have qualified, for though the
number of its parties is rather larger, at least
half those represented tended to have three seats
or fewer, and therefore counted for little in
government-making. In the 1980s the category is
smaller. The number of parties in the states
concerned has not changed much, but their relationship to each other has. Several of them are now
better described as Moderate Polarised Pluralism.

C.   Moderate Polarised Pluralism

This resembles the previous type in all but one
crucial respect. Governments consist of stable
coalitions, committed over the long term to
distinctive policies, whether in economic management or national defence. This means that the
electoral process and the government-creating
process have become merged and elections have
become plebiscites on governmental performance.
Though there are still as many parties as before,
there are now only two poles. The pole that is out
of power has become a recognisable opposition, no
longer merely waiting for the next reshuffle, but
offering alternative policies and declaring in
advance what coalitions it will enter. The elections in Norway, Sweden and Belgium in 1985 and in
the Netherlands and France in 1986 were examples of
an incumbent coalitions seeking a renewed mandate
in a bi-polar contest. In addition, we can include
Austria and West Germany in this category since the
end of their Great Coalitions (1966 and 1969 respectively); the election of 1972 was the first in
West Germany in which the parties gave advance
coalition commitments. The fact that Austria has
enjoyed single-party government for much of that
period does not undermine this categorisation;
polar coalitions are quite consistent with the
Austrian system as it has emerged.
    Moderate polarised pluralism may be a tempo-
rary phase, brought about by the salience of particular issues. It has been given a possibly
accidental lease of life by the re-election of four
of the incumbent coalitions in 1985-6, the re-
election of single-party governments in Greece and
Spain and a direct alternation in France. As long
as there is multi-partism, polarisation is not
guaranteed; the defeat of an incumbent coalition

18

does not guarantee its replacement by an alternative. Polarised pluralism can easily revert to unpolarised. The number of parties in competition, though not necessarily the primary determinant of how a party system works, remains an important criterion, despite the attempts of numerous scholars to refine, qualify or downgrade it.(13)

Two further problems arise from the experience of France and West Germany in the categorisation of opposition in polarised systems. The first is that the concept of an opposition party is derived from parliamentary regimes and is difficult to apply to semi-presidential ones. In France, since the National Assembly elections of 1986, the Socialists, with the Communists, have formed 'the opposition'. But the Socialists still hold the Presidency, with its considerable prerogatives. They are both opposition and power-sharers. In West Germany, though electoral competition has been implicitly polarised since the founding of the Federal Republic and explicitly since coalition declarations became the norm in 1972, there have been changes of government, but no true alternation. In 1966 the Social Democrats (SPD) displaced the Free Democrats (FDP) as the coalition partner of the Christian Democrats (CDU). In 1969 the FDP displaced the CDU as the SPD's coalition partner. In 1982 the CDU displaced the SPD as the FDP's coalition partner. However, by 1982 such a limited alternation, not legitimated by an electoral verdict, was, by general consent and with the agreement of the Constitutional Court, no longer consistent with the conventions of the constitution. The Bundestag was therefore dissolved to enable the new coalition to seek a popular mandate and bi-polar pluralism was preserved.

D.   Extreme Unpolarised Pluralism

This, too, is a variant of category B. It differs from B in having a greater number of parties in competition, which means that a greater number of parties is likely to be needed for a coalition and stable bi-polarity is more difficult to achieve. However, given the trends already described in this section, this type appears to be a dying breed. If the number of parties (a minimum of eight regularly represented in parliament) were the sole criterion, then Finland, the Netherlands, Spain and Portugal would qualify. But in all these except Finland the

19

relative sizes of the parties vary greatly, and the weakness of the micro-parties means that majority-opposition relations are very similar to those under moderate pluralism and government formation no more difficult. Indeed two parties have tended to suffice for a coalition in Portugal and the Netherlands since the late 1970s and in Spain there has been single-party government since 1979.

E. Extreme Polarised Pluralism

This resembles our old friend 'polarised pluralism', launched by Sartori in 1966. This type had three distinguishing characteristics: a multi-dimensional issue structure, a greater distance between the poles than in other multi-party systems and polarity, i.e. the polarisation at extremes. (14) The model was based on the experience of post-1945 Italy, though historical examples, mainly Weimar and the Fourth French Republic, were added. In his revised version of the model, other examples are added, including Chile between 1961 and 1973.(15) The type is analytically interesting and has been influential, but it, too, must now be regarded as primarily of historical interest. To be sure, multi-polar issue structures remain, with clerical-lay or centre-periphery disputes cutting across the socio-economic left-right axis. What is less evident is that the distance between the poles is any longer a threat to the survival of any Western European parliamentary regime, or that there is any Western European state in which the centrifugal drives predominate over the centripetal. In Italy the Communist Party, though stronger than when Sartori launched his model and fluctuating, as Geoffrey Pridham points out, between consensual and conflictual behaviour models, cannot be discribed as 'anti-system'. Its participation in municipal and regional government and its crucial role in legislative committees, especially between 1976 and 1979, suggest that it should not be classified as a 'structural opposition'. Nor should the French and Finnish Communist Parties, which have both participated in coalition governments without apparent damage to the fabric of the constitution. Indeed, the only major European Communist Party that is still a structural opposition is that of Portugal.
   While the old Extreme Left has become less extreme, the new Extreme Left and the old Extreme

Right, whose drives are clearly centrifugal, are not very strong. On the right only the Front National in France has achieved any break-through. On the left, parliamentary representation of revolutionary groups, whether PSIUP and PDUP in Italy, or various Left Socialist parties in Denmark, Norway and the Netherlands, or of 'new politics' parties, like the Italian Radicals or the West German Greens, has rarely exceeded the five or six per cent mark. Indeed, one of the most impor-tant developments in the character of West European parliamentary opposition politics has been the decline of extreme polarisation.

In general Western Europe has seen a conver-gence in the patterns of party competition since the 1960s. Where parties were fewest, their number has grown slightly (e.g. Great Britain, West Germany). Extreme polarisation (e.g. Italy, French Fourth Republic) is no longer a serious factor. Moderate polarisation, turning parliamentary elec-tions into occasions of governmental choice, has increased. Parliamentary opposition has been domesticated. In many of the countries where there was a premium on centrist consensus and inhibitions on oppositional behaviour, the premium and the inhibitions have declined. However, parliament is not the only stage on which opposition can be expressed, and election campaigns are not the only occasions on which it can be measured.

iv) Changes in the Organisation and Channelling of Opinion

The main reason for the diminished polarisation of party competiton has been the secularisation of politics. Inherited loyalties, and the ideological baggage that goes with them, have declined. It is not, however, ideology that has disappeared, but the particular form in which it was organised and channelled in the first stage of European mass politics, i.e. the continental European integration party, representing both a set of interests and a view of the world, bolstered with a mass membership and the affiliation of a pressure group. This process has had a number of consequences, some of which have already been noted. Either the old integration party loses support, or it survives by diluting its appeal. But there are further effects. As more and more voters become detached

21

from strong loyalties they become more mobile in
their voting behaviour. New issues arise, and
their advocacy becomes easier as old political
space is being evacuated. Single-issue promotion
flourishes, either through parties or through
extra-parliamentary organisations. Interest groups
may at certain times become the principal, or at
least the most vocal, forms of opposition.

What we have been witnessing therefore, as a
result of the unfreezing process, is not the end of
ideology, but a destabilisation of the ideological
balance. One form that this has taken is the
decline of what became known as consociationalism,
a set of institutions which may be called a
conspiratorial device arising out of the assumption
by the leaders of the main opinion groups that
their followers cannot be trusted to compete freely
for power in the state.(16) Consociationalism
could take one or both of two forms. At the parliamentary level it consists of wide-ranging coalitions, designed to incorporate as many sub-cultures
as possible and to incorporate them in the polity
through spoils, patronage or a share of legislative
benefits. The extreme case of this is Switzerland,
where the four main parties are permanently joined
in a national coalition. A less extreme case, and
the archetypal one as far as the literature is
concerned, is the Netherlands.(17) At the socio-
economic level it consists of some kind of formal
or informal corporatism, whereby major macro-econo-
mic and welfare decisions are taken in concert
between the main interest groups. The outstanding
examples of this type are Sweden and Austria.(18)
In some instances - Austria until the mid-1960s and
the Netherlands until the late 1970s - consociationalism operated at both levels. But whatever
form it took, its purpose was to inhibit oppositional behaviour and its effect to reduce the
impact of elections on policy-making. It was a
form of cartelised, not competitive, politics.
Since the late 1970s as Ken Gladdish points
out,(19) the pressures to inhibit opposition and to
maintain a permanent centrism, have declined. The
tendency to accept moderate polarisation in
national politics, already noted, has replaced
consociationalism in a number of states. Rokkan's
striking formulation 'votes count, but resources
decide'(20) is not exactly invalid, but applies to
rather less of West European policy-making than
when it was made.

Is There Life After Dahl?

One effect of the decline of consociationalism
has been to exclude some major interests, temporarily or permanently, from the policy process. In
some countries this exclusion was in any case the
norm. In France, for instance, trade unions were
never in the confidence of governments, at least
before the election of Mitterrand, and for much of
the time the same was true of Italy. Trade unions
in these cases saw themselves as forces of opposition and so, at times, did many other excluded
interests - farmers, doctors or whatever. A significant evolution in the status of interest groups
has taken place in Britain. Under the post-war
consensus, or pluralistic stagnation as Samuel Beer
has called it,(21) most major groups, especially
the trade unions, were incorporated in the policy
process, however informally. When the unions
forced Harold Wilson to drop his Industrial Relations Bill in 1969, they did so as an in-group with
veto powers, not as an opposition. Though the
'social contract' of the second Wilson government
was an attempt to restore this corporate consensus,
the trend, initiated by the Heath government and
accelerated by the Thatcher government, has been
towards exclusion, away from centrism and towards
polarisation.(22) Unions have acted in symmetry
with this development and at least some of the
strikes under the Heath and Thatcher governments
have had an anti-government edge to them.

The final development bringing about new forms
of oppositional behaviour has been the rise of new
issues and new opinion cleavages. These have
involved parties and interest groups but also
direct action including, in some cases, violence.
Most of the issues come under the heading of 'new
politics', though one of the most important and
persistent ones, opposition to nuclear weapons, has
an ancient lineage in other forms of war-
resistance. Concern with the arms race and with
the environment in its many forms are the most
prominent of the new issues that have affected
oppositional behaviour. This almost invariably
expressed itself first in the form of extra-
parliamentary organisation, with mass meetings,
protests and marches. Since environmental
questions were often more localised, the organisation was also more fragmented and autonomous, as
with the West German citizens' initiative groups of
the 1970s.

The second stage generally marked some move

23

towards partisan involvement. While the protest
organisations themselves avoided direct links with
existing political parties, they would also try to
get their demands accepted as policies by the
parties that appeared most hospitable to them. The
debates in the British Labour Party over unilateral
nuclear disarmament in the early 1960s and again in
the 1980s, and similar controversies in the SPD,
illustrate this. One can trace a similar evolution
for environmental demands, especially over the use
of nuclear power, and for the feminist movement.

But general concern with ecology also leads
more easily to the creation of new parties. There
are now Ecological or Green parties in most Western
European countries. Though they have national
parliamentary representation only in West Germany
and Belgium, they have much wider membership in
regional and local authorities as well as in the
European Assembly. Green parties, however, are not
all of one type and their role has to be analysed
in relation to the 'new politics' generally, and to
the articulators of other claims, such as those for
women's liberation, homosexual equality and alternative life-styles generally.

Green parties had their origins in pre-
existing pressure groups, such as Friends of the
Earth in Britain or the citizens' initiatives in
West Germany. But some at least of these organisations were part of a wider movement that found
its main expression in the West German extra-
parliamentary opposition (APO) of the 1960s and the
French student revolt of 1968. Their organisational forms were not primarily goal-oriented, i.e.
designed to achieve a particular policy outcome,
but ends in themselves. The concern with the
uncontrolled use of military and civilian
technology was part of a wider dissent from the
dominant values of capitalist society. Hence the
concern with a thorough reform of life-styles and
alternative models of political organisation. In
the case of the West German Greens this meant an
insistence on remaining an 'anti-party party', on
preventing the emergence of oligarchies or bureau-
cratisation by insisting on a mid-term 'rotation'
of elected representatives, a demand finally
abandoned at the Greens' national congress in May
1986. The relationship between ecological movements and 'new politics' is therefore complex. Not
all ecologically-minded parties or voters are in
sympathy with the life-reform demands of the new

politics; not all new politics groups - for instance those in Italy described by Grant Amyot - give priority to ecological concerns.(23)

One other cleavage dimension, which had an indirect link with new politics, gained greater prominence in the 1960s and 1970s, and this was a revived emphasis on regionalism, devolution and centre-periphery conflicts generally. This constitutes one of the oldest forms of political dissent and has a prominent place in the Lipset-Rokkan model. For much of the time this dimension of opposition can be invisible, when existing national parties manage to articulate particular peripheral concerns. The British Liberal Party has for almost a century spoken for the special interests of Scotland and Wales; the Norwegian Labour Party, the Catholic-conservative People's Party of Austria and the French Radicals have been to some extent anti-metropolitan parties. However, during the 1960s and 1970s there was a more emphatic demand for political decentralisation which took one of two forms. One was the defence of specific cultural peculiarities and regional economic interests against the centralising nation-state; the other was a more general programme for the decentralisation of government. Both overlapped with the 'new politics' protest against over-bureaucratisation and the anonymity of modern society.

Of the two, specific regional protest has been more effective than the demand for indiscriminate decentralisation. 'A Europe of the regions' has remained a fantasy, with no evidence that there was popular support for it. Even where regionalisation has been institutionalised within individual states, as in Italy, France and Spain, there is little evidence of popular enthusiasm for it. However, where there is clear cultural or linguistic sub-national identity or an earlier tradition of separate statehood, as for Scotland and Wales, Catalonia and the Basque country, South Tyrol and Bavaria, the demands have been persistent and, in the majority of cases, successful. But success has not led to the disappearance of regionalist or separatist parties; indeed, it has provided them with power bases and they retain a <u>raison d'être</u> as defenders of the new <u>status quo</u> or as articulators of further demands. The one instance where cultural separatism threatened to destroy the state, namely Belgium, is an exception to this trend. There Flemish and Walloon federalist

25

parties were the pace-makers in decentralising
government. Once this was achieved, however, they
declined, partly because the established parties
themselves felt obliged to split into French and
Flemish units.

Conclusion

Is there life after Dahl? Twenty years is a short
time in politics and much that was observable in
the organisation of political interest articulation
in the 1960s has persisted. But the changes that
have occurred are sufficient to merit analysis.

On a party-political level there has been a
trend away from the extremes of polarised pluralism
and consociationalism. There is more confidence in
the ability of the system to absorb peaceful alternation and tolerate policy opposition, except,
interestingly, in Britain. Structural opposition
exists, on both the revolutionary Left and the
radical Right, but it is contained by a general
consensus in favour of system-maintenance. There
is more polarisation, but less polarity.

New forms of opposition reflect new concerns
and new issues, but they are helped by a gradual
unfreezing of inherited loyalties and a weakening
of the old European sub-culture segmentation. The
centralised nation-state and technological progress
evoke less faithful adherence than before.
Autonomous citizens' groups, single-issue mass
movements and groups advocating alternative political styles call into question not only the traditional political agenda but the traditional forms
of channelling opinion. Some of these challenges
take on the whole accepted convention of European
constitutionalism, but that does not necessarily
make them new. The paving-stone, the kidnap and
the stick of gelignite have a recognised place in
the history of dissent. The effect of the new
issues and the new oppositions on political life in
Western Europe has nevertheless been considerable.
For many people the ad hoc extra-parliamentary
lobby is now a source of more intense loyalty and
of greater attitudinal guidance than any political
party. The imperatives of survival have forced
established parties to rethink their agendas. In
spite of this, at least some 'alternative' parties,
in particular the West German Greens and the
Italian Radicals, have acquired a niche in the

mansion of politics.

The secularisation of life in the wake of rapid occupational and educational change has increased the potential for new movements and new political methods. Oppositions will come and go. Opposition will go on.

Notes

1. Ghita Ionescu and Isabel de Madariaga, Opposition: Past and Present of A Political Institution, (C.A. Watts, London, 1968).
2. Gabriel A. Almond and Sidney Verba, The Civic Culture: Political Attitudes and Democracy in Five Nations, (Princeton UP, Princeton, NJ, 1963); Seymour M. Lipset and Stein Rokkan, Party Systems and Voter Alignments: Cross-National Perspectives, (The Free Press, New York, 1967); Arend Lijphart, The Politics of Accommodation: Pluralism and Democracy in the Netherlands, (University of California Press, Berkeley and Los Angeles, 1968).
3. R.A. Dahl (ed), Political Oppositions in Western Democracies, (Yale UP, New Haven, Conn., 1966), pp.349-52, xvii-xviii.
4. For a useful introduction, see Eva Kolinsky, Parties, Opposition and Society in Germany, (Croom Helm, London, 1984), chs 6 and 7; Raymond Aron, La Revolution Introuvable, (Fayard, Paris, 1968).
5. For details see Thomas T. Mackie and R. Rose, The International Almanac of Electoral History, 2nd edn, (Macmillan, London, 1982), and the regular coverage of elections in Electoral Studies, European Journal of Political Research and West European Politics.
6. See, above all, William L. Miller, The End of British Politics? Scots and English Political Behaviour in the Seventies, (Oxford UP, Oxford, 1981); John M. Bochel et al., The Referendum Experience, (Aberdeen UP, Aberdeen, 1981). Also Peter Pulzer, 'Ethnic Protest in Britain in the 1970s' in Kay Lawson and Peter Merkl (eds) When Parties Fail, (Princeton UP, Princeton NJ, 1986).
7. Otto Kirchheimer, 'The Waning of Oppositions in Parliamentary Regimes', Social Research, vol. XXIV, no. 2, (1957) p.147.
8. Lipset and Rokkan, Party Systems and Voter Alignments, p.50.
9. See Ivor Crewe and David Denver (eds) Electoral Change in Western Democracies: Patterns and Sources of Electoral Volatility, (Croom Helm, Beckenham, 1985); Russell J. Dalton, Stephen C. Flanagan and Paul A. Beck, Electoral Change in Advanced Industrial Democracies, (Princeton UP, Princeton NJ,

1985). For individual country studies see Bo Sarlvik and Ivor Crewe, Decade of De-alignment: The Conservative Victory of 1979 and Electoral Trends in the 1970s, (Cambridge UP, Cambridge, 1983); Richard Rose and Ian McAllister, Voters Begin to Choose: From Closed Class to Open Elections In Britain, (Sage Publications, London, 1986); Kendall L. Baker, Russell J. Dalton and Kai Hildebrandt, Germany Transformed: Political Culture and the New Politics, (Harvard UP, Cambridge, Mass., 1981).

10. Giovanni Sartori, 'European Political Parties' in Joseph La Palombara and Myron Weiner (eds), Political Parties and Political Development, (Princeton UP, Princeton NJ, 1966).

11. See David Butler, Governing Without a Majority: Dilemmas for Hung Parliaments in Britain, (Collins, London, 1983); Vernon Bogdanor, Multi-Party Politics and the Constitution, (Cambridge UP, Cambridge, 1983).

12. Allen Potter, 'Opposition with a Capital 'O'', in Dahl, Political Oppositions. See also the contribution by David Denver in this volume.

13. See, for instance, Jean Blondel, 'Party Systems and Patterns of Government in Western Democracies', Canadian Journal of Political Science, vol. I, no. 2, (1968); Stein Rokkan, 'Growth and Structuring of Mass Politics in the Smaller European Democracies', Comparative Studies in Society and History, vol. X/2, (1968); Douglas Rae, The Political Consequences of Electoral Laws, (Yale UP, New Haven, Conn., 1967), pp.48-60.

14. Sartori, 'European Political Parties'.

15. Giovanni Sartori, Parties and Party Systems. A Framework for Analysis, (Cambridge UP, Cambridge, 1976), ch.6, esp. pp.159-63.

16. Kenneth McRae (ed.), Consociational Democracy. Political Accommodation in Segmented Societies, (McClelland and Stewart, Toronto, 1974), p.177. For a development of Lijphart's original typology see his Democracy in Plural Societies, (Yale UP, New Haven, Conn., 1977).

17. In addition to Lijphart, see the references in Ken Gladdish's chapter in this volume.

18. See G.E. Andersen, Politics Against Markets. The Social Democratic Road to Power, Princeton UP, Princeton, NJ, 1985); Peter J. Katzenstein, Corporatism and Change Austria

and Switzerland and the Politics of Industry, (Cornell UP, Ithaca, NY, 1984).

19. See Ken Gladdish's chapter in this volume.
20. Stein Rokkan, 'Norway: Numerical Democracy and Corporate Pluralism' in Dahl, Political Oppositions, p.105.
21. Samuel Beer, Britain Against Itself. The Political Contradictions of Collectivism, (Faber and Faber, London, 1982), pp.23 ff.
22. Cf. the chapter by David Capitanchik in this volume, who sees a more gradual transformation in the role of British trade unions.
23. See Grant Amyot's chapter in this volume.

2. PARLIAMENTARY OPPOSITIONS IN EUROPE

Klaus von Beyme

Introduction: A Footnote to the Research Situation

Focusing analysis on parliamentary oppositions has the advantage that the argument does not get so easily lost in the plethora of the numerous forms of social opposition relevant to modern societies. Central to this analysis are only:

- parties in parliament, and
- more particularly, those parliamentary groups which are strong enough to obtain the quorum necessary to entitle them to an independent parliamentary status. In turbulent times this restricted focus excludes, however, everything which is interesting. To give an example: under the Grand Coalition in Germany, 1966, the Free Democrats (FDP) were 'the parliamentary opposition'. This mini-opposition - not socialised into its new role since it had been a coalition partner in all previous post-war governments, except for the years 1957 to 1961 when Adenauer had an absolute majority - tried hard to be effective. De facto, however, effective opposition power was wielded by the extra-parliamentary opposition, which in some Länder even brought the political system to the brink of a severe crisis.

In most comparative books on political parties the phenomenon of political oppositions is discussed in a rather casual way. Some books do not mention the concept in their index,(1) others mention it only as a subordinate point when treating either party systems or parliamentary groups.(2)

31

Only good old Duverger treats opposition in a special chapter at the end of his book. He seems to imply that there are no difficulties in describing and explaining this phenomenon, apart from the diffuse opposition in presidential systems. For the European countries, he mentions only two types of oppositions: the British type, which he believes to be predominant in Northern Europe, characterised by opposition on 'principes seconds', and the Latin type with conflicts over fundamental principles.(3)

More puzzling is the fact that also the most widely read comparative books on legislatures do not deal systematically with the phenomenon of parliamentary oppositions. Some do not even mention this concept in their index.(4) Studies on legislative behaviour focus on coalition building. The existence of an opposition is frequently only acknowledged in the context of the 'members of the minority'.(5) Again there is a greater readiness on the part of older studies to deal with 'opposition' as a special topic, but again we are left with rather vague typologies such as responsible and irresponsible oppositions.(6) Sartori later added the notion of a semi-responsible opposition - an opposition not attacking the system, but not oriented towards becoming the future government. Sometimes he even uses value-laden variations such as fair and unfair opposition, whereby he sees the latter characterised by 'incessant escalation'.(7) Research in the 1970s concentrated on fundamental oppositions. Comparative books on parliamentary oppositions were extremely rare. A notable exception leaves us with a threefold typology, which is close to Dahl's classifications:(8)

- issue-oriented ad hoc opposition;
- co-operative opposition;
- competitive opposition.

The scarcity of research noted here is surprising, because the 1960s saw an enormous revival of interest in opposition. In the left-wing literature the whole image of the parties of many countries was, above all, shaped by a nostalgia for the good old fundamental opposition characterised by:

- a clear and all-embracing ideology;
- the strong organisation of a permanently

mobilised membership party;
- a clear social target group;
- a wide network of conveyor organisations to guarantee the 'linkage' between party and society. So linkage was not yet understood in the vaguer modern American sense of how to keep a party responsive to policy issues and social demands.(9)

Kirchheimer's complaint about the withering opposition became the credo for many Continental writers for quite a number of years. Those who believed in the transformation function of parties answered in the affirmative to Kirchheimer's suggestion: 'we may come to regret the passing - even if it was inevitable - of the class-mass party and the denominational party'.(10) But, as in general party theory from Michels to Duverger, such a party 'per se', if it ever existed, has only been the SPD - with all its virtues and failures - in the stage of 'revolutionary attentism'. Opposition in the late 1960s and early 1970s was, however, not considered to be a hopeless effort. The paradigm of the transformation of society competed with the two traditional paradigms of 'integration' and 'competition'.(11) But in contrast to the implications of Thomas Kuhn's notion of a paradigm, party theory has developed in a way which proves that competition between these theoretical approaches does not necessarily result in a zero-sum game with inevitable losers and winners. Whole schools of empirically oriented party research - even if they hailed the new oppositions - blurred the notion of opposition within parliaments still further by emphasising internal conflicts of factions.(12) Finally a very German, and a very exhaustive attempt to deal with the concept of the catch-all party as the counter-ideal to a competitive opposition, fundamentally different from the bourgeois class parties, proposed to abandon the concept altogether.(13)

The analysis of this study is restricted to the contributions of German authors. The peculiarities of the German context of the debate on the Volkspartei - with its zeal widely incomprehensible to many researchers in other countries - further decreases its usefulness for finding a definition of modern parliamentary oppositions in a post-ideological environment.

Frustrated by the comparative literature we

could turn back to Robert Dahl's classic checklist to come to an empirical approach to the topic of parliamentary oppositions.(14) This list comprehends:

i) the organisational cohesion or concentration of the opponents;
ii) the competitiveness of the opposition;
iii) the site or setting for the encounter between opposition and those who control the government;
iv) the distinctiveness or identifiability of the opposition;
v) the goals of the opposition;
vi) the strategies of the opposition.

It should be noted, however, that Dahl's checklist does not exclusively focus on 'parliamentary oppositions'. Although comparative research on parliamentary groups is as underdeveloped as are the studies on opposition,(15) it nevertheless provides us with some guidelines for the systematic study of the phenomenon of parliamentary oppositions. In this context I propose to deal with the following topics:

i) the broadening range of oppositions;
ii) the institutionally guaranteed role of oppositions;
iii) ideology and the programme implementation of oppositions in the legislatures;
iv) the improved chances for oppositions to gain access to power and the <u>Koalitionsfähigkeit</u>.

i)   The Broadening Range of Oppositions

The battle-cry identifying the decline of oppositions turned out to be a self-destroying prophecy. But it is not the Marxist wave of new parties that has created new and lasting parliamentary oppositions. Of the new parliamentary oppositions Aksel Larsen's Socialist People's Party in Denmark and the leftist socialist groups   PSU and PSIUP were comparatively the most successful ones. Only for Larsen's party did the question of co-operation arise. The Danish SPP remained in vehement opposition only for as long as the Social Democrats attempted their tactics of encapsulation, a treatment that had worked with the Communists.(16) As soon as the Social Democrats developed a strategy

34

of co-operation in order to keep a possible bourgeois coalition out of office, the SPP was more and more integrated into a tacit voting coalition. The same tactics were practised by the Social Democrats in Sweden and Norway when the support of the Communists was urgently needed. Regional parties and neo-populist groups, such as Glistrup's Progressive Party, became fairly steady semi-oppositions, whose voting power has proved sufficient to influence parliamentary majorities. Only rarely have these new parties entered government, as did the Rassemblement Wallon in Belgium from 1974 to 1977 at the price of creating enormous internal tensions in the party which resulted in contradictory strategies.

The new oppositions, such as the leftist socialists and ecologists, have sometimes articulated class interests, but nevertheless represent in their social composition a very modern, i.e. post-class society. The PSU in France, temporarily the most successful new opposition party in Europe, was also the party with the lowest representation of workers of all those relevant parties claiming to represent workers' interests, if we exclude for a moment some Maoist parties who celebrated class consciousness in groups composed exclusively of academics.(17) There is hardly any connection between social structure and the intensity with which parties exercise their role as opposition, except that a majority of academics in a party can lead to an increase of doctrinaire attitudes and thus perpetuate the party's fate, if it seems doomed to permanent opposition. The new oppositions usually do not have established links with interest groups or associations which could function as conveyor organisations. In this respect they are similar to many liberal centre parties, for these have lost their laicist organisational support of free masons' lodges, which in Switzerland, France and other countries they were still able to command.(18)

Because, generally speaking, indirect membership in parties - except for the British Labour Party and the Austrian ÖVP - is today of decreasing importance, and because the links of social organisations and parties on the whole are weakening, the losses resulting from the lack of such conveyor organisations are slight, especially since the new oppositions frequently compete with the traditional parties for the new middle classes.

ii) The Institutionally Guaranteed Role of Oppositions

The increasingly non-violent character of fundamental oppositions, the extended liberal regulation
of the rights of minorities and counter-reactions
against former practices of authoritarian rule in
some European nations have improved the status of
the opposition in many countries. Hardly ever is
the opposition mentioned in constitutions or statutes concerning parliamentary procedures. But
oppositions benefit from the strengthened role of
parliamentary groups laid down in recent constitutions (Spain, Art. 66,3; Portugal, Art. 183). In
the amended Swedish constitution of 1971 (Chapter
6, 2) the opposition even benefited from the trend
to divest the king of any influence on government
building. For this purpose it is now the Speaker
of the House who has to act, and he is obliged to
consult the leaders of all parliamentary groups.
      In the older constitutional systems most of
the institutional regulations on the opposition
tended to be written down in the parliamentary
statutes on procedure. In hardly any Continental
regulation is there a winner-take-all situation.
Parliamentary minorities are highly protected even
in Britain, though much of what is regarded as the
'usual channels behind the speaker's chair' is
based more on conventions than on statutes. But
even if the Speaker seems to be fair and even
favourable to new oppositions, newcomer parties
have a hard time in the House of Commons, because
of the amazingly close co-operation between Labour
and Conservative Whips in their traditional assertion of the importance of the two-party system. It
is in the interest of the Government and Labour -
'the official opposition' - to squeeze out the
Alliance.(19)
      In many Continental countries the smaller
opposition parties have greater chances. In some
countries, such as in Scandinavia, minority rights
are highly respected and benefit the opposition
parties.(20) This advantage, however, has sometimes come to naught because of the hegemonial
position of the Social Democrats who have been in
power most of the time, thus demoralising the
opposition parties, which have shown little
cohesion during the intermezzi of their government
responsibility. In some countries the strong
position of the parliamentary groups has led to

informal 'co-government' (Nebenregierung) with regard to procedure, as in the 'Altestenrat' of the Bundestag or the meetings of the capogruppi in the Italian parliament.(21)

Such an institutionalised oligarchy can, however, result in severe discriminations against new oppositions, as could be observed in the German Bundestag after the arrival of the Green Party. This new opposition has been barred from membership in some relevant committees dealing with matters of secrecy, and the Constitutional Court in Karlsruhe has been called upon to intervene on its behalf (October 1985). Part of the obstructionist behaviour of new oppositions is also due to this kind of discrimination. In Germany, at least, a line of argument that challenges the majority principle is encouraged by these attempts to encapsulate the new opposition, as is illustrated by the quarrels between 'fundamentalists' and realists in the Green Party.(22)

The political opportunities of parliamentary oppositions vary with the differences in the parliamentary groups' privileges in the committees. Oddly enough, the Westminster model, which has the greatest formal recognition of the opposition, at the same time gives it a comparatively small influence on legislation, because of the relative weakness of parliamentary committees. In Europe the strength of parliamentary committees ranks highest in Italy and Germany, and both countries rank second only to the United States in a worldwide comparison.(23) In Germany the formal institutionalisation of the opposition - which the well-meaning Anglophiles of Hamburg adopted in 1971 - is considered to be of less importance than more substantial changes through parliamentary reform. The introduction of other British habits, such as the formation of a shadow cabinet, has also proved to be hardly compatible with the necessity of coalition-building in Germany. That is why only the 'nucleus of a governmental team' (Kernmann-schaft) has been identified by opposition parties before elections in order not to alienate the future coalition partner. Most of the privileges of oppositions concern functions of control. But even where the opposition can demand a committee of investigation (Untersuchungsausschuss) the majority has sometimes tried to limit the powers of this committee, as, for example, during the Flick affair in Germany, so that in May 1984 the Constitutional

Court once more had to intervene on behalf of the opposition parties.(24)

No European constitutional democracy has gone so far as to follow US constitutional practice and to strengthen the rights of minorities, and give quasi-judicial powers to committees of investigation. The advocates of further intellectual borrowing from America forget, however, that the American model would yield quite different results under the restrictions imposed by homogeneous decision-making units consisting of parliamentary majorities and governments, as are the rule in European countries. The most important institutionalised options open to 'competitive' oppositions can be found in the predominantly German-speaking countries of Europe, with their federalist division of power. This vertical division of power becomes to a certain extent translated into a horizontal division of powers between governing parties and oppositions. In Europe the non-congruence of the national and the state party systems is, however, less developed than in the United States or Canada, or even in Australia. Consociational federations, like Austria and Switzerland, have organised through consensus-building and proportional arrangements national party systems, which are fairly homogeneous. Heterogeneity - if it occurs - does not matter much, because of the non-existence of the notion of a losing opposition. In its structures, German politics used to be a case mid-way between the North American and the consociational model. In the times when a government led by the Social Democrats (SPD) had to survive against a powerful opposition, with strongholds in many important Länder and with almost two-thirds of the votes in the Bundesrat, the structural break between the national and the regional party systems which was said to offer wide possibilities for political obstruction by the opposition was overrated by political scientists.(25)

Since 1982 the new SPD opposition has benefited less from the structural divergence of levels of conflict resolution in the federal state. On all three levels of the federal system the old truism, that in federal systems oppositions are more prone to co-operation than to conflict, has once again proved to be realistic, and it can also be applied to the first experiences with decentralisation and party coalitions on regional and national levels in Italy and Spain.

iii) Ideology and Programme Implementation

Party ideologies are usually not determined by the
decisions of parliamentary groups. It has often
been remarked - and not only in the case of the
British Labour Party - that parliamentary groups in
general are more moderate than party leaders acting
outside parliament.   Ideological distances are
usually measured not by statements of the parliamentary   groups,   but by comparisons of party
platforms formulated outside parliament.

The ideological zeal of an opposition is sometimes shaped by its ability to influence legislation.   This ability is least developed in the
Westminster model of a winner-takes-all situation.
Especially after a landslide victory of the government party, such as Mrs Thatcher had in 1983, the
opposition tends to be demoralised.   Labour attendance in the Commons these days is so poor that it
is beginning to worry even the government Whips,
and Labour Whips appear to have difficulty in
finding speakers.(26)   Loose talk about 'post-
parliamentary democracy' is possible only in
countries with a weak opposition.   Fortunately the
British public still ranks Parliament very highly
because it does not differentiate between the
formal and the real powers of the House.(27)

In studying the impact of ideological orientations we have to concentrate our analysis on the
aspect of programme realisation in parliament.
Here, just as in the electoral arena, oppositions
tend to concentrate on a couple of issues dear to
them.   Specialisation in debate has been studied
for Denmark.(28) The results in a multi-party
system with a high degree of fragmentation can
hardly be generalised, however, since the Danish
party system encourages parties concentrating on a
few issues per se.

The high degree of specialisation especially
for opposition parties is also functional to party
interests with regard to the electorate.   It has
been stated that emphasis on more than six or seven
issues creates confusion, rather than adding to
electoral mobilisation.(29) This observation also
holds more or less true for oppositional parliamentary behaviour. It is less adequate with regard to
the exercise of control powers.   Here the opposi-

tional parties can use all the issues available to inquire, to investigate and to try to mobilise by criticising the government. In most parliaments, however, a good deal of the opposition's control powers is given away, because of the tendency of opposition parties to expand issues to general discussion, as demonstrated in the debates on the annual budgets. This has the side-effect that the bureaucracies responsible for the accounts are increasingly more effective in controlling the governments than the oppositions. The oppositions are - in this case - also handicapped by the fact that 95 per cent of most budgets are not open to annual changes, even if the oppositions win their argument. The opposite handicap of oppositions - such as in France - lies in too much centralisation in the distribution of parliamentary seats. The French 'parachutés' sometimes strengthen localist aspects of the debate in order to gain profile in their constituency. The general powerlessness of parliament also affects localist interests of opposition parties which fail to control government in its major policy orientations.(30)

In the times of modernisation euphoria, the planning functions of parliament were widely discussed. To the benefit of the oppositions, not all of the ideas for a parliamentary involvement in planning were implemented. The exercise of the legislative powers of oppositions demands a much greater concentration on a few issues, simply because the amount of work oppositions can undertake is limited, and because the help of parliamentary staff can not substitute for the direct and indirect help which the bureaucracy gives to the parties in power. The party system and its structure is an important intervening variable here. In a quasi two-party system or in a net division of the political arena into two political camps (Scandinavia, West Germany; Austria is an exception), the opposition usually has greater incentives to introduce counter-proposals to government initiatives than in the consociational climate of a multi-party system with its blurred boundaries between the ruling coalition and the temporary opposition.

The more ideologically-minded the opposition is, the more it tends to apply a 'holistic' strategy of counter-bills, which are alternative in every aspect, as was the case with the SPD under Schumacher. With its growing integration into the

political system the zeal of the SPD for using
legislative initiatives as an instrument of opposition was largely weakened. During their time in
opposition the Christian Democrats (CDU) preferred
to use their power to initiate calculated inputs by
amendments to SPD bills and - especially during the
phase of the withering away of Chancellor Schmidt's
majority after 1980 - did so with remarkable
success, usually concentrating on projects in
economic and social policies.(31)

Sometimes the opposition has to be co-
operative, however, even in the use of its
amending power. Usually it does not press too many
amendments in order not to force the governmental
coalition to abandon the relevant project
altogether, to avoid taking the blame for the
failure to resolve an urgent problem.

Especially with regard to the legislative
function, co-operative opposition is a widespread
phenomenon, a fact which renders the older dualist
typology of co-operative and competitive oppositions irrelevant. The great majority of all bills
in parliaments are passed unanimously or almost
unanimously. In Germany it can be shown that bills
whose content is close to the ideological core
beliefs of the parties, for example concerning the
distribution of wealth or additional rights of
participation, can expect less co-operation in the
legislative process from the opposition.(32) Even
those oppositions which are dubbed 'unfair' by
Sartori, like the Italian Communists, have joined
ranks with the Christian Democrats to support some
three-quarters of legislation.(33)

Is this 'irresponsible' opposition? In many
parliamentary systems highly competitive opposition
parties show traits of 'parliamentary co-government' in times of crisis: in Italy during the time
when Moro was held a prisoner by terrorists, in
Germany from the building of the Wall in Berlin to
the Schleyer incident.

In multi-party systems the differentiations
between oppositional attitudes are much more difficult to identify. Even parties in government are
partly in opposition with regard to some issues.
In a political system with proportional government,
like the one we find in Switzerland, issues
structure areas of conflict. Sometimes occasional
oppositional attitudes of parties in government can
be found only by studying the behaviour of the
parties during the referenda in the various

cantons.(34)   What has been dubbed the 'helvetic malaise' is partly caused by the two-way possibilities of initiating legislation which encourage the blurring of opposition and government parties and invite occasional oppositions on many levels.

Voting behaviour on important issues has frequently been studied, though in the European context roll-call analysis does not make as much sense as it does in the United States.   In some European countries open voting was introduced fairly late (e.g. in Sweden in 1925).   Party cohesion is less dependent on the parties' role in opposition or in government than on ideology.   For Sweden it has been shown that the Conservatives are closer to the Social Democrats in this respect than to some other parties of the centre, with which they have formed the opposition most of the time.(35)

In most countries in matters of Weltanschauung (divorce, abortion, death penalty) no pressure is put on the deputies by the parliamentary groups. The closer an issue is to the heart of party politics, the more homogeneous the voting behaviour in parliament tends to be.(36) Even in systems with a highly dispersed party structure - examples are the French Fourth Republic and Finland - party cohesion increased over time.   In Finland it had reached more than 90 per cent already by the 1950s, except for the Agrarians and the Social Democrats.(37)   In France the Radicals traditionally were the least disciplined group, but in opposition under the new Gaullist regime they became highly cohesive.(38)   In some cases the oppositional function can change the degree of party cohesion, but in most European parliamentary systems this is more the case with bourgeois parties.   Socialist parties - unless fragmented by correnti as in Italy - are more consistent with regard to party cohesion, regardless of the fact of whether they are in power or in opposition.   Only in Britain was the decline of factionalism in the Labour opposition striking.(39)

iv)   **The Improved Chances of Access to Power and Coalitions**

If one agrees with Max Weber that the first goals of party organisations are launching programmes and exercising patronage, then it can be said that the second important goal of a parliamentary opposition is to participate in government. The prospects for oppositions to enter government have become much better than they were during the period of the reconstitution of democracy after World War II. In West European democracies the frequency of alternations in government has been increasing (see Table 2.1). Kirchheimer(40) resented already in the 1960s that the popular legitimation of office-holders emerged as the most important function of modern catch-all parties.

Table 2.1: Alternating governments and coalitions

Austria	1970						
Belgium	1954						
Denmark	1950	1953	1968	1971	1973	1975	1982
France	1981						
FRG	1969	1982					
Ireland	1948	1951	1954	1973	1977	1981	1982 (2 x)
Luxembourg	1974	1979					
Norway	1963	1965	1971	1972	1973	1981	
Spain	1982						
Sweden	1976	1982					
UK	1945	1951	1964	1970	1974	1979	

Source: von Beyme: Political Parties in Western Democracies
p. 334.

The participation pattern of different parties in government since World War II is still very asymmetrical (Table 2.2), but if we were to analyse the composition of governments by decades it could be shown that the chances for party political change have increased over the last few years. Since disintegration of coalitions is - apart from general elections - still the most important reason for the dissolution of governments in West European democracies, oppositions directly participate in government-building, though parliamentarty reasons for the dissolutions tend to be rare. The parties outside parliament remain the motor of change, rather than the opposition in parliament, unless the latter is the leading centre of decision-making within a party, which is rarely the case in modern mass parties. The access to power is, however, very much restricted to older established parties, though in multi-party systems ethnic or new populist groups have recently managed to establish a working relationship with the party in power to

Table 2.2: Parties' share of government in months (1946-83)

Country	Communists	Socialists		Liberals		Christian Democrats	Conservatives	Regionalists
		Left	Right	Radical	Liberal			
Austria	23		407			292		
Belgium			291		250	397	72	60
Canada					376		82	
Denmark			324	304	131		34	
Finland	191		304	406	144			295
FRG			189		406	256	146 (DP)*	
Iceland	124		235	37	223		326	
Ireland			147		144		456	
Italy	24	174	264	241	95	456		
Luxembourg			196		301	387		
Netherlands	6		201	78	253	456		
Norway		21	354	64	61	63	69	
Sweden			381	148	73		56	
UK			227				229	

Note: * (DP) stands for Deutsche Partei.

Source: Ibid., p. 333.

secure a governmental majority even without the existence of a formal coalition.

Generally speaking, it can be said that it has been easier for the new oppositions to become accepted than it was for the historical oppositions in the past, especially the socialists and the communists.

New parties were earlier acknowledged as having Koalitionsfähigkeit - the ability to form coalitions - than older ones. To reach this status took the Communist and right-wing parties, e.g. the Austrian Liberals (FPÖ), decades. On the Land level the German Green Party has already been partly accepted after only a couple of years. Even though the new oppositions, like, for example, the Greens, were initially discriminated against by denying them their fair proportion of committee seats or by applying against them the whole rigour of parliamentary rules which are rarely evoked in cases of poor discipline by deputies of the established parties, they have become candidates for coalitions in a much shorter period of time than used to be the case. In Hesse even after bad experiences the negotiations between the SPD and the Greens continued and a formal coalition agreement was announced in October 1985. Political systems also learn with regard to new oppositions: some SPD members claim that a coalition with the ecologists is necessary for socio-therapeutic reasons, i.e. to further an integration process. (41) Considerations of this kind apparently motivated Mitterrand to accept the Communists in the new government coalition in 1981, though he did not need them for a parliamentary majority. In spite of a lot of noise in some European parliaments, oppositions have not only broadened but have also become more rapidly integrated as well. All the forecasts prophesying transformations of the political systems have proved to be premature, even in cases when national party systems did not gravitate back to normalcy, as in Denmark in contrast to Norway.

Conclusion

Fundamental opposition attracts more attention than the daily routine of co-operative and competitive opposition in parliament. There is no truly comparative work on parliamentary oppositions.

Most of the material on this topic has to be collected from studies on legislative behaviour in general. The power orientation of modern oppositions has its equivalent in the focus of research: coalition-formation is much more frequently studied than oppositional strategies. A good deal of the typologies on oppositions are not very useful for studying parliamentary oppositions exclusively. With regard to the latter, four developments have been shown to be of major importance:

i) The range of oppositions has broadened. New oppositions have gained importance, though not as mass movements comparable to classic mass parties, like the Christian Democrats or the Social Democrats. The new oppositions entering parliament are characterised by an even higher proportion of non-workers among their membership than the traditional parties - even if they claim to represent working-class interests. Ecological, regional and ethnic oppositions to a disproportionately high degree comprise intellectuals.

ii) Institutional guarantees for the oppositions have been strengthened. This has rarely been done via constitutional amendments, but more frequently by changing procedural statutes. Oppositions benefit from the strengthening of parliamentary groups and their role in the committees. In political systems operating with federalism or a regional division of powers co-operative attitudes of oppositions are encouraged.

iii) Ideological distance between parties can hardly be measured on the parliamentary level. Here the implementation of programmes is more important. In the legislative process oppositions tend to favour a great degree of specialisation on a few issues. There is much less specialisation on their part with regard to the controlling functions of parliament. Holistic strategies of counter-proposals which are alternative in every aspect have been losing ground. The amending powers of co-operative oppositions have grown. On the parliamentary level, the distinction between 'competitive' and 'co-operative' oppositions is not a useful typology, since in most West European democracies there are differences in issue areas which simultaneously allow both forms of oppositional behaviour. Parliamentary group cohesion is

more dependent on ideology than on the role of
parties, either as parties in government or in
opposition. Occasionally bourgeois parties have
developed a much greater degree of cohesion while
in opposition than other parties.

iv) Alternation in government coalitions and the
Koalitionsfähigkeit of oppositions are, generally
speaking, phenomena of increased importance. There
is a certain acceleration in the integration of
oppositions. Political systems learn. With regard
to semi-integrated oppositions, sometimes even a
kind of quasi coalition-building for socio-
therapeutic reasons seems preferable.

Some authors have asked modern oppositions to abandon their power orientation.(42) On the one hand,
there is - judging by the experience with the still
quite rare cases of alternations in power - indeed
a tendency of new oppositions arrogantly to ignore
their new role. The CDU in Germany needed some
years to accept that it was not the only 'natural
governing party in Germany', and it had to get rid
of its leader Barzel in the process. On the other
hand, the power orientation of oppositions has
advantages: criticism directed against the government of the day in parliament and during election
campaigns tends to be more competent. The dialogue
between government and opposition is broader than
it used to be.
    With regard to Kirchheimer's nostalgia for the
'denominational parties' it should not be forgotten
that they rarely discussed common problems, and
that there was a strong tendency for them to ride
ideological hobby horses: the bourgeois parties
stressed economic policies, the socialist parties
social and educational policies. The skills of the
party elites were consequently also very limited.
The power-oriented oppositions in party systems
that used to be denominationally structured have
improved this situation very substantially.
Oppositions have gained in universal competence
what they have lost in ideological zeal.

Notes

1. Leon D. Epstein, Political Parties in Western Democracies, (Pall Mall, London, 1967); (second edn., 1980).
2. Giovanni Sartori, Parties and Party Systems, (Cambridge UP, 1976); Klaus von Beyme, Political Parties in Western Democracies, (Gower, Aldershot, 1985).
3. Maurice Duverger, Les partis politiques, (Colin, Paris, 1976, 9th edn.), p.459; Angelo Panebianco, Modelli di partito, (II Mulino, Bologna, 1982), pp.135ff.
4. Jean Blondel, Comparative Legislatures, (Prentice-Hall, Englewood Cliffs, NJ, 1973); Gerhard Loewenberg and Samuel C. Patterson, Comparing Legislatures, (Little Brown, Boston, Mass., 1979); Jean-Claude Colliard, Les regimes parlementaires contemporains, (Presses de la fondation nationale des sciences politiques, Paris, 1978); Michael L. Mezey, Comparative Legislatures, (Duke UP, Durham NC, 1979).
5. Jean-Yves Cherot, Le Comportement parlemen-taire, (Economica, Paris, 1984), p.173; William O. Aydelotte (ed.), The History of Parliamentary Behaviour, (Princeton UP, Princeton NJ, 1977). An exception without empirical data: Andre J. Milnor / Mark N. Franklin, 'Patterns of Opposition Behavior in Modern Legislatures' in: Allan Kornberg (ed.), Legislatures in Comparative Perspective, (McKay, New York, 1973), pp.421-46.
6. Kenneth C. Wheare, Legislatures. (Oxford UP, London, 1968), p.95.
7. Giovanni Sartori, Parties and Party Systems, (Cambridge UP, 1976), p.140.
8. Heinrich Oberreuter (ed.), Parlamentarische Opposition. Ein internationaler Vergleich, (Hoffmann and Campe, Hamburg, 1975), p.20.
9. Kay Lawson (ed.), Political Parties and Linkage, (Yale UP, New Haven, Conn., 1980).
10. Otto Kirchheimer, 'The Transformation of the Western European Party Systems' in Joseph La Palombara and Myron Weiner (eds), Political Parties and Political Development, (Princeton UP, Princeton NJ, 1966), p.200.
11. For the impact of these three models cf. Elmar Wiesendahl, Parteien und Demokratie. Eine soziologische Analyse paradigmatischer Ansätze

der Parteienforschung, (Leske, Opladen, 1980), pp.174ff.

12. Frank P. Belloni and Dennis C. Beller (eds), Faction Politics. Political Parties and Factionalism in Comparative Perspective, (Clio Press, Oxford, 1978); Joachim Raschke, Organisierter Konflikt in westeuropäischen Parteine. Vergleichende Analyse partei-interner Oppositionsgruppen, (Westdeutscher Verlag, Opladen, 1977).

13. Alf Mintzel, Die Volkspartei. Typus und Wirklichkeit, (Westdeutscher Verlag, Opladen, 1983), pp.323ff.

14. Robert A. Dahl, 'Patterns of Opposition' in Dahl (ed.): Political Oppositions in Western Democracies, (Yale UP, New Haven, Conn., 1966), p.332.

15. Cf. Klaus von Beyme, 'Governments, Parliaments and the Structure of Power in Political Parties' in Hans Daalder/Peter Main (eds). Western European Party Systems. Continuity and Change, (Sage, London, 1983), pp.341-67.

16. Erik Damgaard, 'Stability and Change in the Danish Party System Over Half a Century', Scandinavian Political Studies, (1974), p.117.

17. Charles Hauss, The New Left in France, The Unified Socialist Party, (Greenwood, Westport, Conn., 1978), p.78.

18. von Beyme, Political Parties in Western Democracies, p.191.

19. James Naughtie, 'The State of the Parties in Parliament: The Alliance', The Political Quarterly 55 (1984), p.370.

20. Johan P. Olsen, Organised Democracy. Political Institutions in a Welfare State, The Case of Norway, (Universitetsforlaget, Oslo, 1983), p.37.

21. Hellmut Wollmann, Die Stellung der Parlamentsminderheiten in England, der Bundes-republik Deutschland und Italien, (Nijhoff, The Hague, 1970), pp.87ff.

22. Thomas Ebermann and Rainer Trampert, Die Zukunft der Grünen. Ein realistisches Konzept für eine radikale Partei, (Konkret Verlag, Hamburg, 1984), pp.267ff.

23. John D. Lees and Malcolm Shaw (eds), Committees in Legislatures. A Comparative Analysis, (Martin Robertson, Oxford, 1979), p.393.

24. Cf. Rudolf Gerhard, 'Publizität oder

Geheimnisschutz. Eine exemplarische
Auseinandersetzung zwischen Regierung und
Parlament vor dem Bundesverfassungsgericht',
Frankfurter Allegmeine Zeitung, 23 May 1984,
p.12.

25. Gerhard Lehmbruch, Parteienwettbewerb im
Bundesstaat, Kohlhammer, Stuttgart, 1976).

26. Margaret van Hattem, 'The State of the Parties
in Parliament. The Labour Party's second term
of opposition', The Political Quarterly 55
(1984), pp.364ff.

27. cf. Philip Norton, The Commons in Perspective,
(Martin Robertson, Oxford, 1981), p.245.

28. Erik Damgaard, Folketinget under forandring,
(Samfundsvidenskabeligt Forlag, Copenhagen,
1977), p.205.

29. Ian Budge and Dennis J. Farlie, Explaining and
Predicting Elections. Issue Effects and Party
Strategies in Twenty-three Democracies, (Allen
& Unwin, London, 1983), p.15.

30. Pierre Birnbaum et al., Réinventer le parlement, (Flammarion, Paris, 1977), p.34ff.

31. Cf. Klaus von Beyme, The Political System of
the Federal Republic of Germany, (Gower,
Aldershot, 1983), pp.131ff.

32. Klaus von Beyme, 'Elite Input and Policy
Output: The Case of Germany', in Moshe
Czudnowski (ed.), Does Who Governs Matter?,
(Northern Illinois UP, Dekalb, 1982),
pp.55-67.

33. Franco Cazzola, Governo e opposizione nel
Parlamento italiano, (Giuffre, Milan, 1974),
p.99.

34. Henry H. Kern, Parlement et société en Suisse,
(Saint-Saphorin, 1981), p.140; Erich Gruner,
Regierung und Opposition im schweizerischen
Bundesstaat, (Bern, 1969).

35. B. Bjurulf, A Dynamic Analysis of Scandinavian
Roll-Call-Behavior, (Studentlitteratur, Lund,
1974), pp.23ff.

36. S. Holmberg, Riksdagen representerar Svenska
folket: Empiriska studier i representative
demokrati, (Studentlitteratur, Lund, 1974),
pp.218ff.

37. Perti Pesonen, 'Political Parties in the
Finnish Eduskunta' in S.C. Patterson and J.C.
Wahlke (eds), Comparative Legislative
Behavior, (Wiley, New York, 1972), pp.199-233.

38. Duncan MacRae, Parliament, Parties, and
Society in France 1946-1958, (Macmillan,

London, 1967), p.55f; F.L. Wilson and
R. Wiste, 'Party Cohesion in the French
National Assembly 1958-1973' Legislative
Studies Quarterly 1 (1976), p.471.
39. Van Hattem, 'State of the Parties', p.364.
40. Kirchheimer, 'Transformation of Western
European Party Systems', p.198.
41. Bernd E. Heptner, 'Politik als Therapie.
Warum die hessische SPD am Bündnis mit den
Grünen festhält', Frankfurter Allgemeine
Zeitung, 4 October 1985, p.12.
42. Ghita Ionescu and Isabel de Madariaga,
Opposition. Past and Present of a Political
Institution, (Watts, London, 1968), Chapter
III.

3. PARTY AND PROTEST: THE TWO FACES OF OPPOSITION IN WESTERN EUROPE

Gordon Smith

A Choice of Perspectives

The theory of 'political opposition' tends to be somewhat patchy, and this is no surprise, given the diverse forms opposition may take. At one extreme there is the traditional view that treats opposition solely as a formal political institution, that is, in the sense of a parliamentary opposition, and the parliamentary arena as exclusively the preserve of the parties. At the other extreme, opposition can be taken to include virtually all expressions of dissent in society that directly or indirectly impinge on government. In this view it is the concept of political opposition that is of primary significance, not its institutional representation in parties and parliaments. As political phenomena, the angry mob or the dissent of the intellectuals should rank equally with party opposition.

Between these two extremes there is a large middle ground. Not only are we concerned with the parties in opposition as unitary actors but also with the presence of organised opposition within parties - factionalism - which itself can be translated into the sphere of government. The parties also maintain close connections with a range of organised interests, and while their major concerns need not be explicitly political, their demands and the positions they adopt make for a potential source of opposition. Those interests, whatever their nature, may be weakly organised or not at all, and with no party links. Their demands and aspirations may just be treated neutrally as 'inputs' to the political system, and yet it is those claims which, if unsatisfied, can generate new forms of opposition and which can present a challenge to the established parties.

This span of party, para-party and extra-party activity can all legitimately be referred to as 'political opposition'. But it runs counter to the parliamentary perspective, and its proponents would argue that the traditional understanding of opposition should not be watered down by introducing all kinds of extra-parliamentary concern. The counter-argument is that the treatment of opposition easily becomes too compartmentalised. After all, the parties themselves are not bound by a rigid distinction between parliamentary and non-parliamentary action; nor should it be supposed that parliamentary opposition can be neatly divorced from the discontents in wider society.

This latter point is reinforced in considering how much the liberal democracies of Western Europe have been affected by the upsurge of what may be loosely described as 'protest politics' over the past two decades. The multiplication of protest, arising and often continuing quite outside the framework of party competition, inevitably has consequences for the process of decision-making, the standing and role of parties, and for the political system as a whole. Not least are the effects on opposition parties, for in one way or another they have to come to terms with the growing strength of extra-party opposition: it is a rival that has to be tamed or headed-off, not just another input. Political opposition has thus become more fluid, voicing itself in unconventional ways and frequently with more dramatic effect than the mainstream parliamentary opposition. Any debate between opposition as an institution or as a wider concept has to be settled according to the particular interests of the observer. This chapter is concerned with looking at the two versions of opposition together by bringing them into the same type of analysis. In this way it may be easier to appreciate the changes evident in the nature of opposition in Western Europe. First, it is proposed to look at aspects of party and parliamentary opposition before widening the treatment to take account of political protest more generally - and how that again has reacted on the parties.

A Model of Parliamentary Opposition.

The theory of parliamentary opposition - or at least many of the assumptions about it - was for a long time strongly influenced by the British experience. The early evolution in Britain of the institution of the Opposition as a recognisable 'alternative government' was one cause, and the fact that it was also a 'loyal' opposition promised, if not a continuity of policy, then at least that there would be no shattering change in constitutional form consequent upon its accession to office. Moreover, with a ready-made potential government in the wings, problems of securing a smooth succession of government were eliminated. Another reason for the attraction of the British system was that its mechanism would be made to appear almost as a necessary condition for the stability of a parliamentary democracy. A vital part of that mechanism was the existence of a two-party system, for that implied a cohesive governing party faced by an equally united opposition.

The British model - to the extent that it has actually applied in Britain - could never properly fit the situation of a multi-party system, whether or not it managed to produce stable government by other means. The nearest approximation is a two-bloc party system, typically consisting of one group of parties with a 'bourgeois-right' inclination and another of 'socialist-left' parties, the kind of formation that is chiefly associated with the Scandinavian party systems. Such a line-up gives a good indication of how coalitions will be formed, but they may be unstable: parties near the centre will be ambivalent about their loyalties, and others, in coalition or opposition, will be particularly sensitive to signs that they are losing out by a too close association with their allies. This is a feature of most multi-party politics, for it invites a continual jostling for position, whether in government or opposition, but the tendency will be all the more marked if there is no single, clear line of polarisation/division separating groups of parties.

One consequence may be a resulting instability of government, but that is not the contrast with the British model intended here. It is rather the different conception of opposition that is entailed: since there is no single or certain 'alternative government', no one party indubitably bears the 'responsibility' of opposition. The fall of a government by no means guarantees an opposition party a place in a new coalition, and it need not have a particular wish to have one: the

interests of the party and its electorate could be
better served by staying outside and keeping flexible, opposing some measures but supporting others.
The flexibility of opposition will appear in a different form if a party does join in coalition
government, for it can use its position to block
certain policies and push for others. Such 'opposition from within' in the final analysis depends
on a party's ability to bring the government down,
and the problem of placating a difficult coalition
partner may present a far greater danger to the
government than does the parliamentary opposition.

All this means that there are substantially
different conceptions of opposition applying to the
parliamentary democracies of Western Europe. In
the model case, there is the single 'institution'
of opposition, but as one moves away from its
prerequisites, it becomes more accurate to think of
opposition being institutionalised in the individual parties. It is their several and often
quite disparate viewpoints and calculations that
lead to a new outcome of 'opposition'. There is a
whole range of oppositional behaviour ranging from
the co-operative style, through to an ad hoc/
ambivalent stance, finally to strong contestation
and determined confrontation. Given a sufficient
number of parties, all these different renderings
can be represented at the same time.

Faced with all these possible nuances and
variations, it is evident that, unlike formal
coalition theory, the problem of devising any
general or predictive theory of opposition based on
the number and relative size of the parties is too
vast to contemplate, although there are parallels
with coalition theory, and a 'theory' of opposition
might resemble the obverse of its coalition
counterpart with the latter's minimum-winning and
minimum-connected variants suitably transposed.
Yet whatever the merits of concentrating on the
number of parties and related aspects as the most
easily distinguishable set of variables, the nature
and functioning of parliamentary opposition in any
country also has to be related to particular and
possibly more diffuse factors.

Most obviously, opposition will be affected by
constitutional rules and parliamentary practice.
In this respect such matters as the duration of a
parliament, the means of expressing no-confidence,
the extent of governmental responsibility to the
assembly, and the power of dissolution are all

important in determining how opposition parties are likely to behave. Contrast, for instance, the five-year terms of some parliaments with the three-year life of the Swedish Riksdag, the ease with which the House of Commons can be dissolved for a snap election with the extreme difficulty of securing an early dissolution of the West German Bundestag, or the actual impossibility of curtailing the life of the Norwegian Storting. Such constraints inevitably affect the outlook of opposition parties, as do others that determine the exercise of governmental responsibility to an assembly: while in many cases the opposition needs only a relative majority to bring down a government, in others the task is much more difficult - the West German requirement for a vote of 'constructive no-confidence' is a barrier to purely negative opposition, and in Switzerland the opposition parties have an impossible task, faced as they are by what appears to be a permanent governing cartel.

At least in dealing with constitutional aspects, the variables are fairly readily identifiable, but analysis becomes more complex when considering political traditions and the general political culture of a country. For in an indirect way they will point to the role that a parliamentary opposition is expected to play, whether it should act 'responsibly', and the electoral penalties a party may incur if it engages in disruptive actions; in another political climate such behaviour may be rewarded. Important as rules and traditions are in governing parliamentary opposition, ultimately they are subordinate to the nature of the parties themselves, for the ideology they promote must be of decisive importance in deciding how they regard and use oppositon.

This key aspect we shall consider subsequently. It is instructive, however, to take a further critical look at the two-party model of parliamentary opposition. The attribution of governmental stability is certainly correct if applied to the lifetime of a parliament, but that is offset by frequency of change - and a complete one - after an election. Stability of government, as measured by its duration, is lower for multi-party systems,(1) but changes in the party composition of government are smaller - the replacements are usually partial - with the consequence that the continuity of policy is greater. These features

are present in all multi-party systems, but they
have a special relevance for what have come to be
known as the consociational democracies - those
political systems which despite the segmented
character of their societies none the less have a
marked political stability. Various of the smaller
European democracies have at one time or another
been described as consociational - the Netherlands,
Belgium, and Switzerland - and even though the
theory and its applicability to particular
countries has been put into question, it is
apparent that strongly segmented societies are ill-
suited to using government and opposition as sharp
alternatives, and consociational devices aimed at
fostering a consensus are necessarily incompatible
with the majoritarian style of decision-making
which encourages the exposure of differences rather
than their reconciliation.

Even with majoritarian systems there are
significant variations. There is, for example, the
often neglected case of the three-party system. It
is often treated simply as a form of multi-partism,
but its peculiarity is the combination of both
multi-party and two-party characteristics. This is
especially the case if a small third party holds
the balance between two major ones, for the possibility of the small party shifting its support from
one to the other provides the mechanism of governing alternation. On the one hand, two-party
rotation in office is secured, on the other, the
partial replacement of parties in government
encourages a continuity of policy. Much of the
cohesion of bi-partism is maintained, since one of
the three parties will singly constitute the
government or the opposition, and the other two
have to match the united front it presents. The
West German party system has for the most part
corresponded to this format, with the small Free
Democrats occupying a pivotal position between the
CDU and SPD. These illustrations - the consociational form and the three-party system - reinforce
the view that imposing any one model of parliamentary opposition only gives a distorted picture of
how parliamentary democracy works.

Accommodation and Transformation

A party's ideology is arguably the most important
factor determining the style and intensity of its
opposition. A primary distinction can be made

between parties whose aims are compatible with the
existing political and socio-economic orders and
those that seek to replace them. The overwhelming
majority of West European parties belong in the
former category, whether they are on the moderate
right or left. To the extent that their opposition
does imply change, their intentions can be described as progressive or retrogressive, but it is
not a fundamental opposition. It entails pressing
particular demands that have been neglected,
promoting policies to resolve current problems, and
the reversal of existing government policies. But
their intended effect is to buttress the prevailing
order, not to undermine it. The moderation may be
masked by a high level of apparent polarisation:
strong party rhetoric, unscrupulous campaigning,
personal vilification. Yet the fact remains that
they are basically pro-system in character, ready
to rally together if the 'system' is under serious
attack and well able to co-operate despite the
exigencies of party competition.

Whether a tidy pro-system packaging is
entirely satisfactory is open to doubt, since it is
not matched by an equally neat ordering of parties
that in one way or another do stand for fundamental
change. They can all be labelled 'transformative',
but they differ considerably among themselves. The
basic decision to be made by a party with transformative goals concerns the strategy it should adopt,
and it is here that there is a parting of the ways.

In one group belong what may be termed the
'radical' parties (although in allowing for the
difference of perspective between right and left,
it is better to use 'reactionary' as well).
Broadly, such parties take the view that their
goals are attainable within the existing framework
of liberal democracy - retaining its values and
institutions intact while furthering their vital
aims. If their goals are more far-reaching, to
include a basic restructuring of political institutions, they will still work through those institutions in the first instance at the same time as
building up a consensus for more radical change
once some of the initial steps have been taken.
The emphasis throughout is on peaceful change and
majoritarian consent.

In the second group belong parties that deny
that their objectivies can ever be reached by
gradualistic means. Two things can happen. One is
that a party will lose its way in the course of the

long march through the institutions: deflected from its original goals and purposes, it will become more concerned to retain its strength and identity as an organisation, not as a force for change. Alternatively a party may remain true to its ideals, but the road will be blocked well before a transformative programme has substantial effect. Resistance from pro-system parties is to be expected, and behind them are ranged powerful interests which when under pressure will use tricks and force to maintain their position. To insist on peaceful change and rely on consent is thus to play into the hands of an enemy which for its part is prepared to use all available means when necessary. A party agreeing with that line of reasoning or fearful of becoming compromised by too close an association with institutions that it aims to destroy or transform has the option of taking a revolutionary (or equally a counter-revolutionary) course.

What Is an 'Anti-system' Party?

Discussion of parties that have transformative goals, although - in principle or as a matter of strategy - differing in the means by which they try to attain them leads naturally to a consideration of the anti-system party - the most implacable of all party oppositions. But precise as the subdivision of transformative parties into radical and revolutionary categories may appear, it is far from unambiguous when applied in practice.

There are anyway problems in using big labels, and the term 'anti-system' is one of the less satisfactory ways of classifying parties. To say that a party is 'extremist' may be helpful in locating it on the far left or right of the party continuum, but can that be equated with being anti-system? An anti-system party may be defined in terms of its expressing 'fundamental' opposition or 'opposition in principle', but is that by itself a sufficient condition?

Fundamental or principled opposition refers to the transformative nature of a party's ideology, but there may be difficulties in agreeing just what the ideology is. This need not be problematic if it is given precise expression, periodically re-iterated, and fully endorsed within the party, by the leaders and by important factions. But if the ideology is a hazy collection of possibly contradictory ideas or dusty myths, there will be trouble

59

in reaching a firm conclusion. This does not mean
that only parties with clearly laid-out pronouncements can qualify for the anti-system badge:
ideological incoherence should not be confused with
system-conforming pragmatism.
  A further difficulty lies in ascertaining the
extent of transformation that is envisaged. The
use of the term 'anti-system' can imply a total
restructuring of state and society, whereas there
may be a genuine ambivalence, and as already indicated the aim could be to abolish the existing
political institutions along with the socio-
economic system, or else just the one or the other.
Often, what precisely the 'system' is that is under
attack and how it is to be replaced is left con-
veniently vague, reminiscent of the Nazi follower
in the Weimar Republic who believed that the take-
over and the 'new order' would produce 'the opposite of what we have now'.
  There is also the problem of the difference of
strategy between 'radical' and 'revolutionary'
parties. Generally, the former work through the
institutions, while the latter seek to confront
them. Yet frequently it is only a difference of
emphasis. A radical party is anyway not restricted
to the parliamentary arena, and once outside that
framework many of the actions it supports or takes
will result in confrontation, not least because the
'rules' of extra-parliamentary activity are elusive
in comparison with those governing conventional
party competition. Other considerations affect the
revolutionary party. If it were solely dedicated
to revolution it could scarcely be called a party,
so at least it would have to make a token appearance by participating in the electoral contest.
But, in fact, it will normally take a full part,
and in that respect it appears to differ little
from radical parties. However, the resort to
normal parliamentary politics is only one pincer of
a 'dual strategy', the other being a continuing
assault on the system by whatever means available.
The two parts of the strategy are not in contradiction, nor is it a case of spreading the bets; it is
rather that the two are used in combination and are
intended to reinforce one another.
  Sartori approaches the question of defining an
anti-system party in a way that avoids having to
make a sharp distinction between radical and revolutionary parties - as the terms are used here - by
treating ideology and strategy on the same plane.

He does so by using the concept of legitimacy, so
that an anti-system party is one which 'undermines
the legitimacy of the regime it opposes'.(2) Thus
we should judge a party by the <u>effects</u> it has on
the legitimacy of the regime, not by its aims or
intentions or the means it employs. Major consequences of the undermining process include a political destabilisation, unstable and unworkable governments and a general turning-away from parliamentary democracy - a disaffection within important
elites and a growing attraction among the electorate for those parties that promise an end to the
regime.

Naturally, there are difficulties in Sartori's
interpretation as well. Firstly, if a party does
not succeed in undermining legitimacy, despite its
pretensions, should it still be regarded as being
anti-system? Secondly, should we not distinguish
between short-run and long-run effects? The importance of this question is in drawing the attention
to party evolution over a long period. Many West
European parties which we would now hesitate to
label as radical, let alone revolutionary, were
firmly anti-system in their origins and early life.
They questioned the legitimacy of the prevailing
order and were to a degree successful, not least in
harnessing permanent electoral support. Viewed
over the longer term, many of those parties even
became mildly pro-system, and brought their electoral following with them. In other words, they
played a significant role in reconciling a substantial section of the electorate to the political
system.

There is a final twist to the anti-system
problem. Up to this point the discussion has
focused on the self-definition of the party - its
aims, behaviour and strategy. But it is just as
enlightening to see how other parties perceive and
react towards it. Their judgement will lead to
exclusion or wary co-operation, and it will be a
sensitive assessment since they will probably be
the first to be affected by any undermining activities. Yet the matter can not be left there. It is
also the case that it may be quite useful for other
parties to portray one as 'anti-system'. Not only
does this serve as a point of reference and a
justification for their own positions, the strategy
of exclusion serves other purposes as well: it is
helpful in maintaining loyal support from voters
fearful of an anti-system threat, and it is a

useful way of restricting the coalition choices of potential partners if one is excluded from the start. The 'bogeyman' technique can be employed against large or small parties, and to an extent regardless of their destabilising potential.

All of these queries make it difficult to assess the anti-system party with any certainty. The only sure guide is the historical record where a party did succeed in undermining the legitimacy of a regime and help to bring it down. But contemporary assessment is hazardous, and only if the presence of transformative goals is taken to be the sole criterion will many parties qualify, while they mostly fail on any other test. This applies to the present-day Communist parties of Western Europe, since the means they use are strictly parliamentary, and they would not pass the 'undermining' test either. The same applies to parties on the right, with the Italian MSI as the only serious contender, and for both left and right the 'excluded bogeyman' explanation is just as tenable as any threat emanating from the parties themselves. In France, the Front National can be counted as 'extremist' and it may have an anti-system potential, but in most respects it resembles a typical protest movement, and in its concern with immigration could easily remain a single-issue party rather than the base for a wide-ranging attack on the political system.

It is only in moving away from the left-right axis that some unequivocal anti-system parties appear, chiefly those supporting a separatist cause. Thus the separatist movements in the Basque region and in Northern Ireland are strongly transformative in their desire to break the existing state structure, and the 'dual strategies' they employ - electoral competition coupled with the use of violence - are typical of pronounced anti-system parties: they aim to make government unworkable, and in so doing, at least in the eyes of their supporters, they successfully undermine the legitimacy of the state.

A trawl throughout Western Europe nets few anti-system parties, and following Sartori's argument we can conclude that - at least on a party level - the legitimacy of the various political systems is in good standing with their publics. Yet that conclusion does appear at odds with the extent of opposition expressed through non-party channels. The problem is to evaluate the relation-

ship between the two forms of opposition. In
particular, do the 'alternative' manifestations of
opposition act supportively towards party opposition, or is it the case that they are on divergent
courses?

Patterns of Opposition

Robert Dahl distinguishes no fewer than six ways in
which oppositions can differ from one another, and
although in his analysis the focus of interest was
on how party oppositions can vary, the contrast can
just as readily be made between party and non-party
opposition.(3) What he terms the 'distinctiveness'
of opposition is derived from three other characteristics he lists: the 'concentration' of opposition, its 'competitiveness' and the 'sites for
encounters' available to an opposition. Following
the meaning Dahl attaches to these terms, it is
clear that party-based opposition is generally more
distinctive than non-party opposition: party opposition is necessarily based on one or a few parties, it is competitive in the sense that the gains
or losses of one party can be related to the losses
or gains of other parties, and the number of decisive sites - elections, parliamentary voting,
coalition formation - is usually limited. In contrast, non-party opposition is diffuse rather than
distinctive: it is 'unconcentrated' and capable of
rapid growth or decline, it lacks the competitive
pay-off, and the sites it can use are largely non-
institutionalised, with the consequence that they
can be varied according to the issue or the target.
While the first four characteristics give a
sharp contrast between party and non-party opposition, the two final ones detailed by Dahl - the
'goals' and the 'strategies' of opposition - make
for a greater comparability. Thus two questions
can be put about any form of opposition. Are its
goals compatible with the existing regime and its
attendant structures? Do its adherents pursue a
course of action that is acceptable to others, most
importantly including the political authorities?
We can represent the terms of the two
questions - compatibility of aims and acceptability
of behaviour - in diagram form, as in Figure 3.1,
where the 'goals' are either accommodative or
transformative and where the 'strategies' are
either acceptable or unacceptable. Yet the answers
to the questions can be ambiguous, as is evident

for the anti-system party (A) shown straddling the acceptable/unacceptable divide in accordance with its 'dual strategy'. Similarly, the ambivalence of a party (B) towards the political and socio-economic structures is not a rare occurrence - it is, after all, central to the grand debate on the precise character of 'democratic socialism': if a party is committed to upholding the institutions of political democracy at all costs, then its trans-formative goals will have to be abandoned or post-poned indefinitely.

Figure 3.1:   <u>Ambiguities of Opposition</u>

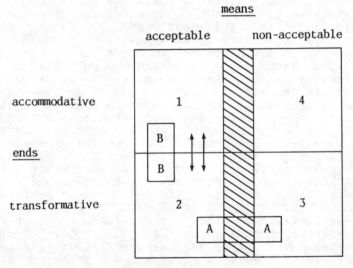

1 = retro-/progressive
2 = radical/reactionary
3 = counter-/revolutionary
4 = anomic/nascent

There is a further ambiguity which concerns the nature of the dichotomies rather than the opposi-tion itself.   Political systems are not static so that goals that are incompatible with the system in one era may be accommodated in other.   Similarly, what is acceptable activity on the part of opposi-tion can vary from one period to another.   While the limits for most party opposition are usually fairly clearly drawn, it is the strategies of non-party opposition that can be of greatest concern.

The Grey Zone of 'Acceptability'

The techniques, tactics and strategies of non-party opposition, unless they are excessively anodyne, are intended to act as a challenge to the political authorities and the <u>status quo</u>. But how those challenges and expressions of dissent should be classified is another matter. Consider some of the choices: parliamentary or extra-parliamentary; constitutional or unconstitutional; legal or illegal; conventional or unconventional; peaceful or violent. There is an overlap from one pair to another, but there are important differences of emphasis. Once one moves beyond the safest criterion, namely that of legality - opposition acting within the law - uncertainty arises, and the law itself is often vague. In practical terms, the distinction between violent and peaceful opposition may seem to be the most satisfactory, but peaceful opposition frequently involves breaking the law, even though it may nevertheless be regarded as 'legitimate' opposition. Moreover, there is still an awkward and ill-defined area between peaceful and violent: one man's peaceful protest is seen by others as an intimidatory pressure, perhaps with a covert threat of violence. These problems are decently veiled by the newer distinction between conventional and unconventional means of opposition, although, as with other formulations, all kinds of tactic are lumped together.

Some of the difficulties can be resolved if the test of acceptability is applied, for it avoids categories that have become over-formalised and it allows greater flexibility over time. The question is of course 'acceptable to whom?'. The major points of reference are public opinion, the provisions of the law and the political authorities. As long as these are not too far apart from one another, there will be some consensus on what is to be accepted as legitimate opposition, but if the three are not in harmony there will be a 'grey zone' of acceptability, and its extent is continually being tested.

Throughout Western Europe, there has been an extension of non-party protest action and an increasing willingness to take up new causes.(4) Without at this point examining the extent to which protest politics and new issues result from new values and a cultural change affecting political behaviour, it is evident that a partial explanation lies in the increasing affluence of the liberal democracies: there are more people with a fairly high educational attainment and greater leisure at their disposal. They can afford to engage in oppositional ventures that require time, organisation and expertise. Technical progress has also helped to magnify the impact of protest, for example, through easing travel and allowing enhanced media coverage. Even a relatively small protest group can show itself to good effect and be sure of fair-minded television reporting - as long as it can make itself 'newsworthy', and that is an open invitation to probe the limits of opposition.

A description of Western societies that has had wide currency refers to the danger of their becoming 'ungovernable'. It was a misleading exaggeration if applied to the broad mass of society which doubtless is as governable as ever, but it does underline the readiness of minority groups and sectional interests to by-pass normal/party channels and resort to 'direct action' regardless of wider consequences, whether this means flouting the law or shocking the sensibilities of the general public. The point, however, is that on one level such opposition is apparently in the shadow zone of 'acceptability'. The conclusions drawn are at odds: at one extreme, the state is thought to be becoming liberal to the point of helplessness, but at the other it is seen as attempting to act more repressively in response. Taken together, they well express the confusion surrounding the contemporary meaning of legitimate opposition.

In the sense used by Dahl, non-party opposition lacks 'distinctiveness' in concentration and cohesion, but its diversity, flexibility and absence of fixed institutional form does not imply a weakness, which would be the case possibly for a divided and diffuse party opposition. One reason for the difference is that non-party opposition is primarily concerned with furthering a particular protest - everything else can be subordinated to that end - whereas party opposition is concerned with the generality of political power. The implication of this reasoning is that, as the scope of non-party protest/opposition is widened, there is a transfer from diffusion to distinctiveness. We can examine this contention by looking at various types of protest movement.

Anomic, Limited and General Protest Movements

Opposition is usually thought of as having a structure, that is, having a rudimentary organisation,
recognisable leadership, explicit goals and not
wholly unrealistic ideas of how they are to be
achieved. Anomic protest has none of these
features: it is completely unstructured, lacks
permanent identity, clear purpose or a coherent
means-end relationship. Disaffection is shown in
the sudden flare-up, random violence, punctuated by
long spells of apparent apathy - all typical of
Britain's inner-city riots of the 1980s. Anomic
protest is a social phenomenon, not in the first
instance an expression of political demands. It
indicates that the needs or aspirations of certain
groups are not being met through political structures, and in a vague way the protests are anti-
system, but if they are given the shape of
political demands they could be satisfied by the
established parties and within the system. Protest
in liberal democracies which takes a shapeless
form, perhaps just seeming to be against 'authority', may be ascribed to political inadequacy and
social isolation. However, it could also signify a
more general breakdown of social norms, as
Dahrendorf indicates in postulating a 'road to
Anomia', in contrast to Utopia, which is a state of
affairs in which breaches of norms go unpunished.
(5)

Although at first sight the anomic/nascent
grouping in Figure 3.1 seems peculiar (in the combination of accommodative ends and non-acceptable
means) and certainly does not belong to party opposition, it should not be disregarded as just an
interesting oddity or only applying to under-
privileged groups. That would be to touch merely
on the fringe of 'protest' in Western democracies
which mostly shows little or nothing of political
inadequacy or social isolation. On the contrary,
participants in protest action are likely to be
articulate, politically aware, and to have a
variety of supporting social ties and connections.

This is a phenomenon recognised early on as a
specifically 'middle-class' radicalism, which in
recent years has turned to using unconventional
strategies in protest action.(6) Yet it is ironic
that those sections of society that are best
equipped to work through the conventional party
institutions should turn instead to 'direct

action'. One type of explanation is the secular
decline in party identification and the concomitant
rise in issue-voting, a falling away of strong
political loyalties without an abatement of
political concerns.

These concerns are taken up by the parties,
but on a whole host of issues it is extra-party
protest that has greater impact than most party
opposition: the struggle for minority and ethnic
rights, the feminist cause, the opposition to
nuclear energy, environmental issues, the mobilising of popular support for the 'peace movement'.
These are the major examples affecting all West
European countries, and they are joined by many
others of purely national or even local concern.
The total impression given is of a fragmentation of
opposition once the parties have ceded their
agenda-setting role.

There are good grounds, however, for querying
the portrayal of opposition as just limited-issue
protest - although not disputing its apparently
fragmentary character. There are two important
considerations. One is the extent to which the
various issues and movements are able to draw on a
common pool of support. The other is that the
issues in question are rarely self-contained but
connect up with others. Thus, behind the limited
and fragmented protest we can discern the outlines
of a general and coherent extra-party opposition.
What are the ingredients of this 'new
politics'? Firstly, it is strongly 'anti-establishment' in flavour. This shows itself in a
mistrust of orthodox parties and their 'cartel of
power', hostility towards political authority, and
a preference for direct action rather than using
conventional channels and tactics. Secondly, the
new politics gives expression to post-materialist
values, that is, the change in personal priorities
away from material preoccupations towards values
emphasising social- and self-realisation. This
shift is gradual, and it is the young, well-
educated and the relatively affluent who are the
first to be affected. Thirdly, and derived from
the other two, the new politics is identified with
the high value placed on active participation;
indeed, the whole movement could be described in
terms of a 'participatory revolution'.(7) This
naturally combines with anti-elitism, for it is the
elitism fostered by the representative parliamentary institutions which effectively stifles wider

participation. Particular protests are about specific issues, but in the background there is this greater claim for a redefinition of liberal democracy. Finally, the new values also have the status of imperatives: the style of this opposition is a 'politics of moral conviction', a Gesinnungs-politik, which is ill-matched to the aura of compromise surrounding contemporary party opposition.

Incorporation of 'General Protest'?

The contrast between conventional party opposition and protest politics is profound. Not only does it raise problems of defining legitimate opposition and the efficacy of party government, it also leads to questions about how the two forms of opposition can co-exist. Will their antagonism lead to a continuing fragmentation of opposition or is there a basis for reconciliation? A 'reconciliation' implies that in one way or another the 'new politics' would be absorbed into the mainstream of party politics, but the terms of that absorption could vary significantly from one country to another. Indeed, there are anyway marked differences in the incidence of new issues within Western Europe, especially as between northern and southern Europe, with the Mediterranean countries the least affected. The disparities can be explained in terms of 'development', so that West Germany, with the most prominent features of a general protest movement, can be seen as prototypical for Western Europe. However, other large countries such as Britain and France, even though fully sharing in the particular issues, show no signs of forming discrete and sizeable entities explicitly based on the new politics.

The relative success of 'Green' parties in West Germany and in several smaller countries does provide some kind of yardstick by which to assess the potential of the new opposition and the consequent effects on party systems. The West German Greens are an exemplary case in harnessing all the major new-issue concerns to an explicit post-materialist value system. Whilst at one time it would have been correct to think of 'ecology' as a single issue and rather far-fetched to consider a 'green' economic programme, let alone foreign and defence policies, a coherent ideology has emerged. It may still appear highly unrealistic to enter the

world of eco-units or contemplate the final consequences of eco-feminism, but they are all threads
running from a central value system, not a hotch-
potch of unrelated ideas. The transformative goals
are not easily separated from strategy, since the
value placed on widespread participation is both an
end and a means: in describing itself as an 'anti-
party party', the movement sees its unconventional
strategies as in themselves valuable in having a
fundamental effect on German politics and society.

Those pretensions apart, it is necessary to
establish how such opposition will fare in
different national contexts. Least plausible is
the view that the new politics represents an additional social cleavage in West European societies.
While it is true that the various strands of
protest are referred to as 'new social movements',
their social make-up is usually heterogeneous, and
they are best thought of as value-sharing communi-
ties. None of the three major indicators - youth,
education, and relative affluence - together or
separately adds up to a permanently identifiable
social interest. Moreover, if these three factors
point to the sections of society that at the outset
are most susceptible to the appeal of new issues,
then subsequent diffusion to other sections makes
the idea of a social cleavage emerging even less
tenable.

There are three other possibilities, each
applicable more to some countries than to others:
the emergence of a new political dimension beyond
left and right, absorption within the left-right
spectrum, or, finally, a fundamental process of
dealignment from the party-political constellation.
Each kind of development has different consequences
for political opposition.

A new political dimension is best visualised
as running athwart the overwhelming left-right
orientation of European parties - thus it is 'new
politics versus old politics'. In this respect
successful Green parties effectively dominate the
new dimension, but all parties are free to move
partly towards them or not, with the consequence
that party positions become 'scattered' in contrast
to the bi-polarity of the left-right axis.(8) On
this score, a really successful Green or similar
party would act as a political catalyst bringing
about a general change in political culture. The
admixture of party types, however, each with its
own version of 'acceptable opposition' leads to an

enduring tension in party systems, and probably little gain in 'distinctiveness' in Dahl's terms.

It might be supposed that in those countries where Greens or their equivalents have made some inroads the case for a new party dimension was established, but this is not necessarily so: the new parties can be a transient phenomenon, ultimately to be merged into the pre-existing party framework. The indications are that the aspirations of the new movements are mainly in accord with the parties of the left, with the important exception of attitudes towards the economy and to economic growth. In the longer term, the case for absorption is strengthened by the generous elasticity attaching to the concepts of 'left' and 'right'. Certain values do stay constant, but the ideas of 'liberty, equality and fraternity' are not the preserve of a single interpretation, and their affinity with the new movements is apparent. It is also evident that absorption can take place with or without the presence of a specifically 'new politics' party. Much depends on the reaction of established left-wing parties. In West Germany the SPD has found a positive move necessary, in part to ward off the perceived threat to its own position.(9) In Britain this competitive challenge does not exist; nevertheless the Labour Party could find it imperative to widen its appeal and move away from its traditional class-image of society. The general effect of absorption on party systems is to enhance bi-polarity, and with a rejuvenation of left-wing ideas that results in increased polarisation, a concentration of opposition leading to greater distinctiveness.

Dealignment poses far greater problems for party systems.(10) It means that there is no 'reconciliation' between party and non-party opposition, although taken by itself the process of electoral dealignment does not automatically point to an escalation of protest or mean that new social movements are bound to attract mass support. Dealignment in the sense of a weakening attachment of voters to parties can be gauged by measures of electoral volatility, and they show a consistent, if modest, rise since the 1960s.(11) Yet it is too early to judge the final outcome - whether it means a permanent loss in party identification or whether we are in the throes of a realignment of parties and electorate affecting all countries to a greater or lesser degree. Gross measures of volatility can

71

anyway be misleading, since they fail to capture
the extent and direction of movement. Thus, much
of the movement could be of the 'intra-bloc'
variety, that is, among the parties of the left or
right, and although the fortunes of particular
parties are greatly affected the actual system-
effects are small.(12) This is an entirely different picture from one in which voters are seen to be
swinging wildly and randomly, supporting fringe or
anti-system parties, not voting at all, or opting
out entirely in favour of extra-party protest. If
the scale of dealignment can too easily be exaggerated, it is still true that any permanent loss
puts parties under pressure, and while on one level
the electorate may continue to vote 'loyally' for
them, there is nothing to prevent the voters simultaneously giving their aid and sympathy to new
causes or themselves engaging in extra-party protest. It is this 'Jekyll and Hyde' aspect of de-
alignment that shows the two faces of opposition to
be closely joined.

Conclusion: Majorities versus Minorities

The case that there is a looming crisis of party
and parliamentary government can easily be overstated. Party government thrives in all West
European countries - at what other period in
history were they all committed to liberal
democracy? The central indicators of institutional
well-being are positive: there is no trend towards
governmental instability, no dramatic upsurge in
the number of parties gaining representation,
little evidence of electorates turning away from
parties in disillusion or apathy, and they have
certainly not switched instead to anti-system
parties, however these are defined. None of the
broad measures supports the argument of 'crisis'.
On the contrary, it is rather that we are faced
with a well-oiled and smoothly-running engine,
complete with the efficient safety-valve of party
opposition. This picture is sharply at odds with
the other one of determined challenges mounted by
diverse minority groups, and they are willing to
press their causes in ways that are antithetical to
parliamentary democracy.
    Although the extent of protest politics makes
the life of governments more difficult, they are
quite equal to the problems of policy implemention
and law enforcement. Their success, in the view of

critics, has its shadow-side in penalising minority
opinion. Thus Pizzorno has argued that it is
precisely the functioning of the pluralist system
which is at fault in wearing down the activism and
political commitment that is generated in the
formation of new collective identities:(13)

> The waste and loss of social commitment
> seems thus to grow unbearable after each
> process of restabilization. Pluralism, the
> proud product of Western political inven-
> tion, increasingly begets indifference or
> pessimism.

If in some sense the response of the pluralist
state is treated as being 'repressive' in
character, this argument should not be transferred
to all aspects of pluralist society including the
parties. From their perspective the problem is not
'waste and loss' of commitment but how to reconcile
competing minority demands, for they are not simply
to be ignored: to the extent that parties can no
longer rely on the old cleavage structures of
European society to produce a stable electoral
following, they are not in a position to dismiss
the claims of new collectivities, and a failure to
adapt to social change hands over the initiative to
extra-party movements and new parties. Party
susceptibility is undeniable, but the multiplication and magnification of protest gives confusing
messages for the parties to decipher. The danger
is that they take on board all kinds of minority
cause along with a style of minority opposition
that is hostile to the parliamentary tradition -
demands for direct action, participation, the whole
range of unconventional opposition.
At the heart of the matter is the relationship
of minorities to majorities: how minority views can
acceptably be translated into majoritarian assent.
This has been a continuing debate. What has
changed is the increased willingness of minority
groups to question the majoritarian principle - at
least as it is interpreted as meaning purely
<u>parliamentary</u> majorities. The institutions of
parliamentary democracy have enjoyed stability
because of their relative insulation from wider
pressures at the same time as being receptive to
demands transmitted through the parties. It is the
balance between insulation and sensitivity that the
changing expressions of opposition have disturbed.

Notes

1. Thus A. Lijphart, <u>Democracies: Patterns of Majoritarian and Consensus Government in Twenty-One Countries</u>, (Yale UP, New Haven, Conn., 1984), p.81, shows that the average durability of minimal-winning one-party cabinets (which is the type most closely associated with a two-party system) is 50 per cent more than minimal-winning coalition cabinets, and further that the former are more than twice as durable as the average for kinds of cabinet.

2. G. Sartori, <u>Parties and Party Systems: A Framework for Analysis</u>, (Cambridge UP, Cambridge, 1976), p.133. Sartori purposely treats 'anti-system' broadly so as to allow for variations over time as well as in the nature of the parties. Their 'delegitimising impact' is thus the lowest common demoninator.

3. Dahl shows that the six possibilities give rise to distinctive 'patterns of opposition', but that the only major variables are the 'goals' and the 'system characteristics'; party strategies are an outcome, with the choice of sites being a mediating variable. R. Dahl (ed.), <u>Political Oppositions in Western Democracies</u>, (Yale UP, New Haven, Conn., 1966), pp.332-47.

4. See for instance, S. Barnes, M. Kaase et al., <u>Political Action: Mass Participation in Five Western Countries</u>, (Sage, London, 1979).

5. R. Dahrendorf, <u>Law and Order</u>, (The Hamlyn Trust/Stevens & Sons, London, 1985), p.24. Dahrendorf further defines the concept of Anomia as 'a state of extreme uncertainty in which no one knows what behaviour to expect from others in given situations'.

6. An early example is F. Parkin, <u>Middle Class Radicalism: The Social Bases of the British Campaign for Nuclear Disarmament</u>, (Manchester UP, Manchester, 1968).

7. For a discussion of the possibly limited consequences of the 'revolution' for the established political institutions, see M. Kaase, 'The Challenge of the "Participatory Revolution" in Pluralist Democracies', <u>International Political Science Review</u>, vol. 5, no. 3, (1984).

8. The 'scattering' of parties across two
    dimensions can, of course, be represented in
    various ways, with the first dimension occu-
    pied by the conventional left-right axis. The
    addition of the 'new politics' as a second
    dimension is often treated as an establish-
    ment-anti-establishment axis. A variation is
    the materialist/post-materialist breakdown
    which applies to value orientations but which
    can be adapted to a party framework as well.
9. The contingent future of the Greens is a
    conclusion reached by W. Bürklin: 'The
    question of the future existence of the Greens
    is less dependent on its own behaviour and
    more on the way the SPD will solve the
    conflict between idealism and realism.' 'The
    German Greens: The Post-Industrial Non-Estab-
    lished and the Party System', International
    Political Science Review, vol. 6, no. 4,
    (October 1985).
10. For an analysis of the various possibilities
    inherent in the proces of de-alignment, see
    R. Dalton, S. Flanagan and P. Beck (eds),
    Electoral Change in Advanced Industrial
    Societies: Realignment or Dealignment?,
    (Princeton UP, Princeton, NJ, 1984). See also
    a critical review of this book by P. Mair in
    West European Politics, (January 1986).
11. In particular, see M. Maguire, 'Is There Still
    Persistence? Electoral Change in Western
    Europe, 1948-1979' in H. Daalder and P. Mair
    (eds), Western European Party Systems:
    Continuity and Change, (Sage, London, 1983).
    Maguire concludes: 'The pattern makes it
    clear that the relatively static period shown
    by the 1948-79 period did in fact mask the
    rather pronounced degree of change experienced
    during the last two decades' (p.91).
12. The concept of 'intra-bloc' volatility is
    explored by S. Bartolini and P. Mair in
    analysing the problem of cleavage persistence
    in the context of electoral change. 'The
    Class Cleavage in Historical Perspective: An
    Analytical Reconstruction and Empirical Test',
    paper presented to the German Political
    Science Association, Mannheim, 1983. One
    difficulty in this approach is the fact that
    parties themselves may change their ideology
    (hence electorate) and so shift from one bloc
    to another.

13.   A. Pizzorno, 'Interests and Parties in
      Pluralism' in S. Berger (ed.), <u>Organizing
      Interests in Western Europe</u>, (Cambridge UP,
      Cambridge, 1981), p.282.

PART II : OPPOSITION AND POLITICAL CHANGE

4. GREAT BRITAIN: FROM 'OPPOSITION WITH A CAPITAL "O"' TO FRAGMENTED OPPOSITION

David Denver

Writing in the mid-1960s, Allen Potter described opposition in Britain as 'Opposition with a Capital "O"'.(1) According to Potter, the two-party system determined the nature of opposition, producing an institutionalised, unified, single-party Opposition in the House of Commons whose role (and duty) was to criticise and oppose the actions and policies of the government of the day. At the same time, the Opposition sought to present itself as a credible alternative government and, given the regular 'swing of the pendulum', could reasonably expect to become the governing party in due course. This ensured that opposition was 'responsible'. Relationships between Government and Opposition, as well as the roles, duties and rights of the Opposition itself, were prescribed by constitutional conventions and an informal consensus among political leaders. All accepted that the majority party in the House of Commons had the right to govern and the minority party the right to oppose.

In similar vein, Dahl suggests that Britain, of all the countries covered in his comparative study, has corresponded most closely to the 'classic model' of opposition:(2)

> the opposition is clearly identified, the principal sites for encounters between opposition and government are the national parliament, parliamentary elections and the national media... There are only two major parties, both highly unified; hence the opposition is highly concentrated in a single party. Finally, the two parties are highly competitive in parliament and in elections. As a result of all these

78

> conditions, opposition is so sharply
> distinguished that it is possible to
> identify unambiguously the opposition. In
> Britain... the distinctiveness of the
> opposition is symbolized, by its very name,
> 'Her Majesty's Loyal Opposition'.

These accounts come close to suggesting that in the
British political system an enviable solution to
the problem of managing opposition in a democracy
has developed. Similar laudatory accounts are
commonly found in textbooks on British government.
(3)

In this 'traditional' view, the nature of
opposition in Britain is inextricably linked to the
existence of a competitive two-party system. In
fact, it was only after 1945 that such a system
became clearly established. From the origins of
modern parties in the late nineteenth century the
British system was complicated by the existence of
the Irish Home Rule party, major party splits, the
rise of Labour and the decline of the Liberals.(4)
Between 1945 and 1970, however, the two-party
system was the most obvious feature of British
party politics. Despite occasional third-party
'revivals' and nationalist upsurges in Scotland and
Wales, the Conservative and Labour parties alter-
nated in government and opposition, won the support
of the overwhelming majority of voters in general
elections, and held all but a tiny minority of
seats in the House of Commons (see Table 4.1).

In the 1970s and 1980s, however, the continued
stability of the two-party system was seriously
threatened and its value called into question by
critics. The adversarial style of politics associated with the two-party system was attacked as
contributing to the political malaise that seemed
to characterise Britain.(5) Even the previously
much-vaunted institutionalisation of opposition was
now seen as a flaw in the system. 'Few systems of
government', commented Johnson, 'can have institutionalised the role of Mephistopheles as effectively as the British'.(6)

As doubts about the desirability and effectiveness of the two-party system were increasingly
expressed, the very existence of the system
appeared to be undermined by a series of developments in the 1970s and 1980s. Electoral support
for the two major parties, especially the Labour
Party, declined sharply (Table 4.1); third-party

support reached levels not previously seen in the post-war period; nationalist parties became a permanent part of the political scene in Scotland and Wales. In 1981 an important new party was formed (the Social Democratic Party) and immediately had a sensational impact on politics. Underlying these clear signs of strain in the party system, political scientists detected an increasing 'partisan de-alignment' among the electorate. Previously the party system had been sustained by the 'twin pillars' of class and party identification. Labour could generally count on obtaining the support of around two-thirds of the manual working class while the middle class usually gave about four-fifths of its votes to the Conservatives. Identification with both parties - a sense of psychological attachment to them among electors - was widespread and strong. These two features meant that each party had a solid bloc of supporters who could be relied on to vote for their party with unswerving loyalty. But in the 1970s the link between class and party weakened markedly and commitment to the parties, as indicated by strength of party identification, declined.(7) Electors became more inclined to depart from traditional party allegiances and the formerly solid blocs of support, which underpinned the stable two-party system, began to crumble.

In the House of Commons too there were signs that the party system was not operating as before. While the two major parties continued to dominate, their behaviour in the House was much less cohesive in the 1970s than before. Norton's analysis of divisions in the House of Commons for the 1945-70 period,(8) broadly confirms Beer's description of MPs' behaviour - 'day after day with a Prussian discipline they trooped into the division lobbies at the signals of their whips and in the service of the authoritative decisions of their parliamentary parties'.(9) But in the 1970s this changed. According to Norton, not only were divisions in which MPs voted against their party more common (6.5 per cent of divisions, 1945-70: 24.5 per cent of divisions, 1974-9) but MPs dissented in greater numbers than before, were more willing to vote with the opposing party(10) and, for the first time in the post-war period, were prepared to inflict defeat upon their own government.(11)

None the less, the operation of the electoral system ensured that the marked changes among the

electorate were not reflected in the legislature.
Relatively speaking, the House of Commons remained
a bastion of traditional two-party politics. This
is illustrated in Table 4.1 which compares the
results of general elections from 1950 to 1970 with
those from February 1974 onwards. The figures for
the earlier period show clearly the complete
dominance of the two major parties in terms of both
votes and seats. In the 1970s, however, while the
major parties lost electoral support and the
distribution of votes became more fractionalised,
two-party dominance in the House of Commons
continued.

Table 4.1: General election results 1950-83

(a) Share of Votes	Mean 1950-70 %	Feb 1974 %	Oct 1974 %	1979 %	1983 %
Con	45.6	38.8	36.7	44.9	43.5
Lab	46.4	38.0	40.3	37.8	28.3
Lib	6.9	19.8	18.8	14.1	26.0
Others	1.1	3.4	4.2	3.2	2.2
Fractionalisation Index	.570	.665	.666	.635	.663

(b) Share of Seats	Mean 1950-70 %	Feb 1974 %	Oct 1974 %	1979 %	1983 %
Con	49.7	47.6	44.5	54.4	62.7
Lab	49.0	48.3	51.2	43.2	33.0
Lib	1.3	2.2	2.1	1.8	3.6
Others	0.1	1.8	2.2	0.6	0.6
Fractionalisation Index	.508	.539	.539	.517	.497
(N)		(623)	(623)	(623)	(633)

Table 4.1: continued

Notes: Northern   Ireland   is   excluded from this   and   all
subsequent tables since the convention has been to treat all
Northern Ireland candidates as 'others' from February 1974.
The figures for the Liberals in 1983 refer to the Liberal/
SDP Alliance.   The fractionalisation index is that devised
by Rae, The Political Consequences of Electoral Laws, op.
cit.
Source: F.W.S. Craig, British Electoral Facts, (Parliamentary Research Services, Chichester, 1981); The Times (1984).

The 1983 general election saw yet further
novel developments in British party politics. With
the   emergence   of   the SDP in   alliance with   the
Liberals, the third-party share of the vote rose to
26 per cent, only two points behind Labour. But in
the House of Commons the Alliance won only 23 seats
while   the   Conservatives   with   397   seats had a
majority   of   188 over Labour and of 144   over   all
other parties combined. One-party dominance of the
legislature   on   this   scale had not been   seen   in
Britain since Labour's triumph in 1945.   In   these
circumstances   the traditional model of   opposition
appeared   to   be at odds with political   realities.
True,   a single party (Labour) formed the   official
Opposition,   but   with   less than one-third of   the
available   seats it was weaker than any Opposition
since the war. Moreover, Labour obtained less than
half   of the votes cast for opposition parties   and
its   electoral weakness was such that its prospects
of forming the next government seemed remote.(12)
        Far from being unified, cohesive and strong,
then,   opposition   after 1983 was weak and divided.
Moreover,   the   whole   context   of   Government-
Opposition   relationships was changed.   Under   the
'classic model' of opposition outlined above, party
relationships were essentially bi-polar and predictable.   Each   party   had   a   single   opponent to
consider,   both   in   the House and among the electorate,   and   the   goal of each was to defeat   the
other. A simple two-way adversary system obtained.
After 1983, however, party competition was multi-
polar   (although more so among the electorate   than
in the House of Commons). The major parties had to
take   the   Alliance into consideration when determining strategy,   while the Alliance itself had to
contend   with   both the Government and the Opposition.   Party   relationships   thus became   more
complex, more unstable and less predictable. The

responses of the opposition parties to this situation are considered in the rest of this chapter.

The Labour Party

Although it subsequently formed the official Opposition, the Labour Party, by any criterion, was humiliated at the 1983 general election.(13) Labour obtained its smallest share of the vote since 1918 and its lowest-ever average vote share per candidate; elected fewer MPs than at any election since 1935; came second in only 132 seats and lost 119 deposits - more than the total lost in all previous post-war elections combined.

If this catastrophe had been the product of an unusual coincidence of short-term forces - such as the relative popularity of the party leaders, the 'Falklands factor' or poor campaign organisation - then it might have been shrugged off as part and parcel of the ups and downs of democratic politics. But evidence had accumulated throughout the 1970s that Labour's electoral problems were, on the contrary, long-term and deep-rooted.

The 1983 election was merely the latest (and worst) in a series which had seen Labour's support steadily slipping. As the figures in Table 4.2 show, Labour support peaked at just over 40 per cent of the eligible electorate in 1951 but thereafter declined in every election, with the exception of 1966, to a low point of one-fifth of the electorate in 1983. Moreover, from 1955 onwards Labour support became steadily more concentrated in the North of England and Scotland and in urban areas.(14) By 1983, 62 per cent of Labour MPs represented constituencies in Northern England and Scotland (compared with 46 per cent in 1955) and 73 per cent of Labour MPs in England were elected from London and the six metropolitan counties. Labour

Table 4.2: Labour's share of the eligible electorate 1950-83

Election	%	Election	%	Election	%
1950	39.3	1964	34.6	1974(O)	29.3
1951	40.8	1966	37.2	1979	28.8
1955	36.4	1970	31.6	1983	20.6
1959	35.3	1974(F)	30.1		

Source: Ibid.

was thus pushed back into the declining regions and
conurbations and almost obliterated in the expanding South, suburban and rural Britain.

What underlies and explains these aggregate
effects, is a crumbling of Labour's electoral base.
The manual working class - Labour's traditional
supporters - is slowly declining as a proportion of
the workforce and within this ever-smaller section
of the electorate Labour support has slumped. In
1966 Labour received almost 70 per cent of the
votes of manual workers but this fell to 50 per
cent in 1979 and collapsed to 38 per cent in
1983.(15) In particular, Labour failed to appeal
to what Crewe calls the 'new working class',(16)
leading the Conservatives in 1983 by just one point
(37 to 36 per cent) among manual workers in the
private sector and coming in third place (with 25
per cent and 26 per cent of votes respectively)
among manual workers who are owner-occupiers or who
live in the South. Ominously for Labour all three
of these groups, unlike the 'traditional working
class', are expanding. Running parallel to the
decline in voting support for Labour, there has
also been a decline in the proportion of electors
identifying with the party. In 1966, 46 per cent
of electors claimed to identify with Labour but
this fell to 32 per cent in 1983. And while half
of the 1966 identifiers described their identification as 'very strong', this was true of only a
third of the much-reduced band of Labour identifiers in 1983.(17)

Thus, the solid core support upon which Labour
could once rely had shrunk dramatically in the
space of 20 years. In addition, over the same
period, there was a marked decline in the electorate's approval of Labour policies and principles. This was true even of Labour supporters.
Harrop concludes from an analysis of identical
policy preference questions asked by Gallup in
1957, 1962 and 1980 that 'there has been a long-
term decline in the proportion of Labour voters
willing to endorse radical policies'.(18) And
Crewe reviewing the period 1964-79, reports:(19)

> Among Labour's ranks there has been a
> spectacular decline in support for the
> collectivist trinity of public ownership,
> trade union power and social welfare. In
> 1964 a clear majority of Labour identifiers
> approved of further nationalisation (57 per

cent) and repudiated the idea that trade
unions were too powerful (59 per cent); an
overwhelming majority wanted more spending
on the social services (89 per cent). By
1979 support for each of these three tenets
was down to barely a third; among manual
workers in general, and the electorate as a
whole, support was of course even lower.
What was already an ideological split in the
1960s had turned into an ideological chasm
by 1979.

The 1983 election was not, then, a temporary
setback for Labour which could easily be reversed.
Rather the election merely highlighted the electoral crisis facing the party.(20)
    These long-term electoral problems were,
however, compounded by developments within the
Labour Party during the 1970s and early 1980s.
There had always been factions and divisions within
the party but generally the 'moderate' parliamentary leadership had retained control over policy,
strategy and organisation. They were usually
assisted in this by the massive votes of trade
unions at Labour conferences. From the late 1960s,
however, some unions began to move to the left and
to use their votes against the party leadership.
In the 1970s the Left gained control of Labour's
National Executive Committee (NEC) and the 'hard'
or extreme Left greatly increased in influence in
the party. Largely in reaction to the disappoint-
ments of the 1964-70 and 1974-9 Labour governments,
the Left sought to commit the party to more left-
wing policies and to make the leadership more
accountable to the rank-and-file. Although the
latter issue centred around three apparently
obscure intra-party constitutional questions - the
mandatory re-selection of incumbent MPs, the election of the party leader and control over the
election manifesto - divisions on these issues
reflected a bitter and highly publicised Left-Right
struggle for control of the party. And increasingly it appeared that the Left was in the
ascendant.(21)
    One major consequence of this was the defec-
tion of leading members of the Labour Right to form
the SDP (see below); another was that amongst the
electorate Labour was widely perceived as a divided
and extremist party. During 1982, for example, an
average of 87 per cent of respondents in Gallup's

monthly polls believed that Labour was divided.(22)
In August and October 1983, 71 per cent agreed that
Labour was 'too extreme'.(23) In September 1970,
25 per cent of respondents had described Labour as
'too socialist' and 14 per cent as 'not socialist
enough'; by October 1983 the respective figures
were 48 per cent and 9 per cent.(24)

Immediately after the 1983 election, then,
Labour was reduced to a third of the seats in
Parliament and had to cope with a shrinking electoral base, a poor public image and unpopular
policies. In addition, the central organisation of
the party was widely believed to have managed the
election campaign ineptly and the party leader,
Michael Foot, was viewed with something approaching
derision by the majority of the electorate.

This last difficulty was swiftly and easily
dealt with. Foot and the deputy leader Healey
announced that they would not seek renomination and
at the party's first post-election conference in
October Neil Kinnock was elected leader and Roy
Hattersley deputy, both easily defeating their
rivals, amid pleas for unity and calls for the
party to face electoral reality. The effect on
Labour popularity was immediate. In September
Labour's share of voting intentions stood at 24.5
per cent, in October the figure was 35.5 per
cent,(26) and since then Labour has never fallen
below 30 per cent (on a three-monthly average
basis). Kinnock quickly set about attempting to
up-date and freshen Labour's image and also to
modernise the party apparatus, encouraging a more
professional approach to the media, in the use of
polls and so on. Indicative of his approach was
the setting up of a campaign strategy unit headed
by Robin Cook MP.

More thoroughgoing organisational change came
later. In June 1985 Labour's general secretary Jim
Mortimer, whose term of office had proved a
disappointment, was replaced by Larry Whitty, aged
41. Whitty introduced a radical restructuring of
party headquarters, aiming to streamline management
by reducing the existing ten departments to three
and rationalising the work of the NEC.

Although the change of leadership and the
sharpening up of organisation were important, they
did not in themselves address the more fundamental
question of the strategy that should be pursued by
Labour as the party faced its second consecutive
term in opposition. Abstracting and simplifying

drastically, it might be suggested that the Labour leadership had four options:

i)   They could try simply to sit out the crisis, attempting to hold Labour's ramshackle coalition together while waiting for the government to make mistakes and run into a period of unpopularity. Previous experience suggested that this would normally happen in due course and Labour would reap the electoral benefit. This traditionally has been the main strategy of the Opposition in Britain.

ii)   They could seek to change the party's 'extremist' image by attacking the Left, expelling factions such as the Militant Tendency (a Trotskyist group which had allegedly infiltrated the party), abandoning unpopular left-wing policies and reasserting leadership control by 'rolling back' the constitutional changes that the Left had won.   This view was associated with the Right in the party and in particular with the Manifesto group of Labour MPs.

iii)   They could continue to promote 'socialist' policies.   In this view, the blame for the 1983 election result did not lie with the Left.   Rather it was a consequence of, among other things, media distortion of Labour policies and the failure of some leaders to espouse key elements of the election manifesto enthusiastically.   The latter point emphasised the need for vigilance on the part of the rank-and-file and the importance of the constitutional changes won in order to prevent 'sell-outs' by the party leadership.   This strategy was associated with the Campaign group of MPs and left-wing groups such as the Labour Co-ordinating Committee and London Labour Briefing.

iv)   They might seek some form of anti-Thatcher electoral pact with the Liberal/SDP Alliance.   In reality, this option was a non-starter given the bitterness with which many in the Labour Party regarded their former colleagues in the SDP.   But the idea was floated by Frank Field MP and also received some discussion in the Communist party journal Marxism Today and in the 'Agenda' page of The Guardian.(27)

For the first two years after his election Kinnock's approach, broadly speaking, appeared to fall somewhere between strategies (i) and (ii). He endeavoured to follow the difficult course of keeping the party united while edging it slowly towards the centre and isolating the far Left. Despite suspicions on the Left of a 'sell-out', he carried the majority of the party with him. By mid-1985 commentators were generally agreed that Labour was in much better shape and that it was beginning to look like a credible electoral force. (28) The Guardian of 28 May suggested in an editorial that:

> Mr Kinnock has rightly tried to jettison some of the bulky policy luggage with which Mr Foot campaigned. Labour is no longer electorally encumbered by policies on NATO, nationalisation, unemployment, the Common Market and on owner occupation which fail to persuade potential voters and which large swatches of Labour loyalists consider unrealistic and ill thought out.

Kinnock's task in steering the course he chose was made considerably easier by the fact that since the election observers have detected a 'realignment' on the left of the party. Sections of the 'hard' Left including the Labour Co-ordinating Committee and individuals such as Ken Livingstone, Michael Meacher and David Blunkett adopted a 'new realism' which involved supporting Kinnock and isolating the 'ultras'.(29)

At the Labour conference in October 1985 Kinnock suddenly moved more clearly towards the second strategy outlined above by fiercely attacking Militant and (later) the 'hard' Left in general. This increased his popularity among the electorate, at least temporarily,(30) and was welcomed by many in the party. Some local parties began to expel Militant supporters and at the end of 1985 the NEC itself instigated an investigation into Militant activity in Liverpool. The 'hard' Left, on the other hand, bitterly opposed Kinnock's stance.

But the replacement of Foot by Kinnock as party leader did not by any means solve all of Labour's problems. In the first place, although he has more electoral appeal than Foot, Kinnock has image problems of his own. He has never been able to shake off the impression that he is something of an inexperienced political light-weight.(31) His

'honeymoon' with the electorate after his election
as leader, according to Gallup's figures, lasted
till mid-1984. Thereafter the index of satis-
faction with Kinnock (percentage believing he was
proving a good leader minus the percentage
believing he was a bad leader) was consistently
negative,(32) in stark contrast to the scores for
David Steel and David Owen, the leaders of the
other main opposition parties whose ratings have
been strongly positive.(33) In addition, Kinnock
consistently trailed Mrs Thatcher and was not far
ahead of ▸Steel and Owen as the leader thought
likely to make 'the best Prime Minister'.(34)

Labour's attempts at electoral recovery were
also hampered by the miners' strike of 1984-5. The
strike was long and bitter and was marked by highly
publicised confrontations between pickets and the
police, often involving violence. It seems likely
that Labour's formal support for the strike with
its attendant violence was electorally damaging.
Within the party, however, the Left backed the
strike enthusiastically, viewing it as a legitimate
form of extra-parliamentary opposition to government policies, and the fragility of the new-found
party unity was underlined by the Left's attacks on
the leadership's allegedly half-hearted support for
the miners. Kinnock's handling of the issue was
indicative of the finely balanced strategy he was
pursuing. On the one hand, he supported the strike
and the miners' case; on the other, he condemned
violence and insisted that court orders should be
obeyed. The effect was that he did not satisfy the
Left within the party and was widely perceived by
the electorate as being indecisive. It was not
Kinnock but Arthur Scargill, the left-wing President of the miners' union, who dominated Labour's
1984 conference. And even at the 1985 conference a
resolution calling upon a future Labour government
to reimburse the financial losses sustained by the
union was passed after a bitter debate, despite
Kinnock's strenuous opposition.

The Labour leadership was placed in a similarly difficult position over the issue of 'rate-
capping' by which the government sought to limit
spending by local councils. Left-wing-controlled
councils determined to oppose and defy the government to the point of illegality. As with the
miners' strike, this form of extra-parliamentary
opposition provided a rallying point for the Left
but the parliamentary leadership, while supporting

89

the councils' cause, steadfastly refused to condone
illegal actions. The issue again emphasises the
strains within Labour's coalition, providing the
Left with ammunition to accuse the leadership of
yet another 'betrayal'.

By far the biggest obstacle to Labour's
regaining its former position was, however, the
existence of the Alliance. In a system of two-
party dominance, such as existed up to 1970, the
Opposition, almost without positive effort, would
expect to benefit electorally from government
unpopularity. As governments made gaffes, took
unpopular decisions or failed to achieve their
economic objectives, the electorate would turn to
the Opposition. And after 1983 the Conservative
Government failed to contain rising unemployment
(which was thought by the electorate to be overwhelmingly the most important problem facing the
country) and made a series of gaffes - such as
seriously underestimating the opposition to its
proposals to reduce expenditure on student grants.
Consequently, it encountered a period of electoral
unpopularity. From the end of 1983 the Conservatives' share of monthly voting intentions declined
steadily. The decline was reversed at the end of
1984 as a result of public sympathy following a
bomb attack at the Conservative annual conference
at Brighton in which the Prime Minister narrowly
escaped death. But as the incident faded from
public memory the government's decline resumed more
sharply than before, although there was a recovery
in popularity towards the end of 1985 (see Figure
4.1).

After the 1983 election, however, two-party
dominance, at least among the electorate was a
thing of the past. To a much greater extent than
had been the case with the Liberals alone, the
Liberal-SDP Alliance constituted a credible alternative opposition and, given Labour's continuing
troubles, an attractive option for discontented
Conservative voters. As a result, Labour acquired
only some of the benefit of government unpopularity
and never rose above 40 per cent of voting intentions. This contrasts with the period following
the 1979 general election when Labour stood at over
40 per cent in the Gallup poll for twenty consecutive months.

A similar story is told by the results of
parliamentary by-elections (see Table 4.3). In all
nine by-elections held between 1983 and the end of

Great Britain

Figure 4.1. Trends in voting intentions 1983-85

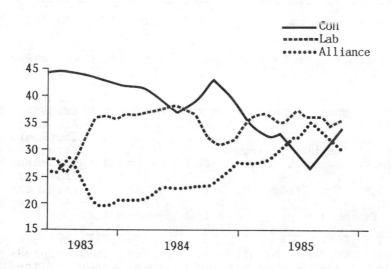

Note: The graphs are smoothed by using a three-monthly moving average. The figure for any month is the mean of the figures for the month in question, the preceding month and the succeeding month.

1985 the Conservative share of the vote declined, which is not unexpected. But Labour, the principal opposition party, made only modest gains in six cases and actually lost ground in three. Much more substantial advances were made by the Alliance (except at Cynon Valley, a Welsh Labour strong-hold), and the two seats which changed hands fell to the Alliance.

In some ways, then, Labour had taken stock of its position after the 1983 election and attempted to do something about it. A new, younger leadership had been elected, and a more professional approach to campaigning and to party management encouraged; there was an evident determination to avoid the bitter conflicts of the recent past and a willingness - at least on the part of the leadership - to modify policies that had proved electorally damaging. By late 1985 Labour had come some way in recovering from the débâcle of 1983.

91

Table 4.3: <u>Change in share of three-party vote in by-elections 1983-85</u>

Date	Constituency	Con %	Lab %	All %	Result
July 83	Penrith & Border	-11.9	-5.6	+17.5	Con Hold
March 84	Chesterfield	-16.7	+0.2	+16.5	Lab Hold
May 84	Surrey SW	-10.1	-1.4	+11.5	Con Hold
May 84	Stafford	-10.8	+3.7	+ 7.1	Con Hold
May 84	Cynon Valley	- 7.0	+6.6	+ 0.4	Lab Hold
June 84	Portsmouth S.	-16.3	+3.9	+12.3	All Gain (from Con)
Dec. 84	Enfield Southgate	- 7.4	-5.8	+13.2	Con Hold
July 85	Brecon & Radnor	-21.1	+9.5	+11.6	All Gain (from Con)
Dec. 85	Tyne Bridge	-14.0	+2.1	+11.8	Lab Hold
All By-elections		-13.2	+1.6	+11.7	

Note: The figure for all by-elections compares the aggregated by-election votes with the aggregated votes in the same constituencies at the 1983 general election.

But long-term problems remained. The battle for control of the party was by no means over. Although open warfare was avoided, skirmishing between Left and Right continued over the selection and reselection of parliamentary candidates and party policy. Moreover, despite the 'new realism' at the top, the Left in the party is probably stronger than ever,(35) and the avowed purpose of the 'realigned' Left is to prevent the party, and Kinnock in particular, falling under the control of the Centre and Right. While it is relatively easy for the party to remain united in condemnation of government policy, Labour has yet to formulate its alternative proposals and determine the content of its next election manifesto, and it is unlikely that the Left will give up their recent gains easily, especially since the constitutional changes made after 1979 have decisively shifted power in the party away from the Parliamentary Labour Party (PLP) to constituency activists and trade unions. Left-Right conflict together with other internal party problems - such as the issue of whether separate black sections should be allowed and the ever-present threat of the deselection of incumbent MPs

by local activists - continue to beset Labour.(36)
The party's preoccupation with internal problems
led Hugo Young to observe in <u>The Guardian</u> of 14
November 1985 that 'In the two years Mr. Kinnock
has been the Labour leader he has delivered no
speech that was not addressed, directly or in code,
to the internal state of the party'.(37)

In addition, despite something of a recovery
in electoral popularity, the long-term problems of
declining support among the expanding 'new working
class', alienation from basic Labour principles,
and reduced commitment to the party among its own
supporters remain. The lost Labour voters will not
be easily regained, especially now that the
Alliance appears to be a permanent part of the
party system as an alternative opposition to the
Conservatives. With a volatile, dealigned electorate, the situation is fluid and unpredictable -
especially given the vagaries of the electoral
system - but the odds are against Labour's being
able to form a government with a clear overall
majority after the next election. Despite this,
Labour continues to act as if it were the sole
opposition party. The leadership, in public at
least, flatly refuses to consider the possibility
that it may have to adjust to coalition politics
after the next election. Strategy towards the
Alliance, apart from the Left's heckling of
Alliance leaders in the House of Commons (which may
itself be counterproductive), appears to be simply
to ignore it and hope that it will prove a short-
term phenomenon. Given the Alliance's performance
since the general election, this seems a risky
strategy.

With the vast Conservative majority in the
House of Commons, there was no possibility after
the 1983 election that the government could be
defeated on a vote of confidence and an election
forced (as had been the case, for example, in the
1974-9 parliament). None the less, one would still
assume that Labour would continue to perform the
traditional role of the Opposition in the Chamber -
opposing, questioning, harrying and seeking to
embarrass the government. In fact, many commentators have reported that Labour's performance in
the House has fallen far short of what would be
expected.

Margaret Van Hattem, for example, suggested
that 'since the General Election, the elected
Labour Opposition has largely ceased to function in

Parliament'. She went on to report poor attendance by Labour backbenchers, both in the House and on committees, to the extent that Labour has difficulty finding speakers even on subjects chosen for debate by the Opposition. Hugo Young made the same points in The Guardian of 27 June 1985:

> the reluctance of Labour MPs to attend their place of work would, by normal employers, be taken as evidence of breach of contract and grounds for the docking of wages, if not dismissal. Even when Labour launches its own debates, the merest dribble of MPs is willing to appear. For practical purposes, the Labour rank-and-file has just about abandoned parliamentary politics.

He concluded that the non-governmental parties had 'opted out of the role allotted them by constitutional custom and practice' and that while there is an Opposition there is no opposition in Parliament. The absenteeism of Labour MPs was highlighted in July 1985. In a vote on 'Top People's Salaries', abstentions among its own backbenchers meant that the government could have been defeated had all Labour members been present.

There seem to be three main reasons for Labour's poor performance in Parliament. Firstly, the overwhelming Conservative majority, and the remoteness of the possibility of even denting it, is very disheartening and a major cause of low morale on the Labour benches. Secondly, the fact that Labour MPs must be reselected by their local constituencies means that members have to spend a good deal of time placating and cultivating their local parties at the expense of their parliamentary duties. Thirdly, the emphasis of Kinnock's strategy was upon campaigning in the country rather than set-piece confrontations in the House of Commons.(38) Van Hattem also suggests that the PLP was not helped by the relatively poor quality of the new intake of backbench MPs and the patchy quality of the front-bench team.

After 1983, then, the official Opposition devoted its energies to sorting out internal problems and preparing for and campaigning for the next election. Oppositions in Britain have, of course, always done this to some extent. Only in unusual circumstances and on rare occasions could the Opposition hope to influence government policy

significantly. None the less, oppositions did use
the Parliamentary arena to inform public opinion
and to portray themselves as an alternative government. Now, however, due to the massive Conservative majority, Labour's internal problems and its
parlous electoral situation, campaigning appears to
have replaced opposing in Parliament as the main
function of the Opposition.

The SDP-Liberal Alliance

Although the period between 1945 and 1970 in
British politics is correctly described as one of
two-party dominance, other parties were never
entirely eliminated. At their lowest point, in
1951, the Liberals obtained 2.5 per cent of the
general election vote and six seats in the House of
Commons. Moreover, from time to time the electoral
hegemony of the major parties appeared to be under
threat. In 1957-8 and in 1962 there were Liberal
'revivals'. In each case a dramatic by-election
result (Torrington in 1958 and Orpington in 1962)
reflected increased support and acted as a spur to
further increases in popularity in opinion polls
and significant gains were recorded in local elections. But in each case too the revivals proved
temporary and support faded as the next general
election approached. Voters, it could be argued,
were willing to experiment with voting Liberal in
by-elections but would inevitably return to their
traditional party when government was at stake in
general elections.

In 1972-3 there was yet another Liberal
revival accompanied by a spectacular Liberal
victory in the Sutton and Cheam by-election. On
this occasion, however, although there was some
downturn, the increased support did not evaporate
at the next general election. In February 1974 the
Liberals obtained just under 20 per cent of the
vote (see Table 4.1) and 14 seats, easily their
best post-war performance, and slipped back only
slightly to 18.8 per cent of the vote in the second
election of 1974.(39) However these results did
not herald a breakthrough for the Liberals. During
the 1974-9 Parliament they returned to the electoral doldrums, losing deposits in 20 of the 29 by-
elections contested. There was something of a
recovery in support just before and during the 1979
election campaign and the party ended up with 14
per cent of the vote. But despite the electoral

turmoil of the 1970s the possibility of breaking the grip of the major parties still appeared remote at the end of the decade.

Between 1979 and 1983, however, this situation was transformed by the appearance of a new party, the SDP. The formation and initial impact of the SDP involved an interlocking of events at the level of political elites and changes in the mass elec- torate. At elite level there was a coming together of two strands. The Labour Party's drift to the left during the 1970s had appalled many of the leaders of the party's right wing. Among these was Roy Jenkins, a former cabinet minister who had become President of the European Commission in 1976. Jenkins had a devoted band of followers and he kept in touch with British politics. In November 1979 he delivered a televised lecture in which he called for a realignment in British politics and floated the idea of a new centre party. This evoked a wide sympathetic response and Jenkins returned to the theme in a well-publicised Press Gallery lecture in June 1980. The more important elite strand arose more directly out of the Left-Right conflict in the Labour party. Initially the leaders of the Right - including the 'Gang of Three' (David Owen, William Rodgers and Shirley Williams) - were hostile to the idea of a new party but the advances made by the Left during 1980 finally convinced them that a break was neces- sary. Gradually the 'Gang of Three' became the 'Gang of Four' as Jenkins and his followers came together with Owen, Rodgers and Williams. The actual break came immediately after a notably confused special Labour conference in January 1981 which voted to remove the power of choosing the party leader from MPs and vest it in an electoral college in which MPs would have only 30 per cent of the voting strength (with trade unions having 40 per cent and local parties 30 per cent). After this, events moved rapidly and the new party was formally launched, with intense publicity, in March 1981.(40)

Elite-level party splits or breakaways do not always evoke a significant response among the mass of voters. But in the SDP's case the formation of the party occurred at a time when both long-term and short-term influences upon the electorate were unusually favourable. In the long term, as we have seen, there had been a progressive de-alignment of the electorate resulting in more electors being 'up for grabs' than ever before.

In the short term, both the government and the Opposition were unpopular. Labour was widely perceived as having moved to the left and in early 1981 the Thatcher Government was regarded as doctrinaire and inflexible. The March Gallup poll found that 'no Prime Minister since the war has been as disliked as Mrs Thatcher, nor any Opposition leader as little respected as Mr. Foot'.(41)

In these circumstances the impact of the SDP was dramatic. In the House of Commons the fledgling party immediately had 14 MPs (13 defecting from Labour and one from the Conservatives); within eight weeks of its formation 52,000 people joined the party; in its March poll Gallup, on the basis of a prompted question, found that the SDP and the Liberals together led the other parties in voting intentions.

After the euphoria generated in setting up a new party, the SDP leadership settled down to the more mundane task of creating an organisational structure. Within two years the party had a constitution approved by postal ballot of the members, a central headquarters with 35 full-time staff, seven regional organisers, an elected leader (Jenkins) and president (Williams), a duly constituted national committee and local organisations covering most of the country. In parliament, SDP strength doubled as more Labour MPs defected to it. But the most significant decision taken was to seek an electoral pact with the Liberals. Following meetings in May/June 1981 a joint statement was issued, called 'A Fresh Start for Britain' which concluded:(42)

> Our two parties wish to avoid fighting each other in elections ... we shall therefore consider jointly and separately the constitutional, organisational and electoral arrangements in our respective parties which will make an alliance effective'.

Thus the Alliance was born.

For a time electoral momentum was sustained. Three successive by-elections were won impressively (Croydon North West, Crosby and Glasgow Hillhead) and the Alliance continued to lead in the polls. After the Falklands conflict of April 1982, however, as the popularity of the government and of Mrs Thatcher sharply increased, the Alliance

drifted down in the polls and by-election perfor-
mances were relatively mediocre.(43) As the 1983
election approached, it seemed that the sceptics
who had dismissed the success of the Alliance as
simply yet another mid-term third-party 'flash'
might be proved right as the Alliance languished -
compared to its pre-Falklands level - at around 20
per cent in the polls. But in the last week of the
election campaign its support began to pick up and
in the event, with 26 per cent of the vote, the
Alliance was only two points behind Labour (see
Table 4.1). This was a new peak in post-war third-
party support and in addition the Alliance lost
only eleven deposits and came second in 312 seats,
ousting Labour as the second party to the Conservatives in rural and suburban areas and in the South
outside London. In terms of seats won, however,
the Alliance's reward was meagre - 23 seats (17
Liberal and 6 SDP) in a House of 650. While the
votes in the country might suggest that the
Alliance was an alternative opposition, in the
House of Commons it was still a fringe group
dwarfed by the Labour Opposition with nine times as
many MPs.

The general election highlighted the problems
faced by the Alliance as it sought to create a
permanent and much enlarged role for a third force
in the British party system. Most obviously, the
electoral system is a major stumbling-block. This
arises because in converting votes into seats the
system rewards geographical concentrations of
support rather than its overall level and the
Alliance vote, unlike that of the other parties,
was very evenly spread throughout the country.(44)
This is unlikely to change and calculations suggest
that the Alliance has a veritable mountain to climb
before its position in the House of Commons begins
to reflect its support in the country. McAllister
and Rose, for example, show that if the Alliance
share of the vote rose to 33 per cent with the
increase coming from the party currently first in
each constituency, then it would still only have 74
seats.(45) Even more strikingly, if there were a
switch of 8.6 per cent of the Conservative vote to
the Alliance and no other movements, then the
Alliance would be first in terms of popular votes
but have only 79 MPs. Given three-party competition and declining uniformity of electoral movements across constituencies, various outcomes of
the next election are possible but it is clear that

a simple increase of a few points in the Alliance's
overall vote share will not result in a flood of
Alliance gains. This is perhaps the single most
important feature of the Alliance's strategic
position and is recognised as such by the leadership.(46)

Almost as important, however, is the nature of
Alliance support. Studies of the Liberal vote in
the 1970s established that Liberal support differed
from that of the major parties in a number of
ways.(47) It was not concentrated in any social
group but tended to be uniform across groups.
Liberal voters were less likely to identify with
their party and, when they did identify, to do so
more weakly than other voters. Motivations for
voting Liberal were more likely to be negative -
dislike of other parties - than positive and
voters' perceptions of the Liberals' policy or
ideological positions were hazy. The Liberal vote
was 'soft' in the sense that few people were
consistent Liberal supporters. Rather, at each
election a large proportion of previous supporters
deserted to other parties and a fresh wave of
defectors from other parties switched to the
Liberals. To use an image suggested by Crewe, the
Liberals were a busy junction on the main party
line but not a terminus for many voters.(48)

To a great extent the Alliance vote both
before and during the 1983 general election
displayed the same characteristics. The social
evenness of support (which contributed in part to
the geographical evenness mentioned above) is shown
in Table 4.4. While there is a slight difference
between men and women in the level of Alliance
support and older voters seem to have been less
inclined to desert traditional allegiances, the
most striking aspect of the data is the even
Alliance support among occupational and housing
classes and in the different employment sectors.
In comparison, the other parties' support is
heavily skewed among these groups. This fits in
with the Alliance's view of itself as a vehicle for
transforming the 'old' class-based politics, but it
also means that the Alliance lacks a secure social
base to provide core electoral support.

This problem is compounded by the weakness of
the commitment of Alliance voters. Whereas 80 per
cent of Conservative voters and 85 per cent of
Labour voters identified with the party they voted
for, this was true of only 51 per cent of Alliance

Great Britain

Table 4.4: Voting patterns in the 1983 general election

	Con %	Lab %	Alliance %
Sex			
Male	46	29	24
Female	43	29	28
Age			
18-22	42	29	30
23-44	44	29	28
45-64	46	27	28
65+	47	34	19
Occupation			
Professional/Managerial	61	12	26
Office/Clerical	55	21	24
Skilled Manual	39	35	27
Other Manual	29	44	28
Housing Tenure			
Owner Occupiers	55	17	28
Council Tenants	22	55	24
Sector of Employment			
Private	49	26	25
Public	37	36	27

Source: Crewe in A. Ranney (ed), Britain at the Polls 1983, Tables 7.5, 7.6, 7.7. (American Enterprises Institute, Washington DC, 1985).

voters. Indeed, 38 per cent of Alliance voters identified with one of the major parties. And of those who did identify with the Alliance, only 16 per cent described their commitment as 'very strong' compared with 37 per cent and 35 per cent of Conservative and Labour identifiers respectively.(49) Despite its good performance, then, the Alliance, like the Liberals alone in the previous decade, was acutely vulnerable to defections in future elections.

Crewe has also shown that the Alliance has not carved out for itself a distinctive ideological space.(50) Voters tend to perceive the Alliance as being vaguely 'in the middle' and Alliance voters are not distinguished by a characteristic set of

100

issue positions. A central position on a perceived
left-right continuum does have advantages in that
disaffected electors can be recruited from both
sides, but it also means that defectors from the
centre do not have far to travel to rejoin parties
on the left or right. Given the negative motivation of much Alliance voting, the danger is that if
the other parties improve their standing with the
electorate - and this is something the Alliance has
little control over - votes may flow away from the
Alliance as rapidly as they flooded in.(51)

The Alliance claimed to represent a new form
of opposition in British politics. It castigated
'opposition for opposition's sake' and the adversarial system. In its place it advocated 'the
politics of co-operation' in which opposition would
be constructive, and 'working together' rather than
conflict would be the dominant theme. But given
that Alliance support in the country was diffuse,
volatile and fragile and that in the House of
Commons the Alliance constituted a small minority
opposition group, its options after the 1983 election were limited. Internally, future relations
between the two Alliance partners had to be determined and, especially in the case of the SDP,
organisation strengthened. Externally, the
Alliance needed simply to stay in the public eye
and hope that the government would run into popularity problems and Labour fail to pull itself
together.

The alliance between the Liberals and the SDP
had been arranged for one election only and had,
therefore, to be renegotiated. This was made
slightly more problematical by the resignation of
Roy Jenkins as SDP leader immediately after the
election. He was replaced by David Owen who was
younger, more energetic, more abrasive (and proved
more popular with the electorate) than Jenkins.
But Owen's relationship with David Steel was said
to be less cordial than Jenkins' had been and he
was more committed to the continued independence of
the SDP. There were some in both parties who
advocated a closer relationship between the
Alliance partners, even to the point of a merger,
but Owen firmly opposed such suggestions and sought
to limit close co-operation over candidate selection at local level. Both Owen and Steel also
opposed a proposal that the Alliance should have a
single leader, agreeing that in the event of the
Alliance forming a government the leader of the

larger party in the House of Commons would be Prime
Minister. But the Alliance was reaffirmed and the
relationship between the two parties remained
cordial. A joint committee consisting of twelve
representatives from each party was set up to
determine strategy for elections, funding, tactics
and policy promotion. Despite occasional sticky
patches, strains over policy (especially defence)
and little local difficulties, the task of
preparing for the next election proceeded on the
whole harmoniously.

In the House of Commons, co-operation between
the two parties has been close. There are weekly
meetings between the party leaders and whips, joint
monthly meetings of all MPs of both parties and a
series of joint policy groups. But the Alliance
has found it difficult to maintain a high profile
in Parliament - which is one way of capturing
public attention. The problem is that the traditions and procedures of the House are geared to a
two-party system. Business is organised on the
basis of close co-operation between government and
Opposition whips and in this process the Alliance
tends to be 'frozen out'. In the 1983-4 session,
for example, only one of the 19 days allotted for
opposition-initiated debates was given to the
Alliance. Alliance spokesmen have also not been
granted an automatic right to respond to government
statements, question ministers or speak in debates
immediately after the official Opposition. They
have, indeed, had difficulty in being called to
speak and have had to wait until well into debates
when there is less chance of making an impact on
the House or of being extensively reported in the
media. In addition, Alliance amendments are rarely
put to the vote and Alliance MPs are poorly represented on select committees. Despite frequent
complaints to the Speaker, the Alliance has made
very little headway on these matters.(52)

Other Alliance attempts to stay in the political limelight also had little effect. In June 1984
the Campaign for Fair Votes - an independent group
heavily backed by the Alliance - presented a petition with over a million signatures to Parliament,
calling for reform of the electoral system. But as
with most petitions this was quickly forgotten.
David Owen's concern with publicity was such that
in 1985 he instigated a court action against Independent Television News claiming that the Alliance
was not given the coverage which its support

warranted. But this was unsuccessful. The major
parties even attempted to minimise the public
impact of Alliance performance in by-elections - a
traditional source of publicity for smaller parties
- by fixing one for the same day as the European
elections and three on the same day as local elections.

Despite these problems, Alliance hopes of a
slide in government popularity were fulfilled and,
as has been noted, the Alliance benefited more
from this than the Labour Party. As Figure 4.1
shows, from late 1983 there was a slow but steady
increase in the Alliance's share of voting intentions in Gallup's monthly poll and, despite slipping back a little towards the end of 1985, they
were still well up with the other parties. This
popularity was reflected in by-elections (see Table
4.3) in which two gains were made. Taking all the
by-elections together, the Alliance had a larger
share of votes (36 per cent) than either the
Conservatives (33 per cent) or Labour (31 per
cent). This dribble of by-elections, together with
local elections such as the county elections in
1985, was sufficient to keep the electorate aware
of the Alliance's existence and helps to explain
why they remained a viable option for disaffected
Conservatives.

At the mid-point of Mrs Thatcher's second term
there were a number of positive features in the
Alliance's position. In the first place, given the
history of breakaway groups in British politics, it
is no mean feat that the Alliance, and in particular the SDP, was still in existence. The SDP might
easily have been a complete flop, but its membership stabilised at around 50,000 and organisationally the party seemed set to be a permanent feature
of the British political landscape. The Alliance
also seemed to have a larger core support than any
previous third force. In Gallup's monthly polls
from June 1983 it dropped below 20 per cent on only
four occasions (and then only to 19.5 per cent), so
that there was a higher platform than before from
which to approach the next election. In addition,
with 312 second places in 1983, the Alliance was in
a good tactical position to capitalise upon any
anti-government feeling. Finally, the leaders of
the Alliance parties were popular with the electorate, consistently eliciting positive scores from
poll respondents in contrast with the negative
ratings usually given to their Conservative and

Labour rivals.

On the other hand, the electoral system over-shadows the Alliance, always threatening to ruin its chances. Given that a large majority of MPs in both major parties remain implacably opposed to changing the electoral system, there is little the Alliance can do about this. Under the present system probably the best that the Alliance can hope for is to hold the balance of power in the next Parliament. In that case, it might be able to negotiate an arrangement whereby it will secure a commitment from one of the other parties at least to raising the question of changing the electoral system. But the outcome of a 'hung' House of Commons is difficult to predict. Finally, however, the nature of Alliance support means that there is an ever-present danger that a volatile electorate might rapidly abandon it, leaving it as a fringe party of protest. While things may appear set fair for a period, the Alliance runs a high risk of being blown off course by squalls and storms.

Nationalists and Others

In addition to the Conservatives, Labour, the Liberals and the SDP, six other parties were repre-sented in the House of Commons after the 1983 election - the Scottish National Party (SNP), the Welsh National Party (Plaid Cymru) each with two seats, and four Northern Irish parties (the Official Unionists, Democratic Unionists, the Social Democratic and Labour Party and Provisional Sinn Fein.(53) Of course, very many more parties of all colours and opinions put forward candidates in the election, but their support was negligible. (54) Only a few of these unsuccessful parties merit a brief mention.

The Communist Party reached a peak of elec-toral support in Britain in 1945 when two Communist MPs were elected. Since them, however, no seats have been won and support has been derisory. In 1983, its 35 candidates averaged only 0.8 per cent of the vote and since then there has been a major split in the party between supporters of the Eurocommunist leadership and supporters of the more pro-Soviet line advocated by the party's newspaper, the Morning Star.

The National Front (NF) was formed in 1967 by an amalgamation of various right-wing groups and for a time in the 1970s polled moderately well -

for a fringe party - especially in by-elections and local elections. In a by-election in 1973, for example, for the first and only time the Front saved its deposit, and in the 1979 general election 303 NF candidates obtained almost 300,000 votes. Even by then, however, NF support was declining and the organisation fell prey to the fissiparous tendencies which seem to characterise extreme right-wing movements. In the 1983 elections one of the Front's offshoots, the British National Party, had almost as many candidates (54) as the Front itself (60) and both performed badly, achieving only 41,000 votes in total.

The most successful fringe party in 1983 was the Bcology Party, renamed the Green Party in 1986, whose 108 candidates totalled 54,000 votes, averaging just over one per cent in contested seats. But this is insignificant compared with the success of the Greens in other West European states.

Parties on the political fringe in Britain add some variety to elections - and even this is likely to decline in future since candidates' deposits have now been increased from £150 to £500 - but their impact upon the electorate and the political system is minimal. This cannot, however, be said of the SNP and Plaid Cymru which are better described as 'minor' rather then 'fringe' parties.

The SNP was founded in 1934 but it was only in the late 1960s that it first became an important force in Scottish politics. Startling advances in by-elections and local elections at that time enabled the SNP to push the 'Scottish question' on to the agenda of British politics and it remained there throughout the 1970s. Table 4.5 details the

Table 4.5: **The SNP in general elections in Scotland 1964-83**

	1964	1966	1970	Feb. 1974	Oct. 1974	1979	1983
% of Votes	2.4	5.0	11.4	21.9	30.4	17.3	11.8
No. of Candidates	15	23	65	70	71	71	72
Seats Won	0	0	1	7	11	2	2

Note: There were 71 seats in Scotland until 1983 when the number increased to 72.
Source: as Table 4.1.

electoral performance of the SNP and it can be seen
that support peaked in October 1974 but has
declined since.

Much of the wind was taken out of the SNP's
sails by the result of the referendum of March
1979, when Scottish voters failed to endorse by the
required majority a proposal to set up a Scottish
Assembly, and the devolution issue gradually
dropped out of the news. The party also experienced internal division between traditionalists for
whom Scottish independence was the paramount policy
concern and radicals who wanted the party also to
adopt a more left-wing stance on economic and
social issues. Public squabbling, including the
expulsion of leading radicals, gave the party a
poor image and its support declined further after
1979 in local elections and in the 1983 general
election. Since then there has been some healing
of wounds but support has not picked up. There has
been no by-election in Scotland to give the SNP
publicity and its rating in the monthly System
Three (Scotland) polls since June 1983 has not been
above 15 (or below 10) per cent.

Although the SNP does not seem poised to make
an electoral breakthrough it does seem a permanent
fixture in the Scottish party system, having fairly
extensive local organisation, a toehold in many
local authorities (and outright control of one),
two seats in Parliament and a core support of
around 10 per cent of the Scottish electorate. The
devolution issue remains simmering. If it boils up
again the SNP could once again threaten the stability of the party system in Scotland.(55)

Political nationalism has been less successful
in Wales. As with the SNP, however, a spectacular
by-election victory for Plaid Cymru in the late
1960s signalled an upswing in the party's fortunes.
In the 1979 referendum, however, devolution proposals were overwhelmingly rejected in Wales and in
subsequent elections Plaid's fortunes have
declined, though the concentration of the party's
support in rural and Welsh-speaking areas has
enabled it to retain two seats. There has been no
evidence of a recovery by Plaid Cymru. In mid-1985
at a by-election in Wales - admittedly in a predominantly English-speaking constituency - the
party received only 435 votes, 1.1 per cent of the
total. Although the party remains in existence, it
has also suffered from internal wrangling between
traditionalist and socialist elements (with the

Table 4.6: Plaid Cymru in general elections in Wales 1964-83

	1964	1966	1970	Feb. 1974	Oct. 1974	1979	1983
% of Votes	4.8	4.3	11.5	10.7	10.8	8.1	7.8
No. of Candidates	23	20	36	36	36	36	38
Seats Won	0	0	0	2	3	2	2

Note: There were   36 seats in Wales until 1983 when the number was increased to 38.
Sources: Ibid.

latter gaining the upper hand in 1985).   Plaid remains very much a minor party and its prospects of making significant advances appear slim.
    The complexities of Northern Ireland politics defy all but the specialist, but for the purposes of this chapter a few points are worthy of note. Up to 1970, Ulster's representation at Westminster (12 seats) was overwhelmingly dominated by the Ulster Unionist Party and Unionist members were indistinguishable from the Conservatives.(56)   In the 1970s, however, the Unionist monolith fragmen- ted, as did the representation of the minority Catholic community, and the almost unconditional Unionist support for the Conservatives in the House of Commons was withdrawn.   This became more signi- ficant in 1983 when the number of Westminster seats increased to 17.   This makes it more difficult for a major party to gain an overall majority in the House of Commons and raises the possibility that in a very tight situation in the House the votes of Ulster MPs might be crucial in sustaining or defeating a government.   Moreover, the Anglo-Irish agreement signed by the Conservative Government in November 1985 and the Labour Party's commitment to the eventual unification of Ireland ensured that the Unionist bloc would continue to withhold support from both major parties.
    Electoral developments in Scotland, Wales and Northern Ireland are certainly not as threatening to two-party hegemony as the rise of the Alliance. They serve as a reminder, however, that in the United Kingdom there are significant areas of opposition not just to the current government but to any government at Westminster.

Conclusion

This chapter began by outlining how opposition in Britain was viewed twenty years ago. The events of the 1970s and early 1980s have rendered that view outmoded in almost all particulars. Opposition is not unified and highly concentrated but divided and more fragmented. The major opposition party cannot be certain to form the next government even if opinion polls point to a desire for change in the country. It is faced with the challenge of defeating the party in government, and also with halting the electoral gains of rival oppositions. The duty of the Opposition to criticise, harry and oppose the government in the House of Commons has taken second place to campaigning in the country and attending to internal disputes. The two major parties are not highly competitive in Parliament or across the country. The adversarial style of politics is thought by many to be no longer a vital component of parliamentary government but at best a charade and at worst a blight upon the political system; an alternative opposition group holding this view and having extensive support among the electorate is excluded from effective participation in the parliamentary process; the electoral system and the House of Commons remain more suited to the politics of the 1950s than to those of the 1980s.

These changes have come about as a result of changes among the electorate and in the party system and it now seems unlikely that there will be a rapid return to the 'good (or bad) old days' of straightforward two-party politics. Even if the 'malignant distortion'(57) of the electoral system continues to produce a two-party dominated House of Commons in which the rituals of government and Opposition are played out, a major disjunction will remain between the balance of forces at Westminster and the balance among the electorate.

Partisan de-alignment, and its attendant electoral volatility, has produced a highly fluid situation in British politics, which makes it idle to speculate about the outcome of the next general election and developments thereafter. Possibilities run from a third successive Conservative victory (which would surely heighten the crisis of the Left in Britain) to an outright Alliance victory (which would change the face of British politics). The range of probabilities is narrower than this, but whatever the outcome it seems safe

to predict that there will be no return to the
'classic model' of opposition that has been a
distinctive feature of British politics and, in its
time, an object of envy and pride.

Notes

1. A. Potter, 'Great Britain: Opposition with a Capital "O"', in R.A. Dahl (ed.), Political Oppositions in Western Democracies, (Yale UP, New Haven, Conn., 1966), D.W. Rae, The Political Consequences of Electoral Laws (revised ed.), (Yale UP, New Haven, Conn., 1971).
2. Dahl, Political Oppositions p.340.
3. A. Birch, The British System of Government, (4th edn), (Allen & Unwin, London, 1980), pp.157-61; I. Jennings, Cabinet Government, 3rd edn, (Cambridge UP, London, 1961) pp.499-503.
4. V. Bogdanor, Multi-Party Politics and the Constitution, (Cambridge UP, Cambridge, 1981), pp.7-10.
5. S.E. Finer, Adversary Politics and Electoral Reform, (Wigram, London, 1975); N. Johnson In Search of the Constitution, (Methuen, London and New York, 1977), pp.425 ff.
6. Ibid. p.69.
7. I. Crewe, B. Sarlvik, and J. Alt, 'Partisan Dealignment in Britain, 1964-1974', British Journal of Political Science 7 (1977), pp.129-90; B. Sarlvik and I. Crewe, Decade of Dealignment: The Conservative Victory of 1979 and Electoral Trends in the 1970s, (Cambridge UP, Cambridge, 1983); I. Crewe, 'The Electorate: Partisan Dealignment Ten Years On' in H. Berrington (ed.), Change in British Politics, (Frank Cass, London, 1984), pp.18-215.
8. P. Norton, Dissension in the House of Commons, (Clarendon Press, Oxford, 1980), pp.425 ff.
9. S. Beer, Modern British Politics, (Faber and Faber, London, 1965), p.351.
10. Dissenting votes in the 1945-70 period tended to be cast when the opposing party abstained; Norton, Dissension in the House of Commons, p.425.
11. Between 1945 and 1970 there were 10 government defeats but none were attributable to the government's own backbenchers. Between 1970 and 1979 there were 65 government defeats, of which 29 were due to dissenting votes by government backbenchers (ibid. pp. xvii, 469).

12. I. McAllister, and R. Rose, The Nationwide Competition for Votes, (Pinter, London, 1984), pp.203-18.

13. It might be noted, however, that by means of idiosyncratic logic Mr Benn and others on the left of the party interpreted the results as something of a triumph for socialism. T. Benn, 'Spirit of Labour Reborn', The Guardian, 20 June 1983.

14. J. Curtice, and M. Steed, 'Electoral Choice and the Production of Government: The Changing Operation of the Electoral System in the United Kingdom since 1955', British Journal of Political Science 12 (1982), pp.249-98.

15. Crewe, 'The Electorate: Partisan Dealignment Ten Years On', p.194.

16. Ibid. p.196.

17. Ibid. p.190.

18. H. Harrop, 'Labour-voting Conservatives: A Survey of Policy Differences between the Labour Party and Labour Voters' in R. Worcester and M. Harrop (eds), Political Communications: The General Election Campaign of 1979, (Allen & Unwin, London, 1982).

19. I. Crewe, 'The Labour Party and the Electorate' in D. Kavanagh (ed.), The Politics of the Labour Party, (Allen & Unwin, London, 1982), p.37.

20. A less pessimistic view of Labour's situation is given by W.L. Miller, 'There was no alternative: The British Election of 1983', Parliamentary Affairs, vol. 37, no. 4 (1984), pp.364-84. He argues that short-term factors such as disunity and leadership incompetence exaggerated Labour's débâcle.

21. D. Kogan and M. Kogan, The Battle for the Labour Party, (Fontana, London, 1982); P. Whiteley, The Labour Party in Crisis, (Methuen, London, 1983); P. Williams, 'The Labour Party: The Rise of the Left' in Berrington, Change in British Politics, pp.26-55.

22. Gallup Polls Ltd., Political Index (GPI) reports 257-68.

23. Ibid. 276; 278.

24. Ibid. 182; 278.

25. P. Kellner, 'The Labour Campaign' in A. Ranney (ed.), Britain at the Polls 1983, (American Enterprise Institute, Washington DC, 1985), pp.65-80.

26. GPI, reports 277, 278.
27. See e.g. E. Hobsbawn, 'The broad attack on Thatcher', The Guardian, 8 April 1985.
28. This judgement appeared to be shared by electors. In June 1985 Gallup reported that 51 per cent of respondents agreed that Labour was 'starting to pull itself together and regain its strength', GPI report 298.
29. See P. Seyd, 'The dawn of the Left's new realists', The Guardian, 26 April 1985.
30. Kinnock's 'popularity index' in the Gallup poll shot from -23 in September to +15 in October and then declined to +7 in November and +8 in December: GPI reports 301-304.
31. In September 1984, for example, 29 per cent of Gallup's respondents spontaneously applied the phrase 'Doesn't seem big enough for the job' to Kinnock compared with 14 per cent who applied it to Steel, 9 percent to Thatcher and 8 per cent to Owen: GPI report 289.
32. Except for the months noted in footnote 30.
33. GPI reports 277 ff.
34. Ibid. 286 ff.
35. A left-wing view of the position of the Left is given by Arblaster:

> Kinnock and his allies, old and new, should beware of treating the Left with the old-style leader's arrogance, and of attempting to drive it into the political wilderness ... socialists, active and committed now form a large section of (the Labour Party's) membership and make up the core of the campaigning Left. They will not accept being either abused or ignored.

A. Arblaster, 'Labour's very own moving right show', The Guardian, 26 April 1985.
36. It should be noted, however, that one potentially very damaging development eventually came to nothing. Under the Conservative Government's Trade Union Act unions were compelled to ballot their members on the question of whether union political funds should be retained. These funds provide the vast majority of Labour Party finance and at one point there seemed a real possibility that some unions would vote to abandon them. By December 1985, all 24 unions which had balloted voted overwhelmingly to retain political funds.

37. M. Van Hattem, 'The State of the Parties in Parliament: The Labour Party's Second Term in Opposition', Political Quarterly 55 (1984), pp.364-8.
38. Thus in June 1985 the campaign unit of the PLP drew up a 'hit list' of 131 seats not held by Labour targeted for special effort. Each seat was allocated to an incumbent MP who was expected to liaise with the local party concerned on a regular basis, in addition to his own constituency work.
39. It should be noted, however, that in the October election there were 619 Liberal candidates compared with 517 in February.
40. ·I. Bradley, Breaking the Mould? (Martin Robertson, Oxford, 1981); H. Stephenson, Claret and Chips (Michael Joseph, London, 1982); The Times Guide to the House of Commons, (Times Books, London, 1984).
41. I. Crewe, 'Why the going is now so favourable for a centre party alliance', The Times, 23 March 1981.
42. The full text of 'A Fresh Start for Britain' is reproduced in Stephenson, Claret and Chips, Appendix 2.
43. No more seats were won until the Bermondsey by-election of February 1983 and in that case the result was clearly affected by specifically local factors. D. Denver, 'The SDP-Liberal Alliance: The End of the Two-Party System?' in Berrington, Change in British Politics, pp.75-102.
44. Over 12 regions the Alliance share of the vote ranged from 33.7 per cent (South West) to 23.2 per cent (Wales). The Conservative share ranged from 57.2 per cent (South East) to 28.4 per cent (Scotland) and Labour's from 37.5 per cent (Wales) to 14.1 per cent (South East). The standard deviation of regional votes for the Alliance was 3.3 compared with 9.7 for Labour and 9.2 for the Conservatives. Regional voting figures are taken from The Times 1984.
45. McAllister, and Rose, Nationwide Competition, p.212.
46. Thus at the end of 1984 David Owen claimed to be confident that the Alliance would hold a balance of power after the next election but merely 'hoped' that outright victory was possible since he was not a 'Cassius Clay

politician', The Guardian, 28 December 1984.

47. P. Lemieux, 'Political Issues and Liberal
Support in the February 1974 British General
Election', Political Studies, vol. xxv, no. 3
(1977), pp.323-42; J. Alt, T. Crewe, and B.
Sailvlk, 'Angels in Plastic: The Liberal Surge
in 1974', Political Studies, vol. xxv, no. 3
(1977), pp.343-68.

48. I. Crewe, 'Great Britain' in I. Crewe and
D. Denver (eds), Electoral Change in Western
Democracies, (Croom Helm, London, 1985),
p.121.

49. I. Crewe, 'How to Win a Landslide Without
Really Trying: Why the Conservatives Won in
1983' in A. Ranney (ed.), Britain at the Polls
1983, (American Enterprises Institute,
Washington DC, 1985), pp.192-3.

50. I. Crewe, 'Is Britain's Two-Party System
Really About to Crumble?' Electoral Studies,
vol. 1, no. 3 (1982), pp.275-313.

51. Some aspects of this account of the nature of
Alliance voting are challenged by A. Heath, et
al., How Britain votes, (Pergamon Press,
Oxford, 1985) but their own data confirm the
relative evenness of Alliance support across
major social groups, and although they argue
that 1983 Alliance voters were relatively
ideologically coherent they none the less
conclude that 'Until the Alliance can find one
or more distinctively and "passionately"
Alliance principles, it is unlikely that it
will rival the other parties in its number of
committed supporters' (p.21).

52. J. Naughtie, 'The State of the Parties in
Parliament: The Alliance', Political Quarterly
55 (1984), pp.364-84.

53. Provisional Sinn Fein's representation is
purely formal since their single MP has
refused to take his seat.

54. The 431 'other candidates' outside Northern
Ireland won no seats and 0.7 per cent of the
votes.

55. For an account of the SNP up to 1978 see J.
Brand, The National Movement in Scotland,
(Routledge & Kegan Paul, London, 1978).

56. An illustration of the extent to which this
was the case is the fact that Craig, the
authorative source on British election
results, labels Ulster Unionists as Conservatives and includes Unionist votes and seats

in the Conservative total up to and including the 1970 election. After that, all Northern Ireland candidates are treated as 'others' in the UK context. F.W.S. Craig, <u>British Electoral Facts</u>, (Parliamentary Research Services, Chichester, 1981) and <u>Britain Votes 3</u>, (Parliamentary Research Services, Chichester, 1984).

57. Crewe, <u>The Electorate: Partisan Dealignment Ten Years On</u>, p.183.

5.   FRANCE: LEGITIMACY ATTAINED

Byron Criddle

French politics has been characterised as plagued
by a crisis of legitimacy. Alfred Grosser, writing
in 1965, saw France as 'nothing but opposition'.(1)
He summarised the prevailing, indeed traditional,
conventional wisdom that all governments were, in
effect, minorities; that all governments were
denied the essential ingredients of a national
consensus, the right to speak for the whole
country; France was perceived as being divided into
les deux Frances(2) although real socio-economic
and political divisions may have been less deep.
Under these conditions, all governments had to
remain unequal to a thankless task. Grosser wrote
of 'conflicts of legitimacy', of a tradition of
contesting not merely governmental authority, but
the legitimacy of the regime itself. Thus the
legitimacy of the Third Republic was challenged by
Catholics and workers; that of Vichy by de Gaulle's
appeal in June 1940 and the Resistance thereafter;
that of the Fourth Republic many times in its
twelve-year history (not least when the Gaullist
Debré observed that Prime Minister Mollet would
answer to a court of law for signing the Treaty of
Rome) and most convincingly in 1958 when the
Algiers coup de force finally felled the regime.
The ensuing Fifth Republic was established by a man
who in 1960 could proclaim that he had embodied
national legitimacy for twenty years. There was,
moreover, the French tradition of government opponents conflating government and state, so that
before 1958 de Gaulle could blame 'the system', and
after 1958 the Left could blame 'the regime'; nor
was it insignificant that the 'system' installed in
1946 was approved initially in a referendum by a
mere one in three electors, and the 'regime' of

116

1958 by an albeit more healthy two in three.

Grosser's analysis was expanded by Macridis(3) who stressed the multiplicity of oppositions and their negative character; that they came from every possible combination of political parties, many of which were themselves fissiparous. Governments were merely defensively derived responses to parties opposed to the very regime: in 1951 ten out of nineteen million voters voted for two 'anti-regime' parties, the Communists and the Gaullists. Political life, though historically bifurcated into 'Left' and 'Right', in fact consisted of a number of mutually hostile parties on either side of that divide; a situation, in short, of 'polarised pluralism' as identified by Giovanni Sartori.(4) In addition to divided governments facing a variety of parliamentary oppositions, there also existed extra-parliamentary oppositions in the form of violent demonstrations, and the menace, and ulti-mate reality, of coups d'état. In 1976 the third president of the Fifth Republic, Valéry Giscard d'Estaing, wrote of his hope of 'once and for all committing our country to modern democracy'(5), by which he meant implanting in France political atti-tudes and procedures familiar, as he believed, to the Northern European democracies, which he saw as preferable to 'the Latin liking for extremes' and a style of political debate taking the form of a confrontation between two mutually exclusive truths.(6)

The National Consensus

In fact, between the Fourth Republic as described by Grosser and Macridis and President Giscard's book in 1976, the negative character of governments and oppositions had been replaced by a coherent governing majority built first around President de Gaulle and the Gaullist party. Thus, when Giscard took up his pen France had at least positive and stable government; what it lacked, however, was an opposition capable of alternating in power with the governing majority. The stability of government thus comprised a situation in which one half of the country (the Right) permanently ruled the other half (the Left), and where certain liberal democra-tic norms, such as the legitimacy of party (a perennial target in Gaullist discourse) and more specifically the rights of opposition parties appeared denied, thus preventing the achievement of

the Giscardian objective of <u>cohabitation raison-</u>
<u>nable</u> - a Gallic version of Anglo-Saxon consensus
and fair play, with government and opposition
parties alternating undramatically in power.
Despite these enduring shortcomings, it was
nevertheless asserted in 1978 by Frears that 'legitimacy is well-established'.(7) This assessment
was made, moreover, in the wake of a parliamentary
election in which for the eighth time in succession
over a twenty-year period the electorate had voted
for the <u>status quo</u>, for the incumbent government,
eschewing a vote for opposition parties whose
access to power was always presented by those in
government as bearing the risk of constitutional
crisis. Nevertheless, for that observer, even
without <u>alternance</u>, the regime had by 1978 attained
legitimacy. As a checklist of legitimacy indicators, Frears offered the following: is there alternation? is it peaceful? is it accepted? is it
followed by monetary collapse or constitutional
crisis? does the new government seek to modify
fundamentally political institutions? is there a
broad consensus between the old government and the
new on the main lines of foreign and defence
policy? In short, is alternation of parties in
power compromised by the presence of governing
parties unprepared to accord legitimacy to their
opponents, or opposition parties or groups with
structural, as distinct from routine policy orien-
tated, objectives?
For Maurice Duverger, writing in 1985, a
national consensus of a kind similar to that found
in other Western European states, had finally been
accomplished.(8) It comprises first a consensus on
democracy, the monarchist and authoritarian
tendency on the Right having disappeared, along
with celebrated divisions over foreign and colonial
policy; and the force of extremism on the Left
having been eroded with the apparent renunciation
by the Communist party of the harder aspects of
Stalinism. Meanwhile, although Le Pen and the re-
emergent extreme Right and the still recidivist PCF
would probably <u>not</u> respect liberal democratic
values, were either to obtain power on their own (a
wholly fictional notion), the fact that they do not
draw attention to their authoritarian predilec-
tions, through fear of electoral disavowal,
confirms that a consensus on democracy does indeed
exist and that even extremist parties have to
respect it. The consensus comprises secondly, a

consensus on institutions. This was finally
secured in 1981 when <u>alternance</u> at last occurred as
the opposition coalition of the Left replaced the
governing coalition of the Right in power for
twenty three years. The capture of the presidency
by the Left candidate, Mitterrand, in 1981 effectively removed the reservations of an anti-
caesarist type, which the Left had expressed for
two decades about the presidential nature of the
Fifth Republic. In 1981 what reservations remained
were reduced to a token reference to certain
anodyne changes in presidential powers. The Left's
occupancy of a directly-elected executive presidency, designed by and for the Right, legitimated
the 1958-62 constitutional arrangements by removing
their partisan associations, and Mitterrand's con-
duct in office confirmed the reconciliation of the
Left to the presidential monarchy it had rhetoric-
ally denounced in earlier years. Mitterrand's own
reflections on assuming office were revealing
enough; 'Les institutions n'etaient pas faites à
mon intention; mais elles sont bien faites pour
moi'.(9) Furthermore, the Socialist Government
after 1981 made full use of all the devices available in the constitution to side-step parliamentary
obstruction of its programme, notwithstanding the
Left's traditional sensitivity to the legitimacy of
parliamentary constraints on the executive.

There remained, of course, the reservations of
the PCF, its opposition to a popularly elected head
of state (and of government) being understandable
given that no Communist candidate could ever expect
to reach the Elysée, even if Marchais delayed dis-
paraging the whole question of presidential power
until after his votes had been counted in April
1981. But the PCF has equally to take account of
the popularity both of presidential dominance and
the system of direct election among the voters,
even Communist voters, only 17 per cent of whom (as
compared with 13 per cent of all voters) favour a
diminished role for the presidency.(10) It is
true, of course, that the March 1986 parliamentary
election produced a vote for 'extremist' parties
(PCF plus <u>Front National</u>) of some 20 per cent,
implying that the consensus is flawed, but such a
calculation is notional given the essentially
protest nature of much voting for such parties;
hostility to government policy, or lack of it,
should not be seen as evidence of support for a
challenge to the legitimacy of the regime or its

institutions. There is, in any case, some problem
with the word 'extremist'; how 'extreme' are
'extremist' parties? Lavau's analysis of the PCF
as performing a tribune function, acting as spokesman for the poor and defenceless, implies that,
regardless of whatever its leaders may <u>say</u>, the
party's electoral significance is more conventional.(11) Furthermore, notwithstanding the radical rhetoric of the leadership - as evidenced by
L'Humanité's defiant declaration in the wake of the
party's worst electoral performance for fifty years
in March 1986, that it was a 'revolutionary party'
- the PCF acts conventionally enough within French
liberal democratic structures, indeed to the
extent of sharing in government for three years
after 1981. And in any event, the 20 per cent vote
for 'extremist' parties (PCF plus FN) in 1986 was
less than half the 'anti-system' (Communist plus
Gaullist) aggregate of 1951, and barely half that
(Communist plus Poujadist) of 1956. It seems
possible, therefore, to agree with Duverger that
'for the first time since 1789, the consensus on
the regime is quasi general; differences concern
only minor points',(12) and, one might add, involve
only minor parties. The point is simply put: in
1981 the Fifth Republic came of age with alternation finally reconciling the Left to a regime
installed by the Right, and thus possessing like
all French regimes, partisan associations; whilst
the Right, in having to surrender office, could
hardly contest a regime it had itself founded and
in which it could reasonably hope soon to recapture
power.

The third aspect of the consensus, according
to Duverger, is social. Economic modernisation has
increased living standards and transformed social
structure and cleavage patterns. Some groups, once
influential, such as the self-employed petty
bourgeoisie, have diminished; others, such as the
white collars, have greatly expanded. With rural
contraction has come suburban expansion. The poor
are cushioned by welfare and inequalities diminished. Meanwhile, the blue-collar working class
both enjoys higher standards and slowly declines in
size, thus denuding the electoral force of its
would-be proprietor, the PCF. For Duverger, in
consequence, 'révolutionnairisme' gives way to
'réformisme'.(13)

As evidence of the new consensus, the form
taken by opposition in the Fifth Republic after the

120

mid-1960s was bipolarised, 'bipolarised' implying
something very different from 'polarised'.
Bipolarisation, after an initial division of the
electorate into Gaullist and anti-Gaullist alliances, has taken the form of Right versus Left, but
no longer in the sense of warring camps implacably
opposed, rather of diversely composed coalitions
led by the moderate elements of each alliance. The
origins of this moderate bipolarisation lie not
only in the social and attitudinal changes already
described, but more immediately stem from two
important institutional devices affecting the terms
of competition, namely the two-ballot electoral
system reintroduced for parliamentary elections in
1958, and the direct election of the presidency,
introduced in 1962 and first implemented in
1965.(14).

The electoral system of 'scrutin majoritaire à
deux tours' had always, when used before during
most of the Third Republic, had a bipolarising
effect at the second ballot. The nature of the
bipolarisation after reintroduction of the system
in 1958 differed, however, from that before 1940,
in that it was nationally standardised rather than
regionally diverse, and this essentially because of
the national focus given to elections in the early
years of the regime by its charismatic leader,
Charles de Gaulle. Thus political culture ('heroic
leadership') and electoral contrivance combined to
prompt party system realignment. Parties of the
Right with few significant exceptions assembled
behind de Gaulle at the second ballot, leaving
parties of the Left to form, faute de mieux, a pole
of opposition. Because heavy penalties awaited
parties that ignored the alliance-building strategies required to win seats at the second ballot,
the Left, though bitterly and historically divided
between Communists and Socialists, established
first a national electoral pact (1967) and then a
programmatic agreement (1972) in order to contest
the Right's enduring incumbency. Thus opposition
strategies became essentially co-operative, but not
- and significantly not - exclusively so. The crux
of each alliance's electoral pact was withdrawal
before the second ballot in favour of the best-
placed candidate; this led, especially on the Left,
where the alliance was essentially a negative
matter, to intense competition between Socialist
and Communist parties at the first ballot in order
to assume the leading position necessary to proceed

to the occupation of winnable seats after the
second ballot. Thus at the 1978 election, the PCF,
obsessed by the growing Socialist threat to its
dominance, did everything it could to beat its
mortal ally at the first ballot in order to staunch
the flow of left seats from Communist to Socialist
at the second ballot. This rivalry dominated the
election and ultimately determined its outcome:
defeat for the once-favoured Left.(15) The same
election also saw a record number of first-round
contests between allied Gaullist and Giscardian
candidates, each vying for supremacy within the
governing majority. Nevertheless, bipolarisation
has implied co-operative strategies, a requirement
serving to pull 'extreme' parties such as the
Communists, albeit reluctantly and thus ultimately
unconvincingly, away from Stalinist orthodoxy and
towards 'Eurocommunist' moderation.

Bipolarisation involves, however, much more
than mere electoral tactics. It has involved a
radical refashioning of the party system, the most
prominent and durable feature of which was extreme
fragmentation into a large number of small and
poorly disciplined parties. From a large number of
small parties, France has moved to a small number
of large parties. By the late 1970s only four
parties of significance were operationally significant, though one of these was in fact an alliance
of three smaller parties. During the Fourth
Republic, the four largest parties - and it is
important to note that they were not the same four
parties from one election to the next - averaged 77
per cent of the vote over the three elections
between 1946 and 1956; during the Fifth Republic
from 1958 to 1978 over six elections, the four
largest parties collected 85 per cent, and in 1981,
99 per cent. The same trend was reflected in the
distribution of parliamentary seats; by 1981 97 per
cent were occupied by the big four. There had also
developed a genuine government-opposition bifurca-
tion, replacing the varied oppositions of earlier
republics. Parliament was now divided into permanent supporters and permanent opponents of government. Furthermore, this pattern of permanent,
disciplined bipolarity came by 1977 to extend down
into local government.

Presidentialisation of Politics

A second institutional stimulus to a bipolarised

122

pattern of opposition, and arguably the more important, was the presidentialisation of politics
produced by the elevation of the presidency to full
executive status and its direct election. The
mechanism of election was particularly important,
involving a deliberately two-cornered contest at
the second ballot, requiring the victor to aggregate nationally some fifteen million votes, a
figure well beyond the reach of any single party-
based candidate. Presidential elections have
become the central event of national political
life, and although rare on account of the seven-
year term of office they are more important than
the intervening parliamentary elections, even, in
the long run, the election of March 1986 which for
the first time produced a result hostile to the
incumbent president. Legislative elections have
become subordinate to presidential contests, each
dominated by the frankly explicit rallying cry of
'une majorité pour le Président'. More than this,
presidential elections with votes counted in one
national constituency have served to nationalise
political life, eroding the importance of regional
particularisms on which some of the older parties
had relied.

The impact on the parties has been far-
reaching. To be taken seriously a party has to
have a presidentially-credible leader, and has to
evolve long-term strategies. In effect, of the big
four parties dominating political life by the
1970s, three were largely purpose-built to promote
presidential candidates. The RPR (Rassemblement
pour la République), created in 1976 by Jacques
Chirac, though having been formed under a different
label as nothing more than an unconditional supporting force for President de Gaulle, has an avowedly
presidentialist mission. Equally, though less
effectively, the UDF (Union pour la démocratie
française) was established to provide parliamentary
backing for President Giscard d'Estaing. It is a
less secure growth, suffering the traditional
resistance of its component parts to organisation,
failing to provide as was intended an effective
counterweight to Gaullist strength and by the 1980s
compromised by the presence of a rival, and more
popular présidentiable, Raymond Barre. The
Socialist Party provides the third example of a
presidentialised party. Risen like a phoenix from
the ashes of Mollet's moribund SFIO, it was
'demolletised' by François Mitterrand at the Epinay

Congress of 1971 only to become wholly
'mitterrandised' thereafter, with everything subordinated to the task of propelling Mitterrand into
the presidency on the backs of a mathematically
necessary and thus essentially expedient alliance
with the Communist Party, all of which was dignified with the phrase 'La ligne d'Epinay'. What
RPR, UDF and PS have in common is that their essential function is to launch presidential candidates
and sustain them in office.

Presidentialisation has meant that parties
lacking this vocation are pushed to the margins.
The Communists, the one party of the big four
unable to play the presidential game, certainly
owes part of its electoral demise to its new-found
irrelevance in a presidential system. The candida-
ture of Marchais in 1981, like that of Duclos in
1969, was far from evidence of the PCF seriously
entering the presidential stakes, but rather of a
defiant gesture designed to clip the wings of its
Socialist rival. Meanwhile, leaders of small
parties who entertain presidential ambitions are
obliged, in the manner of Michel Rocard, to join
'presidential' parties. Equally, the subsequent
difficulties encountered by Rocard inside the
Socialist Party, where he lacks activist support,
confirm the need for présidentiables to have a
secure and reliable base within the party in order
to secure the party's backing for a presidential
bid. Barre's similar lack of a secure and significant partisan base appeared in the 1980s somewhat
to complicate his prospects.

It has been suggested that presidential hopefuls have either to conquer parties or to neutralise them.(16) Conquest, in the case of weakly
structured parties is relatively easy, as confirmed
by Servan-Schreiber's capture of the Radical Party,
though this was a largely futile accomplishment
given the marginalised and moribund condition of
the party. Chirac used his power and status as
Prime Minister to take over the Gaullist party in
1976 from the barons he had treacherously deserted
in the presidential election of 1974; in this exercise he was assisted both by the Gaullist party's
inherent desire to equate with power and its receptiveness to strong leadership. In the case of the
Socialist Party, seizure of power by a présidentiable is a more subtle business. Thus at the 1979
Congress ambitious Young Turks such as Fabius and
Chevènement backed Mitterrand against Rocard on the

basis of the former being a candidate 'acceptable
to the party'. This was a means both of ditching
Rocard and of lining Fabius and Chevènement up to
succeeding in legitimate fashion to the presidential mantle in the future.

Candidates, such as Rocard, popular with
public opinion but lacking internal party support,
have to adopt the alternative neutralisation
strategy. Thus Rocard sought to mobilise his
extra-party popularity by waving his poll ratings
and frequent television appearances in Mitterrand's
face. This somewhat foolhardy defiance entirely
failed to undermine the position of a leader like
Mitterrand, around whom the very electoral resurgence of the party appeared to have been built and
whose legitimacy could be justified moreover in
terms of the party's democratic culture. Elements
of the neutralisation strategy emerged in the run-
up to the 1986 legislative election as Raymond
Barre, a présidentiable with no adequate partisan
base and in competition with at least two other
right-of-centre presidential hopefuls, sought to
manoeuvre for the presidency by denigrating the
notion of partisan strategies around a beleaguered
President Mitterrand, all of this in the name of
preserving the status of the presidency. Men
without parties naturally extol the virtue of
presidents above parties. Experience, however,
suggests that it is only presidents with secure
partisan backing in parliament, such as de Gaulle
from 1962-69, Pompidou from 1969-74, and Mitterrand
from 1981-86 who have the means to be fully presidential presidents. Anything less than a secure
partisan base leads to weakness and compromise, as
in the latter part of Giscard's presidency, or
indeed to a different 'reading' of the constitution, as was suggested with the defeat of the
Socialists in 1986.

Presidential strategies not only require
secure partisan bases, but also involve long-term
inter-party alliances in order to establish electoral credibility. Thus alliances cannot be spatch-
cocked together in the run-up to an election. The
Socialist-Communist alliance originated in 1965 and
involved a long march through two consecutive
presidential defeats before Mitterrand finally and
unexpectedly won in 1981. The two Gaullist presidents profited from the largest available partisan
base, allied to the virtually (until the death of
Pompidou) unconditional support of the 'Giscardian'

125

Right. Giscard himself, with, of all the four presidents since 1958, the least solid party base, was in the happy position, on the death of President Pompidou, of comparing favourably with an undistinguished rank of Gaullist presidential aspirants; yet he too had been tenaciously plotting his ascent to the Elysée since forming his own party in 1962. Faulty strategies, on the other hand, are those put together in a rush, or based merely on a single partisan base devoid of alliances; the 1969 election afforded examples of each. The candidacy of Alain Poher made little sense: no partisan negotiations preceded it, it being an ad hoc response prompted by the sudden and surprising exposure of Poher as interim president for a few weeks (in his capacity as President of the Senate) following the unexpected resignation of de Gaulle. The Poher phenomenon was little more than the creation of his television appearances and of the pollsters (whose importance also re-emerged in 1974 when polling showed Chaban-Delmas running consistently behind Giscard d'Estaing, thus effectively putting paid to the former's chances). Poher was also able to profit from the temporary vacuum created on the left by the May evènements and electoral rout of 1968. Meanwhile, the candidacy of the Communist Duclos was an example of how an isolated partisan base of some 21 per cent was valid only if the intention was to remind a disorientated Socialist Party of the reality of Communist dominance.

Presidentialism has also imposed structural modifications on the parties.(17) The first relates to organisation; organisationally geared for parliamentary elections, the parties have had to adapt to presidential politics. A presidential-ised culture has permeated the parties, enabling leaders to wield much arbitrary power, though to be fair, in some parties cultural dispositions of this sort already existed. The presidential dominance of Chirac over the RPR is but the presidential dominance of the regime in microcosm. In the case of Mitterrand and the Socialist Party, the institutional model of the Fifth Republic has also become the prevailing model inside the party, notwithstanding the fact that the party has, of all French parties, the most self-consciously democratic tradition, and retains representative bodies with decision-making powers. Yet Mitterrand's party has seen its leader rightly regaled with a variety of

titles: <u>patron</u>, <u>seigneur</u>, <u>roi</u>. Formal power struc
tures count for little; Mitterrand's back-up team
of advisers, both during and between election
campaigns, was quite separate from the formal
agencies of the party. As in the United States,
presidential support teams tend to be built around
a network of chums and cronies dating back to the
leader's political youth or middle age, in
Mitterrand's case, confidants such as Badinter,
Dreyfus and Hernu. From these people, quite as
much as from amongst those with clout inside the
party, were drawn the senior appointments in office
after 1981.

A second, and important, impact on the parties
is in the matter of ideology. Presidential
politics involves wide vote aggregation, calling
for a 'catch-all' strategy involving an enhanced
role for leadership, a commensurately reduced role
for the rank-and-file, a discarding of ideological
baggage, and a detachment from too specific class
clienteles. Parties of the Right, and commonly in
power, normally have little autonomy from their
leaders anyway, nor much in the way of dogma to get
in the way of electoral campaigning. Parties of
the Left, however, languishing long in opposition,
like the Socialists before 1981, find the process
more awkward. Such parties are programmatic in the
sense of having certain policy objectives common to
socialist parties and, moreover, the additional
preoccupation of sustaining a programmatic alliance
with a difficult and demanding Communist ally.
Even so, the Socialist Party was effectively
constrained by Mitterrand. In 1981, even more
obviously than in 1974, he ran as his own man,
campaigning on his own '110 Propositions' and most
significantly not the <u>Projet socialiste</u>, a draft
produced by the party's Marxist left wing and
accordingly containing much material of an electorally indigestible sort. The campaigning emphasis, as befits a personalised contest such as a
presidential race, is more upon the man than the
measures. The marketing of Mitterrand in 1981
indeed spoke volumes for the transformation of a
Socialist Party; in his nationally ubiquitous
campaign poster the Socialist Party leader was
portrayed against the backdrop of a rural scene,
with church tower prominent and alongside that most
reassuringly bland of slogans: <u>la force tranquille</u>.
The Left's victory of 1981, to the extent that it
was much more than merely the defeat of the Right,

was almost certainly a victory for la force tranquille, and categorically not for one of the central nostrums of the Projet socialiste, namely la rupture avec le capitalisme.(18)

The demise of ideology in a country noted for 'a taste for language and a pleasure in ideas',(19) where ideas indeed are taken seriously and where revolutionary rhetoric has long been an integral part of much left political discourse, may seem like a contradiction in terms. Yet the Marxist-sounding Project socialiste of 1980, and the call at the 1981 Socialist Party congress for 'rolling heads' in the civil service, did little more than provide examples of how the form should not be mistaken for the substance. The Projet was never taken seriously by party leaders as a viable campaigning tool, and very few senior civil servants' heads did roll when Socialist ministers took up office in 1981. One should not be misled by a unique mix of radical discourse and conserva-tive practice; thus even Giscard's strictures rather overstated the case for political disability when he wrote of France being characterised by 'ideological divorce'.(20) In effect no leaders of significance dispute the desirability of Giscard's 'cohabitation raisonnable', nor Pierre Mauroy's socialist version of the same concept: 'dialogue républicaine'.

To all intents and purposes, the taste for ideology has become a victim of the application of the Downsian model in French electioneering, at least at bipolarised second ballot contests.(21) The Downsian model assumes that candidates give priority to winning the election and therefore act rationally to maximise votes; that the electoral arena has a centre; that enough voters exist capable of being moved from one side to the other to make competition for their votes worthwhile; that floating voters are to be found at the centre rather than at the extremes; and that candidates may moderate their positions without losing partisan supporters with more extreme views. Whilst this model does not apply to first-ballot electioneering, where the Socialists, for example, have had traditionally to fight a campaign on two fronts (communist and centrist), it does in other respects apply in every particular, and most notably in connection with the unimportance of partisan discontent. The full retreat of the Socialist Government from ideology, its throwing

into reverse of the Keynesian dash for growth and
application of rigeur was met with little resistance in the party, whose stand-in leader, Jospin,
maintained throughout the five years of government
a stance closer to apologist for government than
representative of activist hopes. Weekly meetings
between Mitterrand, Prime Minister Mauroy and
Jospin during the three years of the Mauroy Government served essentially to ensure that the party
was kept in harness behind the President and
government. Even on the emotionally powerful issue
of church schools, the government's monumental
climb-down in 1984 was met by substantial rank-and-
file acquiescence. The docility of the Socialist
Party after 1981 confirmed that even Socialist
parties can become pliant supporting forces for
incumbent presidents, perhaps more especially if
they have been out of power for a generation.

Not even the highly factionalised character of
the Socialist Party - its unique distinguishing
mark compared with all other parties - insulated it
from the presidential infection: in effect, factional life was reduced to a competition of rival
présidentiables (Rocard, Mauroy, Chevènement,
Fabius). Only currents with a présidentiable in
the van count, though this is somewhat less true
of the left-wing CERES (Centre d'etudes, de recherches et d'éducation socialistes) faction. Effectively ideology has become the servant of ambition,
as indeed was illustrated by Mitterrand's own
dexterous weaving amid the factions in the ten
years before 1981, as he moved from the marxisant
emphasis required of a new party leader with only
shallow Socialist roots in 1971, through a rejection of the left wing in the cause of broadening
electoral appeal in the period before 1978; back to
an alliance with the CERES in order to disqualify
and isolate a dangerous rival, Rocard, in 1979; and
finally to the manifest pragmatism of the 1981
campaign, when victory was won with a strategy
indistinguishable from that advocated by Rocard.
Factional conflict focused upon presidential ambition clearly carries some destabilising potential,
but less seriously than factional conflict in which
ideology counts per se.

The 1980s Elections

The pattern of bipolarised, presidentialised opposition thus far described was put at risk by the

electoral outcomes of the 1980s. Whilst the 1981
elections provided for alternation without tears,
that is, in the least disruptive fashion, by way of
first a presidential victory followed by the new
president's use of the dissolution weapon and the
subsequent election of a congruent parliamentary
majority, the electoral majorities by which such
alternation was effected were highly ephemeral.
Mitterrand's 52 per cent presidential majority of
May 1981 and the Left's 55 per cent aggregate in
the June legislative election had vanished within
six months, as confirmed at all important elections
(parliamentary by-elections, cantonal elections,
municipal elections and European Assembly elections) after January 1982. This rapid vaporisation
of the Left's majority opened up the prospect of
the French being exposed on the expiry of the
shorter (five-year) parliamentary term in 1986 to
an attempt at alternation the wrong way round, with
a newly ascendant right-wing parliamentary majority
confronting, but having no capacity to remove, an
incumbent Socialist President. This duly occurred
in March 1986 and was dignified with the term
'cohabitation'.
    What this electoral outcome served to reveal
was the purely behavioural basis of the presidential dominance which has so fashioned the character
of competition in the Fifth Republic. Presidential
dominance has no real constitutional foundation.
Whilst the presidency has certain explicit powers
of appointment and decision-making in respect of
dissolving the National Assembly, invoking emergency powers and sanctioning referenda, the constitution specifically does not allot the President a
governing function; that rests with the Prime
Minister and government, which must, under the
concept of responsibility to the legislature,
command a majority in the National Assembly. In
effect, the President has two sorts of powers: the
few and rather special powers listed in the constitution, and the many available to him only if he is
the leader of the parliamentary majority and able
to rule by proxy through a loyal and docile Prime
Minister. Without the latter capacity the President of the Republic combines simultaneously some
of the functions of leader of the Opposition
à l'anglaise, though admittedly with more powers
than the holder of that British office. Thus
presidential dominance - the keystone of Fifth
Republic politics - rests upon the happy coinci-

dence of the electorate ensuring that incumbent presidents are never compromised by being denied a parliamentary majority; upon electoral behaviour, not constitutional precept.

The originality, not to say eccentricity, of French political life was reflected in the campaign for the March 1986 elections. Most spokesmen of the Right up-ended the political nostrums of their generation by affecting to believe in a parliamentarist interpretation of the constitution which, in the words of the Gaullist Chaban-Delmas, meant that the Président should preside and the Government govern. Even de Gaulle's once-expressed belief that the constitution was 'elastic' was dusted down.(22) But in as historically conscious a country as France it took no time for others to invoke the spectre of Gambetta challenging the defeated President MacMahon in 1877 'to submit or resign'. The advocate of that course in 1986, in the name of preserving the power and authority of the presidency, was Raymond Barre. There was every indication that the invoking of confrontation and crisis by Barre slowed down the Right's electoral progress and contributed to the unexpected narrowness of its March 1986 victory, as voters rallied to a President whose legitimacy was being threatened by Barre's posture.

A 4 per cent swing from Right to Left over the period of the campaign in February-March pointed to the presidentialisation of the election by Mitterrand's numerous interventions. Not only did the Socialist Party run on the presidentialist slogan 'Avec le Président', but the President addressed two major Socialist rallies, and gave a number of press and television interviews in which he made clear his view that he would not become an 'inert' president; that he would continue to command in foreign and defence policy; and that he would protect the social policy gains made by his Socialist governments since 1981. Ironically, though equally predictably, in an election whose certain outcome threatened presidential dominance, the March 1986 election, more than any other parliamentary election since 1958 was thoroughly presidentialised by a party struggling to retain a governing status so tenuously won in 1981.

In effect, for all the uncertainties opened up by the outcome of the March 1986 election cohabitation of the Socialist President Mitterrand with the Gaullist Prime Minister Chirac - the

131

essential features of Fifth Republic politics
remained intact, or at least were no more than
temporarily compromised. First, presidential
dominance, if interrupted, was certainly not broken
by the clash of presidential and parliamentary
mandates. All major political leaders of the new
parliamentary majority retained their belief in a
dominant presidency and many personally sought the
office. Thus for Chirac, occupancy of the Matignon
after March was intended merely to put himself in
an unassailable position for running as the Right's
most likely successor to President Mitterrand in
the presidential election due in 1988. Barre's
tactics, though different, were equally focused on
the presidential race; ambitious, but lacking a
strong base, he had to hope that Chirac would
destroy his credibility amidst the muddied waters
of cohabitation, a process serving also to
disengage or neutralise the force of the RPR and
permit Barre with clean hands to lead the Right to
a presidential victory. Meanwhile, the Socialist
Party, sustained in parliamentary strength and with
all its leaders returned to the Assembly by
Mitterrand's deft recourse to proportional representation in 1986, had every reason to hold ranks
behind the President as never before. Fully
socially democratised by five years of office,
acclimatised to power, the party seemed likely even
to avoid a war of succession to Mitterrand, should
he risk leaving his party to fight without him.
The mood of realism in the party after five years
was arguably sufficient for it even to acquiesce in
the dauphinisation of Fabius so as to short-circuit
a war of chiefs, though the ambitions of Rocard
were likely to have a destabilising impact. But
essentially, the commitment of all political
leaders to the restoration of a governing presidency served to guarantee that the short period of
cohabitation would be a mere parenthesis.
      Secondly, bipolarisation could also be
expected to survive the limited damage done to it
by the reversion to proportional representation in
March 1986. Designed by the Socialists to repro-
duce on the right the sort of disaggregation which
had by 1985 come to characterise the erstwhile
'union of the Left', proportional representation
was intended to award seats to the extreme Right
(FN) at the expense of the respectable Right (RPR-
UDF), and this it duly did, almost denying the
respectable Right a parliamentary majority. Apart

from containing the Right's victory and so
strengthening Mitterrand's hand over the cohabitation interregnum, proportional representation
sustained the declining extreme Left (PCF) and
encouraged the rising extreme Right (Front
National). Each with 10 per cent of the vote and 6
per cent of the parliamentary seats, the extremes
secured what they would not have obtained under the
discarded electoral system, which would have
reduced the Communists to an all-time low of nine
seats and delivered no more than seven (and arguably fewer) to the Front National.(23) Proportional representation in 1986 thus had a mildly
fragmenting effect, exacerbating centrifugal
strains in contrast to the centripetal forces
encouraged by the discarded two-ballot system. Yet
the retention by the RPR-UDF and the PS of almost
80 per cent of the vote testified to a broad
consensus around the larger moderate parties with
governing potential. Moreover, the promptly
announced intention of Chirac's government to
restore scrutin majoritaire à deux tours, if
successfully accomplished, would restore one of the
twin pillars on which bipolarisation had been
built; without it, and the mechanics of the presidential election, it has been suggested that
bipolarisation would founder, particularly on the
left.(24) Thus it appeared that the ground-rules
set for party competition in the Fifth Republic
were intact, and that large, cohesive parties with
presidential leaders and catch-all strategies had a
future in a way that declining sectarian parties
(PCF) or temporarily effervescent parties (FN) did
not.

The most significant development in the 1980s
was not the rise of the 'extreme' Right, but the
demise of the 'extreme' Left, as reflected in the
decline of the Communist Party and the affirmation
of a 3:1 electoral dominance over it of the
Socialist Party. Reduced by 1986 to under 10 per
cent of the vote, the PCF had lost half its electorate in the space of eight years. Marginalised
by electoral devices and institutional factors, as
well as by social forces and its leaders' own
resistance to change, the Communist Party had been
reduced to a force d'appoint on the left, leaving
the Socialist Party free to campaign overtly as a
social democratic party shorn of the radical
verbalism forced on it by an alliance with a big
Communist party, and to bid for the support of

conservative voters. With the veto power of the
PCF broken, the social democratisation of the Left
made possible a version of the alternance souple
characteristic of Northern Europe.(25) The major
parties of Left and Right could anticipate the
routine exchange of national office on the periodic
swing of the pendulum, and as a small consolation
when ousted nationally, could retreat into the
regional and local power bases which the Socialist
government's reforms after 1981 had made more
significant.

Cohabitation and the substantial policy
consensus it implied - even if symbolised by an
albeit uncomfortable dyarchy of Mitterrand and
Chirac after the 1986 election - was a long way
from the electoral rhetoric of the 1970s, when the
Right dramatised elections as a choix de société.
A French-style consensus on the regime, on foreign
and defence policy and on substantial tracts of
social policy (the latter symbolised and safe-
guarded by the emergence of a large pragmatic
social democratic party) might not exactly amount
to the British Butskellism of the 1950s, still less
to a 'grand coalition' of 'historic compromise',
but it did decidedly challenge the vision of French
politics as presented by Sartori, Grosser and
others in the earlier post-war decades.

Notes

1. A. Grosser, 'France: Nothing but Opposition', in R., Dahl, Political Oppositions in Western Democracies, (Yale UP, New Haven, Conn., 1966), pp.284-302.
2. D. Johnson, 'The Two Frances: the Historical Debate', West European Politics (October 1978), pp.3-10.
3. R. Macridis 'Oppositions in France: An Interpretation', Government and Opposition, (Summer 1972), pp.116-85.
4. G. Sartori, 'The Case for Polarised Pluralism' in J. La Palombara and M. Weiner (eds), Political Parties and Political Development, (Princeton UP, Princeton NJ, 1967).
5. V. Giscard D'Estaing, Démocratie française, (Fayard, Paris, 1976), pp.154-5.
6. Ibid.
7. J.R. Frears, 'Legitimacy, Democracy and Consensus', West European Politics (1978), p.13.
8. M. Duverger, Le système politique français, (PUF, Paris, 1985), pp.494 ff.
9. Le Monde, 2 July 1981.
10. SOFRES poll, L'Express, April 1985.
11. G. Lavau, 'Le partie communiste dans le système politique français' in F. Bon et al., Le communisme en France (Armand Colin, Paris, 1969).
12. Duverger, Le système politique, p.502.
13. Ibid. p.503
14. For an examination of the effect of the voting system in France see D. Goldey and P. Williams in V. Bogdanor and D. Butler (eds), Democracy and Elections, (Cambridge UP, Cambridge, 1982) and S. Bartolini, 'Institutional Constraints and Party Competition in the French Party System', West European Politics, vol. 7, no. 4, (1984), pp.103-27.
15. Frears, 'Legitimacy, Democracy and Consensus', p.23.
16. H. Portelli, 'La présidentialisation des partis politiques', Pouvoirs 14, (1980), pp.97-106.
17. Ibid.
18. See G. Grunberg, 'Causes et fragilités de la victoire socialiste de 1981' in D. Boy et al., 1981: Les élections d'alternance, (FNSP, Paris, 1986).

19. Grosser, 'France: Nothing but Opposition'.
20. Giscard d'Estaing, Démocratic française.
21. A. Downs, An Economic Theory of Democracy, (Harper & Row, New York, 1957).
22. A. Peyrefitte, Encore un effort, Monsieur le Président, (J-C Lattes, Paris, 1985).
23. Bull-BVA estimate, Libération, 18 March 1986.
24. O. Duhamel, La gauche et la Ve République, (PUF, Paris, 1980). p.553.
25. M. Duverger, Bréviaire de la cohabitation, (PUF, Paris, 1986), p.112.

6. THE FEDERAL REPUBLIC OF GERMANY: THE RE-EMERGENT OPPOSITION?

William E. Paterson and Douglas Webber

Introduction

In his essay on the 'vanishing opposition' in the Federal Republic of Germany, written in 1964, Otto Kirchheimer distinguished between three modes of political opposition. These were: 'opposition of principle', where the opposition advocated a degree of 'goal displacement' incompatible with the constitutional requirements of 'the system'; 'loyal opposition', which involved 'some form of goal differentiation' in harmony with these constitutional requirements; and 'political competition', a state of affairs in which the 'opposition' in fact ceased to articulate different goals or objectives from those of the government, but still competed with it for office and in which government and opposition could conceivably differ, for example, over the order in which their agreed objectives should be fulfilled.(1)

Kirchheimer's essay stressed the weakness of the second of these modes of opposition, that of the 'loyal opposition', in Germany and in the Federal Republic. In Imperial Germany and the Weimar Republic, there had been an abundance of 'opposition of principle', while the Third Reich permitted no legal opposition at all. The history of the Federal Republic since 1949 had been one of the rapid erosion of any opposition which espoused alternative goals to those of the government. By 1964, opposition politics had given way completely to mere 'political competition'.(2) The political landscape in the Federal Republic was characterised by the existence of a wide-ranging consensus over fundamental policy issues.

This chapter is devoted to an analysis of the

development of opposition politics in the Federal
Republic of Germany since the mid-1960s. In the
first part, however, the changing concepts and
practice of opposition in Germany and the Federal
Republic up until this period are investigated. In
the subsequent part on opposition politics since
the formation of the 'Grand Coalition' federal
government in 1966, particular attention is given
to developments since the accession to office in
1982 of a federal coalition government of the CDU/
CSU (Christian Democratic Union/Christian Social
Union) and the FDP, (Free Democratic Party). This
focus is justified by two factors. First, the
dismissal of the SPD (Social Democratic Party) into
the federal opposition with the fall of the old
Social-Liberal coalition offers the chance to
compare its opposition strategy to the one it
followed when Kirchheimer wrote his seminal essay.
Second, following the 1983 federal elections, the
SPD was joined on the opposition benches in the
Bundestag by the Greens and was thus faced - for
the first time since the early years of the Federal
Republic - by a significant competitor for the
left-wing vote. The existence of the Greens
changed the context of the SPD's opposition
strategy greatly compared with that which had
prevailed in the first half of the 1960s.

This chapter does not deal with extra-
parliamentary opposition, except in so far as this
has shaped the strategies of the opposition parties
in the Bundestag (cf. chapter 12 in this book).
Our concentration on the politics of parliamentary
opposition(s) in the Federal Republic is not meant
to signify that extra-parliamentary opposition has
not been an important - sometimes the most important - dimension of opposition. It is also important to bear in mind, when looking at parliamentary
opposition(s) in the Federal Republic, that it may
be necessary to distinguish between 'symbolic' and
'effective' opposition or between oppositional
rhetoric and oppositional practice and that the
allocation of government and opposition roles in
practice may not coincide with the formal allocation of roles between the majority and minority
parties or coalitions in the Bundestag.

Historical Background

The weakness of the concept of opposition in
Germany reflected the defeat of the 1848 revolution

and the failure of parliamentary government to
develop. The institutions of Imperial Germany were
dualistic in form, but it was the Kaiser rather
than the Reichstag who played the decisive role.
Bismarck had designed the institutions specifically
to inhibit the development of parliamentary government. The governmental executive was nominated by
and ultimately dependent on the support of the
Kaiser rather than the Reichstag. In such a
constitutional construction, opposition as a
developed concept was bound to be still-born.(3)

> The opposition in the Reichstag was not a
> potential government party or member of a
> governing coalition, since there were no
> governing majorities.

Rather than a unified opposition developing,
parties in such a system remained groups of special
interests looking, often in vain, for opportunities
to exert influence. This, of course, was the role
foreseen for them in Hegelian state theory. Here
the state personified by its monarchically-based
government represents the general interest, while
political parties represent only partial and
incomplete interests.

The Social Democratic Party, which emerged as
the largest party in the Imperial period, did have
a concept of opposition. Representing as it did
the working class, which was camped on the margins
of society in Imperial Germany, its conception was
one of rejection, of principled opposition to the
prevailing system. The SPD attempted, in theory at
least, to offer a radical alternative within the
existing system. As Imperial Germany became more
prosperous and as the trade unions at least became
more integrated within the existing system, the SPD
was urged by its revisionist wing to pursue opposition from within the system in theory as well as in
practice. Such a step would have involved significant costs for the SPD leadership in terms of self-
perception and party unity and, more basically,
there was no incentive to change since such a
change could never have led to government in the
prevailing institutional system.

Opposition in the Weimar Republic

The establishment of the Weimar Republic led
neither to stable parliamentary government nor to

elite or mass acceptance of the concept of opposition. The circumstances of the creation of the Republic meant that the incumbents of military and bureaucratic positions of power remained largely in post. The persistence of a traditional pattern of cleavage, reinforced, but not created, by an electoral system of proportional representation produced a multi-party system of some complexity. This meant that parliamentary government was invariably coalition government. The fact that a number of parties were not available for participation in any potential coalition, since they were opposed in principle to the Weimar Republic, meant that democratic opposition was normally both weak and lacking in credibility, as chronic governmental instability implied that it would very probably coalesce at some future point with the government party it was criticising. A further consequence of the endemic governmental instability was that the military and bureaucratic office-holders were much less subject to political control than they otherwise would have been, and government often had to be carried not on the basis of parliamentary majorities but under Article 48 of the Emergency Law of the Weimar Constitution. Thus, despite a democratic constitution, there was, in practice, considerably continuity with the Imperial period and very little opportunity for the development of a credible parliamentary opposition.

A marked feature of Weimar was the strength of principled opposition to the system. The German Communist Party (KPD) tried to take power by revolutionary means between 1919 and 1923 and remained unreconciled to the Weimar Republic throughout its existence: 'Demokratie - das ist nicht viel. Sozialimus ist das Ziel' - ('Democracay - that's not much. Socialism is the goal'). On the right, a number of extreme nationalist groups, of which the National Socialists (NSDAP) became by far the most significant, were equally consistent in their pursuit of principled opposition to the regime. Both right and left oppositions were contemptuous of parliamentary institutions and invested a great deal of their . strength and ingenuity in extra-parliamentary opposition, occasionally, as in the Berlin transport strikes, joining forces against the elected Democrats. Both oppositions originally envisaged coming to power by the violent, frontal overthrow of the state. This period ended with the crushing of the last of the Communist insurrections in 1923 and the defeat of the Munich Putsch in the same year. Large paramilitary forces were retained by both the extreme Left and Right, but they were henceforth used more against each other than in a frontal attack on the state.

The Machtergreifung of 1933 very quickly ended any legitimate opposition to the regime. A one-party regime was created and, in theory at least, the pluralistic nature of German institutions was abolished by a process of Gleichschaltung.

The Establishment of Opposition in the Federal Republic

In his essay published in 1957, 'The Waning of Opposition in Parliamentary Regimes', Kirchheimer developed a simple tripartite typology of opposi-tion in democratic systems.(4) These were the classical English model of the loyal (systemkon-forme) opposition, the opposition of principle (systemfeindliche Opposition, the kind constituted by the NSDAP and the KPD in Weimar) and what he labelled Bereichsopposition ('sectoral opposi-tion'). In the last, the opposition does not seek to articulate a comprehensive alternative as is the case with a loyal opposition, but rather provides an alternative in particular policy areas from within a coalition. The example that Kirchheimer had in mind was the post-war Grand Coalition in Austria.

With the establishment of the Federal Repub-lic, the prospects for the establishment of a loyal opposition looked better than at any previous time in German history. The Basic Law, which envisaged a parliamentary system, had been supported by all the democratic parties. The parties themselves had been given a legitimacy through Article 21 of the Basic Law which they had never hitherto possessed. Great efforts had also been made by the drafters of the Basic Law to constrain the impact of any oppo-sition of principle. Plebiscitary devices such as existed in the Weimar Constitution are absent from the Basic Law. The emphasis is on stability and representative parliamentary democracy and against mass political participation. The position of the Chancellor could no longer be threatened by the temporary coming together of anti-system majorities (negative majorities). In order to displace a Chancellor, the Basic Law insisted in Article 67 that there be a majority for a successor candidate.

The result of the 1949 election had been very close and Konrad Adenauer was elected Chancellor by the margin of one (his own!) vote. Kurt Schumacher, the first leader of the post-war SPD, was committed to upgrading the role of opposition and his first statement in the Bundestag was an ambitious description of the role of a loyal opposition:(5)

> The opposition can not be expected to function as a substitute party for the government and to accept responsibility for acts which many governments would be reluctant to endorse. Opposition is an important part of the life of the state and not a second-rank auxiliary for the government. The essence of opposition is a permanent attempt to force the government and its parties by concrete proposals tuned to concrete situations to pursue the political line outlined by the opposition.

Schumacher's dominance in the Fraktion (parliamentary party) was never seriously threatened. Of special relevance to the development of opposition was his reliance on a group of former emigrés, notably Erich Ollenhauer (his deputy), Fritz Heine, Erwin Schoettle and Willi Eichler. Like Bernstein before them, they had all been deeply influenced by the experience of exile in Britain. The views which they developed in exile were amazingly close to Schumacher's and included a very similar view of the function of opposition.

Table 6.1: Percentage of bills passed against SPD opposition in the first Bundestag, 1949-53

Budget	78.9
Foreign affairs	55.0
Agriculture	19.4
Finance	15.4
Internal affairs, police, culture, etc.	14.8
Labour, social policy	11.8
Economy	7.4

Source: W. Kralewski and K.H. Neunreither, Oppositionelles Verhalten im ersten Deutschen Bundestag, 1949-1953, (Westdeutscher Verlag, Cologne, 1963), p.92.

In practice, the factors which militated

against the development of loyal opposition in the sense articulated by Schumacher proved to be overwhelming. Even in his period of leadership (from 1949 to 1952), the amount of goal differentiation (which is a defining characteristic of Kirchheimer's loyal opposition) was both fairly low and concentrated particularly in one sector, that of foreign policy.

Several explanations have been offered as to why the SPD even in these early years adopted a form of opposition which stressed co-operation at the expense of competition.(6) Any explanation has to begin with the economy, as it is here that a Social Democratic opposition might be expected to concentrate.(7) Opposition in this area was initially constrained by the basic imperatives of reconstruction which continued to apply until well into the 1950s. The SPD suffered a major reverse in this area before the establishment of the Federal Republic with the currency reform of 1948 and the adoption in the same year of the 'Social Market Economy'. Most important, however, was the onset of a long and sustained economic boom following the outbreak of the Korean War in 1950. By the end of the first legislative period, the SPD was well on the way to dropping alternative economic conceptions. In matters of economic policy, then, the SPD simply yielded to the overwhelming success of the German economy of the 1950s.

The division of Germany into two states and the mutual hostility of the Federal Republic and the German Democratic Republic reduced the space for opposition in the former, since opposition, particularly on the left, could always be portrayed as aiding, if not in fact emanating from, the GDR.

The use of this tactic by the governing parties was all the more likely to be effective, given the degree of continuity in German attitudes towards the role of opposition. Not unsurprisingly, in the light of the unparalleled prosperity, it continued to be viewed in a somewhat negative light, whereas government, especially that of Adenauer, basked in public support. This lack of approval of the function of opposition was reflected in public reactions to two later episodes. In the two cases where opposition parties made perfectly legitimate use of the constructive vote of no confidence in the Chancellor (Article 67 of the Basic Law), the public reaction displayed striking similarities. In both cases, despite the fact that the first attempt to unseat the Chancellor (1972) was unsuccessful and the second (1982) succeeded, the public's reaction was to side with the Chancellor, although, in the latter case, a contributory factor was also the widespread indignation at the FDP's perceived failure to honour its 1980 election pledge to maintain the Social-Liberal coalition with Helmut Schmidt as Chancellor. The popular sympathy for Brandt in 1972 contributed to his election victory, but the wave of support for Schmidt in 1982 ebbed quickly and had practically died out before the 1983 federal election (in which Schmidt was no longer the SPD's Chancellor candidate).

The difficulties of the opposition in the Federal Republic were heightened by institutional obstacles to its role. The organisation of the Bundestag worked against the institution of opposition. The Bundestag's design, with the government sitting on raised benches above the deputies, expressed more vividly the government-Parliament dichotomy than the classic opposition-government dichotomy supported by the architecture of Westminster. The Bundestag's organisation, with its emphasis on committees and committee work and its self-conception as a 'working Parliament', also militated against the establishment in the public mind of the role of opposition. Further difficulties were introduced by the existence of a bicameral legislature and the frequent need for legislation to obtain a majority in the second (Länder) chamber, the Bundesrat, as well as in the Bundestag. Being confronted by an opposition majority in the Bundesrat is a factor which has pushed successive governments in the direction of consensual law-making. This may well help to increase the influence of the opposition, but it does often make it difficult for it to develop the role of opposition as an alternative. Indeed, the distinctive West German model of 'co-operative federalism' contains an in-built bias towards consensual decision-making.

The final specifically German obstacle to the institutionalisation of competitive opposition was the existence of judicial review by the Federal Constitutional Court (Bundesverfassungsgericht). The comprehensive nature of the Basic Law, which is notable for its enshrining of goals and values as well as prescribing the mechanisms of government, acts to inhibit the propagation of alternatives,

since it is perfectly clear that certain 'alternatives' would be ruled out by the Federal Constitutional Court, even if the opposition were somehow
to obtain a majority for its proposals in the
Bundestag. (At the same time, the Basic Law and
the existence of judicial review constrain the
freedom of action of the government too and thus
serve to narrow the scope for political conflict in
the Federal Republic.)

In his article on the 'vanishing opposition'
in the Federal Replubic, Kirchheimer also emphasised the general role of the welfare state in
moderating political conflict and diminishing the
scope for opposition. The provision in the Basic
Law that the Federal Republic be a democratic
Sozialstaat raised the welfare state to a constitutional obligation and some important milestones
in its growth were laid by Christian Democratic-led
governments in the 1950s and 1960s. The progress
of the SPD towards a co-operative opposition
strategy was a little more traumatic, however, than
Kirchheimer describes it. His article rested on
the assumption that the SPD had adopted the
Volkspartei model, which in his view meant that the
leadership enjoyed a high degree of autonomy from
the extra-parliamentary party and was basically
able to take the key decisions. In particular, the
controversy surrounding the question of rearmament
at times appeared to be pushing the SPD towards a
strategy of extra-parliamentary opposition. Opposition to rearmament was so wide and intense,
particularly among the rank-and-file of the trade
union movement, that it could not all be safely
contained within parliamentary channels. In 1955,
the SPD leadership helped found the 'Paulskirche
movement', which organised gigantic demonstrations
against rearmament. However, the SPD leadership's
support for the movement was ambivalent and eventually the scepticism of Herbert Wehner triumphed:(9)

> I queried then how things would develop if
> one were to come to a point where the
> parliamentary opposition was exhausted and
> no longer capable of increased efforts,
> whether one wanted, with all the ensuing
> consequences, to take to the streets or not.
> Since I presumed that no-one wanted that,
> and since I myself saw no possibility, even
> if one wanted to, of achieving in this way
> anything which could prove of use for our

> people, I considered these actions to be
> dangerous. I considered it dangerous to
> arouse moods, to gather people with whom
> Social Democracy from a specific point
> onwards could not progress any further and,
> in addition, to destroy thereby the way to
> the so-called average man.

The SPD's abandonment of alternatives culminated in
the Bad Godesberg programme of 1959. In foreign
policy, where it had maintained a more distinctive
stance, Wehner's Bundestag speech of 30 June 1960
committed the SPD to the main positions of the
Adenauer Government. The accent was on a co-operative rather than competitive role as opposition, as
epitomised in Willy Brandt's statement that:(10)

> In a sound and developing democracy, it is
> the norm rather than the exception that the
> parties put forward similar, even identical,
> demands in a number of fields. the question
> of priorities in the rank order of tasks to
> be solved and of methods and accents thus
> becomes ever so much more the content of
> opinion formation.

It is significant that the SPD's strategy for
coming to power by this time more or less ignored
the contribution that the performance of the
opposition role could make to achieving this goal.
The SPD strategy had major and minor themes. The
minor theme involved stressing the governmental
performance of the SPD at the local and Land level.
The adoption of Brandt, then the Mayor of Berlin,
as Chancellor candidate and the party's front
runner (Aushängeschild) in 1960 symbolised this
strategy. The major strategy, which was closely
identified with Wehner, was to come to power
through a coalition with the CDU/CSU and to advance
electorally by demonstrating competence in government.

The Grand Coalition, 1966-69

In 1966, the SPD - in line with the above strategy
- joined the CDU/CSU in a Grand Coalition. The
FDP, the only party now in opposition, simply
lacked the necessary size to be credible as an
opposition. There was not even a great deal of

'sectoral opposition' (see above) within the coalition. Those issues on which the coalition partners
had different opinions were simply excluded from
the political agenda through a number of coalition
mechanisms, of which the most famous was the informal inter-party committee known as the <u>Kressbonner
Kreis</u>. As in other periods, foreign policy constituted an exception to some extent, but even here
the differences were relatively small after the
Soviet invasion of Czechoslovakia in 1968.

The absence of parliamentary opposition
produced a quantum leap in extra-parliamentary
opposition, which was concentrated largely on the
left. The right-wing extremist party, the NPD,
fearful of being banned by the Federal Constitutional Court as anti-democratic, took some care at
the level of official party pronouncements to
remain within the restrictive confines of the Basic
Law.

It was the Left which claimed a monopoly of
the extra-parliamentary opposition - expressed in
its description of itself as the APO (<u>Ausserparla-
mentarische Opposition</u>, extra-parliamentary Opposition). The APO drew its support from a number of
quarters, including the student movement, disillusioned members of the SPD and Marxists hostile to
the 'bureaucratic' socialist regimes of Eastern
Europe. It failed in its attempts to influence
policy towards Vietnam, it failed to prevent the
passing of the Emergency Laws in 1968 and it failed
electorally when it paradoxically contested the
1969 election. It did, however, appear to demonstrate the relatively fragile hold of parliamentary
institutions on the generation of Germans which had
grown up in the Federal Republic.(11)

The CDU/CSU in Opposition

The 'change of power' (<u>Machtwechsel</u>) in 1969 was
widely perceived to be a very important milestone
in the consolidation of parliamentary government in
the Federal Republic. Despite the bold statements
of Brandt in his first government declaration in
1969, it was always clear that the SPD's freedom of
manoeuvre in government would be constrained by its
dependence on its coalition partner, the FDP. How
the CDU/CSU would perform the opposition role was
unclear, particularly in the period immediately
after the formation of the SPD/FDP coalition. Its
first reaction - as the largest party and one which

saw itself as the natural party of government - was to query the outcome. This could not last very long, however, and was superseded by a phase in which it anticipated the imminent collapse of the government. The CDU/CSU had the scope to pursue a more competitive style of opposition than the SPD had done earlier. It was numerically in a strong position to carry out the role. Moreover, a number of reforms initiated during the period of the Grand Coalition to strengthen the visibility of the opposition role came into force after 1969. These included enhanced rights of initiative in plenary sessions and some improvements in the control functions of Bundestag committees.(12)

There were, in fact, some important changes in both the style and substance of the opposition role during the CDU/CSU's period in opposition. The style of debate in the plenary sessions was more adversarial than at any period since the 1950s. As in the 1950s, this adversarial style was most pronounced in the field of foreign policy. In its bitter opposition to the SPD/FDP government's Ostpolitik, the CDU/CSU reminded many of the SPD under Schumacher, both in style and, in part, in content. Just as the SPD had opposed the policy of the Western integration of the Federal Republic because of its implications for the prospects of German reunification, the CDU/CSU insisted that the treaty commitments with Eastern European states entered into under the Ostpolitik must not compromise the reunification option. Bitter conflicts over foreign policy were pre-programmed in the Federal Republic. Through the division of Germany, governments in the Federal Republic have been continuously involved in defining and redefining their relationships with other states in the international system. The treaties defining these relationships have centred ultimately around the consequences of World War II. Any West German opposition was thus likely to focus on the costs of the treaties.(13) The problem for both the SPD opposition in the 1950s and the CDU/CSU opposition two decades later was that, despite a high level of formal commitment to reunification in the Federal Republic, the policies of European integration in the 1950s and the Ostpolitik in the 1970s, both of which in different ways appeared to compromise this goal, were enormously popular.

The CDU/CSU also echoed Schumacher, especially in the legislative period from 1969 to 1972, in

advancing many 'concrete proposals' of its own. It
was more effective in terms of achievements in this
area since it was able to make use of its long and
recent ministerial experience. Of its 122 draft
bills between 1969 and 1972, 36 were accepted by
the Bundestag, 18 in their original form and 18
embodied in other bills. This constituted a
success rate of about 30 per cent. In the third
and fourth legislative periods, the SPD had
achieved a success rate of about 10 per cent -
which was also the rate which the CDU/CSU achieved
in the 1976-80 legislative period.(14) This
strategy of advancing its own 'concrete' legislative proposals was not pursued so avidly by the
CDU/CSU after 1972, as its governmental experience
became more of a wasting asset and as it in any
case failed conspicuously to deliver any electoral
dividend.

A major change of emphasis in the CDU/CSU's
performance of the opposition role seemed to be
rendered possible by its possession of a majority
in the Bundesrat. The CDU/CSU tried to make, and
was to some extent successful in making, the
Bundesrat a major site for opposition, but its
success in this respect was only partial. The
system of 'co-operative federalism' militates
against a very antagonistic relationship between
the federal government and the Land governments and
a determinedly-followed policy of confrontation in
the Bundestag would have generated considerable
political tensions. Moreover, the CDU/CSU's
possession of a majority in the Bundesrat served to
encourage the SPD/FDP Government to make concessions at a very early stage in the formulation of
legislation. Bills were either not introduced
because it was felt that the Bundesrat would block
them or significant alterations were made in them
to try to ensure that they would pass. In this
way, the opposition in the Bundesrat was highly
effective in preventing unwelcome outcomes for the
CDU/CSU and it often did 'force the government and
its parties ... to pursue the political line outlined by the opposition' (Schumacher).(15) The
disadvantage for the CDU/CSU in this was that it
did not necessarily yield an electoral bonus, as
the opposition's influence was exerted at such an
early stage of the legislative process and the
government was thus not seen - in any very obvious
way - to have been defeated. Paradoxically, the
CDU/CSU's pursuit of a partisan strategy in the

149

Bundesrat reinforced the bias towards consensual law-making, and so made the task of the CDU/CSU opposition in the Bundestag in attacking the government more difficult. The CDU/CSU's difficulties in maintaining a distinctive opposition role and profile were further exacerbated by the FDP's successful pursuit of a strategy of 'sectoral opposition' (especially in the spheres of economic and social policy) within the governing coalition. The powerful impact of the 'liberal corrective' in many policy areas left little for the CDU/CSU to attack.

Christian Democratic expectations that the Brandt Government would collapse were dampened by the failure of the constructive vote of no confidence in April 1972 and then completely dashed by the crushing defeat of the CDU/CSU in the November 1972 election. It was no longer the largest party and it looked very unlikely that any attempt to detach the FDP from the SPD would succeed.

This realisation provoked considerable tension within the CDU/CSU as to how it should perform its opposition role in future. This tension was increased by the knowledge that the phase of dramatic foreign policy conflicts was over for the time being, as the treaties made under the Ostpolitik had been ratified. The Christian Democrats' difficulties in developing a clear opposition profile were added to by Brandt's replacement by Schmidt, whose managerial style of government seemed to go down very well with the electorate.

The response of the CDU/CSU to this situation was divided. The federal party leadership concentrated on modernising the organisation of the CDU, which it (rightly) believed would pay large dividends in the long run. Rainer Barzel was replaced first by Karl Carstens and then by Helmut Kohl in an attempt to find a more attractive leader. This change had a limited impact on the performance of the opposition role, since Kohl remained as Minister-President of the Rhineland Palatinate until after the 1976 election.

The CSU leader, Franz-Josef Strauss, was the most prominent advocate of an alternative line. In his view, the CDU/CSU's initial opposition strategy had failed and there ought now to be much more emphasis on obstruction and confrontation. Strauss was strengthened in this view by the CSU's striking success in the Bavarian Land election in October 1974, when it polled 62.1 per cent of the vote. In

a speech at Sonthofen on 18 November 1974, distributed some time afterwards by the SPD, Strauss
articulated a strategy of confrontation and
obstruction and welcomed the idea of a crisis,
which, in his view, needed to be a prolonged one in
order for voters to be persuaded to desert the
Schmidt Government. The opposition had to 'criticise and warn' but to avoid putting forward
concrete policy proposals. It had to emotionalise
political debate and generate fear and anxiety
among the electorate. It could not create too much
confrontation.(16)

Strauss was in a minority, however, in the
CDU/CSU - a fact which became brutally apparent
when he tried to detach the CSU from the CDU and
form a nation-wide conservative party after the
1976 election. After a short period, it became
clear that Kohl enjoyed much more support and
Strauss had to back down. He stood as the CDU/
CSU's Chancellor candidate in 1980, but a heavy
election defeat signalled the failure of his
opposition strategy of providing the electorate
with a clear political alternative.

The dominant theme of the CDU/CSU's parliamentary opposition was co-operation. In the period
from 1972 to 1983, some 64.8 per cent of all bills
were passed unanimously.(16) The percentage did
actually decline during this period, but this was
partly attributable to the opposition of some SPD
parliamentarians to some government bills.

Historically, both the SPD and the CDU/CSU
have thus adopted predominantly 'co-operative'
strategies of opposition, regardless of the strategies which they initially followed. In pursuit of
their main goal of gaining power, they have both
given priority to the task of finding a coalition
partner at the expense of the opposition function.
In both cases, this approach was successful. The
SPD entered the Grand Coalition in 1966 and the
CDU/CSU was able to persuade the FDP to switch
allegiance and form a Christian-Liberal coalition
government in 1982.

The SPD in Opposition

By the time the SPD went into opposition (at the
federal level) in 1982, the underpinnings of the
political consensus identified by Kirchheimer had
been seriously eroded and the main constituent
elements of this consensus had become politically

151

controversial:(17)

i) Declining economic growth had made it more
and more difficult for the state to finance
the welfare state, which in turn had ceased
to be politically taboo.

ii) An increasing proportion of the electorate
viewed technological change, and its 'revolutionary social implications' with ambivalence.(18)

iii) Arms spending and more general issues of
foreign and defence policy had become major
rallying points of political opposition. The
widespread opposition to the stationing of
American medium-range nuclear missiles in the
Federal Republic betrayed a loss of faith in
the NATO philosophy of nuclear deterrence.
Some political forces, most notably the
Greens, espoused a neutralist foreign policy
and thus called the cornerstones of German
foreign and defence policy into question.

iv) The strength of support for the continuation
of a policy of maintaining good relations
with the GDR and the other Eastern European
Communist states signified that anti-Communism and the former 'external threat' had
ceased to function as major sources of political cohesion in the Federal Republic.

v) In addition, the advance of 'post-
materialist' values had loosened the old
consensus over the desirability of economic
growth. This process was manifested above
all in growing protest against environmental
destruction and the construction of nuclear
power plants. This change in values, and the
issue of the stationing of American nuclear
missiles in the Federal Republic, were primarily responsible for the emergence of the
Greens and their clearing the 5 per cent
'hurdle' in the 1983 Bundestag elections.

Among the established parties in the Federal
Republic, the SPD was the one which registered the
tremors in the old political consensus most
strongly. During Schmidt's Chancellorship, the
policy differences between the government and the
(formal) CDU/CSU opposition had gradually become
indistinguishable in practice and the role of opposition in a variety of policy spheres had increasingly been occupied by the left wing of the SPD,

and by extra-parliamentary movements in which some
Social Democrats occupied leading positions. Thus,
as early as 1979, Wehner, then SPD parliamentary
party leader, felt compelled to warn that:(19)

> The party must ... not allow itself to be-
> come the opposition, as it were, to a
> government in which it is the bigger part-
> ner. It must support the Social Democrats
> in the executive. The line of conflict must
> run principally between the Social Democrats
> and their political opponents and not be-
> tween the party, on the one hand, and its
> government members, on the other, or between
> different groups within the party.

Following the 1980 federal elections, the conflict
over the NATO twin-track decision and over the
Social-Liberal coalition's austerity policy inten-
sified the SPD's internal divisions. The party's
transition from government to opposition gave rise
to widespread fears, including within the SPD
itself and especially among right-wing Social
Democrats, that it might now develop into a 'left-
wing protest party'. This, of course, would have
implied the SPD's pursuing a clearly competitive
opposition role. Had this not happened, after all,
to the Labour Party in Britain after its election
defeat in 1979 and to the French Socialists during
their long period of opposition in the Fifth
Republic, when, according to Pierre Mauroy, 'we all
played the game of overtaking each other on the
left'?(20) Given that the SPD Left had been active
in mobilising extra-parliamentary protest against
the policies of an SPD-led government before 1982,
and that the SPD was now confronted for the first
time since the early years of the Federal Republic
with a serious competitor for the left vote, the
Greens, these fears were not entirely groundless.
    There are two closely intertwined dimensions
of opposition politics. The one relates to the
content of the policies propagated by the formal
opposition and the extent to which these policies
differ from those pursued by the government. The
other relates to the methods or instruments used by
the opposition and their effect upon the government.
    The most striking aspect of the SPD's perfor-
mance in opposition with regard to policy formulation has been the prolific rate at which it has

produced policy proposals. This could be explained partly by the fact that the party took with it into opposition numerous bills which it had formulated while still in government, and which had been vetoed by the FDP. It also wanted to display a higher profile in policy areas where the challenge of the Greens was strongest, notably the environment and women's issues. Here, the parliamentary party established new portfolios. More generally, the high output of bills and other policy documents reflected the party leadership's explicit rejection of an opposition strategy à la Sonthofen (see above) and its belief that open confrontation would be electorally harmful in a society in which many still had an 'ambivalent' attitude to political conflict and a predilection for social harmony.(21)

The party's prolific output of policy proposals does not indicate that it has adopted or propagated policies which are sharply distinguishable from those of the government. In fact, over wide areas of policy, the SPD's policy 'alternatives' have differed from the government's policies in nuances only. This has been the case most notably in the general area of economic management. The SPD has taken a different stance to the government on issues such as the role of cuts in working time and public investment in combating unemployment but, despite continuing mass unemployment, it has not weakened its basic commitment to the market economy enshrined in the Bad Godesberg programme. On the contrary: the party's new programme is likely to contain a more positive appraisal of the market economy that its forerunner.(22)

In certain policy spheres, however, the SPD has adopted positions which contrast sharply with those of the Christian-Liberal coalition. The Social Democrats' opposition profile has undoubtedly been most visible in defence policy. The SPD's decision, after it left federal office, to oppose the stationing of American nuclear missiles in the Federal Republic implied a substantial weakening of its commitment to the NATO strategy of nuclear deterrence. On the other hand, there has been no change in its fundamental allegiance to the Federal Republic's membership of NATO. Also since having left office, the SPD has developed a much more sceptical attitude towards nuclear power and towards mass media policy. It has also striven to present a distinctive opposition profile in questions of social policy, where it has opposed most

ot the Christian-Liberal coalition's cuts in
welfare provision, although without promising to
restore all of them upon its re-election. In this
area, the government was probably most vulnerable
to opposition attack and the SPD has been eager to
rebuild its reputation as the 'party of the welfare
state' following the final phase of the Social-
Liberal coalition, which also made deep cuts in
welfare benefits. However, to the extent that the
government and the SPD occupy conflicting positions
on social policy issues, this reflects the government's drift away from the old welfare state
consensus more than any change of position on the
part of the SPD. On the issue of a long-term
reform of pensions' insurance, for example, the SPD
made an explicit offer to co-operate with the
government on formulating legislation and put
forward proposals not radically different from
those of the Christian Democratic Labour Minister.

In terms of policy content, Social Democratic
opposition strategy has thus contained elements of
both co-operation and competition. It is only in
selected policy areas that it has propagated clear
alternative policies to those of the government.

The second dimension of opposition politics
mentioned above referred to its instruments, to the
methods employed by the opposition to try to
influence the political course of the government.
To the extent that the SPD opposed government
policy, it did so predominantly within parliamentary channels, in the Bundestag and the Bundesrat.
Alternative policies have been put forward above
all in the Bundestag; government policies and the
government's performance in office have been
attacked, and government-sponsored legislation has
been opposed. The SPD also initiated parliamentary
investigatory committees to inquire into scandals
involving the dismissal of a Bundeswehr general by
the Defence Minister and the defection of several
alleged spies, and it supported the Greens in
establishing the committee which investigated the
'Flick Affair' - although less to express opposition to government policy as such than to embarrass
the government by exposing its incompetence or
unsavoury financial linkages with the business
world.

Social Democratic opposition strategy has none
the less not had an exclusively parliamentary
focus. Firstly, like the CDU/CSU in the 1970s, the
SPD has also mobilised the possibility of judicial

155

review as an instrument of opposition by taking, or threatening to take, the government before the Federal Constitutional Court. The most notable example of this tactic was the federal parliamentary party's threat to take the 'road to Karlsruhe' to try to thwart the government's plan to implement an amnesty for persons or organisations which had evaded paying taxes on donations to political parties - a proposal which ultimately foundered on opposition from within the FDP as well as on a storm of public protest. The SPD has thus given further momentum to the process of juridification of political conflict initiated by the CDU/CSU when it was on the opposition benches.

Support for, and participation in, protest campaigns and demonstrations has formed the other pillar of the SPD's extra-parliamentary opposition. After fierce internal conflicts, the party leadership approved Social Democrats' participation in the peace movement's protest demonstrations against the stationing of the American medium-range nuclear missiles in the autumn of 1983 and, in an act which symbolised the party's changed posture on the issue, the party chairman, Brandt, addressed the central demonstration in Bonn. The first mass rallies of the peace movement two years earlier had not only <u>not</u> been supported by the party leadership; the then Chancellor, Schmidt, had wanted any Social Democrats taking part in the demonstrations to be formally disciplined.

The course and outcome of the debate within the party on the tactics which could legitimately be employed to try to prevent the missiles' stationing underlined, however, how much the SPD remained a <u>loyal</u> opposition (that is, a 'prosystematic') party. The debate was fuelled especially by a left-wing Social Democrat, Oskar Lafontaine, who, referring to the 'right of resistance' (<u>Widerstandsrecht</u>) in the Basic Law, pleaded for a general strike - albeit initially for only two or three hours - against the missiles' stationing.(23) This proposal was rapidly quashed by the Deutsche Gewerkschaftsbund leadership and the SPD's trade union council, and the party and the DGB linked their participation in the anti-missile demonstrations to the condition that their non-violent character be ensured and that the SPD and the DGB be able to articulate their own standpoints on the missiles issue. Moreover, neither was prepared to countenance a referendum over the issue. It was not seen as of such fundamental importance as to warrant compromising the principle of representative democracy. A five-minute stoppage of work against the missiles' stationing in East and West eventually decided on by the DGB was ridiculed in the peace movement - because of its timing from 11.55 a.m. to midday - as an 'extended lunch-break'.(24) SPD support for a protest week against the government's economic and social policies in 1985 points to the close co-operation at extra-parliamentary level between the SPD in opposition and the trade unions.

All in all, the party has pursued a more competitive opposition strategy since 1982 than in the pre-Grand Coalition period of 'embracement'. Yet, it has not become a 'left-wing protest party' in opposition, but has remained fairly pragmatic, slightly left-of-centre, a 'people's party' (Volkspartei). Its opposition strategy has been dictated by the overriding objective of extending its power base at the level of Land and local government and mobilising the support of an - ideologically and socially - broad spectrum of voters with the goal of reconquering federal office under its own steam or of expanding its electoral support at least to a point from which it could negotiate its entry into a coalition government from a position of strength. (25) In practice, this means developing a programme and profile which enable the party to appeal simultaneously to supporters of the 'new' social movements (and thus eliminate the Greens as a long-term competitor for the left-wing vote), to its traditional core electorate among the organised working class, and to broad sections of the salaried middle classes, including floating voters who supported the governing parties in 1983, but may be persuaded to vote SPD. The orientation of the SPD towards electoral advance and success was particularly evident in the increasing instrumentalisation for vote-maximising purposes of the debate over a new long-term party programme, and in the designation of the most popular leading Social Democrat, Johannes Rau, as its new Chancellor candidate in 1985 for the 1987 elections.

What reasons may be adduced for the SPD's not having developed in opposition into a 'left-wing protest party'? First, the opposition period has been marked by a strong continuity in the party's federal leadership personnel, who continue to exert a pre-eminent influence on its direction. The

157

withdrawals of Schmidt and Wehner from the inner circles of the leadership were accompanied, however, by an enhancement of the importance of the extra-parliamentary party and a modest shift in the intra-party balance of forces, which has strengthened the centre around the party chairman, Brandt, and the new federal parliamentary party chairman, Vogel. The consequence of these developments has been the party's Zentrierung ('centrisation', that is, the re-positioning of the party in its centre following its effective leadership from the right by Schmidt while he was Chancellor). The opposition strategy of the SPD, with its combination elements of competition and co-operation, and the shifts in party policy on some issues may be interpreted as reflecting these developments.

A second reason has to do with the federal structure of the West German state. Although the party's power base in local and Land government was weaker by 1982 than it had been at any stage since the 1950s, it still governed four Länder and a host of large, medium-sized and smaller cities. In the Federal Republic, the major federal opposition party is never out of office completely. The Social Democratic-controlled Land and local governments constitute a natural constituency and force for 'realism' when the party is in opposition. They are faced with the task of translating party policy into practice on the ground. Moreover, the weight of the Land governments within the party may be expected to increase when the party is in opposition federally, as they command the bureaucracies with the expertise and resources required for policy formulation. Thus, Social Democratic Land premiers played a central role in the formulation of the party's election programmes.

A third bulwark against radicalisation of the SPD in opposition is constituted by the concentration of parliamentary work in committees, and the pressures that this tends to generate in favour of the development of expertise in specific policy sectors and a problem-solving approach to politics and political issues. The emphasis on committee work in the Bundestag, coupled with the need to adapt as a pre-condition of ascent within the hierarchy of the parliamentary party, where the right wing of the party is more strongly entrenched than in other leading party organs, helps to explain why left-wing Social Democrats regularly undergo a considerable deradicalisation upon their

The Federal Republic of Germany

election to the Bundestag, possibly irrespective of
whether the party is in, or out of, office.

Fourthly, the absence since 1982 of any major
or intense class or ideological polarisation
(except over the missiles issue) means that the
party leadership has not come under significant
pressure from the rank-and-file membership or its
core electoral clientele to adopt a more radical
opposition strategy. In some policy areas, the
SPD's primary role was to defend the status quo
with one or more segments of the governing coalition against those currents in the coalition which
aspired to change or overthrow it, as in the intra-
governmental conflicts over issues of Ostpolitik.
Moreover, when the government decided in 1985 to
try to legislate to make it more difficult for the
trade unions to strike, this afforded the SPD a
welcome opportunity to present itself as the only
party capable of, and willing to, maintain the
'social peace' and as the political attorney of the
trade unions.

The fifth reason why the SPD has not veered
more sharply to the left in opposition is connected
with the close alignment of its policies and
strategy in opposition with those of the mainstream
of the trade union movement and the disinclination
of the majority of the unions to follow any opposition strategies which they feared could bring them
into conflict with the law or the constitution.(26)
The unions acted as a conservative force within the
party on the issue of how to deal with the American
missiles issue. The essentially cautious character
of union opposition politics is visible also, for
example, in the IG Metall's discouragement of
factory occupations as an instrument for defending
jobs, and the cool to hostile response within the
DGB to an IG Metall executive member's suggestion
that the unions could legitimise strenuous opposition to planned government legislation on labour
and workplace co-determination by reference to the
'right of resistance' in the Basic Law. The institutions of company and workplace co-determination
provide the unions' and workers' factory councils
in the Federal Republic with a power base which is
not immediately vulnerable to changes in the
economic and political conjuncture and which serves
as a functional equivalent to the SPD's occupation
of Land and local government when it is in the
federal opposition, discouraging radicalism and
encouraging 'realism' and 'responsibility'. This

159

tendency is reinforced by a highly legalised framework of industrial relations.

None the less, there were limits beyond which the government could not go without precipitating massive union opposition. Those limits appeared to have been reached when the government introduced legislation in 1985/86 on the reimbursement from public funds of wages lost due to strikes elsewhere in industry; SPD and trade unions interpreted the proposals as interference with the right to strike. The proposed legislation led to a wave of union protests of a kind which had not been witnessed in the Federal Republic since at least the conflict over the emergency laws in the late 1960s. Thus, relations between the (Christian-Liberal) Government and the unions had changed since Kirchheimer had observed the 'vanishing opposition' in the early 1960s. Not only the emergence of the Greens, but also the growing atmosphere of confrontation between the government and organised labour ruled out the SPD's pursuing a new 'embracement' strategy as a means of (re-)conquering federal office. Moreover, also unlike the situation in the 1950s and early 1960s, the performance of the government in the field of economic management and other areas had by no means been so impressive and positively assessed by the electorate as to pull the SPD along with it in its ideological 'tow'. Indeed, on issues relating to the labour market and the distribution of income, the government's record left it very vulnerable to attack by the opposition. There were sound vote-maximising (and other) motives for the SPD's not burying all its political differences with the government, as well as for it not developing into a 'left-wing protest party'.

The New Opposition

Until the election of the Greens in 1983, the SPD had not been confronted by a rival to its left in the Bundestag since the Communist Party failed on the 5 per cent hurdle at the 1953 federal elections. The 'established' parties (SPD, CDU/CSU and FDP) had enjoyed a monopoly of Bundestag representation since 1961. The new party in the Bundestag had risen on a wave of extra-parliamentary opposition - of the ecology, peace and other 'new' social movements - and had its predominant social basis in the 'mass intelligentsia', among highly educated younger people in service sector occupations in the

metropolitan areas and university towns.(27) The
Greens prided themselves on being different from
the other parties. They set out to be, in the
words of one of their early leaders, the 'anti-
party party', one which had grown up out of
frustration with the policies and performance of
the existing parties. The Greens were for 'basis
democracy', the strict accountability of MPs to
grass-roots members, and the biennial rotation of
MPs, and against vote-maximisation and office-
seeking as the primary objects of political
activity, and against compromise and coalitions
with other parties. They were also for extra-
parliamentary protest action. In their self-
conception at least, the Greens were a party - and
opposition - of a 'new type'. A major focus of
this opposition was extra-parliamentary. The 'new'
social movements provided the 'legs' on which the
Green Parliamentary parties stood. 'Basis democracy' was meant to ensure that the parliamentary
wing of the Greens served as the transmission belt
of the extra-parliamentary party and movements.

Contesting elections and participating
actively in parliamentary work must not be incompatible with the Greens' self-conception. Parliament could be used as a forum for propagating Green
policy, for criticising the government (and the
other opposition) and existing social and economic
conditions, and for highlighting the distinctiveness of the Greens and their programme. In practice, none the less, parliamentary representation
(at the local and Land, as well as the federal,
level) appears to have changed the Greens more than
they have changed the parliaments.(28) The Greens
have become more and more like the other parliamentary parties. This process has manifested itself
in several ways. First, not only among Green MPs,
but also among the party rank-and-file, the rotation principle has fallen increasingly into dis-
favour, even if it has not yet been discarded.
Second, the federal parliamentary party at least
has developed a division of labour like that of the
other parties, with MPs being allocated specific
policy-area responsibilities in accordance with the
demands of a 'working Parliament'.(29) Third, in
proportion to its size, the Greens' federal parliamentary party has been even more industrious than
the SPD in formulating and proposing alternative
policies to the government's.(30) Like the SPD, it
has also in practice eschewed Strauss's Sonthofen

161

strategy of opposition, even if the intention in
drafting bills has been to show that the Greens'
proposals stand in 'fundamental contradiction ...
to the possibilities of this Parliament and this
society' to bring about concrete changes.(31)
Fourth, there are signs of the emergence of clientelistic relationships between the Greens in
parliament and their electoral constituencies, such
as teachers and the participants in 'alternative'
business projects. Fifth, the Greens have proved
no less eager than the other parties to exploit the
possibilities afforded by judicial review as
instruments of opposition. Sixth, a growing proportion of the Greens seems to be prepared to
contemplate co-operating with other parties, most
frequently with the SPD, and even forming coalition
governments, as with the SPD in Hesse in 1985.(32)
    This process by which the Green parliamentary
parties have increasingly assumed the traits of
their 'established' counterparts is not synonymous
with a 'parliamentarisation' of the Greens as a
whole - that is, with the subordination of the
Green party to the requirements of parliamentary
and electoral politics. To be sure, the apparently
growing support for Green co-operation with other
parties and participation in coalitions, the
involvement of a growing proportion of the party
membership in parliamentary work, and the parliamentary parties' increasing independence from
extra-parliamentary control all constitute indicators of a progressive 'parliamentarisation' of the
Greens.(33) This trend, however, is contested
among the Greens, especially by radical environmentalists and green-tinged left-wing socialists. On
the crucial issue of whether, and under what conditions, the Greens ought to co-operate or coalesce
with other parties, the Greens' 1984 and 1985
congresses brought no clear decision one way or the
other. The fundamental conflicts of opinion
between Green 'realists' and 'fundamentalists'
echoed those between reformists and revolutionaries
in the pre-World War I SPD.(34)
    The unstable balance of forces within the
Green movement, despite some evidence of a growth
in the influence of the 'realists' makes it difficult to predict what kind of opposition the Greens
will constitute and it is no easier to predict
whether or for how long they might survive as a
parliamentary force. The 'realists' seem set to
turn the party into an essentially left-wing Social

Democratic   party with an ecological   bias   - which
may   stand   for   far-reaching social   and   economic
reforms.   It would operate within the boundaries of
'the   system' and could coalesce with the   SPD.(35)
A   Green party dominated by the   'fundamentalists',
on   the   other   hand,   would   have   an   ambivalent
relationship to representative parliamentary   democracy   and   a   state   based on   the   rule   of   law.
Radical   reforms would be aimed at existing   economic,   social and political structures, while such a
party   would   not   be   available   as   a   coalition
partner.   For its part,   the SPD has been,   on the
whole,   no less sceptical about the possibility   or
desirability of co-operating or coalescing with the
Greens;   in the Bundestag,   it has followed the 'no
cuddle-muddle   with the Greens' line laid   down   by
Brandt   and declined to make common cause with   the
Greens in opposition.
   The   argument   of this chapter has   been   that
parliamentary   opposition   in the Federal   Republic
has had a preponderantly co-operative   cast.   This
is   not   to say that there is not a great   deal   of
polarisation   and   confrontation   at the   level   of
rhetoric on the hustings and in plenary sessions in
Parliament,   but this rhetoric masks a <u>practice</u>   of
opposition   which is much more   co-operative.   The
most significant new feature of opposition politics
in the Federal Republic is the rise, to the left of
the   SPD,   of   the Greens.   Although   the   Greens'
emergence   has   had some impact on   the   opposition
strategy of the SPD,   this has not been so great as
to   move the SPD away from an essentially co-operative position.

Notes

1. See O. Kirchheimer, 'Germany: The Vanishing Opposition', in Robert Dahl (ed.), Political Oppositions in Western Democracies, (Yale UP, New Haven, Conn., 1966), p.237.
2. Ibid.
3. D. Grosser, 'Die Sehnsucht nach Harmonie: Historische und verfassungsstrukturelle Vorbelastungen der Opposition in Deutschland', in H. Oberreuter (ed.), Parlamentarische Opposition: ein internationaler Vergleich, (Hoffmann und Campe, Hamburg, 1975) p.211.
4. O. Kirchheimer, 'The Waning of Opposition in Parliamentary Regimes', in Social Research, vol. 24, no. 2, (Summer 1957), pp.127-57.
5. Quoted from Deutschen Bundestag, Protokoll der Verhandlungen, 20 September 1949, p.32.
6. The distinction between competitive and co-operative opposition was made originally by Dahl. It is developed at length in H.J. Veen, Opposition im Bundestag. Ihre Funktionen, institutionellen Handlungsbedingungen und das Verhalten der CDU/CSU-Fraktion in der 6. Wahlperiode 1969-1972, (Bundeszentrale für politische Bildung, Bonn, 1976).
7. See A. Ashkenasi, Reformpartei und Aussen-politik: Die Aussenpolitik der SPD Berlin-Bonn, (Wissenschaft und Politik, Cologne, 1968), for the argument that Social Democratic parties should concentrate on economic policy as a focus of opposition.
8. Kirchheimer, 'The Vanishing Opposition', p.245.
9. Wehner, quoted in G. Gaus, Staatserhaltende Opposition oder hat die SPD kapituliert? (Rowohlt, Reinbek, 1966), p.26.
10. Cf. Willy Brandt, Plädoyer für die Zukunft, (Europäische Verlagsanstalt, Frankfurt, 1961), p.17.
11. For an influential article which stressed a tradition of hostility to representative democracy, see Kurt L. Shell, 'Extra-Parliamentary Opposition in Postwar Germany', Comparative Politics, vol. 2, (1970), pp.653-80.
12. See G. Pridham, 'The Government/Opposition Dimension and the Development of the Party System in the 1970s. The Reappearance of Conflictual Politics' in H. Döring and

G. Smith (eds), Party Government and Political
Culture in Western Germany, (Macmillan,
London, 1982), pp.130-54 and especially
pp.146-7. See also Veen, Opposition im
Bundestag, pp.120-5.

13. See W.E. Paterson, 'Political Parties and the
Making of Foreign Policy', Review of International Studies, vol. 7, no. 4, (1981),
pp.227-37.

14. Veen, Opposition im Bundestag, p.54.

15. Deutschen Bundestag, Erste Wahlperiode,
Stenographische Berichte, vol. 1, session 6,
21 September 1949, p.32.

16. See V. Nienhaus, 'Konsensuale Gesetzgebung im
Deutschen Bundestag: Zahlen und Anmerkungen
zur 7. bis 9. Wahlperiode', in Zeitschrift
für Parlamentsfragen, vol. 2, (1985),
pp.163-9, especially p.164. In assessing the
significance of such statistics, it is important, of course, to bear in mind that the
proportion of politically significant legislation passed unanimously may be considerable
lower than the overall figure - as Kralewski
and Neunreither found, for example, in their
analysis of voting patterns in the first
Bundestag. During its period in opposition
from 1969 to 1983, for example, the CDU/CSU
regularly opposed the government's budgets.
Arguably, the character of such opposition was
often largely ritual. On these points, see
Peter Schindler. Datenhandbuch zur Geschichte
des Deutschen Bundestages 1949 bis 1982
(Presse- und Informationszentrum des Deutschen
Bundestages, Bonn, 1983), pp.703-12.

17. Kirchheimer, 'The Vanishing Opposition'.
pp.247-9.

18. See, for example, the opinion poll data
published in Michael von Klipstein and
Burkhard Strümpel, Der Überdruss am Überfluss
(Olzog, Munich, 1984), p.183, which indicate
that between 1966 and 1981, the proportion of
the population which held technology to be
'all in all, a blessing' declined from 72 to
30 per cent. The proportion which thought it
'partly a blessing and partly a curse' grew
from 17 to 53 per cent and that which regarded
it as a 'curse' from 3 to 13 per cent.

19. Herbert Wehner and Olaf Sund, 'Unvollstandiger
Versuch eines Beitrags zum Selbstverständnis
der Sozialdemokraten über die Rolle der

gemeinsamen SPD', in Die Neue Gesellschaft, vol. 26, no. 11, (November 1979), p.3.

20. As quoted in Die Zeit, no. 43, 18 October 1985, p.11.

21. See the interview with Vogel, 'Kohl ist mitunter schlicht nicht fleissig genug', in Vorwärts, no. 30, 19 July 1984, p.14.

22. See the guidelines for the Godesberg programme's revision and 'up-dating' published by the party's 'fundamental values commission', 'Godesberg heute', (SPD-Vorstand, Bonn, 1984), especially pp.9-10 and 'Anlauf zum grossen Wurf', in Wirtschaftswoche no. 8, 17 February 1984, p.24.

23. Article 20 of the Basic Law states that 'all Germans have the right to resist anyone who takes action to abolish' the constitution of the [democratic, social and federal] state, 'if no other redress is possible'.

24. See Martin Kempe, 'Eine rot-grüne Option ist von der DGB-Spitze nicht zu erwarten', in Frankfurter Rundschau, 27 July 1985.

25. The conquest of an absolute majority of seats in the Bundestag was proclaimed by the party leadership as its objective in the 1987 election, with particular confidence following the party's excellent showing in the 1985 Land elections in North Rhine-Westphalia and the Saarland, and it was calculated that, under certain conditions, this majority could be obtained with little more than 45 per cent of the vote. It is not easy to believe, however, that the party leadership regarded such an outcome as a realistic possibility, and it may pin its principal hopes of re-entering government on being able to play a fulcrum role in the formation of a new coalition (or minority) government, should a Christian-Liberal coalition with a substantially reduced Bundestag majority collapse in the course of the next legislative period. One of the main reasons why the strengthening of the SPD's power base in the Länder plays such a prominent role in the leadership's thinking is that it would naturally prefer a future SPD-led federal government to be underpinned (in contrast to the position in the 1970s) by a majority in the Bundesrat.

26. The SPD has not, however, agreed with all of the unions on all policy issues and, for

example, did not take the same view as the
chemical industry workers' and mine workers'
unions on the controversial issue in 1984 of
whether a coal-fired power station should go
into operation without a filter to reduce its
pollution emission.

27. For an analysis of the social basis of the
Greens, including a discussion of the concept
of 'mass intelligentsia', see Joachim Raschke,
'Soziale Konflikte und Parteiensystem in der
Bundersrepublik', in Aus Politik und
Zeitgeschichte, vol. 49. (1985), pp.27-30.

28. According to one estimate, some 7,000 Greens
sat in local councils in the Federal Republic
at the beginning of 1985 and the Greens were
also represented in six of 11 Land
Parliaments. See Wolfram Bickerich, 'Das
Mögliche und das Wünschbare', in W. Bickerich
(ed.), SPD und Grüne: Das neue Bündnis?
(Rowohlt, Reinbek, 1985), p.13.

29. See Wolfgang Ismayr, 'Die Grünen im Bundestag:
Parlamentarisierung und Basisanbindung', in
Zeitschrift für Parlamentsfragen, vol. 16,
no. 3, (September 1985), pp.302-6.

30. See ibid., p.319. Up to the end of 1984, the
Greens had put forward 32 bills in the
Bundestag, three fewer than the SPD, since the
beginning of the parliamentary period. They
had placed far more parliamentary questions
than the SPD. Cf. Ibid., pp.316-17.

31. Quotation from report by the federal parliamentary party to the Greens' federal congress,
ibid. p.313.

32. All opinion surveys revealed that an overwhelming majority of Green voters supported
the idea of the Greens co-operating or
coalescing with the SPD.

33. Following the local elections in North Rhine
Westphalia in 1984, for example, about a
quarter of all Green party members in the Land
had a seat in the local councils. If they all
rotated, according to party rules, after the
first two years of the legislative period, a
half of the party's members would have served
on councils by the time of the next local
elections. See 'Ganz schön alt', in Der
Spiegel, no. 49, (3 December 1984), p.62.

34. See, for such a comparison, the essay by Horst
Heimann, 'Gehen die Grünen den Weg der SPD?',
in L'80, no. 33 (March 1985), pp.58-67.

35. A leading group of 'realists' listed the
    following demands for possible negotiations
    for the formation of a federal coalition with
    the SPD: removal of American medium-range
    nuclear missiles in the Federal Republic and
    closure of all nuclear weapon depots, the
    closure of all nuclear energy plants, no
    orders for any new weapons systems, and an
    annual 10 per cent reduction in military
    expenditure. See 'Harte Bedingungen für
    Bündnis mit SPD', in Kölner Stadt-Anzeiger, 31
    October 1985. The description of this cata-
    logue of demands as a 'basis for discussions'
    seemed to suggest that, for the 'realists',
    such demands were negotiable and not an abso-
    lute pre-condition of their supporting an
    SPD-led government.

7. OPPOSITION IN ITALY: FROM POLARISED PLURALISM TO CENTRIPETAL PLURALISM

Geoffrey Pridham

Introduction: The Waning of Anti-System Opposition?

It is really a truism to say that the nature and role of political opposition in Italy reflect that country's liberal democratic state. And yet it merits repetition if only because the reverse contextual argument, that the nature of the system conditions the opposition role, gives us the necessary direction for approaching it and facilitates analysis of its recognised complexities.

In identifying salient characteristics of the opposition in Italy, we note, for instance, its structural fragmentation in the Parliament against a background of strong cleavages, although, numerically and politically, it has been dominated by the Communist Party (PCI), since the system is not so much a classic multi-party system as one with dominant elements. At the institutional level, the opposition has been marked by both conflictual and consensual patterns of legislative behaviour and it is possible to recognise variation over time in the balance between the two. Politically, and 'most obviously, Italy is exceptional among West European democracies for its absence of alternation in power, so that one is effectively talking about a permanent opposition, at least so far as the Communist Party is concerned. This lack of alternation as a result of ideological division relates directly to the growing problem of 'governability' or concern over the system's ineffectiveness in Italy, given that in liberal democracies the possibility and acceptance of alternation is widely seen as fundamental to political choice and a competitive party system.(1) One may go further by noting that the new crisis of confidence at the

169

mass level in the established parties is in part a
direct outcome of the problems surrounding political opposition mentioned above. That is, the
system is seen as blocked, and offering little
scope for policy initiative. The apparently
increasing gap between society and the parties as
agents of mediation dates back to the disillusioned
hopes attached to the emergence of the PCI from
opposition to support and thereby influence the
governments of the later 1970s (as a weak substitute for alternation), in response to a demand for
reform and change.

This kind of approach integrating the role of
opposition within the wider framework of the
evolving system and of society is all the more
imperative in the Italian case since that system is
commonly described as a partitocrazia, whereby the
parties individually and collectively not only
'populate' the state but also penetrate society to
an extent not replicated in most other West European countries. Hence, it is essential to discuss
political opposition with respect to linkages
between parties as institutional actors and as
organisational and societal actors. Despite this
basic feature of the Italian system and some
acknowledgement of the importance of contextual
variables in the sparse literature on opposition in
Italy, the latter has, however - whatever its
intrinsic value - been distinguished by two deficiencies of approach.

On the one hand, there has been an absence of
engagement between empirical theory relevant to the
subject and detailed work on opposition in Italy.
With the first, attention has been drawn most of
all to models or abstractions of the Italian party
system with implications for the role of opposition. Most notably, there is Giovanni Sartori's
thesis of 'polarised pluralism' and Giorgio Galli's
alternative one of an 'imperfect two-party system'
(bipartitismo imperfetto), both presented in the
1960s and repeated subsequently with some modification. More recently, theories of consociative
democracy on elite convergence or co-operation
between opposing political forces have occasioned
much debate in Italy, while Farneti's thesis of
'centripetal pluralism' has been offered as a
replacement for Sartori's now much contested
model.(2) Although such abstractions, most of all
Sartori's, have dominated much thinking about the
Italian (party) system, there has been little

attempt to apply them and draw conclusions specifically with respect to the role of opposition.

Secondly, trends of empirical research on
opposition in Italy both there and abroad have
revealed an interest in one or other problem
relating to the subject rather than in a more
comprehensive approach. For example, opposition in
the Parliament has been examined by Cazzola (1974)
and Di Palma (1977), both focusing on legislative
concurrence between government and opposition as an
increasing pattern in Italy since the late
1960s.(3) Barnes based his discussion of 'oppositions on left, right and centre' in Italy on the
evolution and structure of the party system, with
little direct attention given to the actual performance of the opposition role at the parliamentary
and societal levels.(4) Otherwise, if there has
been any overriding theme in work on the Italian
case it has been the problem of 'anti-system'
opposition. This was true of Sartori (1966 and
1976) and Tosi (1966 and 1975) as well as
Barnes.(5) The theme has persisted notwithstanding useful evidence from attitudinal surveys by
Putnam (1973) and Sani (1980) pointing to the need
for more careful handling of this problem and
emphasising, in the latter's case, changing perceptions of it.(6) More recent work by Putnam and
others has underlined a trend of elite-level
depolarisation, (7) thus calling into question the
assumptions of Sartori and others about 'anti-
system' politics in Italy. Indeed, polemics in
Italy among political scientists about this overriding theme have dwelt among other things on the
datedness of the Sartorian model.

Inevitably, this dispute over the meaning of
'anti-system' politics has focused concretely on
the evolution of the PCI and its strategy since the
1960s, from a position of relative isolation in
opposition to the centre-Left governments (the
Socialists had earlier broken their oppositional
alliance with the PCI and joined the Christian
Democrats (DC) in coalition) to the adoption of the
'historic compromise' strategy and acquisition of
power in many regions and most large cities
combined with policy-based external support for the
'National Solidarity' governments led by Andreotti
(1976-9). Even though the PCI's strategic re-
direction with the 'democratic alternative' adopted
in 1980 (abandoning the proposed alliance with the
DC) was eventually followed by a retraction in its

171

local and regional governmental role, this has not
involved a reversal to the situation of the 1960s,
in terms of both party system dynamics and political culture. For the DC is not nearly so dominant
as it was before, the PCI has since then been much
legitimated and there has been a gradual decline in
anti-Communism.(8) This leads us to ask whether
the debate over 'anti-system' opposition in Italy
has simply been a problem of time-boundness of
political models (i.e. they have been overtaken by
party development itself, as with the case of the
PCI), or whether there is some other explanation.
The fact that Sartori, Tosi and others have by and
large held to their positions of the 1960s suggests
the latter. So, we then have to ask whether the
concept of 'anti-systemness' has been applied
systematically enough.

At first sight, the terms 'anti-system' and
'loyal' as types of opposition appear too bland to
be useful as analytical tools; that is, they may be
conceptually neat but in practice they are not so
clearly distinguishable, not least because they do
little justice to the complexities and ambiguities
of party behaviour. Indeed, if we look closely at
the Italian scene something of this problem is
reflected in the profusion if not confusion of
terminology on this matter; also because of the
habit among political elites there of coining
conceptual phrases to describe their differences of
position. However, so far as political scientists
are concerned, some attempt has been made to
differentiate qualitatively in the face of this
mushrooming of terminology. Tosi, for instance, in
his later essay (1975) distinguished between what
was historically evident and what was constitutionally determinable, seeing that constitutional law
does not consider ideology, namely that a difference be drawn between 'anti-constitutional' and
'anti-system'.(9)

But Sartori himself subsequently (1976)
defined what he understood by 'anti-system', arguing that this was not equivalent to 'revolutionary': (10)

> Over time the degree and the intensity of
> an 'anti-attitude' are bound to vary. Fur-
> thermore, not all the anti-system parties
> are such in a same sense: the negation
> covers, or may cover, a wide span of differ-
> ent attitudes ranging from 'alienation' and

total refusal to 'protest'. Now, clearly,
alienation and protest are different in
kind, not merely in degree. Yet the distinction cannot be easily applied on empirical grounds, because large electorates cover
all these sentiments or attitudes. Voters
can be protesters, while the party activists
can be alienated. Likewise, the party
leadership can be ideologically motivated,
whereas the rank and file may simply lack
bread. On the other hand, at the level of
the political system the consequences of
alienation and/or of protest are not
markedly different: whatever the nature, at
the source, of the anti-attitude, a government faces the same daily difficulties.

Sartori does, therefore, provide here the kind of
differentiated approach required, particularly as
some of the terminology used with respect to 'anti-
system' politics has been at best ambiguous. While
some terms overlap - such as Kirchheimer's 'opposition of principle' as being equivalent to 'anti-
system' opposition - and others relate more to
style than substance (e.g. 'intransigent' opposition, even though it implies a possible tendency
towards 'opposition of principle'), further terms
are not so clear in this respect. For example,
although Sartori distinguishes between 'opposition
of principle' and 'opposition on issues', the
latter does not exclusively imply loyalty to the
system, since an 'anti-system' party might choose
for tactical or other reasons to mount its opposition selectively. Nevertheless, taking Sartori's
helpful definition, the distinction between 'anti-
system' and 'loyal' opposition is a valid one as a
starting-point for examining the Italian case,
especially as it subsumes many of the other termin-
ological distinctions and as it has been at the
centre of debate on this question in Italy itself.
It remains to decide on how to apply it.

As indicated by Sartori, much of the confusion
about the nature of opposition in Italy has derived
from uni-dimensional or stereotyped views of the
problem of change in the system. If we survey, for
instance, general texts on Italian politics and
comparative studies of opposition with references
to Italy, there is (apart from sparse mention of
the subject in the former case) an overall tendency
to adopt the original Sartorian model and label the

PCI in an unspecified way as 'anti-system', or even
in one source as performing a 'ghetto function' of
'buffeting and eroding' the government and exploit-
ing the parliamentary institution in a manner
comparable to that of the Nazis during the Weimar
Republic.(11) Some formula for accommodating a
strategy of system change or reform with loyalty to
it is therefore necessary, but this has not been
satisfactorily done in the case of Italy because of
the identification between party (i.e. the DC) and
state. As Tamburrano has written, in explaining
the lack of alternation in power in post-war Italy,
'the real problem is the Italian political system'
itself or specifically the system of power con-
structed and enjoyed by the ruling DC (in power
continuously since 1945), whereby the DC is seen
not only as a party but also as an institution of
the state.(12) Accordingly, the <u>alternativa di
sinistra</u> (alternative of the Left) is regarded as
equivalent to an <u>alternativa di sistema</u> (system
alternative); hence, alternation would involve a
conflict between political power (the PCI) and
state power (the continued 'occupation' of the
state structure by the DC), (13) a conflict that in
a modest form has not been absent at the city level
where the PCI assumed political office from 1975.
It is this apparent inability of the system to
absorb alternation - so far, however, untested -
that is at the heart of the widespread view that
Italy has a 'difficult democracy'.(14) In short,
it does not take much to realise that political
affiliation or tendency is strongly present in
perceptions of the opposition role in Italy, involving among others the political science world; and
we of course return here to the relationship
between that role and the nature of liberal democracy in that country.

For our purposes here, operationalising any
dichotomy between pro-/anti-system or alternatively
between pro-/anti-status quo within the system (the
latter depending on how far we see the PCI as
essentially a reformist party prepared to accommo-
date to the system's basic structure, but at the
same time committed to changing its functioning and
policy direction) would at the outset involve
analysing both what parties say (their strategies
and basic policy positions) and what parties do
(whether their behaviour lends support to the
thesis that they support the democratic structure
or otherwise). The former is realistic in so far

as the trend of publicly stated commitments by a
party may reveal a consistency of strategy (something which the PCI has always strongly claimed),
and therefore possibly an element of convictional
adaptation to the system.(15)   That is, whatever
the reasons for Togliatti's strategic decision in
1944 to reject the revolutionary course, the
pursuit of the 'Italian road to socialism' through
Berlinguer's 'historic compromise' and beyond has
itself had a powerful conditioning influence on the
party, a view supported by the PCI's adaptive
capacity and its persistent search for legitimation.   Judging the action of parties may, of
course, be largely a matter of 'the proof of the
pudding is in the eating'.   As one PCI leader
(former chairman of the party group in the Chamber
of Deputies) has written: (16)

> It is not relevant to know what are the
> intentions of a politician who performs a
> particular political action ... what counts
> is the political process a politician sets
> in motion, and after that its further
> developments, which also depend certainly on
> the intentions that have inspired him, but
> can occur in a way completely opposite to
> his intentions.

Clearly, however, the interplay between attitudes or intentions and actual behaviour is crucial
to our assessment of the nature and role of opposition in a given country, but here a threefold
problem is encountered.   Firstly, the relationship
between party strategy and political choice -
including, as in Italy, the selection of alliance
partners - is rarely a straightforward one.(17)   In
fact, it is very arguable that party strategy may
be intrinsically ambiguous - a point frequently
made about the PCI.   This is usually because of the
enduring weight of a party's history and tradition
despite its adaptation to change, resulting in the
juxtaposition of the 'old' and the 'new' and
possibly conflicting tendencies.(18)   Secondly,
this draws attention to the area of internal party
relationships much neglected when evaluating a
party's performance as opposition.   This was
acknowledged by Dahl when, noting the enormous
variation in the internal unity of parties, he
commented that 'what is formally a single opposition party may in fact disintegrate into a number

175

of factions'.(19)   The point is especially pertinent for Italy, because of the high incidence
there of institutionalised factionalism, even
though with the PCI we are talking about a strongly
disciplined party. It does, however, emphasise the
need to consider the relationship between parliamentary groups and extra-parliamentary party
organisations, not least because in the PCI case
the latter is the more important.   Thirdly, return-
ing to our theme of defining what is meant by
'change', this is best viewed in terms of a dynamic
relationship between parties individually and
collectively, the political system and the wider
environment rather than simply a one-dimensional
perspective as to whether parties are 'anti-system'
or not.   This is the approach developed by
Panebianco in his theory of party organisation,
where he sees the relationship between this and the
environment as an interdependent or interactive
one.(20)   Such an approach is also in line with
Dahl's identification of different types of oppositional goals (specific policies, those relating to
the political structure and those relating to the
socio-economic structure).   Indeed, his whole discussion of different patterns of opposition in
democratic systems is based largely on assessing
the nature of the system as a whole.(21)
    It is with the preceding points and problems
in mind that we are able to formulate an approach
to the question of opposition in Italy.   This
starts by considering the Italian political system
as the context in which oppositon has been pursued
(the institutional structure and its evolution, the
nature of government/opposition relations within
it).   Then we look more closely at the performance
of the opposition role within Parliament and how
this relates to party strategy.   Following from
this, the discussion turns to the interplay between
this role and the national party leadership and
organisation, 'horizontally' as well as considering
'vertical' pressures within parties, before,
finally, viewing the parties' oppositional role
with respect to their function as societal actors
against the background of extra-parliamentary opposition in the proper sense and the wider socio-
economic environment.
    Given the thematic approach just outlined, the
salient characteristics of the opposition in Italy
listed at the beginning of this introduction and
the focus of the debate in the 1960s about the

opposition in Italy on the PCI, this chapter will
concentrate essentially on the role of this party.
In view of the Communist Party's numerical size,
its political importance and relevance to the
system, and in particular its strategic evolution
during the period under review from the 1960s, it
is seen as best exemplifying the complexities as
well as dynamics of the opposition role in Italy.
Other parties in opposition will not be discussed
at length, although they will be mentioned where
relevant to the thematic concerns of the chapter.
So far as the neo-Fascist MSI (Italian Social
Movement) is concerned, this has by contrast with
the PCI been numerically small, it has remained
largely isolated from alliance politics and it has
continued to be widely regarded as anti-system.
This view of the MSI has held because of the anti-
Fascist consensus in Italian politics and because
of its firm right-wing policy lines and sympathy
with the extreme Right elsewhere in Western Europe,
not to mention its links with 'black' political
violence in Italy. While the MSI's strategy has at
times appeared ambiguous, this has, unlike the
PCI's, remained more static than evolved, although
in recent years it has sought to break out of its
political isolation.

The Political System and the Role of Opposition

The problem of coming to terms with the role of
opposition in Italy is a consequence of the late
arrival of liberal democracy there and more broadly
of historical experience, of which Fascism must be
salient. As Putnam has written on 'the beliefs of
politicians' (based on an attitudinal survey of the
late 1960s), the effects of Fascism in Italy were
both consensual and conflictual (22): consensual
because of the anti-Fascist unity in the Resistance, which continued for a few years after the
war and has subsequently been a point of reference
at moments of party-political convergence (as by
the PCI during the 'National Solidarity' governments in the later 1970s); and conflictual as the
Fascist experience sharpened political perceptions
in general and these in turn affected the intensification of traditional cleavages, above all the
divide between the Marxist and Catholic sub-
cultures, in the Cold War period which had such a
formative influence on the new post-war Republic.
And this historical influence has, as we have seen,

been a powerful factor in inhibiting the legitimation of the opposition role in the new post-war
democracy. In the view of Sani, in his analysis of
perceptions of anti-system parties with reference
to both the PCI and the neo-Fascist MSI, the
'battle over the democratic legitimacy of these
political forces has left deep scars in Italy's
political culture'.(23) In other words, while it
is possible to trace the growth of the PCI's own
legitimation as a political force in Italian
politics (a process generally seen as incomplete),
we are talking about little more than a generation.
Ultimately, therefore, acceptance of the opposition
role - dominated as it has been by the PCI - has
been conditional on changes in the political
culture.

This historical background is relevant to our
discussion of the political system as the institutional framework within which the opposition role
has been pursued, because these consensual and
conflictual patterns have both been embodied in it.
The Constitution of 1948 was itself an outcome of
the immediate post-war consensus including the PCI
and, among other things, it accorded a central role
to Parliament in the policy-making process (it
could legislate on many matters left in other countries to the executive) as a direct reaction to
Fascism, to avoid executive predominance. In practice, however, with the expulsion of the PCI from
the national government in 1947 and the DC's acquisition of political dominance from the 1948 election, several provisions of the Constitution remained inoperative for some time, such as for
example establishing the Constitutional Court and
especially regional government. So far as Parliament was concerned, the high polarisation between
the Left opposition (Communists plus Socialists)
and the DC-dominated governments meant that the
consensual features of the Constitution were subordinated to the political struggle. Parliament was
not as prescribed central to the policy process,
and accordingly the role of opposition was constrained. Quite apart from the problem this posed
for the legitimation of that role, the very legitimacy of the system itself appeared called into
question at this time. The parties' views of
Parliament remained controversial, so that during
the 1948 and 1953 elections a major issue was the
relationship of their own opponents with the
Parliament, which was seen as threatened.(24)

Even though eventually the Parliament became more
accepted and established as an institution, the
general question of its 'decline' was highlighted
in the 1960s - a theme common to many other Western
European democracies at that time.

Meanwhile, the PCI had begun to emerge as a
proponent of the power of Parliament - where, after
all, it was accorded official recognition - against
the control and 'abuse' of executive power by the
DC and its allies.(25) This was paralleled by the
PCI's change of position on introducing regional
government, for having started with a Jacobin line
here it now strongly advocated devolution of power
(the DC performed a turnabout in the opposite
direction, out of a desire to prevent the Communists gaining control over the new sub-national
structures in their strongholds). Party interest
(including the pursuit of legitimacy) evidently
combined with this line in favour of 'democratising' the system in the case of the PCI over both
these issues, altogether suggesting a growing
commitment to this system on its part. As a
further illustration of this interplay between
party-political considerations and institutional
evolution, we have to mention the reform of parliamentary procedure in 1971 which effectively
strengthened the Parliament vis-à-vis the executive
and brought the PCI as main opposition party more
openly into the legislative process. This amounted
to an abandonment of the conventio ad excludendum
against the PCI, and it accorded Parliament the
centrality originally provided for in the Constitution. The change was an important outcome of the
centre-left governmental alliance, in particular of
the desire of the Socialist Party (PSI) to promote
progressive policies using the support of the
Communists.(26) It is no exaggeration to see a
relationship between the new possibilities created
here for the opposition and the decline of DC
dominance.

While diachronically it is possible to identify cycles in executive/legislative relations and,
in the case here of Italy, to speak of a trend
opposite to that of 'parliamentary decline', it is
necessary also to look at the functioning of
opposition within this modified system since the
late 1960s (the growth of legislative concurrence
between the government and the PCI had been evident
a few years before the 1971 reform). Although the
broad issue of 'parliamentary decline' was as such

simplistic since it has to be qualified by examining the balance between different parliamentary functions, (27) the specific matter of 'direct controls' over the executive most highlighted in the debate over this would indicate greater institutional opportunities for the opposition role in this recent period.   But we still have to ask - to dwell on the peculiarities of the Italian case - how this has worked out in relation to the consensual/conflictual patterns embedded in the system, juxtaposed and in contradiction as they are.

The starting point is to consider the usual view that Italy's political institutions are weak (most of all this has focused on the restricted role of the head of government, as rather in contrast with the UK, France and West Germany); furthermore, to see this within the context of Italy's <u>partitocrazia</u>. Duverger's point that in multi-party systems the line of government/opposition demarcation is not clear, and that moreover solid and homogeneous coalitions promote opposition coherence and vice versa, is only too true in Italy, and in fact more so than when he wrote his book.(28) This is because of the decline of DC dominance (hence, less homogeneous governments), together with the practice of institutionalised factionalism within government parties (among other things deriving from holding office) and an element of cross-party inter-factional co-operation.   To this must be added the informal aspect of coalition politics in Italy, whereby some parties might commit themselves to supporting the government from outside the cabinet on a policy-agreement basis, so that entering and leaving the government is not automatically equivalent to entering and leaving the opposition.   Given therefore the incohesion of Italian coalitions, and a habit now increasing of government party backbenchers (known as 'snipers') voting against individual government policies, a distinction has usually been made between the formal majority (the coalition) and a 'working majority' (i.e. legislative coalitions). In Italy, because of the dictates of the Constitution in its revised form (especially the blocking power of the PCI in the important committees) and the conventional preference for 'over-large' coalitions whether formal or informal, this practice of co-opting the opposition has become institutionalised and has been raised somewhat to the level of a value system. For instance, Di Palma has talked of a syncretic model as essentially different from the 'Anglo-Saxon' government/opposition model, while he and others have seen in this a modern version of the historical phenomenon of trasformismo practised during the liberal period in Italy (1870-1922) when government policies were passed by ad hoc majorities including opposition groups .(29) Whether this does amount to neo-trasformismo or not, the opposition has consequently not been seen clearly as representing the 'alternative government', to use a good 'Anglo-Saxon' phrase. At the same time, Sartori's assumption that systems of polarised pluralism produce 'irresponsible opposition' has come to be proved incorrect (if it was ever true of Italy, it was in the 1950s). However, this pattern of legislative consensualism needs to be examined further as it is not so clear-cut as it might first appear.

It is important to look more closely at the parliamentary structure and the process of legislation in the light of the 1971 reform. This reform placed the power of deciding on the parliamentary schedule in the hands of the committee of party group leaders in place of Speakers of the two chambers (hence, indirectly controlled by the government before). Since decisions here were to be made unanimously, this allowed the main opposition party an important co-influence. The 1971 changes also strengthened the investigative powers of Parliament by providing for committee hearings, committee access to official information and a role in drafting some legislation.(30) Given the constitutionally powerful function of the committees and their chairmen, the way was open for the opposition to acquire an important say in the policy process, especially as the PCI's discipline was such that the activity of its committee representatives could be well co-ordinated. The PCI's role here was of course upgraded once it was allotted four committee chairmanships in the 1976 legislature, together with the presidency of the Chamber (for the first time since the 1945-7 period). These appointments, made on the basis of agreement among the parties, formed part of the 'institutional' pact in support of the 'National Solidarity' governments; once that ceased in 1979 the PCI lost its committee chairmanships, although it has since retained the presidency of the Chamber (plus, in the 1983 Parliament, two non-permanent committee chairmanships). One might add to this

institutionalisation of legislative concurrence
between government and opposition the extensive use
made by the PCI of the large amount of private
legislation in the Parliament in which it has
sought to promote the interests of its party
constituents.(31)

While this does generally confirm the conclusion earlier about consensual patterns with respect
to the opposition role, one major point of differentiation has to be emphasised. Although roughly
two-thirds of government legislation has over the
years been approved with Communist votes, the
figure should be qualified as this has occurred
more often than not over minor legislation and
especially _leggine_ or 'small laws' concerned with
administrative questions (reflecting the fact,
mentioned earlier, that the Parliament also legis-
lates over routine matters left in other countries
to executive order).(32) On the other hand, this
quantitative lack of opposition is accompanied by
the qualitative tendency of the opposition to mount
its attack on the government over major bills.(33)
A dichotomy between consensual and conflictual
patterns in the opposition role is evident here
since, with the PCI, the former has focused on
committee work and the latter on the plenary.
Cazzola saw, in his study of the Parliament, the
PCI as performing two very different opposition
roles depending on the institutional 'site' (34)
(to use Dahl's word).

One may take this point one stage further by
relating it to Sartori's well-known distinction
between the 'visible' and 'invisible' levels of
politics, i.e. between electoral politics and elite
or parliamentary committee work (usually carried
out behind closed doors). Except for the 1976-9
legislature, accommodation between the PCI and the
DC and other government parties has belonged mainly
to the 'invisible' level while - no real surprise -
press coverage is more intense when the Communists
berate the government in the plenary sessions.
However, in recent years, growing issue consciousness among the public has apparently increased
awareness of some contradiction between these
consensual and conflictual patterns, which has in
turn made it more difficult for the PCI to make its
opposition role convincing. Some PCI leaders have
gone on record expressing disquiet over what Galli
has called this 'hybrid situation' of regular
attacks on the government combined with helping it

to pass its legislation.(35) One recalls the
colourful phrase of Giorgio Napolitano, now PCI
group leader in the Chamber, about the PCI being
in mezza al quado ('halfway across the ford'), used
at the time of 'National Solidarity', a position
which caused internal conflicts over its role
between its leadership's pursuit of the entente
with the DC and growing disaffection here among its
activists amid signs of electoral loss. To
complete this situation of a vicious circle so far
as the PCI opposition role is concerned, it is
important to note that one important motive among
the government parties for seeking the co-operation
of the PCI has been societal apart from instititu-
tional considerations, as outlined in interviews
with the author. In the words of one Liberal
leading activist, the PCI's influence over legislation existed not only because of government
incohesion but also because of its control over
(part of) the trade-union movement and the need for
social consensus behind government policy.(36)
Similarly, the Republican Party (PRI) group leader
in the Chamber argued that 'the PCI represents
important interests, a relevant part of our
society; therefore, it is impossible to disregard
it even in parliamentary work, for it is not as if
the government can go ahead without taking account
of the importance of the force represented by the
PCI'. (37)
       This situation as it has emerged raises a
variety of pertinent questions about the opposition
role in Italy. Most importantly, it suggests the
existence of a (conflictual) opposition-versus-
government dynamic irrespective of the consensus-
promotive elements in the institutional structures.
This would correspond with the strong evidence that
the Left/Right ideological spectrum has remained
uppermost in Italian political attitudes, at both
elite and popular levels, notwithstanding institutional and political change.(38) Survey results
from Putnam and others, indicating a trend to
elite-level depolarisation since the end of the
1960s, have meant a decline in the intensity of the
ideological divide, but by no means its disappearance; moreover, as they show, this trend has not
been replicated at the popular level.(39) In the
PCI's case, von Beyme's argument that 'supporters
of the opposition party are likely to be more
critical of the system than supporters of the
government party', and that there is a relationship

here between political roles and party identification, (40) is very applicable. In so far as they
would perceive the system as being the 'DC state',
Communist supporters and especially activists would
be reflecting the long years of PCI opposition and
its conditioning of party behaviour. In a sense,
we are talking about historical pressures operating
in the direction of the PCI remaining in opposition, unless the DC were to be displaced in power
(which for the foreseeable future is not a realistic expectation); although this does not exclude
that these pressures might eventually diminish with
generational change and the evolution of the
political culture.

All this underlines the linkages between
parties' institutional and societal roles, as an
important dimension of - not to mention lending
visibility to - the inherent contradiction in the
opposition performed by the PCI. As of late, this
contradiction has become less manageable because of
a growing divide between elite behaviour and a more
critical public. Interestingly enough, the elite
response to the latter over the issue of institutional reform could indirectly affect the role of
opposition, as increasing the Prime Minister's
powers (thus possible government cohesion) as well
as electoral reform (which might reduce the number
of parties or at least alter their relative
strength) would probably in turn enhance the
coherence of the opposition. All these different
problems do, of course, throw some light on the
interactive relationship between institutional
structures and political culture, with respect to
the PCI's active and 'responsible' role as opposition promoting its own legitimacy. Presumably, the
contradictions in this role have not made any such
interaction straightforward. But that is a
question that leads us to the next stages of this
analysis.

Parliamentary Opposition and Party Strategies

Although the evolution and patterns of the main
parliamentary opposition (the PCI) have already
been highlighted, it is important to look more
closely and selectively at the parliamentary
opposition as a whole since this directly broaches
the first of the analytical problems identified in
the introductory section of this chapter concerning
the interplay between intentions and actual

behaviour in applying the pro-/anti-system dichotomy: that the relationship between party strategy and political choice is rarely a straight-forward one. This problem is very similar to Dahl's view in differentiating between types of opposition goals: (41)

> Although it is obvious that oppositions differ in their goals, it is exceedingly difficult to reduce differences in goals to a manageable analytical scheme. Political actors, as we all know, have long-run aims and short-run aims, and their short-run goals are not necessarily deduced from their long-run goals: the short-run goals may so much dominate their choice of strategies that their 'long-run' goals are, realistic-ally speaking, nothing more than the outcome of their short-run goals. Everyone knows too that the ostensible goals of a political actor may not be his real goals; his public objectives may differ from his private objectives. There is no simple way to get round these complexitites in the notion of aims or goals...

Conceivably, the relationship between short- and long-term goals is, among other things, determined by the number and variety of political actors. Or, taking other criteria of Dahl - the concentration of the opposition, and its competitiveness - party strategy is conditioned by the structure of the party system.

In Italy, while the PCI has numerically and politically dominated the parliamentary opposition (especially once the PSI left it to join the centre-Left coalitions in the earlier 1960s), it has nevertheless had to function within a multi-party setting. The parliamentary opposition in Italy has been structurally fragmented, though with some variation over time. Literally or numeric-ally, it has diachronically contained a multipli-city of small parties ranging between the two traditional extremes - from Proletarian Democracy (DP) which first entered the Parliament in 1976 and the left socialist, PSIUP (1964-72) through the protest-oriented Radicals (also joined it in 1976) and the traditional centrist parties of the PRI and PLI to the Monarchists (who disappeared in 1972) and the neo-Fascist MSI, not to mention some regionalist parties of which the Tyrolean SVP has remained up to the present time.(42) What concerns us most, however, is the political dynamics within this fragmented opposition.

In his study of the Italian opposition up to the 1960s, Barnes distinguished between the parliamentary opposition of 'anti-constitutional' parties (PCI and MSI) and constitutional parties which remained outside the government, and he also included opposition from within government parties. (43) Today, this schema requires modification both to include the appearance of new parliamentary parties and to reflect the changed position of others, above all of the PCI. We can therefore differentiate as follows: parties which are temporarily in opposition or 'halfway across the ford', but which normally or potentially form part of the 'government camp' (more often than not the small centrist parties); the main opposition, the PCI, which is now (re-) recognised as part of the 'constitutional arch' (the phrase refers to those parties which together formulated the 1948 Constitution and has been much in use both during 'National Solidarity' and more recently with consensus formation over institutional reform); thirdly, the MSI as remaining essentially 'anti-system' in Tosi's sense of 'historically evident'; and parties on the extreme or radical Left, specifically the DP and the Radicals. Given these changes in the structure and positions of the parliamentary opposition, we are of course better able to appreciate the changing styles of this role since World War II, as moving from a polarised bloc-versus-bloc situation, with a largely illegitimate opposition, to the semi-consociational situation, with the PCI offering 'different opposition'. While again underlining the PCI as the dominant opposition, this does not do full justice to the political dynamics within the parliamentary opposition as a whole. It is necessary to remember that the latter is multi-polar, and that it has been characterised by internal antagonisms. This leads us to consider the strategies of the different parties in opposition. In doing so, we concentrate on the recent period of the past decade as that is bound to cast most light on the basic question of 'anti-system' opposition with which we opened this discussion.

Taking the PCI first of all, we have to start by taking into account various features of party

structure which bear on the relationship between
strategy and the activity of the PCI in Parliament.
They tend to illustrate the close co-ordination or
discipline within that party, although they equally
do not negate the earlier assumption that this
relationship is rarely straightforward. Based on
the statements of relevant leaders, the role of the
two parliamentary groups is broadly seen as that of
'interpreting the party line'. This is possible as
there is close and regular contact between the
parliamentary leadership (in particular, the two
group leaders) and the national executive organs of
the PCI, for the group leaders are members of the
party directorate. There is also the special
procedural problem presented by Italy's bicameral
legislature, for the Chamber of Deputies and the
Senate have an equal role in the legislative process. However, the PCI's co-ordinative mechanisms
are such that it largely manages to overcome this
problem, for the two group leaders are not only
together in the directorate but also meet informally outside it including in meetings of PCI
committee chairmen when these have existed.(44)

Nevertheless, two points have to qualify what
may seem at first sight a well-oiled system for
regulating the PCI's performance of the opposition
role. This close co-ordination involves directly
only a small group of leadership personnel, and it
does not exclude that individual parliamentarians
or groups of them might 'interpret' the party line
variously at least over detailed policy matters,
given the PCI's practised role in promoting
sectional or local interests noted earlier. The
control of the parliamentary group leadership over
PCI deputies was particularly high during the
'National Solidarity' governments when government
ministers under Andreotti were meeting with their
opposite numbers in the party, but since then there
has apparently been 'greater freedom of movement'
in the parliamentary groups, (45) meaning that the
group leaders have reverted to a more consultative
relationship with their backbenchers. In effect,
there is significant room for 'interpreting' PCI
strategy in the context of daily parliamentary
business. The other point worth noting here is
that there is no convention or practice in Italy of
a 'shadow cabinet', to use a good 'Anglo-Saxon'
term; and it was only used informally for a time
during 'National Solidarity'.(46) If there is any
equivalent in the PCI, it must include the heads of

187

the six departments in the party organisation. In
other words, however effective internal party co-
ordination might be, the opposition 'team' has to
straddle the parliamentary group/party organisation
relationship even though the PCI's national leaders
are also usually in Parliament, while its recognition as such has been inhibited by the lack of a
clear government/opposition divide. Such structural complexities inevitably imprint themselves on
the application of party strategy to parliamentary
activity.

The other angle on the PCI is to consider the
relationship between its parliamentary opposition
and strategy change. We do have in this recent
period an important example of such a change with
the PCI's abandonment of the 'historic compromise'
(originally formulated by Berlinguer in 1973) in
1980 and its adoption instead of the 'democratic
alternative'. A correlation between strategy and
parliamentary activity is evident in that the first
strategy was eventually expressed in the PCI's
support for the Andreotti Governments of 1976-9, a
process initiated by the DC's inability to form an
adequate majority after the 1976 election without
Communist involvement. Since the PCI's withdrawal
from this legislative coalition, its oppositional
line in the plenary (though not in committees) has
hardened towards successive governments, though it
has mounted frontal attacks only on an issue basis.
These have been most fierce over economic policy
(as in PCI opposition to the Craxi Government's
departure from the scala mobile indexing system of
incomes policy), issues concerning the 'moral
question' (notably, the implication of ministers in
the P2 scandal) and selected cases of terrorism
(e.g. the attack on the Cossiga Government over the
Donat Cattin affair). On the other hand, there has
been 'convergence' over institutional reform even
taking account of the different proposals here from
the different parties. The difference between the
PCI line in the 1979 and 1983 Parliaments and that
of 1976 essentially revolves around the fact that
in the latter it was somewhat pre-determined by a
'preventive' policy pact with the government, while
its support of the government in the former cases
has been ad hoc and not always predictable. There
is also a political consideration behind this
difference, for as Cazzola noted in his study of
parliamentary opposition, the PCI line has varied
according to the type of coalition and has notably

been stronger when the government has been more compact.(47) For instance, the <u>pentapartito</u> or five-party coalition in office since 1981 has enjoyed a self-sufficient majority in parliament, thus making PCI support less necessary to the government.

It could also be said that the PCI's isolation since 1979 in terms of political alliances has influenced its style of parliamentary opposition, but from the foregoing discussion of oppositional style we have to beware of simplistic labels. Certainly, its oppositional style has become more 'intransigent' of late, just as its use of obstruction as notably over the <u>scala mobile</u> in 1984 gained it visibility in this respect, but more to the point is to relate this to the balance between consensual and conflictual patterns. Compared with the 1976 Parliament, the two legislatures since have seen a change in this balance back towards conflictual tendencies. This is well illustrated by the PCI's own definition of its oppositional role at the time of the formation of the Craxi Government in 1983. Following a meeting of the party central committee in July, this role was explained in the form of various strategy proposals involving 'constructive opposition' (seeking to influence government policy) combined with firmness on particular policies, where the PCI would seek to implement its 'alternative' by means of programmatic projects presented to the other parties.(48) On this and other occasions, various PCI leaders have gone out of their way to emphasise that the change of oppositional lines since 1979 does not amount to a return to the situation before the 1970s and that '1948' (the high point of post-war polarisation) is 'not repeatable'.(49) As Natta claimed in an interview late in 1984, the PCI's attacks on the government's anti-inflation policy did not mean it was acting in a 'subversive' or 'Leninist' manner; rather, he claimed, this was no different from the opposition role in other European democracies.(50) He also indicated that the main opposition party's Communist identity in Italy evidently made for a difference of perception.

Finally, whatever the balance between consensual and conflictual patterns in the PCI's parliamentary opposition, the first of these has demarcated it from the other opposition parties. Most of all, this has been behind the mutual antag-

onism between the Communists and the Radicals. The
latter have been numerically smaller than the PCI
with 4 seats in the Chamber in 1976 and 18 in 1979
(compared with the PCI's 227 and 201 respectively),
but politically they have acquired a distinct
profile on a very issue-specific basis, notably
issues concerning civil rights from the time of the
referendum on divorce in 1974, of which the
Radicals were the chief proponent. The Radicals
have pushed since then for other referenda, and
their line of hostility towards the established
parties has characterised their parliamentary
opposition, e.g. the use of obstruction over such
issues as world hunger, state finance for parties
and over government finance bills. The antagonism
between them and the PCI is rooted in electoral
competition among certain groups of (mainly young)
voters; the belief on the PCI side that the
Radicals are not truly of the Left (they were
originally formed as a party splinter from the
right-wing Liberals in the 1950s) as they lack a
convincing economic policy; and the belief on the
Radical side that the PCI is very much a part of
'the system'.

In particular, the Radicals have consistently
and bitterly attacked the PCI's consensual
behaviour as 'anti-democratic', (51) and in this
sense they have overtly presented themselves as
'anti-system'. That is, they have in blanket
fashion opposed all the established parties,
refusing alliance relationships, and among other
things have advocated pulling out of NATO.(52)
When the Radicals first entered the Parliament in
1976, they chose provocatively to sit on the left
of the PCI instead of using the places assigned
them on the right of that party, thus touching on
the Communists' sensitivity about parties to their
left; (53) and, since then, physical fights have
occurred between deputies of the two parties thus
highlighting this antagonism. Among PCI deputies,
the regular complaint has been that 'the Radical
party has not opposed the government but rather the
Communist Party; it has prevented us Communists
from modifying the policy proposals of the government', although it was admitted, however, that the
role of the Radicals was 'somewhat a caricature of
our position in the past'.(54) Evidently, the
opposition line of the Radicals has aroused some
concern within the PCI over its own identity; and
most of all, this has appeared over the issue of

terrorism and specifically the Radicals' association with some terrorist figures, notably Toni
Negri. While the PCI has taken a firm line in
opposing terrorism and defending the Italian state,
the 'Red' origins of the main terrorist groups have
at the same time made the PCI itself defensive at
times on this issue. This is also because the
Radicals - and more so DP, which is close to them
in their hostility to the PCI - have accused the
Communists of reneging on their historical tradition. As opposition party, the PCI has therefore
felt itself caught as it were between the hammer of
Marxism and the anvil of system-supportiveness.

Relations with the MSI have been far less
complicated because the divide between this party
and the Communists has for obvious historical and
ideological reasons remained unbridgeable; also,
since the neo-Fascists have throughout the post-war
period been politically isolated and excluded from
virtually all alliance arrangements. Moreover,
there has been no problem here of electoral competition between the two parties. If anything,
this has more affected the DC at various times such
as the early 1970s, when the MSI enjoyed some
electoral expansion until its association with
'black' terrorism did much to harm any credibility
it might have acquired. More recently, the MSI has
attempted to capitalise on the New Right trend in
European politics and to break out of its 'ghetto'
by adopting a line of 'constructive' opposition
towards the Craxi Government; but this is unlikely
to have any great impact on the PCI's position as
opposition. As regards the small parties of the
centre, the PCI line has generally to be viewed
within the context of its overall relationship with
the government of which these parties have often
formed a part; while their intermittent absence
from the cabinet has not essentially modified this
situation of <u>confronto</u> or issue-based entente with
the PCI. In the past, there have been some differences here between the Liberals (PLI) and the
Republicans (PRI). The former have adhered to an
anti-Communist line which has made any co-operation
with the PCI difficult; while the PRI has over the
past decade moved in favour of an 'opening' towards
the PCI (notably, under La Malfa during 'National
Solidarity'), and it has entered some coalitions
with the Communists in local politics.

In short, the political dynamics within
Italy's fragmented opposition have varied consider-

ably according to the parties in question as well
as the evolution of the party system as a whole.
The complexities of these inter-party relationships
aside, the general pattern of these dynamics
confirms the importance of the Left/Right ideological spectrum in Italian politics. While ideological space both between government and opposition
and within the latter may be seen to expand or
contract, it is not, however, a simple matter of
individual party strategy determining such movement, for party competition and party identity also
act as influential intervening variables. The
interplay between attitudes and behaviour in the
roles of opposition is multi-dimensional, as will
be seen further in assessing linkages between
parliamentary parties and their own organisations.

The Role of Opposition and Extra-Parliamentary Linkages

The other two problems identified in the introduction as affecting the relationship between intentions and actual behaviour in the opposition role,
reflecting therefore on the pro-/anti-system
dichotomy, are relationships within party structures and the impact of the wider environment, the
latter being pertinent to the definition and
requirements of 'change'. These may be taken
together as they both bring the discussion of the
opposition role outside the institutional framework
and therefore into the more 'visible' areas of
politics, or as Italians commonly say - from the
palazzo into the piazza. To some extent, this
wider environment has been approached earlier in
dealing with the general structure of the party
system, but we need to look additionally at parties
as individual structural entities and more especially as societal actors. It should hardly need
emphasising that party strategies involve factors
other than elite-level behaviour, in particular the
mobilisation of social groups, a point most explicitly developed in the case of the PCI.(55) In
effect, we are employing Sartori's distinction
between different forms of social protest in his
definition of 'anti-system (see above).
    Such extra-parliamentary linkages may schema-
tically be seen as 'horizontal' or 'vertical'
according to the level from which pressures
emanate. That is, the former would include leaders
of national parties and their executive organs as

192

distinct from leaders of the parliamentary opposition as well as relevant economic leaders or leaders of interest groups; while the latter, among other things, refer to party bases and electorates as well as new social movements and other forms of extra-parliamentary opposition. Again, the discussion will concentrate on the past decade.

There has already been some random reference to such linkages impinging on the role of parliamentary opposition, so that for the purpose of this present analysis the following categorisation should assist in evaluating their relative importance. This is appropriate to all Italian parties, but it will be applied specifically to those in opposition:

(a) intra-party structural relationships, both horizontal and vertical;
(b) extra-parliamentary opposition in the proper sense of movements in competition with established parties within the same sectors of the ideological spectrum;
(c) social forces which have a semi-institutionalised relationship with political parties, e.g. trade unions and other interest groups, the Church and the media;
(d) crypto-pressure groups which have some linkage with political parties, e.g. secret finance groups, the Mafia;
(e) cleavages and electoral pressures.

(a) Intra-party Structural Relationships. Clearly, among the opposition parties, the PCI is in a class apart from the others simply because its structure is highly articulated as a mass party; but it is still necessary to explore the relationship between parliamentary parties and their national organisations more systematically. It is best to see this relationship as a two-way process and also as one which is not necessarily static - that is, the balance of power between the two elements may shift over time. Conceivably too, this balance is itself affected by the parties' political roles as to whether they move between government and opposition or remain fixed in the latter role. Klaus von Beyme has rightly argued that this relationship is more complex than commonly assumed.(56) Contrary to Duverger, he does not see it as 'a one-way road' for there are certain factors overarching this rather dichotomous relationship and different

variables affecting it, written party rules often
being a misleading indicator here. Von Beyme
concludes on 'this complicated network of influences' in the relationship: (57)

> The distribution of power within the differ-
> ent bodies of the parties and its impact on
> parliament and government is an intervening
> variable, dependent on the type of party
> (bourgeois or socialist), on the party
> system (degree of fragmentation), on insti-
> tutional variables (such as the power of the
> head of state, parliamentary rules, party
> laws, incompatibility rules) and the rela-
> tions between parties and pressure groups.

It is possible first of all to differentiate
between the various Italian parties with respect to
the balance in this relationship. Percy Allum, for
instance, sees the PCI as an apparatus party rather
than primarily a parliamentary party - for Parliament is viewed as one of the arenas of its
political activity - while the DC is the oppositie,
being essentially a party of power. The PSI as the
third party, however, underwent a change with a
shift towards being more of a parliamentary party,
this being related to its entry into government
with the centre-Left coalition.(58) So far as the
small parties in opposition are concerned, one may
generalise that they are really parliamentary
parties since their organisations are small and
usually loosely structured; and they have been
particularly dependent on charismatic leaders for
their appeal (Malagodi, La Malfa, Spadolini and
Pannella). While it is also true they may have a
sense of representing a 'movement' (i.e. political
tendency), they have lacked a structured relationship here and hence adequate direct channels for
activist pressure on their respective parliamentary
parties. For example, although the Radicals'
political outlook is strongly anti-elitist and
their activity places much importance on issue-
based mobilisation (e.g. collecting signatures for
referenda or for protest motions), structurally
their party is top-heavy as their handful of
parliamentarians - not to mention Pannella in
person - dominate their strategy line, given the
small membership (only 2,190 late 1985). They have
in fact chosen to emphasise the 'autonomy' of their
parliamentary group.(59) With the MSI, the problem

has been somewhat different in that its internal
divisions between a cautious and a radical or
populist line have most affected relations within
the leadership, though at times weakening its
control over party activities. Therefore, von
Beyme's argument about the complexity of the power
balance between parliamentary party and national
organisation is only really applicable to the PCI.

With the PCI, we have earlier noted the
mechanism for close consultation between its
parliamentary leaders and the national party
organisation, whereby the application of party
strategy is regularly discussed within the executive organs of the latter, though not normally
detailed legislative work.(60) This point does,
however, require some elaboration. On the one
hand, a formal distinction is made in the party
'horizontal' structure on practical grounds of the
division of labour between the PCI's parliamentary
leaders and the party's national leaders, e.g.
Berlinguer was a deputy in the Chamber, to which he
had been elected since 1968, but he played no
special role there apart from making speeches on
big occasions, for the party secretaryship is
incompatible with holding a parliamentary post.
Similarly, Napolitano lost his position in the
party secretariat on becoming PCI group leader in
the Chamber in 1983, and no longer had an office
in the PCI headquarters in the Botteghe Oscure. On
the other hand, there has in effect been much
interweaving of political experience between the
two arenas seeing that some three-quarters of the
PCI directorate are in parliament, and remembering
for instance that Alessandro Natta (Berlinguer's
successor as PCI secretary from 1984) was also
previously leader of the PCI group in the Chamber
(1972-9). One might emphasise the discipline
exerted by the party over its parliamentarians by
noting its deliberately high turnover among the
latter, thus promoting mobility between party work
and parliamentary activity.(61)

This close co-ordination between the two
arenas does not necessarily mean that the relationship is always free from tensions, the latter
invariably fought out within the party executive or
sometimes the central committee. Tensions over the
opposition role have been more visible in
'vertical' relations with the party. What is
interesting here is the continued conditioning from
the PCI's longevity as opposition force in Italian

195

politics. As Galli and Prandi observed in the
1960s, the PCI leadership tended in its relation
with its members and supporters to 'assume an attitude and employ a language that set it apart as a
party of opposition'.(62) Under Berlinguer with
his 'historic compromise', this style of language
changed with the new emphasis on co-operation with
the DC; but this strategy met no serious problems
until it was actually transmitted into concrete
support for the DC in Rome - that is, when the PCI
moved closer to government. Survey research by
Barbagli and Corbetta has shown that the behaviour
of party activists differed in their reception of
the 'historic compromise' as a strategy proposition
compared with their (more negative) reaction subsequently to the economic policy of austerity of the
Andreotti Governments of 1976-9 and their generally
disappointed policy expectations then.(63) Growing
restlessness within the party together with signs
of electoral loss (in local elections in 1978) and
trade-union demonstrations provided a powerful
influence on the PCI leadership in its decision to
withdraw its support from the DC Government and
return to the opposition role. As Di Giulio, then
vice-chairman of the parliamentary group, has
written, the break between the government and the
unions had an 'explosive' effect on the PCI which -
reflecting a common mood of self-criticism in the
party after this turn of events - was seen as
having 'sheltered itself too much in the _palazzo_'
at a cost to the party itself.(64)

A direct consequence of this searing experience for the PCI was the strategy change of 1980,
one motive behind which was to allow the party
organisation greater freedom to revive itself, for
there had been a sharp membership drop in the
preceding few years. Implicit in this new strategy
of the 'democratic alternative' was a clear
distinction between government and opposition
roles, whereas previously the PCI had underlined
its purpose as 'a party of government and struggle'
(partito di governo e di lotta), a phrase which
itself combined the consensual and conflictual
approaches with all their ambiguities.

(b) Extra-parliamentary Opposition. The first point
that requires stating about opposition in the
extra-parliamentary arena is that this has been far
from hegemonised by the PCI as the main opposition
at the parliamentary level. This is especially the

case in the period under examination, which has
seen the growth of extra-parliamentary opposition
in the proper sense in different forms; the student
movement and the New Left from the late 1960s, the
appearance and persistence of terrorism and more
recently the peace movement and the ecologists,
both late arrivals in Italy compared with many
other West European countries. The fragmentation
of opposition in Italy has been all the more
evident outside the Parliament than within it. If
the PCI came close to hegemonising opposition in
the extra-parliamentary arena, that was more during
the earlier half of the post-war period when the
dominant theme in interpreting Italian politics was
that of the 'institutionalised sub-cultures', the
Catholic and the Marxist - the DC in government
representing one, the PCI in opposition representing the other.

There would appear to be some connection
between this appearance of new forms of extra-
parliamentary opposition and the strategy shift of
the PCI in the 1970s. In so far as the 'historic
compromise' involved or was perceived as moving the
party towards the centre-Left, one may speak of
ideological space being vacated on the left of the
spectrum. This seems confirmed by the fact that
all the extra-parliamentary forces mentioned above
(except for the 'black' version of terrorism)
relate to this side of the spectrum. 'Black'
terrorism's appearance during this period (especially in the early 1970s) complicated the MSI's
pursuit of respectability, for while the former was
fairly autonomous the latter chose not to disasso-
ciate itself. So far as the New Left is concerned,
it arose in part as a protest against the perceived
prevalence of orthodoxy in the traditional parties
of the Left; (65) while subsequently the 'historic
compromise' line and the PCI's pursuit of an
alliance with the parties in government, including
the DC, was an object of bitter attack from the
radical or extreme Left including 'Red' terrorist
groups. The uneasy and tense relationship between
the PCI and these extra-parliamentary forces,
reflected in the Parliament, as already noted, was
replicated more volubly and visibly outside it. In
this sense, it is possible to see this pattern as
involving political rivalry within the same sector
of the ideological spectrum. For instance, the
Radicals as a self-styled anti-establishment movement have been able to relate more comfortably to

197

some of these new forms of extra-parliamentary opposition than the PCI - such as with the peace movement, with the new verdi (greens) and, somewhat controversially, with some terrorist figures. It has only been since the PCI's strategy change of 1980 that it has been able to establish new linkages, mainly with the peace movement following the issue of the nuclear base at Comiso in Sicily. One may identify the new line of the 'democratic alternative' as involving some kind of shift back away from the centre-left of the spectrum - at least that is evident on some issues more than others, e.g. defence, economic policy with the more pronounced stress on workers' interests - but at this point of the discussion we are verging on oversimplified judgements.

It is important to realise that these new forms of extra-parliamentary opposition have their own intrinsic motivation and, more broadly speaking, derive from the changing social and economic environment of Italy since the 1960s. However much they have attacked the PCI for its orthodox behaviour within the system, that has been as much a feature of self-demarcation and search for political space as it was one among several reasons for their original appearance. In other words, it is more correct to see the PCI's strategy and the line followed by these various forces as independent though interacting variables. Clearly, the fact that the state has performed unimpressively in coping with the recession since the early 1970s has had some repercussions on the standing of the PCI (whose association with the austerity policy during 'National Solidarity' was only too visible); but it is also true that new participatory tendencies have been an outcome of social change itself. We are, therefore, talking about a case of the familiar problem of established parties having to adapt to social change, an exercise not made easy for the PCI because of its combination of consensual and conflictive approaches in its opposition role.

However, the problem for the PCI as opposition goes beyond this problem, and returns us once more to the leitmotiv of 'anti-system' politics. The inclination of these extra-parliamentary oppositions has been to present themsevles as 'anti-system', but this also in turn reminds us of the definition of that term. It cannot clearly be said that they represent the same 'anti-system' approach

that the PCI once did or was perceived to do in the
early post-war decades, except possibly for the new
small parties or groups on the extreme left. In
the case of the Radicals, 'anti-system' politics is
directed primarily against the collective hegemony
of the established parties, and one is tempted to
say this is as much an attitude of mind as it is
evidence of systematic political thinking. The
PCI's defence of the state is no more evident than
it its hard line over combatting terrorism, so that
in its rivalry with these extra-parliamentary movements its advocacy of change in the system risks
being disregarded just as it is in the interest of
these movements to de-emphasise it. The extra-
parliamentary oppositions do not present a serious
threat to the PCI in terms of electoral competition, for they either do not compete or in doing so
they remain on the fringe (except for the Radicals
in national elections, although in local elections
they do not participate). But the problem is that
their very existence and rivalry with the PCI
complicate the latter's credibility within the
overall left of the spectrum and also its pursuit
of legitimacy, not to mention highlighting the
ambiguities in the PCI's opposition role. And
beyond all this is the fact that Italy's partitocrazia, very much including the PCI, has been
showing signs of coming under greater challenge.

(c) Social Forces in a Semi-institutional Relationship with Parties A traditional feature of Italy's
partitocrazia has been the major parties' collateral organisations as central to the institutionalisation of the two sub-cultures; and, in addition,
one may include reference to those independent
institutions (notably the Catholic Church) which
have enjoyed a close relationship with one or
other party. For them all, the collective term
'social forces' is used in Italy. The question we
are concerned with here is, therefore, their importance for the performance of the role of opposition. Since the Church and economic elites have
been largely allied with the DC or, in the latter
case, to some extent with the DC's coalition
partners (notably, the Liberals with business
interests), we are principally talking about the
PCI's relationship with the trade-union movement so
far as the opposition is concerned.
    This relationship has changed over time,
especially during the period since the late 1960s,

with some bearing on the PCI's role in opposition. Until the end of the 1960s, the role of the Communist-allied CGIL paralleled that of the PCI as a party, for it was strictly its collateral; but, since that time, the growth of trade-union autonomy leading to co-operation between the three main organisations (later institutionalised in a unitary federation between the CGIL, the Catholic CISL and the moderate Left UIL) together with Berlinguer's strategy of convergence with parties in government produced a more complicated relationship between the PCI and the CGIL. While the government sought to co-opt the PCI among other reasons for its influence over the CGIL, concrete support by the PCI for government economic policies created a rift between party and union. This was most evident during 'National Solidarity' when the PCI went along with Andreotti's policy of austerity.(66) With the move of the PCI away from co-operation with the DC, the relationship eventually became smoother, and of late there was close co-operation between them in opposing Craxi's anti-inflation policy, including the use of strikes, though at the cost of the final rupture in trade-union co-operation. Given the influence of trade-union pressure (and notably of the metalworkers' strike against Andreotti's policy), it may be concluded that the CGIL forms an important component in the PCI's performance as opposition, though this is a two-way relationship. For instance, Berlinguer was at times accused by government circles of 'using the threat of the piazza' in trying to steer government policy in an alternative direction.

The other parties in opposition, seeing their lack of organisational articulation, have not had an equivalent semi-institutionalised relationship with the main social forces; and, in this particular sense, their role in opposition has been somewhat easier to perform. The only possible exception here relates to the role of the media which, considering their important influence and the background of state control, may be grouped under the heading of semi-institutionalised in their relationship with (certain) parties. That is, in the past, the media have been effective channels for the parties in government, so that parties in opposition have been at a disadvantage. However, changes in the 1970s in the statutory position of the media (i.e. radio and television) have loosened government control, and this has been accompanied by a tendency in the main daily newspapers to report more fully and somewhat more impartially the activity of the PCI. This may be seen as part of the further legitimation process of that party, quite apart from giving the opposition as a whole much more visibility in the media. A special feature here has been the Radicals' use of their own Radio Radicale - in line with the growth of private radio - as an arm of their opposition activity, including the regular transmission of parliamentary debates.

(d) Crypto-pressure Groups and Political Parties
This category may be discussed briefly as it only really applies to parties in government, since broadly speaking such groups have been attracted to the sources of power in Italian politics. The relationship between groups like the Mafia as providing something of a 'state within a state', agencies of secret finance (which are not entirely domestic) and underworld networks (most notoriously, the P2 masonic lodge) and the parties in question is a difficult one to describe, not least because this has operated via individuals rather than party organisations, but together these represent an important power factor. They are, however, conspicuous for their lack of any relationship with the main opposition party in Italy, and hence they have had no direct bearing on that role. Nevertheless, worthy of mention is the 'moral question' (increasing exposure of scandals involving such groups, linked as this is to the greater autonomy of the media from the state, and public disquiet over these scandals), for this has presented the PCI with an issue which plainly demarcates the PCI - as well as the Radicals - from the parties which have exploited power in the 'DC state', even accepting the involvement of some Communist local administrators in corruption cases; and therefore, it is an issue on which the opposition parties may seek to enhance their credibility.

(e) Cleavages and Electoral Pressures This subject is important in its own right and is well researched in Italy, so that simply points of reference for the role of opposition will be identified. These are fourfold, all illustrating the relationship between parties and the electorate as one of reciprocal conditioning. Firstly, as noted previously, electoral pressures have been

evident at the parliamentary level both in relations between government and opposition, but also
affecting those within the latter. This confirms
Di Palma's comment in his study of the Italian
Parliament that electoral pressures stretch ideo
logical distance between parties, especially if
they crowd a certain space.(67) But such pressures may also produce conflict within parties, and
this has particularly been true of the PCI among
the opposition parties. As Lange noted in his
review of PCI strategy in the 1970s, its pursuit of
the 'historic compromise' produced, on the one
hand, pressures from the economic situation and
from terrorism - whereby it underlined its state-
supportive role - and on the other hand, electoral
pressures operating against its concrete support
for DC policies.(68)

Secondly, following an extraordinary level of
voting stability for the first two post-war decades
and more, electoral behaviour has since the Divorce
Referendum of 1974 revealed increasing volatility,
among other reasons because of public disaffection
with the main parties. This has created both
opportunities but also greater risks for the PCI,
the latter relating to its general recognition as
one of the established parties. Party strategies,
most notably that of Craxi's PSI, have come to base
their appeals more on winning over this new body of
'opinion voters', but altogether it has made the
opposition role more difficult to manage for the
PCI. Thirdly, as one other reason for this growth
of volatility, the impact of social change has, as
one would expect, begun to have a profound effect
on the party system, notably in the loosening up of
the traditional sub-cultures. In particular, Italy
has undergone substantial socio-economic changes
since the 1960s, such as with increased urbanisa-
tion, not to mention the bite of the recession.
However, with regard to the role of opposition,
this has not had a straightforward effect. We may
recall Sani's conclusion on mass constraints on
political realignments, that such realignments take
time and that (as of 1976) the ground for building
them had hardly been broken, for 'political images
at the mass level have a great inertia'.(69) He
also drew attention to coalition-induced cleavages,
and the fact that the denial of full legitimacy to
the PCI (and also the MSI) had produced 'anti-
system' hostility among its supporters.(70)
Fourthly, despite this, on the later evidence of

Sani himself, the process of legitimation of the PCI has continued even if not completed according to opinion research.(71) Political culture is never truly static, but we have to bear in mind once again that attitudes are not automatically translated into behaviour, and that acceptance of the PCI moving into national office - let alone as leading party in government - would be a difficult operation. The evidence presented in this chapter alone only emphasises the difficulties that would surface in such an event in marrying different party alliance preferences with activist pressures, electoral trends and public opinion, interest groups and, not least, international opinion.

In general, two concluding points about the role of opposition in relation to extra-parliamentary linkages come to mind. Looking at these undoubtedly highlights the difficulties in performing the role of parliamentary oppposition; most of all for the PCI, not only because of the combination of consensual and conflictual patterns in its strategy but also simply because it is a mass party. In addition, focusing on these linkages does call into question any blanket definition of 'anti-system' politics. Quite apart from the strong evidence that the PCI has become much more integrated into the Italian political system since the 1960s, this term begs for differentiated and careful handling.

Conclusion

The basic question of 'anti-system' opposition has dominated much of the preceding discussion of the role of opposition in Italy, as this was the centre of debate on the subject in the 1960s and therefore demanding some updated answer; but also since the evolution of the PCI as the main opposition party has caused more confusion than clarity, raising problems of definition and questions concerning the Italian political system as a whole. The PCI as political party has not obviously remained static, nor has the system itself, not to mention the wider environment. Yet, the legitimation of the PCI is generally regarded as not complete, even though it has repeatedly demonstrated its firm if not growing commitment to the system in the face of various challenges to it - from the recession, from terrorism and, one might add, from the system's own ineffective performance. But one might also simi-

larly ask: when is any system completely consolidated? Or are we largely talking about perceptions
of the PCI conditioned by history, to which there
have been various allusions in this chapter?
Clearly, some framework is required that manages to
place this problem in perspective; and the lack of
any systematic work on the opposition in Italy
since the early 1970s reinforces that need. Accordingly, the theoretical handling of opposition has
to be opened up.

Sartori, who more than anyone else provoked
discussion on this very question of 'anti-system'
opposition, nevertheless later on argued in favour
of approaching this subject in a differentiated
manner. Subsequently, Farneti, who attempted to
replace Sartori's thesis of 'polarised pluralism',
offered the alternaive model of 'centripetal
pluralism', whereby (72)

> the social and political centre, as a con-
> tinuous reference point for any governmental
> majority, is fed by the heterogeneity, the
> contradictions and the tensions of the two
> poles of the system, namely the right and
> the left, that causes them to be feared ...
> as non-viable and unacceptable governmental
> alternatives, by a great majority of the
> electorate. The centre is not, as such, a
> highly homogeneous and cohesive area. It is
> usually internally divided into centre, left
> and right. It contains several social
> strata and above all several strata of
> collective mentalities, ideologies and forms
> of <u>Willensbildung</u>.

In other words, he indicated the basic idea of this
model as 'not the strength of the centre, but
rather the weakness of the right and left poles of
the political and ideological alignment which
results from their heterogeneity'.(73) Farneti
also saw this model as in practice favouring a
tendency towards agreement and bargaining, with a
stress on procedural cohesion, thus postponing the
'final ends' of politics.(74) This reminds us of
the problem identified earlier of accommodating a
demand for 'change' with defence of the system, as
lying behind the difficulties facing the role of
the PCI.

One might, when examining the position of the
PCI as it has developed, adopt Dahl's criteria for

assessing oppositional goals on the question of
fundamental change, and arrive at the following
broad conclusion: yes to changing the personnel of
government; yes to changing specific government
policies, no to changing the political system,
except by consensual reform; and probably more yes
than no to changing the socio-economic structure,
if this meant gradual transformation. But this
does not do full justice to the problem of party
competition in Italy in which it may remain in the
interest of the PCI's rivals to beat the anti-
Communist drum - as, notably, Craxi did in a famous
polemical attack on Marxist-Leninism in 1978 as
part of his newly embarked upon strategy to acquire
more space for his party in the political spectrum.
Equally, if 'anti-system' opposition - in the sense
understood in the 1960s - has indeed waned, opposition as such has not nor has 'anti-system' opposition of more specific varieties; and the PCI as
main opposition party has had to relate to this
changing situation. In short, the question of
'change' in the system has to be related to the
dynamics of that system, just as the latter colours
perceptions of the former.
     From the foregoing, it is obvious that the
role of the opposition in Italy has to be treated
in some way as multi dimensional. Criteria must
include the concepts of opposition in the country,
the nature of the institutional framework as well
as societal responses to opposition activity. Our
study of the consensual and conflictual patterns in
the performance of the opposition role would identify the PCI as both transformative and accommodative as a party, but this role has to be examined
more closely, particularly with reference to the
balance between the two and its various ambiguities
as well as to different specific questions. The
reasons for the consensual pattern are clear to any
student of Italian politics: the PCI's long search
for legitimacy, the need to come to terms with the
persistent dominance in government of the DC and
its coalition allies, the dictates of the institutional arrangements in parliament, and all this
against historical precedents of trasformismo in
the Italian state. The conflictual pattern draws
significantly on the PCI's own history and identity
as a party as well as its ideological drive. But
one is forced to ask, in the light of the discussion in the chapter, whether or not the PCI's long-
term opposition makes it almost impossible to break

out of that role, given also the nature of the system outlined in Farneti's model.

It is perhaps difficult to draw any comparative lessons from the case of Italy for studying the role of opposition. While legislative concurrence between government and opposition has occurred in other European democracies, there are too many national-specific factors in Italy. This is not so much because of particular institutional arrangements, but rather because of the nature of coalition and alliance politics in that country and the fact that the PCI is not easily classifiable as a type of Communist party. One is perhaps left with the general lesson from the comparative study of political parties that these are complex entities, especially the larger parties; and, that it is important to analyse them in a three-dimensional way, as institutional actors, internally and as societal actors.

Notes

1. Gordon Smith, Politics in Western Europe, (Heinemann, London, 1983), p.2.
2. See G. Sartori, 'European political parties: the case of polarised pluralism' in J. La Palombara and M. Weiner (eds), Political Parties and Political Development, (Princeton UP, Princeton NJ, 1966), pp.137-76; Giorgio Galli, Il Bipartitismo Imperfetto, (Il Mulino, Bologna, 1966); on consociational democracy, L. Graziano, 'The historic compromise and consociational democracy' in International Political Science Review, (1980), pp.345-68; Paolo Farneti, The Italian Party System, (Frances Pinter, London, 1985).
3. Franco Cazzola, Governo e Opposizione nel Parlamento Italiano, (Giuffre, Milan, 1974); Giuseppe Di Palma, Surviving without Governing: the Italian parties in Parliament (University of California Press, Berkeley, 1977).
4. Samuel H. Barnes, 'Italy: oppositions on Left, Right and Centre' in R. Dahl (ed.), Political Oppositions in Western Democracies, (Yale UP, New Haven, Conn., 1966), pp.303-31.
5. Sartori, 'European Political Parties' and his Parties and Party Systems, (Cambridge UP, London, 1976); S. Tosi, 'Italy: anti-system opposition within the system', Government and Opposition, (1966), pp.49-61, and his 'Systemkonträre Opposition und Stabilität des Regierungssystems: oppositionelles Verhalten in Italien' in H. Oberreuter (ed.), Parlamentarische Opposition, (Hoffmann und Campe, Hamburg, 1975), pp.106-27.
6. R. Putnam, The Beliefs of Politicians: ideology, conflict and democracy in Britain and Italy, (Yale UP, New Haven, Conn., 1973); G. Sani, 'The political culture of Italy: continuity and change' in G. Almond and S. Verba (eds), The Civic Culture Revisited, (Little Brown, Boston, 1980), pp.273-324.
7. R. Putnam et al., 'Polarisation and depolarisation in Italian politics, 1968-81', paper for the 1981 conference of the American Political Science Association.
8. e.g. Sani, 'Political culture of Italy',
9. Tosi, 'Systemkonträre Opposition', p.106-7.
10. Sartori, Parties and Party Systems, p.132.

11. G. Ionescu and I. de Madariaga, Opposition, (Penguin, Harmondsworth, 1972), pp.80-128.
12. G. Tamburrano, Perche solo in Italia no (Laterza, Bari, 1983), p.32.
13. G. Tamburrano, PCI e PSI nel sistema democristiano, (Laterza, Beri, 1978), pp.14, 61-2.
14. Ibid. pp.63-4.
15. This is the view of S. Tarrow, for example, 'Political dualism and Italian Communism' in American Political Science Review, (1967), pp.39-53.
16. F. Di Giulio and E. Rocco, Un Ministro-ombra si confessa, (Rizzdi, Milan, 1979), p.59.
17. This point is developed systematically as part of a comparative framework for analysing coalitional behaviour in G. Pridham (ed.), Coalition Behaviour in Theory and Practice: an inductive model for Western Europe, (Cambridge UP, Cambridge, 1986), esp. introductory chapter.
18. This point is developed, for example, in G. Smith, 'Europäische Parteiensysteme - Stationen einer Entwicklung?' in J. Falter et al. (eds), Politische Willensbildung und Interessenvermittlung, (Westdeutscher Verlag, Opladen, 1984), pp.14-22.
19. Dahl, Political Oppositions, p.335.
20. A. Panebianco, Modelli di Partito, (Il Mulino, Bologna, 1982), esp. chapter 11.
21. See Dahl, Political Oppositions, chapter 11.
22. Putnam, Beliefs, pp.145-6.
23. G. Sani, 'Mass Constraints on political realignments: perceptions of anti-system parties in Italy', British Journal of Political Science (1976), p.32.
24. G. Galli and A. Prandi, Patterns of Political Participation in Italy, (Yale UP, New Haven, Conn., 1970), p.257.
25. Ibid. pp.261-2.
26. D. Hine, 'Thirty years of the Italian republic: governability and constitutional reform', Parliamentary Affairs, (Winter 1981), pp.68-9.
27. This is usefully summarised in Smith, Politics in Western Europe, pp.158-60.
28. M. Duverger, Political Parties, (Methuen, London, 1964), pp.414, 418.
29. G. Di Palma, Political Syncretism in Italy: historical coalition strategies and the

present crisis, (University of California
Press, Berkeley, 1978); G. Pasquino, 'Il
sistema politico italiano tra neotrasformismo
e democrazia consociativa', Il Mulino (1973),
pp.549-66.

30. Hine, 'Thirty Years of the Italian republic',
p.69.

31. G. Di Palma, 'The available state: problems of
reform', West European Politics (October
1979), p.154. See also the case study in this
respect of pensions policy in E. Maestri,
'Partiti e sistema pensionistico in Italia:
un'analisi dell'azione parlamentare della DC e
del PCI, 1953-75', Rivista Italiana di
Scienza Politica (1984), pp.125-59.

32. See F. Cazzola, 'Consenso e opposizione nel
Parlamento italiano: il ruolo del PCI dall I
alla IV legislatura', Rivista Italiana di
Scienza Politica, (1972), pp.71-96;
F. D'Onofrio, 'Committees in the Italian
Parliament' in J.D. Lees and M. Shaw (eds),
Committees in Legislatures: a comparative
analysis, (Duke UP, Durham NC, 1979), pp.89-
90.

33. D'Onofrio, 'Committees in the Italian
Parliament', p.87.

34. Cazzola, 'Consenso e opposizione', p.93.

35. G. Galli, Panorama, 23 January 1984, p.25.

36. Interview with Andrea Orsini, PLI leader at
Milan, Rome, July 1983.

37. Interview with Adolfo Battaglia, leader of the
PRI group in the Chamber of Deputies, Rome,
November 1981.

38. See Putnam, Beliefs; Sani, 'Political
culture'.

39. Putnam et al., 'Polarisation and depolarisation'.

40. K. von Beyme, Political Parties in Western
Democracies, (Gower, Aldershot, 1985), p.299.

41. Dahl, Political Oppositions, p.341.

42. See useful table in Farneti, The Italian Party
System, p.25.

43. Barnes, 'Italy: oppositions on Left, Right and
Centre', p.305.

44. Interview with Enea Cerquetti, PCI member of
Chamber of Deputies, Rome, August, 1983.

45. Ibid.

46. The term is used in the title of Di Giulio and
Rocco's book, Un Ministro-ombra si confessa,
which describes in detail the policy consulta-

tions between PCI leaders and the government during this time.

47. Cazzola, 'Consenso e opposizione', pp.85-6.

48. Corriere della Sera, 20 July 1983.

49. H.R. Penniman (ed.), Italy at the Polls, 1979, (American Enterprise Institute, Washington DC, 1981), p.138; cf. comment of Antonio Tato, close adviser of Berlinguer, that 'the idea that the PCI could return absolutely to opposition and become an "inheritor" party on the lines of the Wilhelminian German Socialists, in "splendid isolation" ... must be dismissed as historically impossible for the PCI', an interview in J. Ruscoe, The Italian Communist Party, 1976-81, (Macmillan, London, 1982), p.117.

50. Interview, Panorama, 12 November 1984, p.55.

51. In this connection, the Radicals compiled a report on the PCI's voting patterns in the 1979-83 Parliament, see Notizie Radicali, 16 May 1983.

52. Interview with Ildo Santori, leading Radical Party activist, Rome, August 1983.

53. The Times, 9 October 1976.

54. Interview with Enea Cerquetti.

55. See P. Lange, 'Crisis and consent, change and compromise: dilemmas of Italian Communism in the 1970s' West European Politics (October 1979), p.112.

56. K. von Beyme, 'Governments, parliaments and the structure of power in political parties' in H. Daalder and P. Mair (eds), Western European Party Systems: continuity and change, (Sage, London, 1983), pp.341-67.

57. Ibid. pp.366-7.

58. P. Allum, 'Italy' in S. Henig (ed), Political Parties in the European Community, (Allen & Unwin, London, 1979), pp.156-9.

59. Interview with Michela Buonfrate, functionary in Radical Party headquarters, Rome, August 1983.

60. Interview with Enea Cerquetti.

61. See G. Pasquino, 'From Togliatti to the compromesso storico: a party with a governmental vocation' in S. Serfaty and L. Gray (eds), The Italian Communist Party: yesterday, today and tomorrow, (Aldwych Press, London, 1980), pp.83-5.

62. Galli and Prandi, Patterns of Political Participation, p.274.

63. M. Barbagli and P. Corbetta, 'Una tattica e due strategie: inchiesta sulla base del PCI', Il Mulino (1978), pp.922-67; and 'After the historic compromise: a turning point for the PCI', European Journal of Political Research (1982), pp.213-39.
64. Di Giulio and Rocco, Un Ministro-ombra, pp.33-5.
65. S. Hellman, 'The "New Left" in Italy' in M. Kolinsky and W. Paterson (eds), Social and Political Movements in Western Europe, (Croom Helm, London, 1976), pp.243-73.
66. This situation is summarised in Penniman, Italy at the Polls, pp.110-15.
67. Di Palma, Surviving without Governing, p.220.
68. Lange, 'Crisis and consent', p.122.
69. Sani, 'Mass Constraints', pp.31-2.
70. Ibid. pp.4, 32.
71. See Sani, 'Political culture'.
72. Farneti, Italian Party System, p.182.
73. Ibid. p.183.
74. Ibid. p.185.

8. OPPOSITION IN THE NETHERLANDS

Ken Gladdish

In the mid-1960s, Hans Daalder contributed a classic survey of the dynamics of the Dutch party system to Dahl's major anthology on opposition. His study was entitled 'Opposition in a Segmented Society'.(1) The focus upon opposition however was dictated less by the nature of Dutch politics than by the requirements of a comparative study. The emphasis of the account was upon the essentially non-oppositional character of organised national politics in the Netherlands, for reasons which he showed to be both historical and practical.

Writing about Holland in the mid-1980s, one would be less likely to characterise it as a primarily or even substantially segmented society. The social context has changed significantly over the past twenty years to the point where the importance of segmentation has become a matter for quasi-historical debate.(2) Yet the deployment of political forces at national level still displays the features of a system which emerged under conditions of differential sub-culture socialisation. Changes within society have not so far been translated into thoroughgoing changes of political behaviour.

The ultimate task of this account will be to try to explain why this is so. It will require, to be intelligible, a catalogue raisonné of the various contenders for influence in the national political arena, and an account of their fortunes during the post-war period. It will also entail some analysis of the apparently imperfect relationship between social change and political expression, although in most societies that presents formidable conceptual difficulties. Both aspects will stimulate comparative references because

212

although the Netherlands constitutes a very distinctive case of political mobilisation, it is
distinctive in terms of its location within the
wider setting of political mobilisation in Western
Europe.

The current distribution of party strengths in
Holland, and its relation to the three preceding
elections, is set out in Table 8.1.(3)

Confessional Supremacy

Daalder's review of political practice up to the
mid-1960s offers an ideal reference point for the
assessment of subsequent developments. For it was
written when Dutch society was embarking upon a
vertiginous transition from a relatively stable
hierarchical social order to a more open, less
controlled, experimental era of social relations.
This had its parallels of course throughout the
Western world. But in the Netherlands there was a
special factor: because neither society nor
politics had hitherto been predominantly secular.

Both realms had long been deeply coloured by
confessional attachments, and had continued to be
very much governed by those attachments into the
post-1945 universe. Subtle compromises had
perforce been contrived between the material and
the spiritual, within a polity dominated by the
major confessional parties since comprehensive
democratisation in 1918. Thus even the various
secular formations had needed to recognise that a
substantial proportion of their supporters had
confessional connections.

Systematic confessional politics had its
origins in the 1870s with the instrumentation of a
mass movement of militant Calvinists, culminating
in the formation of the Anti-Revolutionary Party
(ARP) in 1879. Political organisation of the
Catholic population followed more slowly; but by
1888 it was possible for a Calvinist-Catholic
coalition cabinet to take office with a small
overall majority in the parliamentary Second
Chamber. In 1894 the Calvinist movement split, to
add a third strand, the eventual Christian Histori-
cals (CHU), to the confessional nexus. All three
parties governed as a trio from 1901-5, and from
1908-13.

During the First World War, when Holland was
neutral, a major re-appraisal of political arrangements resulted, among other things, in universal

213

Table 8.1: Elections to the Second Chamber

	1977 %	1977 Seats	1981 %	1981 Seats	1982 %	1982 Seats	1986 %	1986 Seats
PvdA	33.8	53	28.2	44	30.4	47	33.3	52
CDA	31.9	49	30.8	48	29.3	45	34.6	54
VVD	17.9	28	17.3	26	23.1	36	17.4	27
D'66	5.4	8	11.0	17	4.3	6	6.1	9
SGP	2.1	3	2.0	3	1.9	3	1.8	3
PPR	1.7	3	2.0	3	1.6	2	1.3	2
CPN	1.7	2	2.1	3	1.8	3	0.6	–
GPV	1.0	1	0.8	1	0.8	1	1.0	1
PSP	0.9	1	2.1	3	2.2	3	1.2	1
BP	0.8	1	0.2	–	–	–	–	–
DS'70	0.7	1	0.6	–	–	–	–	–
RPF	–	–	1.2	2	1.5	2	0.9	1
BVP	–	–	0.5	–	0.7	1	0.2	–
CP	–	–	0.1	–	0.8	1	0.4	–
Turnout	87.6		86.1		80.6		85.7	

Abbreviations:

PvdA	Labour Party	GPV	Reformed Political Union (Calvinist)
CDA	Christian Democratic Appeal	PSP	Pacifist Socialist Party
VVD	People's Party for Freedom and Democracy (Liberals)	BP	Farmers' Party
D'66	Democrats 1966	DS'70	Democratic Socialists 1970
SGP	State Reform Party (Calvinist)	RPF	Reformist Political Federation (Calvinist)
PPR	Radical Party	BVP	Evangelical Peoples' Party (Calvinist)
CPN	Communist Party of the Netherlands	CP	Centre Party (Ultra-Right)

male suffrage (to be shortly followed by female suffrage) and proportional representation on the basis of a single national constituency. By this point the confessionals had organised their adherents into zuilen: exclusive communal networks which embraced church activities, labour movements, newspapers, sporting and cultural bodies, and eventually broadcasting, alongside schools, educational foundations and political parties. To an extent this pattern was also adopted by the socialists, who had launched themselves as a mass political movement in the 1890s. A further secular column, broadly liberal, though less concerted or specific than the others completed the process of 'pillarisation'. These developments have been extensively researched and rehearsed in the literature,(4) and although there has been some recent iconoclasm about their precise significance,(5) they constitute the definitive picture of social relations in the Netherlands from the late nineteenth century on. They also symptomise the principal elements of the political system at least up to the mid-1960s.

The latest benchmark for Daalder's account of political dynamics was the outcome of the 1963 elections, in which the Catholic People's Party (KVP), the ARP, and the CHU (see Table 8.2 below), jointly secured 76 out of the 150 seats in the Second Chamber. This was an outcome they had re-enacted consistently since the elections of 1922. Over 40 years the confessionals had thus been able to determine the composition of virtually every cabinet and to have a major influence upon the orchestration of successive governmental programmes.

The disruption of defeat, occupation and devastation between 1940 and 1945 proved a mere caesura in confessional dominance, though there ensued some significant variations of the operational style of inter-war politics. One was that after 1945 the confessionals no longer chose to take office without wider support, having been prepared to govern exclusively for two-thirds of the period between 1918 and 1939. Another was that the socialists, in the shape of the freshly minted Labour Party, the PvdA, became a party of government, after their absence from all cabinets in that same period. A third variation of previous practice was that in the immediate post-war phase, the major confessional parties did not always operate as a concerted phalanx. The ARP remained

215

out of government from 1946 to 1952, as it had done briefly in the cabinet of 1939-40, which incidentally included two socialist members.

These developments were of great importance for the complexion of governments and the momentum of public policy, but there was no fundamental reordering of the prime facts of political geometry. The confessionals retained their unerring capacity to secure at least half the seats in the lower house. Throughout the first dozen post-war years when Labour was in government, chiefly under a widely respected Labour Minister-president, it was the confessionals who ensured continuity and maintained ultimate control of both parliaments and cabinets. Acting in concert they could virtually have governed without Labour, whereas Labour's parliamentary strength, never more than a third of the Chamber, entirely precluded it from governing without the concurrence of a majority of the confessionals.

A further development post-1945 was the formal espousal of corporatism as a system of policy formulation. Much has been written about official corporatism in the Netherlands, and many interpretations of its consequences have been offered.(6) To neo-Marxists it exemplified a case of capitalist dominance translated into the language of a bogus inter-class consensus. To most confessionals it afforded the opportunity of co-operation between interests without stirring up inter-group antagonism. To many socialists it seemed a formula for the direct expression of labour interests at the highest levels; whilst to some liberals it represented a successful way of neutralising potential trade-union militancy.

These various perceptions serve to underline the salience of corporatist practices and to mark their importance in any account of party dynamics vis-à-vis public policy from 1945 up to the late 1960s and indeed beyond.(7) The institutional essence of corporatism was the establishment of a set of bodies which were given the task of recommending to governments formulas for the basic distribution of the national economic product. The three most important of these bodies were the Foundation of Labour, the Central Planning Bureau and the Social and Economic Council. Their recommendations extended to wage agreements, income levels, and social welfare provisions. One overriding consequence of corporatist approaches was that issues which would otherwise have been framed in terms of inter-party competition, were to an extent resolved outside the parliamentary arena.

Clearly, the acceptance of corporatism by the major political parties signified a high consensus about the management of public policy by extra-parliamentary means. This consensus reflected a new phase in the politics of accommodation. The inclusion of the Labour party in cabinet after 1946, and of the re-fashioned Liberal party (VVD) in 1948, meant that the principal secular forma-tions now had access to office alongside the confessionals. The confessionals remained the dominant grouping, but at least all major political contenders could now expect some share of power and influence.

Detached Relations of Government and Parliament

At this point two features of political practice in the Netherlands deserve attention. One is what Daalder neatly characterised as 'the detached relations of government and Parliament',(8) and which Lijphart christened the 'semi-separation of powers'.(9) The other is the unusually laborious process of cabinet formation after elections.(10) Both these items have received extensive treatment in the literature, but their consequences for the style of party behaviour need to be noted.

The 'detached relations' between cabinets and the lower house had their origins in the pre-party phase of parliamentary development. This is not distinctive to Holland if one adverts to comparable phases in the history of other European states. What is, however, special to the Dutch experience is its survival into the era of mass politics, programmatic parties and comprehensive democratisa-tion. Lijphart provides data on the proportion of cabinet members who had never held seats in parlia-ment,(11) bearing in mind that post-1918 MPs were not elected on a constituency basis. Even more notable is that this feature was underlined by a late institutionalisation of the separation of cabinet and parliamentary membership. In 1938, Ministers were formally debarred from holding or retaining parliamentary seats, and in 1948 this was extended to State Secretaries (junior ministers).

One effect of this decoupling of parliamentary and cabinet roles was to generate a complex spec-trum of relations between the holders of cabinet

office and the parliamentary parties to which they
were affiliated. Cabinets did not need to be
staffed from parliamentary parties, but they needed
to be staffed by parties, or at least by the
leaders of the parliamentary groups. This often
resulted in long-serving chairmen of <u>fracties</u>
fielding cabinet teams over a generation of successive elections, whilst themselves enjoying the
status of non-playing captains.(12) The composition of governments reflected the disengagement of
cabinet and Parliament, but the necessary continuity was provided largely by the party leadership in
Parliament, which would imply that cabinets were
somehow subordinate in their status.

Yet it is difficult to offer a conclusive
theorem about the lines of force because procedures
varied with each party, and each cabinet formation
had its own particular features. Once installed,
cabinets had certain advantages over Parliament in
that whatever they presented to the legislature was
the product of a more intimate resolution of
interests than Parliament could easily replicate.
Also cabinets did not necessarily have to rely
solely upon the endorsement of their supportive
parties. As Daalder points out, 'nominal government supporters have often opposed particular
cabinets on particular issues' but equally 'governments with a fairly narrow official basis have in
practice enjoyed considerable support from parties
not represented in the government'.(13) Relations
between cabinet and Parliament in the Netherlands
are unusually hard to generalise about; but their
principal long-term characteristic has been that of
a diffusion of power, which tends to muffle clearly
etched oppositional tactics at parliamentary level
- or indeed at cabinet level.

Problems of Government Formation

The Dutch approach to cabinet-making has always
aroused incredulity among comparativists. Although
much effort has been deployed in considering which
aspects of coalition theory best fit the case, in
reality the jigsaw has invariably consisted of a
limited number of eligible pieces.(14) And the
composition of cabinets has traditionally hinged
upon whether the major confessional parties either
wished or needed to take in other partners. On
occasions the achievement of a workable majority
coalition has presented difficulties. But that

hardly explains why, even when the options have been relatively straightforward, the compilation of a ministry has usually taken from one to two months.

One factor has been that the confessionals, although regarded as a bloc within the party system, were themselves alliances of a number of interests which had to be reconciled within each coalition, even without the further complication of incorporating a secular partner. Thus post-war cabinet formations, despite the inclusion of secular parties, did not take conspicuously longer to complete than pre-war - at least until 1956 when a record of 122 days was achieved for the assembly of a confessional-Labour government. Over the next four elections, from 1959 to 1971, cabinet parturition reverted to an average length of two months. It then soared to five and a half months in 1972-3, seven months in 1977 and three and a half months in 1981.

The habit of leisurely cabinet formation can at times seem as much a matter of style as of necessity. In other states (Denmark springs to mind) the problems of parliamentary arithmetic do not produce interminable interregna. That politicians in the Netherlands are accustomed to such elaborate rituals could imply a lack of a sense of urgency about assuming office - a partial truth though one which mirrors the facts of political geometry rather than an indifference to power. The inescapable pattern of overlapping coalitions has meant substantial continuity of party representation in government. The most strenuous attempt post-war to break this mould, by the Labour party leadership after the 1972 election, left the outgoing government in office for almost half a year.

It has been urged that the deliberate and meticulous process of cabinet-making served to ensure that parties and politicians would respect the outcome of so much effort, and that, once formed, cabinets could rely upon parliamentary support for the duration of their term. But the evidence does not warrant this assumption. Few governments since 1946 have completed a full parliamentary term and fewer still have escaped crises of support whilst in office.(15)

The truth seems rather that, given the strength of the confessionals, there has never been a basis for solid, unified, majority government in Holland. Instead, there has been a need for

219

endless pacts within unstable alliances, including between the confessionals themselves, which have to be presented as carefully devised and potentially shock-proof in order to offset the forces of fission. This does not signify radical dissent nor the presence of militant opposition between parties, but rather the shifting sands of a multi-party system, condemned to revolve around a persistent and resilient centre grouping.

The Quest for Polarisation

To embark upon the study of Dutch politics in the early 1970s was to encounter the inquietudes of a political system apparently poised on the brink of radical change. The accommodationist style, which for more than half a century had served to diminish conflict within the party-parliament-government nexus, was under attack from many sides. In the latter 1960s Western Europe seemed to have taken a new lease upon ideological politics; and in the view of many Dutch commentators the Netherlands now needed to jettison the anachronistic modes of centrist confessional politics and to proceed to a new secular pattern of polarisation.

The recurrent mobilisation of half the voters by the confessionals had, in their judgement, reduced national politics to the level of board-room manipulation and mutual pay-offs. The confessional parties, as alliances of workers, employers, agriculturalists and city-dwellers, blurred the compilation of clear-cut socio-economic strategies and prevented the emergence of a genuine left-right dichotomy. That at least was the 'progressive' position, roundly expressed and exemplified by the 'new left' movement in the Labour party,(16) and echoed more discreetly by the Liberals (WD) at the other end of the secular spectrum.(17)

There were a number of elements which contributed to the frustration with the old politics. Most evident at the electoral level was the decline of confessional support, which first surfaced nationally in 1967, but was to continue through the 1971 and 1972 elections. This, to the progressives, was the signal that centre-based politics were no longer invincible and that a new alignment was both possible and necessary. Also Labour had its own problems, having itself paralleled the confessional subsidence between 1963 and 1967, and,

as a result of its ousting from the cabinet in
1966, having lost its rapprochement with the KVP.
Tarred with the brush of accommodation politics,
and unable to make it work to its advantage, the
PvdA's own fortunes seemed to depend upon incul-
cating some fresh dynamics within the system.

Iconoclasm of a different tone stemmed from a
new formation, Democrats '66, launched in that year
with an Appeal 'to every Dutchman who is concerned
about the serious depreciation of our democratic
form of government'.(18) The D'66 onslaught upon
accommodation politics was essentially structural
rather than strategic. Its chief nostrum was a
quasi-presidential system, to be achieved by the
direct election of the Minister-president, accompanied by a reversion to a constituency basis for
parliamentary elections.(19) In procedural terms
this implied a switch to a direct competition
between adversarial blocs. But D'66 was uncertain
about its own role in this kind of power play,
given its wish to avoid the blunt ideological
choices of a straight left-right dichotomy.
Indeed, one of its leaders spoke in the more
visionary style of a quest for a new political
organum, in which the anachronisms of confessionalism, socialism and late capitalism would somehow
be transcended.(20)

The radical mood which infused both the new
guard of the Labour party and the constitutional
crusaders of D'66, also had resonances within the
confessional parties. To their intellectuals, the
charge of anachronism translated into the view that
the trio of separate Calvinist and Catholic parties
ought to give way to the more fashionable formation
of a Christian Democratic front. Ideas about this
were already circulating in the late 1960s and
gradually became more orthodox as the costs and
perils of traditional mobilisation grew more
vivid.(21) Confessional politicians could rebut
allegations of irrelevance so long as they were
able to secure half the seats in the lower house.
When, by 1972, they could no longer ensure even a
third of the seats, a drastic re-appraisal became
inescapable; for, having controlled Dutch politics
for three or more generations, the confessionals
had no wish for extinction.

The 1971 elections provide a critical vantage
point from which to assess the Dutch party system,
on what seemed to be the threshold of a new adversarial style of politics. The Labour party, in

221

alliance with D'66 and another recent formation, the PPR,(22) embarked upon the election with an unprecedented stratagem: a shadow cabinet ostensibly formed to take office if the alliance succeeded in capturing a majority of seats in the Second Chamber.

To appreciate the audacity of this manoeuvre, some overall model of the party system at this stage of its development is indispensable. The most effective way to present such a model is to structure it along two cross-cutting axes: one embodying the secular parties, the other the confessional. The term confessional covers all parties which had some direct connection with a denominational group, whether a church, a sect or a quasi-religious association. The term secular covers all parties which had no such connection, even though an ideological stance on the distribution of resources within society might not be their prime determinant.

Party representation in the Second Chamber from 1967 to 1972 is set out in Table 8.2.

Table 8.2: Seats in the lower house of Parliament

	1967	1971	1972
PvdA	37	39	43
KVP	42	35	27
ARP	15	13	14
CHU	12	10	7
VVD	17	16	22
D'66	7	11	6
SGP	3	3	3
PPR	-	2	7
CPN	5	6	7
GPV	1	2	2
PSP	4	2	2
BP	7	1	3
DS'70	-	8	6
NM	-	2	-
RKPN	-	-	1
	150	150	150

Abbreviations (of parties other than in Table 8.1)

KVP   Catholic People's Party
ARP   Anti-Revolutionary Party (Calvinist)
CHU   Christian Historical Union (Calvinist)

Table 8.2: <u>Abbreviations</u> (continued)

NM   Small Business Party
RKPN   Roman Catholic Party of the Netherlands

After the 1971 election, 14 parties constituted the parliamentary arena. To present their
positions <u>vis-à-vis</u> each other in terms of a linear
model is to distort the complexities of the party
system. Nevertheless the picture would be unintel-
ligible without such a presentation as is attempted
in Figure 8.1

Figure 8.1: <u>Secular and Confessional parties on a left-
right scale</u>

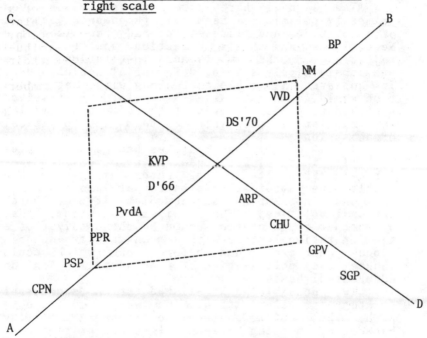

The A-B axis is the line along which the
secular parties might be positioned, reading from
left to right. The C-D axis is the line along
which the confessional parties might be positioned,
<u>also</u> in relation to a left-right dimension, but
given that their rationales derive from denominational imperatives. The rectangle at the crossing
of the two axes encloses the parties which in 1971
were potential candidates for entry to a governing

coalition.

The attempt of the PvdA, in conjunction with D'66 and the PPR, to polarise Dutch politics at this point was, in effect, a bid to form an alliance of parties in opposition to both the confessionals and the secular parties in the B quadrant of the model. Judged by the 1971 election results the odds against such a strategy might seem impossible, but Labour was gambling on an acceleration of forces which already appeared to have inexorable momentum: the decline of confessional support, the volatility of Dutch voters in the face of that decline,(23) and the radical wave of the late 1960s in Western Europe generally.

The signals here were not solely or even primarily political. Seemingly fundamental changes of attitude and life-style had convulsed the Netherlands and their direction was towards a rejection of the symbols and institutions of a previously highly stable, deferential social order. It appeared inevitable that along with that rejection would go an increasingly secular 'progressive' approach to politics, even if there were a time-lag in translating this into new forms of political organisation.

In 1956 only seven parties had gained representation in the lower house. In 15 years, therefore, a fragmentation of voter allegiance had doubled the number of parties in parliament. This was one index of the sudden volatility of Dutch national politics. The key issue had become that of whether fragmentation would be the catalyst of a new operational style with a much greater oppositional character than before - one which could induce the polarisation of representation on an adversarial basis.

Two possible paths existed for a successful strategy of polarisation. One was to contrive to push the confessionals into either splitting between or choosing between a leftward or rightward stance. The other was to hope that the decline of confessional support would so erode the ambivalent centre that eventually it could be left out of account in the formation of secular coalitions. The result of the unexpected election of 1972, called because DS'70 (24) deserted the five-party coalition dominated by the confessionals, seemed a further step along the second path. The confessional trio lost ten more seats, whilst Labour and Liberals increased their joint holding by that

224

amount.

In the prolonged cabinet formation of 1972-3, the PvdA alliance did manage to divide the confessionals. The CHU declined to join a Labour dominated coalition, whereas both the KVP and ARP eventually provided members willing to participate in a 'progressive' cabinet, though their parliamentary groups were not willing to offer unqualified support. This blow to confessional unity was countered by an intensification of the pressure towards amalgamation. First mooted as early as 1967, this improbable merger slowly gained credence as the threat to confessional survival magnified.

The chief advantages of amalgamation, despite all its discomforts and inconveniences, were seen to be twofold. First the protection of a united front against the secular parties, and secondly the impact of a united appeal to all sections of the diminishing confessional electorate. The strategy was not linked with any ideological position. It was a tactical move designed to restore both confidence and bargaining power vis-à-vis the other parties. It was thus an anti-polarisation device, and a direct counter to the ground plan of the PvdA and its uncertain allies.

In 1977 the confessional trio fought the elections as a single bloc with a common list of candidates. This followed joint conventions, inaugurated in 1975, under the banner of the Christian Democratic Appeal. The elections therefore saw the battle joined between the forces of polarisation, led by Labour, and the counter forces of a reorganised centre grouping. Both sides enjoyed some success. Labour, after four years in office, made striking gains of ten seats, whilst the confessionals, though gaining only one seat, held their ground for the first time since 1963. The Liberals won six seats to round off a re-consolidation by the larger parties, after a decade and more of mounting fragmentation.(25)

There resulted an ironic dilemma for the main victor, the PvdA. Although nearer to dominance than ever before, Labour had unleashed a threat which had shored up the major confessionals and strengthened the appeal of the Liberals. The outcome was a coalition of confessionals and Liberals, which meant a further extension of centre group politics, with a new inflection towards the right. The confessionals had neither been bifurcated nor reduced to impotence. They remained

225

an entrenched obstacle to a radical re-alignment of national politics, and therefore still needed to be accommodated on the old lines of post-election deals and compromises.

That accommodation still ruled was aptly demonstrated by the manifestos of the major parties in the run up to the 1981 elections. All give evidence of having been drafted with an eye to maximum flexibility in subsequent negotiations between contenders for office. The sole clear-cut divergence was on the issue of cruise missiles, the PvdA rejecting their installation outright and the VVD committing itself to their acceptance 'unless talks with the Soviet Union ... have resulted in a satisfactory reduction in Soviet nuclear arms'.(26) D'66 regarded them as unacceptable in existing circumstances, whilst the CDA adopted a position from which virtually any outcome might be legitimated.

Apart from the missile question, there was little to suggest that the parties were competing for office in clearly oppositional terms. Which was just as well because after three and a half months of manoeuvre the CDA, PvdA and D'66 found themselves in a three-party coalition, albeit one that was destined to be short-lived.(27)

The Rise of the Liberals

The 1970s saw Dutch political parties on the left endeavouring to translate the social changes of the previous decade into a new style of political competition. The prime mover in this endeavour, the PvdA, improved its fortunes in the process, though in 1981 it reverted to its 1972 position, to recover somewhat in 1982, and substantially in 1986. What is now evident is that the chief beneficiary of the bid for more polarised politics was not Labour but the Liberals, whose support increased fairly steadily from 10 per cent in 1971 to 23 per cent in 1982. The loss of 9 seats in the 1986 election was a palpable setback largely attributed to defects in the leadership. Nevertheless the level of support still equalled the position achieved in 1977 and 1981.

In the elections of 1948 the newly-formed VVD as the sole vehicle of the secular right of centre, had polled a mere 8 per cent of the vote, and it made little advance beyond this over the next quarter-century. The drop in confessional support

which surfaced in 1967, accompanied by a poor
result for the PvdA, did not translate into a
significant improvement of Liberal strength. This
came only in 1972, when Labour was itself recovering, with a further boost in 1977 when Labour did
exceptionally well. Indeed the combined Labour and
Liberal holdings in that election could have sustained a coalition cabinet with 81 seats, an adequate working majority.

The rise of the Liberals is one of the more
clear-cut developments on the secular front since
the 1960s. It has, of course, to be considered in
relation to developments which go beyond the
phenomenon of deconfessionalisation. The most
significant has been a shift to the right in the
approach towards public policy. This has affected
the Christian Democrats and thus produced an easier
pairing of the CDA and VVD as 'natural' partners in
government. The shift reflects most obviously the
widely perceived need for retrenchment in the face
of oil crises and recession.

There has also been a distinct change of ethos
within the Christian Democrats. In its erstwhile
traditional form the mentality of the confessional
parties differed sharply from that of the Liberal
party and its supporters. Individualistic in
economic affairs and libertarian on issues such as
abortion, homosexuality and euthanasia, the
Liberals were far from being the next resort of
communally minded, socially conservative ex-confes-
sionals.

In 1982, however, the greatest volume of
inter-party traffic on the part of voters was
between the CDA and the VVD.(28) This was repeated
in 1986, albeit largely in the reverse direction.
(29) For this to happen is striking testimony to
the increasing secularisation of the Christian
Democrats.

At the beginning of this account reference was
made to the apparent inconsistency of the survival
of a confessional bloc in the face of massive
social change, and the adoption of a more secular,
material way of life by the vast majority of the
citizenry. To elucidate this requires a clearer
focus upon the fundamental dynamics of the Dutch
party system than mere lists and labels can
provide. The most essential point to be made is
that the entire system in its structure, operation
and output, has retained its predominantly centrist
character. Although long presented as a divided

227

society, and residually felt to be so by many of
its members,(30) there is an extremely high consensus about the way problems should be tackled and
policy produced, which reflects the conditioning of
generations by accommodation politics.

The decline of confessionalism, in all its
indices, did not therefore result in the elimination of either the centre bloc or a centripetal
mentality. Indeed, the deconfessionalisation of
the centre served, inter alia, to make centre
voting more attractive to non- or ex-denominational
voters. The CDA, as a now non-sectarian entity, is
thus able to offer open-ended options which can
capitalise upon the uncertainties of a fluid
electorate. The more the major parties to its left
and right are tempted to beef up their prescrip-
tions, the potentially greater the appeal of a
latitudinarian centre, agnostic about all but
certain ethical issues which can themselves be
transmuted into respectable compromises.

Opposition in a centre-based system is both
difficult to orchestrate and inherently hazardous.
The centre can invariably sidestep any single
opponent and invite a rival to share power. By the
late 1970s the PvdA could count the cost of its
strategy of polarisation in terms of its exposure
to the antipathies of a still entrenched centre
formation. Only an alliance of major left and
right parties against the centre could overcome
this problem, and it is both interesting and significant that such a prospect has been voiced within
Labour and Liberal circles.(31) This would, of
course, require an accommodation between the two
which would further reduce any disposition towards
militant oppositional politics.

Extra-parliamentary Opposition

The obsequies for the end of ideology in the West
were, in the mid-1960s, rudely interrupted by an
explosion of direct action, in contrast to the
laborious indirectness of the representative
parliamentary process. Within that frame, the
Netherlands provided an unusually vivid case of a
society whose traditional preoccupations were
abruptly challenged by protest groups and quasi-
popular movements. Daalder, writing on the eve of
these developments, mentions earlier modes of
pressure and agitation but wisely refers to their
'fugitive quality'. That same quality can now be

said to have characterised many of the manifestations of the latter 1960s.

Nevertheless it would be cavalier to overlook
the continuing presence of extra-parliamentary
opposition in Holland, even though its significance
in the mid-1980s appears much reduced. Optimistic,
intravenous participation seems to have dwindled on
the ebb-tide of affluence. Various factors could
be adduced to explain the relative decline of
direct action. One is that a number of the
concerns of the earlier activists have been
absorbed into the bloodstream of social and political practice. Another is that recession, in the
wake of comprehensive welfare, has switched the
emphasis to balancing the books rather than re-
writing them. A third is that the political
system, which once seemed arthritic in the face of
radical challenge, has proved surprisingly resilient and resourceful.

Two forms of extra-parliamentary oppositions
are, however, extant, one major, the other spora-
dic. The major form is that of the orchestrated
national campaign, most notable in the assault
against nuclear confrontation and hyper-destructive
weaponry. The other symptom is that of local
groups, mainly in the larger cities, who confront
the authorities over planning decisions, the evic-
tion of squatters, the liberalisation of drugs etc.

The most impressive national campaign of
recent years has been one mounted by the Inter
Church Peace Council, the IKV, to prevent the
installation of cruise missiles in the Netherlands.
Mass rallies, on occasions graced by royalty, and
an intensive programme of pressure upon politicians
have accompanied each stage of the long-running
debate about whether or not Holland, already
committed to certain nuclear tasks within NATO,
should become a site for medium-range land-based
missiles.

Other pressure groups such as 'No to Cruise'
and Onkruid, an anti militarist formation pledged
to undermine military security, have helped to
provide further momentum; whilst political parties
on the left, notably the PvdA, have strenuously
opposed installations. Even the CDA Minister for
Defence in the 1982-6 government was not in favour
of deployment. Yet after much procrastination, and
elaborate efforts to defuse and obscure the sharp-
ness of the issue, the CDA/VVD cabinet decided, in
November 1985, to deploy and be damned. Both the

intra- and extra-parliamentary oppositions were
thus defied, in what had been presented as a
crucial matter of national survival.

As the 1986 election approached there were
fears that the gulf between the PvdA and the eventual CDA position over the deployment of the
missiles might sabotage the future formation of a
majority coalition. For if the Lubbers cabinet
were to lose its combined parliamentary majority
and Labour were to make impressive gains, negotiations on the basis of a CDA/PvdA combination could
have resulted in impasse over this issue.

The election results resolved these fears by a
further assertion of the centrist disposition of
Dutch voters. Its most vivid manifestations were
the switch of voters from the Liberals to the CDA,
and the CDA's capacity to draw substantial support
from both new voters and former Labour voters. The
centrist tendency was also reflected by the gains
of D'66, a substantial part of which came from its
left, whilst the movement rightwards to Labour of
former supporters of the smaller left-wing parties
(leaving the Communist party without parliamentary
representation for the first time in its long
history) accented the retreat from more exposed
positions.(32)

Once again the capacity of the system to
mobilise support around the centre, despite the
long-term change of orientation on the part of the
centre's major representative, was strikingly
demonstrated. So long as this propensity endures,
the muting of opposition will continue to be a key
characteristic of party behaviour in the Netherlands.

Notes

1. In R.A. Dahl (ed.), <u>Political Oppositions in Western Democracies</u>, (Yale UP, New Haven, Conn., 1966).
2. See M.P.C.M. van Schendelen (ed.), 'Consociationalism, pillarization and conflict-management in the Low Countries', <u>Acta Politica</u> XIX, (Amsterdam, January 1984).
3. Derived from Ken Gladdish, 'The 1982 Netherlands Election', <u>Western European Politics</u>, vol. 6, no. 3, (July 1983), Table 1.
4. For a comprehensive bibliography of <u>Verzuilung</u>, see van Schendelen, 'Consociation-alism'. Accessible texts in English include: H. Bakvis, <u>Catholic Power in the Netherlands</u>, (McGill UP, Montreal, 1981); L. Dutter 'The Netherlands as a plural society', <u>Compara-tive Political Studies</u>, (1978); A. Lijphart, <u>The Politics of Accommodation</u>, (University of California Press, Berkeley, 1968 and 1975).
5. See R. Kieve, 'Pillars of Sand, a marxist critique of consociational democracy in the Netherlands', <u>Comparative Politics</u> (1981); I. Scholten, '<u>Does Consociationalism</u> Exist? A Critique of the Dutch Experience', in R. Rose (ed.), <u>Electoral Participation</u>, (Sage, London, 1980).
6. A useful bibliography of Dutch corporatism is contained in S. Wolinetz, <u>Wage Regulation in the Netherlands</u>, (Council for European Studies, Washington DC, October 1983). Valu-able texts are: J.P. Windmuller, <u>Labour Rela-tions in the Netherlands</u>, (Cornell UP, Itheca NY, 1969); R. Griffiths (ed.), <u>The Economy and Politics of the Netherlands since 1945</u>, (Martinus Nijhoff, The Hague, 1980).
7. For the consequences of economic management of the decline of corporatism, see Ken Gladdish, 'Coalition Government and Policy Outputs in the Netherlands' in V. Bogdanor (ed.), <u>Coalition Government in Western Europe</u>, (Heinemann, London, 1983).
8. Daalder, 'Opposition in a Segmented Society', p.422.
9. Lijphart, <u>Politics of Accommodation</u>, p.135.
10. See R.B. Andeweg, Th. van der Tak and K. Dittrich, 'Government Formation' in Griffiths <u>Economy and Politics</u>; J. Vis,

'Coalition Government in a Constitutional Monarchy' in Bogdanor, Coalition Government.

11. Lijphart,Politics of Accommodation, p.135.
12. Amply illustrated by J.A.W. Burger, former chairman of the PvdA parliamentary group, in an interview with the author, April, 1971.
13. 'Opposition in a Segmented Society', p.422.
14. See Andeweg et al., 'Government Formation', and A. de Swaan, Coalition Theories and Cabinet Formations, (Amsterdam, 1973).
15. On a strict construction only two cabinets have served a full parliamentary term during this period without any periods of demission due to crises, i.e. those of de Jong (1967-71) and of van Agt (1977-81).
16. See S. Wolinetz, 'The Dutch Labour Party' in W. Patterson and A. Thomas (eds), Social Democratic Parties in Western Europe, (Croom Helm, London, 1977).
17. Interview with W.J. Geertsema, then chairman of the Liberal (VVD) parliamentary group, April 1971.
18. The heading of the English text of the founding letter from the D'66 Initiating Committee, 15 September, 1966.
19. A proposal submitted to the Cals-Donner Committee on Constitutional Reform, set up in 1967. For a summary of the committee's origins and outcome see H. Daalder, 'Extreme P.R. - The Dutch Experience' in S.E. Finer (ed.) Adversary Politics and Electoral Reform, (Anthony Wigram, London, 1975).
20. Interview with Hans van Mierlo, then chairman of the D'66 parliamentary group, June 1971. Other D'66 notables who were interviewed at this point were perhaps less visionary but certainly sought a fresh basis on which national politics might be conducted.
21. Accounts of this process in English were presented at the European Consortium for Political Research workshops in Salzburg, April 1984, by Hans J.G.A. van Mierlo, and by Bert Pijnenburg and Jan de Jong.
22. Formed in 1968 by former members of the KVP.
23. See R.B. Andeweg, Dutch Voters Adrift. On Explanations of Electoral Change, (Leiden UP, Leiden, 1982).
24. Formed in 1970 as a breakaway from the PvdA in reaction to the New Left influence. It was wound up in 1981 after its support had

dwindled to below the threshold tor parliamentary representation.

25. For figures for small party representation overall see Ken Gladdish 'The Netherlands', in V. Dugdanor (ed.) Representatives of the People? Parliamentarians and Constituents in Western Democracies, (Gower, Aldershot, 1985), p.148.

26. 'Main points from the Manifesto of the Liberal Party', English summary, p.6.

27. The coalition took office in September 1981 and finally collapsed in May 1982 when the PvdA members resigned over proposed public expenditure cuts. See Gladdish, 'The 1982 Netherlands Election'.

28. See H. Dandt, 'Wisslende Kiezers', Acta Politica, Amsterdam, 1983/2.

29. Intomart exit poll, analysed by Rudy Andeweg and Galen Irwin, de Volksrant, 22 May 1986.

30. A view strongly advanced by the audience at a lecture by the author at Erasmus University, Rotterdam, in November 1982.

31. Attested by interviews with senior politicans in both parties in 1984 and 1985.

32. Intomart exit poll, 22 May 1986.

9. OPPOSITION IN CONTEMPORARY SPAIN: TRADITION AGAINST MODERNITY

Benny Pollack and Jean Grugel

The successful inauguration of a liberal democratic regime in Spain after the death of Francisco Franco legitimised the political parties, movements and interest-group organisations, whose demands remained unmet in more than forty years of authoritarian rule. Indeed, the first elections in the new democracy (1977) were remarkable for the extent to which they reproduced the cleavages and patterns of political identification which Francoism had merely frozen. In this respect alignments in Spanish politics which appear to be the consequence of the installation of a parliamentary monarchy are new in a limited sense only, in as much as they have used the opportunities given to them by the liberal Constitution. Their fundamental patterns of organisation, interest representation and ideological commitments do not suggest a truly radical departure from previous patterns. They are, in more than one way, a refurbished version of old historical alignments.

Three factors in particular have ensured that Spain's democratic transition is not merely superstructural: firstly, and perhaps most important, the consistent and at times courageous stand taken by King Juan Carlos in protecting the young democracy; secondly, the economic development of Spain in the 1960s and early 1970s, responsible for the contradictions within the authoritarian regime, which led to the inauguration of democratisation by a team of ex-Francoists; and, thirdly, the progressive 'Europeanisation' of Spain, culminating in Spain's membership of both the EEC and NATO. It would now be political suicide for any grouping not to endorse, at least verbally, the democratic constitution.

For this reason, democracy versus authoritarianism remains to an extent a valid framework for an analysis of Spanish political parties. At the same time, the political system has rapidly become as sophisticated and complex as any in Western Europe, in terms of party competition, organisational patterns, electioneering and sensitivity to public opinion.

Currently, the main parliamentary opposition comes from the right-wing Popular Alliance (AP), whose origins and ideology can be traced back in a clear line of descent to the last years of Francoism and the 'political associations' which blossomed under the Arias Navarro Government. The parliamentary opposition also incorporates small centrist parties and the nationalist parties of Catalonia and Euzkadi (the Basque country). Non-regional centrist opposition is also articulated through informal contacts between government personnel and bureaucrats, professional associations and the media, especially the independent Madrid daily paper, El Pais. All of these can be regarded as effective channels of communication and indicate the ideological affinity between the modernising Socialist Government of Felipe Gonzáles and the technocrats and businessmen of the 'new' Spain. However, for reasons of space and problems of evaluation, they will not be considered in any detail in this chapter. Instead, we shall concentrate on parliamentary and extra-parliamentary opposition which is articulated through organised channels, parties or movements.

Opposition under the parliamentary monarchy can best be understood according to the following categorisation:

i) parliamentary or extra-parliamentary, according to the methods used to gain access to power, exercise influence, and/or control instances of power;

ii) national or regional, according to the territorial scope of representation, the type of interests articulated, and the nature of their political goals;

iii) pro-democratic or anti-democratic, reflecting commitment to or rejection of a liberal-democratic value system, policy-formulation, political action, and institutionalisation; and,

235

iv)   <u>consensual or conflictive</u>,   reflecting   the
degree of identification with, or alienation from
the government in power, without being part of it,
and without questioning the legitimacy of the political regime.

Despite   the   success   of   the   transition   to
democracy, the scars of the Civil War have far from
disappeared.   The legacy of authoritarian rule   is
even more important, given that democratisation was
not   the result of a radical and sudden break   with
an   authoritarian past - such as the recent transition in Argentina or in Portugal in 1974.   Instead,
it involved a gradual dismantling of the   Francoist
state   with the co-operation of personalities   from
the old regime.(1)   For this reason, a brief introduction   on   opposition   in   the   final   years   of
Francoism and the first tentative years of the   new
democracy is necessary.

Opposition under the Authoritarian Regime

Only   in the narrowest of senses could   the   Franco
regime   be characterised as 'totalitarian',   though
this was probably the case in the immediate   aftermath   of the Civil War,   and part of the decade   of
the   1940s.(2)   The   totalitarian   nature   of   the
Francoist   regime during its first decade is difficult to contest, not only because of the 'totalist'
scope   of   its repressive   apparatus but,   equally
important, because of the self-declared neo-fascist
leanings   of   the   <u>Falange</u> ideology.   True,   this
falangist 'fascism' was more real on paper than   in
reality,   as no participatory or mobilising impetus
was ever part of its doctrinal core.   The defeat of
the Axis powers in 1945,   therefore,   only confirmed
what   the   ambiguity   of   Francoism   had   already
revealed: that the regime was to become an authoritarian   rather than a totalitarian one.   The   distinction   is   one of substance,   for   the   changing
nature   of the regime in the 1950s would   gradually
allow   for   the   development   of   various   forms   of
opposition,   which   would   otherwise not have   been
tolerated.
By   the end of the 1950s,   both an   opposition
from   within   and from without had already   formed.
The character of the organisations/groups developing at the time varied in scope, exhibiting different   organisational patterns,   interest representation and articulation,   ideology and tactics.   The

opposition from within was first articulated by Catholic personalities influenced by the progressive social thought of French philosopher Jacques Maritain; by factions of the clergy shocked by the abucoc of human rightc; and by tho ocorot Catholic fraternity, the Opus Dei, which represented a highly elitist concept of the Church as an ethos (see Figure 9.1). Politically, most of the first acts of opposition came from those linked in one way or another to CEDA, the centre-right Catholic party which had once supported the Republic but had shifted towards the Franco camp before the Civil War.

The tight control of the state by Franco in the 1950s and 1960s did not allow for any opposition within his regime, other than what could be termed as either 'authoritarian' (monarchists, sections of the Church and the Army) and 'conservative-moderate' (Opus Dei, Carlists, Social-Christians, intellectuals). Other forms of opposition, namely by socialist and communist movements, and associated groups, gradually became relevant, and acquired consistency and coherence as 'legitimate', though still illegal, groupings in the 1960s. By then, the transition from a traditional agrarian economy into a relatively modern, urban and industrialised one, had dramatically altered the sociological and political map of Spain. The expansion of both a proletariat and a middle class was just one of the new factors in the Spain of the 1960s. With it came the transformation of the political system as well: alternative trade unions, student unions, a radicalised petit bourgeoisie, even political parties. All these organisations were illegal, but they were already putting a number of demands on the system which, without changes, could not possibly be met.(3)

It was in the 1960s that a de facto coalition of the Spanish proletariat, the Church, the more progressive Catholic intellectuals and the more advanced sectors of the national bourgeoisie, began to take shape. It ultimately became such a powerful conglomerate that its opposition to the Franco regime in the mid-1970s provided the impetus for a number of significant changes. Some of these, like the legalisation of 'political associations' (euphemism for political parties) during the Arias Navarro Government, the pacto de la Moncloa (the Moncloa agreements), and the legalisation of the Communist party during the first Suárez Government

237

Figure 9.1: Opposition in the 1950s and 1960s

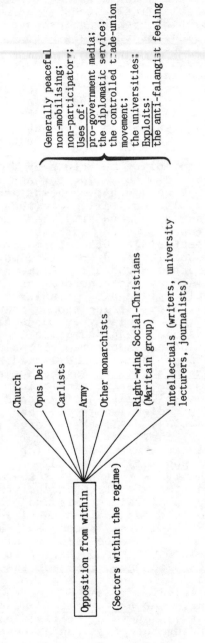

Church
Opus Dei
Carlists
Army
Other monarchists

Right-wing Social-Christians
(Maritain group)

Intellectuals (writers, university
lecturers, journalists)

Opposition from within

(Sectors within the regime)

Generally peaceful
non-mobilising;
non-participatory;
Uses of:
pro-government media;
the diplomatic service;
the controlled trade-union
movement;
the universities;
Exploits:
the anti-falangist feeling

were instrumental in convincing King Juan Carlos to
provide the ultimate impetus for democratisation,
by way of a categorical commitment to the new
democratic system.(4) But these developments would
not have been possible without the clear lead given
during the 1960s by three broad groupings outside
the regime, namely:

i) a left-wing (both inside and outside Spain)
coalition of socialists, communists, anarchists,
Basque and Catalonian nationalists, trade unionists, students and intellectuals;

ii) a growing number of disenchanted traditionalists (mainly former falangists) now identified with
various currents of the Church's Social-Christian
thought; and

iii) a right-wing amalgamation of dissident
Carlists who supported Don Juan's claims to the
throne, and other varieties of frustrated monarchists who had supported Franco at one time or
another (see Figure 9.2)

By and large, the left-wing coalition favoured
popular mobilisation and protest, rallies, circula-
tion of leaflets, and strikes, while the disenchanted Francoists and Monarchists concurred with
the need to introduce broad changes, including the
legalisation of political parties, the elimination
of censorship, freedom of association and protection against torture.(5) The result was a broad,
socially and politically heterogeneous coalition
against the authoritarian regime. The 'modern'
opposition had begun.

Opposition During the Transition to Democracy: from Illegality to Legality

The main leader of the opposition to the Spanish
authoritarian state during the mid-1970s was to be
King Juan Carlos, the monarch chosen by Franco
himself to succeed him. Ironically, Juan Carlos
dismantled the repressive apparatus so studiously
mounted by generations of Francoist bureaucrats and
policemen, legitimising both de facto and de jure
the organisation of political parties and their
operations. A formidable coalition, comprising
virtually all but the ultra-right recalcitrant
sectors of society, made possible what had seemed a

239

Figure 9.2: Opposition in the 1950s and 1960s

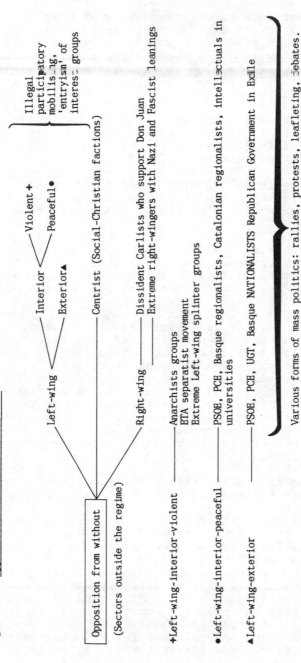

```
                                                          Violent +
                                         Interior
                                                          Peaceful ●
                            Left-wing
                                         Exterior ▲

Opposition from without                  Centrist (Social-Christian factions)
(Sectors outside the regime)
                                                      Dissident Carlists who support Don Juan
                            Right-wing                Extreme right-wingers with Nazi and Fascist leanings
```

```
                                                Illegal
                                                participatory
                                                mobilising,
                                                'entryism' of
                                                interest groups
```

```
+ Left-wing-interior-violent    ———— Anarchists groups
                                     ETA separatist movement
                                     Extreme Left-wing splinter groups

● Left-wing-interior-peaceful   ———— PSOE, PCE, Basque regionalists, Catalonian regionalists, intellectuals in
                                     universities

▲ Left-wing-exterior            ———— PSOE, PCE, UGT, Basque NATIONALISTS Republican Government in Exile
```

Various forms of mass politics: rallies, protests, leafleting, debates.

romantic dream just a few years before: the establishment of a full liberal democratic regime. This
alliance, according to Jonathan Story, was 'between
the monarch and all political forces in the country
opposed to the status quo'.(6)

The period of instability which affected Spain
from Prime Minister Admiral Carrero Blanco's assas-
sination in 1973, until the appointment of Prime
Minister Adolfo Suárez by King Juan Carlos in 1976,
was defined as being in favour of the opposition
owing to a combination of factors. Firstly, the
Opus Dei had gained significant influence already
in the last of Arias Navarro's cabinets. Committed
to gradual change through the modernisation of the
country's political, economic and social institutions, its members provided the technocratic/
modernising/pro-European wing of the old regime,
and acted as a natural link with the more progressive sectors that became prominent during the first
Suárez administration in 1976. These constituted
the second relevant factor in the road towards
democracy, especially Gil Robles' Social Christians
('Democratic Left', Izquierda Democrática) and
Joaquin Ruiz Giménez' Christian Democrats. The
latter acted as broker between the more conservative opposition sectors and the Left, namely, the
Spanish Socialist Workers party (Partido Socialista Obrero Español, PSOE), and the Spanish Communist party (Partido Communista Español, PCE).
These two parties, the third most significant
element in the broad socio-political coalition, co-
ordinated the mass mobilisation against the authoritarian regime.

All three blocs were led by radicalised
sectors of the bourgeoisie and petit bourgeoisie.
Spanish political culture is very much shaped by
strong interactions between what could be categorised as essentially intellectual endeavours, and
politics. This tradition, not uncommon in other
Latin European and Latin American countries, has
contributed to enrich the quality of political
argument, and to 'ideologise' politics, including
policy-making and operational politics. The
development of a radicalised, modernising, pro-
European, generally social democratic, secular,
anti-traditionalist and liberal-democratic intelligentsia, with cross-party, cross-class, cross-
cultural affiliations, helped to create the homo-
geneity and coherence without which the opposition
movement in the final years of the 1960s and early

241

to mid-1970s, would have been a failure. The combination of mass mobilisation plus a coherent radicalised cross-sectional leadership made the task of those still resisting change all but impossible. Furthermore, there were at least two very important factors which enhanced the potentialities of the all-embracing democratic alliance in Spain: the support given to the reforms by King Juan Carlos and Prime Minister Adolfo Suárez, and the regional identification with them, notably in Catalonia and the Basque country. These circumstances strengthened the relative weight of the opposition not only in Madrid, but in the provinces as well. The authoritarian, ultra-conservative sectors, still reluctant to accept defeat, were pushed to the corners of political society where, for the most part, they remain.

The Moncloa agreements of October 1977 between Prime Minister Suárez and most of the opposition signalled the most categoric break with the past ever witnessed in contemporary Spain. It demonstrated the commitment of the governing elite, the centre, the left, and the labour movement to the restoration of liberal democracy. The express sanction of the King added weight to the new parliamentary monarchy. It is not without significance that the Popular Alliance, led by Manuel Fraga, ex-Minister of Information of Franco and Minister of the Interior in the cabinet of Arias Navarro, was not signatory to the pact.

The Dilemmas of Opposition in Democratic Spain: Tradition Versus Modernity

The concept of a modern opposition, as practised in liberal democracies, did not develop in Spain until after the first democratic elections in June 1977. It was only then that the patterns normally associated with the exercise of electoral rights, a competitive party system and political pluralism could be identified as features of the new regime. The concepts of parliamentary, extra-parliamentary, consensual and conflictive, pro-democratic and anti-democratic forms of opposition were added to the already valid categories of national and regional opposition. The appointment of Adolfo Suárez as Prime Minister by the King in 1976 marked the turning-point in the evolution of the Franco regime towards democracy, though the mild liberalisation enacted by the previous Prime Minister,

Arias Navarro, had already led to the creation of about 200 parties, of which 'only' 156 presented candidates for the first elections.

The most dramatic result of these elections, since confirmed by the elections of 1979 and 1982, was the configuration of a multi-party system, with the potential for the development of a two-party system. The proliferation of parties in the mid-1970s proved to be nothing more than the expression of the excitement of a new-born democracy. While several survived the next polls, only four could be considered national-based parties: the Union of the Democratic Centre (Unión de Centro Democrático, UCD) led by Prime Minister Suárez; the Socialist Workers party (PSOE), led by Felipe González; the Popular Alliance (AP) by Manuel Fraga, and the Communist Party (PCE), led by the anti-Franco veteran, Santiago Corrillo.(7) The UCD and the PSOE were the dominant parties in Parliament with 283 of the 350 seats in the Chamber of Deputies between them.

The UCD, however, cannot properly be described as a political party, if by this we mean an organisation with a shared ideology or a membership reasonably united behind a set of principles or a programme. It was rather an electoral coalition of diverse sectors, temporarily united around the charismatic figure of Suárez. Indeed, Suárez's appointment as leader of the government in July 1976 predates by some months the formation of the UCD (May - December 1977). The UCD was composed of those individuals and groups within the old elite who were, for various reasons, prepared to democratise Spain's formal political institutions. They included Christian Democrats, liberals, social democrats, technocrats and independents such as Suárez himself. In so far as we can speak of an ideology, the UCD was democratic, moderate, secular, capitalist and pro-Western. In spite of serious organic weaknesses and internal divisions, the UCD's position as the single largest party in Parliament was consolidated in 1979, when it won 35 per cent of the vote, almost certainly as a consequence of its identification with liberalisation and reform. Although the electoral base of the UCD had collapsed by 1982, during its brief existence it was distinguished by an appeal that was nationwide, reaching even into Catalonia, where it displaced the Catalan right, and to a lesser extent into Euzkadi.

243

Parliamentary opposition before 1982 was mainly from the left, from the Socialist and Communist parties. However, at the political level, though officially both the PSOE and the PCE performed as opposition, this was always mellowed by their enthusiastic support for, and identification with, the political reforms enacted by the Suárez administration. The Moncloa Agreements gave institutional sanctioning to the Left's <u>opposition to the government</u> but <u>support to the regime</u>. The Basque and Catalonian nationalists could also fit into this category during the transitional period, though they could be said to have been broadly more sympathetic to the Suárez Government.

Because an all-embracing consensus on the nature of the political regime could not - and in the opinion of many commentators, still cannot - be taken for granted, the scope of parliamentary opposition in this period was limited by the need to protect the democratic system. At no time was this made more obvious than in the wake of the <u>coup</u> attempt by Colonels Tejero and Milaans del Bosch in February 1981, during which the entire Cortez was held captive overnight. Although the new Prime Minister, Calvo Sotelo, declined González's offer of a government of national unity, the PSOE none the less assumed a more co-operative attitude towards the government.

According to José Amodia,(8)

> moderation was possibly the most salient feature of the process of transition from dictatorship to democracy... The decision to bring about change by constitutional means and the constant threat of military intervention at the slightest sign of deviation or radicalism imposed perforce a careful and deliberate tempo. All political parties except for those on the extreme Right and the extreme Left showed centripetal tendencies from very early on.

Nowhere were these 'centripetal tendencies' more in evidence than in the PSOE, and its period of 'loyal opposition' to Suárez's transitional team coincided with the party's break with its revolutionary past. At the Extraordinary Party Conference of 1979, the PSOE defined itself as 'a class, mass, democratic and federal party' - with an express commitment to marxism noticeably absent. Henceforth, the PSOE

would be an electorally-oriented, modernising
political party, making no effort to hide its
attempt to appeal to Spain's expanding middle
sectors, as well as to workers and to regionalist
sentiments. The Left in Spain can rightly lay
claim to having sacrificed its deep historic
commitment to socialism in order to make the democratic transition possible. Without this level of
co-operation of the Left in Parliament and in the
labour movement, the success of the transition
might have been in doubt.

The Right, by and large, however, did not show
much sympathy for the liberalising reforms, and
rather accepted what it recognised as a product of
the changing social and political circumstances
against which little or nothing (short of a military coup) could be done. The two frustrated
attempts against the new democracy have to be seen
within the context of a deeply distressed authoritarian Right, displaced from the central axis of
power and desperate to gain influence again. The
right-wing Popular Alliance should not be dismissed
in this period as utterly irrelevant, but it was
only a minor party, winning 6 per cent of the vote
in 1979.

Overall, opposition to governments, not to the
political regime, became the distinguishing feature
of the democratic party system emerging in Spain
after 1977, marking a drastic departure from the
government/opposition system of relationships
existing under the authoritarian regime. Under
this latter system, the nature of these relationships was conditioned by its extremely closed,
inward-looking, non-participatory structure. The
opposition had no alternative but to be against the
political regime. Opposition under the authoritarian regime could not be other than extra-parliamentary, and conflictive. Its main goal was the
destruction of the regime, and its replacement by a
different one.

However, not all the opposition under the
authoritarian regime could be categorised as pro-
democratic. Indeed, sectors to the right of the
Falange, and to the left of the PCE, were looking
for even more authoritarian forms, either to the
right or to the left, than the existing one.
Though in both cases their importance is questionable (ultra-rightist, neo-Nazi and neo-Fascist
cells, ultra-leftist splinter movements like GRAPO
and fractions of the mainstream separatist ETA

245

group in the Basque country), they made an unwitting contribution to the unification of the pro-democratic opposition, which included right, centre and left, and both national and regional groups (see Figure 9.3).

It is interesting to notice that the anti-regime commitments of the anti-democratic Right and Left are as strong now as they were under the Francoist state, while the anti-regime definition of the pro-democratic opposition under authoritarianism has been replaced by an anti-government stand. Indeed, the anti-government or anti-regime behaviour of the opposition parties and/or movements is still an essential element in the analysis of government/opposition relations.

Parliamentary Opposition After 1982: the Development of a Bi-Polar System

Immediately following the demise of the authoritarian state, national (and most regional) opposition in Parliament had been more nominal than real. Opposition was from the left, but was consensual and supportive, indicating the PSOE's and the PCE's desire to re-establish democratic norms. In 1982, the PSOE reaped the benefits of identifying itself with the institutionalisation of a modern, democratic value system, rather than offering the electorate a socialist alternative.(9) It was not until after the 1982 general elections that we can speak of government/opposition relations which are truly comparable with those of other Western European countries. The high turn-out (79.6 per cent) and the maturity of the electorate did much to convince both the Spanish people and the international community of the inexorability of the democratic transition. The elections dramatically altered parliamentary politics; there were, moreover, profound changes in relative party strengths and the composition of the Chamber, indicating a high degree of electoral volatility, hardly surprising in a party system which has still to establish itself firmly in the minds of the voters. It is worth noting that the PSOE is an exception to the general trend of low party identification. Although the ideology of Spanish socialism has undergone a radical transformation since 1936, the PSOE voting returns since 1977 suggest electoral stability in traditional (i.e. pre-Civil War) left-wing regions (Valencia, Andalusia, Catalonia and

Figure 9.3: Opposition during the Transition and the Democratic Regime

1. Left-wing opposition during the transitional period and elected Suárez Government
   - PSOE-UGT
   - PCE - Workers Commissions
   - PSOE Cataluna
   - PCB Cataluna

2. Right-wing opposition during the transitional period and elected Suárez Government
   - Alianza Popular
   - Fuerza Nueva (ultra-right, neo-falangist)
   - Nationalist groups
   - ETA - GRAPO

3. Centrist opposition during the transitional period and elected Suárez Government
   - Basque Nationalists

4. Opposition from 'non-political' organisation, institutions, movements, groups during the transitional period and elected Suárez Government
   - Church (fractions)
   - Opus Dei (fractions)
   - Confederation of Business Associations
   - Professional associations (lawyers, journalists, writers, diplomats)

5. Left-wing opposition during the PSOE Government
   - PCE (mainstream)
   - PC (Carrillo)
   - ETA

6. Centrist opposition during the PSOE Government
   - CDS (Suárez)
   - Christian-Democrats
   - Nationalists (Buzkadi and Catalonia)

7. Right-wing opposition during the PSOE Government
   - Alianza Popular (Fraga)
   - Terrorist neo-nazi and neo-fascist groups

8. Opposition from 'non-political' organisations, movements, institutions, groups to the PSOE Government
   - Church (fractions)
   - Army
   - Opus Dei
   - Confederation of Business Associations
   - Agricultural Society
   - Professional Associations
   - Trade Unions
   - Environmentalist Groups

Madrid). This points to a process of ideological transmission in these areas, a process which is sometimes referred to as the persistence of 'political memory'.(10)

Three major blocs still seem to reflect the spectrum of alignments within the Chamber of Deputies (see Table 9.1)

i) the Left, represented by the PSOE and the PCE;

ii) the Centre, represented mainly by the UCD, the Social Democratic Centre (CDS) of ex-Prime Minister Suárez, and the Nationalist parties; and

iii) the Right, represented by the Popular Alliance.

To a certain extent, however, this typology is also misleading. The PSOE has become the hegemonic party of the Left, reducing the PCE in Parliament to an unimportant handful, while the UCD, dispirited by inter-party rivalries and secessions, found itself squeezed between the PSOE on the left and the Popular Alliance on the right. Almost 75 per cent of the total votes cast in the election were concentrated on the two main parties. In 1975 the voting percentage of the UCD and the PSOE combined was 60 per cent. It should be recognised that Spain is moving towards a nationally-based two-party system, with some regional variations in Catalonia and Euzkadi. Some words of caution are necessary, however: firstly it is still not possible to speak in terms of long-term electoral trends because of the brevity of the democratic period, and secondly, the Popular Alliance, Spain's second largest party, has yet to prove that it has established a stable base within the electorate.

In one sense, the most surprising result of the 1982 elections was the spectacular rise of the Popular Alliance (AP), a right-wing party whose democratic credentials remain to some extent in doubt.(11) None the less, this is the party which now heads the parliamentary opposition. The AP appeared on the political scene in October 1976 and was initially a disparate coalition of personalities from the previous regime, some from the fascist movement, the _Falange_, others from the conservative Catholic organisation, Opus Dei, so

Table 9.1: Results of the 1982 Elections to the Chamber of Deputies

	Party	% of Total Vote	No. of Votes	No. of Seats
	Spanish Socialst Workers Party (PSOE)	48.4	10,127,092	202
The Left	Spanish Communist Party (PCE)(a)	4.1	846,802	4
	Herri Batasuna (HB))(b) Euzkadi Left (EE))	1.4	310,927	3
	Union of the Democratic Centre (UCD)	6.7	1,393,574	11
The Centre	Social Democratic Centre (CDS)	2.8	604,309	2
	Basque Nationalists Party (PNV)	1.8	394,656	8
	Convergence and Union (CIU)(c)	3.7	772,726	12
The Right	Popular Alliance (AP)	26.5	5,548,336	107

a) The PCE vote includes that of the autonomous Catalan Communist Party (PSUC).
b) Together, Herri Batasuna and Euzkadi Left represent the Basque extreme left, and the vote represents 20% of the total vote in Euzkadi.
c) Convergence and Union is the bourgeois party of Catalan nationalism.

Source: Ministry of the Interior.

well-represented in Franco's last cabinets. The minor parties which were integrated into the AP (Democratic Reform, Regional Action, Democratic Spanish Action, Social Democracy, the Union of the Spanish People, Liberal Action, and the Popular Social Union) were all markedly conservative or ultra-conservative organisations. On its creation, the party had no national or regional organisational structure of any description.

Between 1976 and 1977, the AP had tried to occupy the centre ground, only to find that King Juan Carlos preferred to trust the democratic transition to Suárez and the UCD. Thereafter, until 1982, the AP was on the whole perceived of as an ideological party of the extreme Right, rather than a pragmatic party capable of winning power (at least electorally), the populist rhetoric of its leader, Manuel Fraga, notwithstanding.(12) In 1982, the AP would seem to have seized the opportunity to occupy the electoral space on the right/centre-right vacated by the disintegration of the UCD.

In so far as such comparisons are valid, the AP likes to identify itself with the British Conservative Party, the Republican Party of the United States, and the right wing of European Christian Democracy. It expresses sympathy for a free-market economic model, is secular but would like to see some recognition of the Catholicism of the Spanish people, supports limited regional autonomy, and is a civilian party. For all its protestations of democratic convictions, however, the AP has not as yet proved completely capable of shedding its image as the party of the old regime. A major reason for this has been the disparity between the AP's official programme, characterised by ambiguity and moderation, and the aggressive revanchism of its leaders in off-the-cuff declarations at public and semi-public meetings. Furthermore, the AP seems to have accepted without a qualm the votes and the militants of <u>Fuerza Nueva</u> (New Force), a small right-wing, anti-system party which went into liquidation in 1982. In 1982, the AP consciously projected a new image of moderate conservatism, but it is still seen by many (including the influential <u>El Pais</u>) as too far to the right to pose a real threat to the PSOE, especially under the leadership of Fraga whose attempt to appear as Spain's elder statesman in contrast to the youth of the Socialist team has been a noticeable failure.

The AP's phenomenal growth in 1982 can be attributed to three factors in the main:

i) the ignominious collapse of the UCD left it virtually the only national alternative to the Socialists on the right;

ii) the persistence of a conservative political culture and a traditional right-wing bias in Spain's rural areas, a cleavage predating and contributing to the Civil War. The AP appeals to a set of conservative values deep-rooted in Catholic agricultural areas, many of which are seen as threatened with extinction in Spain's new modernising, open, industrial society. Emotive words and phrases such as the family, the home, law and order, respect for the elderly, national self-respect are never far from Fraga's lips; and

iii) an extraordinary degree of electoral volatility. It has been estimated that 50 per cent of voters in 1982 either changed party allegiance or were voting for the first time; 60 per cent of the AP's electorate in 1982 were voting for the first time.(13) This group was not by any means made up of newly-registered voters, but had not felt sufficient identification with any previous party to vote in the past.

The opposition to the PSOE Government by AP should be seen not only in parliamentary terms, but also as part of a comprehensive, all-embracing opposition which articulates the demands of various sectors of society, including sectors of the armed forces, in favour of a return to at least some form of traditional/authoritarian regime, if only this time (at least for most of those involved) within a democratic framework. For these sectors, and indeed for the electorate at large, the PSOE has become the party of modernisation and of rupture with the old regime. In this sense, the PSOE does not represent those wanting a 'radical' transformation of society (a commitment which has been abandoned for the sake of stability of the democratic system), but more significantly, it represents also those who aspire to modernise society as a whole - at the economic, social and political levels. Rightly or wrongly, the Popular Alliance is seen as exactly the opposite, the party which wants to preserve as much as possible of the status quo, the voice of those still nostalgic about the Francoist past.

The size of the PSOE's majority (it has 202 deputies to the AP's 107) and the government's popularity mean that the AP's parliamentary opposition can only be formal and it has only a very limited effect on policy outcome. At the same, time, a democratic system of government requires the existence of a democratic opposition, and it is by no means clear that the Spanish electorate has fully accepted the democratic credentials of the AP.

To the left of the PSOE, the PCE and the smaller Carrillo fraction propose models of popular participation and mobilisation which could eventually put the stability of the regime at risk. At the centre, the Christian Democrats headed by Oscar Alzaga and the Social Democrats headed by Adolfo Suárez hope to weaken the modernising/centrist credentials of the Socialist Government, something which could have happened had the government been defeated in the referendum of March 1986 on the issue of NATO and the American bases. The development of a strong, left-wing faction within the PSOE and the trade-union movement could no doubt harm the party's claim to be the 'natural party of government' and enhance the prospects of the centrist opposition. The dispersal of the UCD means that Suárez's CDS and the more recently formed Democratic Reform party (Partido Reformista Democratico, PRD) of Miguel Roca are the two organisations most prepared to dispute the vital centre ground with the PSOE. In the absence of any electoral base or significant representation in Parliament, both depend upon leadership by well-known personalities.

Extra-Parliamentary and Regional Opposition: Anti-Regime Opposition, Separatism and Pressure Groups

The following categorisation is useful in assessing the importance of those politically organised sectors which do not articulate their demands through national political parties:

  i)   national-based ideological anti-regime opposition;
 ii)   democratic regional opposition;
iii)   separatist regional opposition; and
 iv)   single-issue opposition.

National-based ideological anti-regime opposition is at the moment institutionally unstructured. With the demise of <u>Fuerza Nueva</u>, this type
of opposition can be traced mainly to the armed
forces, though the actual size or institutional
legitimacy of such groups remains open to question.
There can be no doubt that the anti-democratic
militaristic right wing presented the greatest
threat to Spain's liberal democratic state during
the early years of its existence, but the massive
repudiation by the King and the Spanish people of
Colonel Tejero's ill-timed and ill-fated <u>coup</u>
attempt left the armed forces with their fingers
badly burnt.(14) For how long it is more difficult
to predict. This type of opposition is significant
not because it is visible or organised or public or
open (it is not on all counts), but precisely for
the opposite reasons. The extent to which the
armed forces, one of the pillars of the Francoist
state, are now a source of ideological anti-regime
opposition is an area of considerable speculation.
The truth is, it is simply impossible to know with
any reasonable degree of certainty. Whether the
Popular Alliance's participation in democratic
elections is a blind for its anti-regime sympathies
is another much-debated topic in Spain.(15) Once
again, the degree of success with which the party
at large has internalised the new democratic value
system is a question that only the future will
answer.
The <u>ideological anti-regime opposition</u> could
be defined as a socially conservative, politically
authoritarian, anti-democratic, anti-liberal, anti-
participatory, Catholic/integralist value system
whose central aim is to stop, and if possible to
reverse, the changes taking place under the democratic regime. The core of this value system is a
doctrinaire commitment to ultra-traditional social
values (emphasis on individualism and corporatism
over co-operation and democracy; pre-eminence of
the family over the individual; and defence of
hierarchy against equality, to mention a few
examples) and political authoritarianism which is
generally manifested by a rejection of all forms of
participatory democracy and its institutions. Most
recently, the Socialist Government has had to
confront opposition from traditional groups which
have mobilised right-wing sectors of public opinion
in the media and even in the courts over the legalisation of abortion and divorce.

253

Territorial opposition with an established electoral base is now confined to Euzkadi and Catalonia, the most economically developed regions of Spain. Other national minorities have also put forward claims to independence at different times and current conflicts of varying intensity exist between Madrid and Catalan, Canarian, Valencian, Balearic and to a lesser extent several other regionalist/separatist groups. Historically, regionalism has taken the form of opposition to the centralist organisations of the state, when the main policy-making institutions are in Madrid, and these are seen as strongly biased toward satisfying the interests of the capital city to the detriment of the provinces.(16)

Parties and movements expressing territorial opposition do not always look for total independence from Spain. Indeed, a clear distinction has emerged, particularly notable since the transition to democracy, between those organisations which are prepared to accept limited autonomy and therefore work within the democratic system at national and regional levels, and those groups whose opposition to the territorial integrity of Spain is total and who refuse to recognise the legitimacy of any government in Madrid, whatever its ideology.

Both the mainstream nationalist movements in Euzkadi (Basque Nationalist Party - Partido Nacionalista Vasco (PNV)) and Catalonia (Convergence and Union - Convergencia i Unio, (CiV)) offer consensual, parliamentary opposition to the PSOE Government. Ironically perhaps, both are, in origin, ideologically bourgeois, centre/centre-right parties, but the resentment and grievances created by years of total denial of their national aspirations by the Franco regime has made it impossible to reach any accommodation with the Popular Alliance, which is seen as the heir to Francoism-Falangism. Instead, the granting of limited autonomy through the establishment of Basque and Catalan administrations and parliaments has made possible the development of a harmonious relationship of mutual respect with the Socialist Government. Separatist violence from the Basque terrorist organisation, ETA, which is currently perceived as an anti-system, anti-democratic movement, has served to strengthen this relationship. The 1982 general elections witnessed the consolidation of the democratic nationalist parties. The number of PNV deputies in the national Parliament

Increased its representation from seven to eight,
while the Catalan CiV increased its representation
from eight in 1979 to twelve.

In Catalonia, left-wing nationalist sentiment
is channelled democratically through the regional
organisations of the Socialist Party (Partido
Socialisto Unificado de Cataluña - PSUC) and the
autonomous Catalan branch of the PSOE. By
contrast, radical nationalism in Euzkadi is distinguished by separatist violence and anti-system
opposition. In the view of ETA, not much has
changed since the days of Franco, and it will
remain antagonistic to any political system which
does not grant sovereign status to the Basque
nation. Basque terrorism in the late 1960s and the
early 1970s did much to undermine the stability of
government during the last years of the dictatorship and for this reason was initally applauded by
the Spanish Left. It is no exaggeration now, however, to say that ETA is the only extra-parliamentary opposition group with the potential for
damaging the democratic system. Even more disturb-
ing is the fact that the consolidation of democracy
and a Socialist victory in 1982 have made no impact
on the sizeable electoral constituency which Herri
Batasuna, the political wing of ETA, has carved out
for itself. The increase in the percentage of
Herri Batasuna's vote in Euzkadi from 13.5 per cent
in 1979 to 20 per cent in 1982 can only indicate a
degree of disaffection with the Madrid government
which is worrying in the extreme.

It could be argued that actions by interest
and/or pressure groups should also be considered a
form of extra-parliamentary opposition. However,
until the anti-NATO campaign of 1986, there had
been little independent development of movements
which operate outside party lines as seems to be
the case in Italy, West Germany, and even Britain
and France. Interest and pressure groups emerged
in the open in Spain with the return to democracy
and argue the case of similar, relevant causes
elsewhere in Europe (greens, environmentalists,
gays, women, gypsies, peace activists, etc.), but
until recently they generally operated through, or
at least very closely to, sympathetic political
parties, especially the Socialist and Communist. A
consensus among political activists on the primor-
dial need to preserve democracy rather than win
power or change public policy meant that a high
level of autonomy, such as has been developed by

some of these pressure groups in Germany or Italy, was not achieved in Spain. Their initial integration into the political system was made via the political parties, rather than through separate institution-building. This phenomenon is also observable, though less significantly, in the relationship between the various trade-union movements and the political parties with which they operate. It is through these parties that the trade unions get access to the instances of power, though the rather conservative economic policies of the González Cabinet have strained the partnership between the PSOE and the UGT, the Socialist-controlled trade union, and its leader Nicolás Redondo is showing increasing signs of wanting to follow some autonomous forms of political action. Whether these will end up in total opposition to the Socialist Government is, however, in much doubt.

One of the most interesting features of the referendum on NATO membership in March 1986 was the independence of the pressure groups which came together to co-ordinate opposition to Spain's membership, in spite of the hostility of their previous political broker, the Socialist Party. This was a natural consequence of the confusion which the issue created among the political parties: the Popular Alliance chose to boycott the referendum but remained favourably disposed to NATO, while the PSOE Government, distinguished historically for its commitment to a neutral Spain and its opposition to military pacts, succeeded in reversing party policy and campaigned vigorously on behalf of joining NATO. The Communist Party and those dissident Socialists unhappy with the PSOE's volte-face chose to offer low-profile opposition to membership for fear of destabilising the democratic transition. Indeed, all the pressure groups involved in campaigning for a 'no' vote were careful to stress that their opposition to the PSOE's new defence policy did not constitute a form of ideological anti-regime opposition.

Two umbrella organisations led the opposition to NATO: the Autonomous Co-ordinating Front of Pacifist Organisations (Frente autonoma, coordinadora estatal de organizaciones pacifista - CEOP) and the Civic Platform for an End to Spanish Membership of NATO (Plataforma civica para la salida de España de la OTAN). Trade unionists, church leaders, pacifists, intellectuals, students and members of the Communist Party were prominent in the campaign. Lacking financial resources, organisational experience and equal access to the media, (17) CEOP and the Plataforma civica none the less drew vast enthusiastic crowds to all their public meetings throughout Spain, to the extent that a government defeat was widely predicted. In the event, the government won by a margin of more than 12 per cent.

Of the seventeen regions (not including Ceuta and Melilla which have colonial status but which also participated in the referendum), the government lost in only four - Catalonia, Euzkadi, Navarra and the Canary Islands. The turn-out (59.7 per cent was the lowest in any democratic elections since 1977.(18) Although it is too early to hazard a complete explanation of the results, we suggest that the following were important factors: firstly, Prime Minister González's charismatic leadership and total personal commitment to the pro-NATO campaign; the media bias toward the government, especially from the national broadcasting corporation, RTVE; and the anti-NATO campaign's reluctance to confront the government head-on since such a policy carried the risk of rocking the foundations of Spanish democracy. Single-issue opposition which directly confronts government policy stands little chance of success, while the PSOE, and Felipe González personally, can continue to identify their strength and credibility with those of Spain's democracy. And this will probably be the case for some years to come.

Conclusion

The tradition-versus-modernity cleavage is idiosyncratic to Spanish political culture. It has permeated virtually all areas of societal behaviour ever since Spain became a nation state, and is at the forefront of current political debates on the content and style of the political reforms being attempted by the Socialist Government.

While opposition to Franco represented the forces of modernity, opposition to the new democratic regime represents the opposite. There has therefore been a distinct shift in the political/ideological/sociological alignments of the opposition. Furthermore, during both the authoritarian regime and the democratic regime, an all-pervasive ideological anti-regime opposition co-existed with more specific forms of opposition to the government. The Left and the Centre generally provided the ideological anti-regime opposition under Franco, while the extreme Right, presumably in hiding within the armed forces and even factions of Alianza Popular, performs as ideological anti-regime opposition to the Socialist administration.

More ad hoc forms of opposition to the government, or to particular policy issues, were only possible under the authoritarian regime from within. Opposition from outside was generally ideological anti-regime opposition. Under the parliamentary monarchy, ad hoc opposition against the government, or particular policy issues, does exist at various levels, i.e. political parties, interest and/or territorial groups or movements. Only the territorial opposition from ETA can be categorised as ideological anti-regime opposition.

The success/failure of opposition to the democratic governments of Suárez and González has been conditioned by a competition for the political space at the centre of the spectrum. While Suárez's Unión del Centro Democrático (now Centro Democrático y Social) was seen initally as the legitimate centre, his and some of his partners' Francoist credentials harmed their credibility as 'moderates' and 'modernisers', while these labels passed to the PSOE. The Right in Suárez's time, mainly Manuel Fraga's Alianza Popular, was and still is seen by a large proportion of the electorate as the natural heir to Franco's authoritarianism. If and when the Socialists are defeated, a new revamped Right will have to convince the voters that they, and not the Left, represent modernity, and offer therefore the best guarantee for the continued existence of a democratic system. As it is, the Left (especially the Socialists) has succeeded in being accepted as the 'natural party of democracy', while the Right has failed in ridding itself of its image as the 'natural party of authoritarianism'. The existence of one of the two more enthusiastic 'Eurocommunist' parties in the world (together with the Italian Communist party) has helped the Left to strengthen an image of moderation, adherence to democratic beliefs, and support for modernisation, three conditions to which the Spanish electorate seems to attribute the greatest importance. The integration of the electorate to the new political system has been made predominantly through party politics, which has

258

thus acquired legitimacy. The ever-increasing percentage of voters, and membership of political parties, seem to indicate that the Spanish electorate will continue to be incorporated into the political system via a competitive parliamentary party system. Alternative models of integration, or of rejection, do not offer any prospects. As things stand, the main beneficiary of this situation will be the democratic regime in general, and the PSOE, in particular. Challenges from the Left and Right will fail unless they can de-legitimise the PSOE as the natural party of democracy, moderation and modernisation.

Notes

1. The idea that the transition to democracy involved a negotiated break (ruptura pactada) with the Franco regime has been hotly contested in recent years. For a discussion of the issue, see Bruce Young, 'The 1982 Elections and democratic Transition in Spain' in David S. Bell (ed.), Democratic Politics in Spain, (Pinter, London, 1978).

2. For a discussion on the nature of the Franco regime, see Juan Linz 'An authoritarian regime : Spain', in E. Allardt and Y. Lithunen (eds), Cleavages, Ideologies and Party Systems, (Transactions of the Westermaark Society, Helsinki, 1964); Juan Linz, 'Opposition in and under an Authoritarian Regime : the case of Spain', in R.A. Dahl (ed.) Regimes and Oppositions, (Yale UP, New Haven, Conn., 1974); Paul Preston (ed.), Spain in Crisis : Evolution and Decline of the Franco Regime, (Harvester, Brighton, 1976); Jose Maravall, Dictatorship and Political Dissent: Workers and Students in Franco's Spain, (Tavistock, London, 1978); Sergio Vilar, La Naturaleza del franquismo, (Ediciones Peninsular, Barcelona, 1977); Armando de Miguel, La Herencia del franquismo, (Cambio, Madrid, 1977); and Pedro Pages, Historia de la resistencia anti franquista, (Planeta, Madrid, 1978).

3. For an illuminating account of Spain's economic development patterns, see E.N. Baklanoff, The Economic Transformation of Spain and Portugal, (Praeger, New York, 1978); and Joseph Harrison, The Economy of Modern Spain, (Manchester UP, Manchester, 1979).

4. For a summarised account of the transition process in Spain, see B. Pollack, 'Spain : From Corporate State to Parliamentary Democracy', Parliamentary Affairs, vol. 31, no. 1, (Winter 1978), pp.52-66; also idem, 'The 1982 Spanish General Election and Beyond', Parliamentary Affairs, vol. 36, no. 2, (Spring 1983), pp.201-17, and B. Pollack and J. Taylor, 'The Transition to Democracy in Portugal and Spain', British Journal of Political Science, vol. 13, no. 2, (1983), pp.209-42. More detailed accounts are provided by V. Alba, Transition in Spain :

From Franco to Democracy, (Transaction Books,
New Brunswick NJ, 1970); R. Carr and
J.F. Fusi, Spain : Dictatorship to Democracy,
(Allen & Unwin, London, 1979);
Preston, Spain in Crisis; John Coverdale,
The Political Transformation of Spain After
Franco, (Praeger, New York, 1979); Pedro
Pages, Transition in Spain, (Transaction
Books, New Brunswick, NJ, 1978); Rafael Lopez
Pintor, 'El estado de la opinión publica
española y la transición a la democracia',
Revista Española de Investigaciones Socio-
logicas, no. 13 (1981), pp. 7-47; and Peter
McDonough et al., 'The Spanish Public in
Political Transition', British Journal of
Political Science 2 (1981).

5.   For a discussion of the opposition in Spain in
the 1960s, see J. Amsden, Collective Bargaining and Class Conflict in Spain, (London
School of Economics, London, 1972); Preston,
Spain in Crisis; Linz, 'Opposition in and
under an authoritarian regime'. Aspects of
left-wing opposition over several periods are
discussed by Richard Gillespie, 'The
Clandestine PSOE', Spanish Studies, no. 6,
(1984), pp.34-47; B. Pollack, 'Factions in The
Spanish Socialist Workers Party; the case of
the 1979 extraordinary congress', paper
presented to the Workshop on Factionalism in
the political parties of Western Europe,
European Consortium for Political Research,
Florence, 25-30 March 1980; Luis E. San
Miguel, 'Para una sociologia del Cambio
politico y le oposición en la España actual',
SISTEMA - Revista de Ciencias Sociales,
no. 4, (January 1974), pp.89-107; Paul
Preston, 'The PCE's Long Road to Democracy
1954-1979', in Richard Kindersley (ed.),
In Search of Eurocommunism, (Macmillan,
London, 1981); and idem 'The PCE in the
Struggle for Democracy in Spain', in Howard
Machin (ed.), National Communism in Western
Europe, (Methuen, London, 1983). For right-
wing opposition see S.M. Ellwood, 'Franco's
Single Party: Falange Española de los Jons',
Ph.D. thesis (unpublished) University of
London 1983.

6.   Jonathan Story, 'Spanish political parties :
before and after the elections' Government
and Opposition, (Autumn 1977), p.474.

7.   For a discussion of the programmes of these

four parties in the period 1977-79, see Raúl Morodo, Los partidos politicos en España, (Editorial Labor, Barcelona, 1979), pp.156-86.

8. José Amodia, 'Union of the Democratic Centre' in Bell, Democratic Politics in Spain, p.5.

9. On the PSOE, see José Maria Maravall, 'The Socialist Alternative: The Policies and Electorate of the PSOE', in Howard R. Penniman and Eusebio M. Mujal-León, Spain at the Polls, 1977, 1979 and 1982, (Duke UP, Durham NC, 1985); S. Julia, La Izquierda del PSOE, (Siglo XXI, Madrid, 1977); and Elizabeth Nash, 'The Spanish Socialist Workers Party Since Franco: from Clandestinity to Government, 1976-82', in Bell, Democratic Politics in Spain.

10. See Maravall, 'The Socialist Alternative'.

11. Little research has been carried out so far on the Popular Alliance. See especially, Rafael López-Pintor, 'Francoist Reformists in Democratic Spain : The Popular Alliance and the Democratic Coalition', in Penniman and Mujal-León, Spain at the Polls, which is excellent, but unfortunately does not cover the 1982 elections; Manuel Fraga Iribarne, Alianza Popular, (Albia, Bilbao, 1977); and Jorge de Estéban and Luis López Guerra, Los partidos politicosen la España actual' Coleccion Tablero, (Planeta, Barcelona, 1982).

12. See, for example, Morodo, Los partidos politicos en España.

13. Rafael López-Pintor, 'The October 1982 General Election and the Evolution of the Spanish Party System' in Penniman and Mujal-León, Spain at the Polls.

14. For a good description of Colonel Tejero's attempted coup and its consequences, see Paul Preston, The Triumph of Democracy in Spain, (Methuen, London, 1986).

15. Fraga's much-quoted remarks on his 'understanding' of (though not 'sympathy' with) plots in the armed forces caused an uproar in the Spanish media.

16. See Juan Linz 'Early State-Building and Late Peripheral Nationalisms against the State : The Case of Spain', in S.J. Eisenstadt and Stein Rokkan (eds), Building States and Nations : Analysis by Region, (Sage, San Francisco, 1973); Stanley Payne, 'Catalan and Basque Nationalism', Journal of Contemporary

History, vol. 6, no. 1 (1971), pp.15 51;
Kenneth Medhurst, 'The Prospects of Federal-
ism : The Regional Problem After Franco',
Government and Opposition, vol. 11, no. 2
(Jan.-Oct. 1976), pp.180-97; Kenneth Medhurst,
The Basques and Catalans, (Minority Rights
Group Report No. 9, London, 1977); Juan F.
Marsal and Javier Roiz, 'Catalan Nationalism
and the Spanish Elections', in Penniman and
Mujal-León, Spain at the Polls; and John
Coverdale, 'Regional Nationalism and the
Elections in the Basque Country' in ibid.

17. All Spain's national newpapers supported
     membership of NATO except the Communist Party-
     controlled Mundo Obrero, and El Pais, which
     took a neutral stand on the issue.

18. The result was as follows: 59.74 per cent of
     the electorate voted; 52.53 per cent
     (9,042,951) voted in favour of NATO; 39.84 per
     cent (6,859,977) voted against; 42.26 per cent
     (11,604,327) of the electorate abstained,
     El Pais (International Edition), 17 March
     1986.

PART III : OPPOSITION OUTSIDE PARLIAMENT

10. NON-PARLIAMENTARY OPPOSITION IN GREAT BRITAIN: THE CASE OF THE TRADE UNIONS

David B. Capitanchik

The British political system accepts the legitimacy
of opposition. Organised groups and institutions
contend for influence over the distribution of
material resources and the promotion and implementation of favoured interests and beliefs.(1)
Political opposition is as important to the functioning of politics as is social consensus to the
decisions ultimately arrived at.   In Britain,
opposition is seen as a bulwark, not as a challenge, to the nominally supreme institution within
the British political system, namely Parliament.
That the supremacy of Parliament is nominal is not
a subject of contention, despite the success of the
occasional 'backbench revolt'.   On the contrary,
the complexity of contemporary society on the one
hand, and the decline of the country's international standing on the other, mean that the
ability of Parliament to determine effectively the
course of the nation's affairs has been reduced.
There has been a corresponding extension of the
legitimacy of action to groups outside the historically narrow confines of Parliament proper in
the ever-expanding sphere of what has come to be
called pressure group politics. The trade union
movement has been a beneficiary, along with other
social and economic groups, of this widening of
political opposition.
　　　Pressure groups have come to be regarded as
focal points within the broad distribution of
political power.(2) At times they have been seen
as sharing power with the formal state institutions
and operating upon them in order to influence
government decision-making in their favour, as well
as gaining popular support for the particular
interests they represent. Broadly, pressure groups

fall into two categories: (i) those that seek to protect a particular economic and/or occupational interest, and (ii) those that seek to promote some 'moral' cause.

In a mixed economy such as that of the United Kingdom, public policy frequently and intimately affects, among others, business, labour and agricultural interests. Consequently, pressure groups claiming to represent such interests are prominent in attempting to influence policy-making. They include such organisations as the Confederation of British Industry (representing employers), the Trades Union Congress, the National Farmers' Union, the British Medical Association and the Law Society, and they can be classified under the heading self-oriented pressure groups. The hallmark of this type of group is that it represents a 'social and economic stake in society', and its most salient features stem from this fact. Significantly, the self-oriented pressure group has, as it were, a fixed target. The major part of its activities are aimed at influencing the appropriate government decision-makers. It can more readily extract money and work from its members on a continuing basis, and it is likely to be less subject to disintegration and be more capable of unified action than pressure groups of the second type. It is typical of such a group that its more important activities take place in the corridors of power rather than in the public arena.

The Howard League for Penal Reform, the National Council for Civil Liberties, the Campaign for Nuclear Disarmament and Amnesty International are examples of pressure groups of the promotional type. They exist to promote a cause and represent interests in a different sense from those in the previous category. Whereas the latter seek to protect what are essentially self-interested material concerns, this type of group seeks to promote a 'moral' interest which is seen as being of concern to society as a whole. A further distinguishing feature is that promotional groups do not necessarily represent those with a social or economic stake in the existing society. They do not have specific targets for their pressure, although they may seek to further their cause by securing its adoption either by a political party or by some official or semi-official body (e.g. Royal patronage). As opposed to the exclusive membership of self-oriented groups, they tend to be open to all like-minded persons.

In Britain, it must be said, the trade union movement has never challenged the legitimacy of the prevailing socio-political system. As ruefully noted in the 1960s by an English Marxist: 'Trade unions do not challenge the existence of society based on a division of classes, they merely express it ... They can bargain within the society, but not transform it'.(3) The formation of the Labour Party to fight anti-trade union legislation from within Parliament can be seen as a legitimation of the system, albeit one that needed modification, rather than a confrontation in order to restructure the core values and norms of the prevailing society. In Beatrice Webb's description, trade unions were 'a continuous association of wage earners for the purpose of maintaining or improving the conditions of their work lives'.(4)

However, to present the unions as institutions confined to wage bargaining, diligently guarding their members' economic welfare narrowly defined, is to misrepresent the contemporary social history of the United Kingdom. The expansion of central government - intervening, as it regularly does nowadays, in the lives of ordinary people - has seen the corresponding expansion of trade union activity in the shaping of government-initiated social legislation. For the national leadership, especially those involved in running the affairs of the Trades Union Congress, the concern with local factory floor working conditions has been overtaken by their preoccupation with the general economic climate and the application of social welfare. Many trade unions have been determined to prevent government intrusion into wage negotiation. Paradoxically, however, the very effort to resist government interference, and hence political determination, in the economic sphere, has drawn the trade union movement into wider political participation. This extension of trade union activity has been aided and abetted by contemporary governments of every political complexion; for the unions have benefited from the growth of interest group politics. Thus not only are trade unions prominent in the early stages of the legislative process, with their attempts to influence specific aspects of government planning, but they have also been important channels of supervision once legislation has been enacted.

This chapter focuses upon two aspects of the

relationship between the trade union movement and society in Great Britain. First it deals with the effect of recent social and economic change upon and within the trade unions themselves. The underlying assumption is that such opposition as unions have sought to exercise against government policy has been prompted more by the desire to resist the impact of change, than to bring change about. Second, it is concerned with the relationship between the trade unions and governments since World War II, the underlying question here being whether the trade union movement has been anything other than a pressure group competing with other interests in society for the allocation of scarce social and economic resources.

Social and Economic Change

The 1970s and 1980s have been marked by a significant shift away from employment in the traditional industries of manufacturing, transport, construction and agriculture towards the service industries. In the same period, employment in manufacturing declined by 24 per cent, in agriculture by 19 per cent and in energy and water supplies by 11 per cent. In sharp contrast, there has been a substantial increase in the numbers of those working in the professions and management; a 27 per cent increase in banking and finance and a 15 per cent increase in employment in public service occupations including recreation and personal services. By 1981, these two groups, together with the distribution, hotel and catering and repair groups, made up 53 per cent of the British workforce. (See Figure 10.1.)

The shift out of manufacturing has been interpreted with typical British pessimism. Political analysts choose to see the trend as yet another example of the country's relentless decline. All this in marked contrast to their American counterparts; consider Daniel Bell's optimistic forecasts and anticipation of a post-industrial America where the shift of resources from manufacture to services has been more pronounced and dramatic than that experienced in the United Kingdom. Where British commentators see decay and erosion, Bell regards the shift as a positive transition - a natural progression much in the way that nineteenth-century men heralded the first industrial revolution as a natural and necessary step towards unceasing social

268

Figure 10.1: Change in employment: by occupation, 1971-1981 (England and Wales)

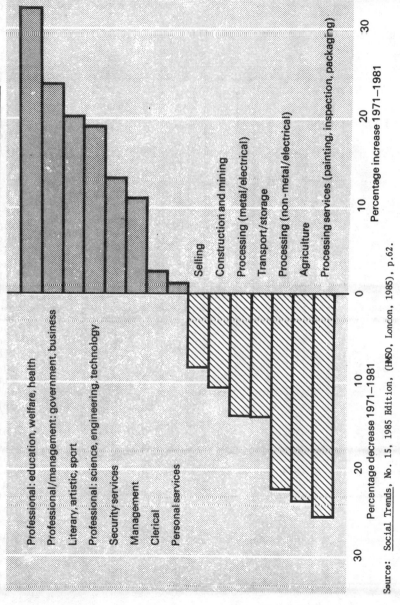

Source: Social Trends, No. 15, 1985 Edition, (HMSO, London, 1985), p.62.

Figure 10.2: <u>Trade union membership: by size of union</u>
(millions)

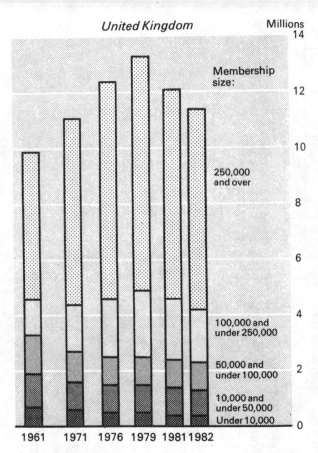

Source: Ibid., p.164.

progress.(5)

For the trade union movement, however, the decline of manufacturing occupations has brought far-reaching change in the composition and size of individual unions and an overall drop in the membership of the movement as a whole. For example, at the end of 1982, TUC affiliated unions had a combined membership of 10.5 million; twelve months later this had fallen to 10.1 million, a decrease of 4 per cent. From the end of 1979, when it stood at 12.2 million, to the end of 1983, membership had declined by 17 per cent. (See Figure 10.2.)

The largest relative falls in membership during the four-year period in question occurred in unions covering employees working mainly in manufacturing. Thus in 1982, the number of people in unions covering manufacturing fell by around 12 per cent against a fall of just over 5 per cent in employment in manufacturing industries. The fall in union membership can be seen as a direct consequence of changes in the economic structure; it has been exacerbated, not caused, by unemployment. The smallest relative falls (and some increases in membership) occurred in unions with members engaged mainly in service industries.

The number of trade unions declined between 1979 and 1982 from 453 to 401. Many unions are relatively small; over half the 1982 total had fewer than 1,000 members and together they accounted for no more than 0.5 per cent of total trade union membership.

Table 10.1 shows that the growth in total membership up to 1979 was concentrated entirely in unions of 100,000 or more members. There were 22 such unions in 1982 and these together accounted for nearly 80 per cent of the total membership.

The overall picture of the trade unions shows a declining membership in fewer larger unions and reflects a general trend in industrial life. Business mergers and rationalisation have characterised corporate life and this has been paralleled by a similar trend in the trade union movement.

The absorption of small individual unions into larger organisations has not led to a simplification of trade union affairs. Quite the contrary, for the linking of groups and sub-groups within an umbrella organisation has led to complexities that owe their existence to history, rather than rational organisational practice. An example of

271

Table 10.1: Membership of selected trade unions (thousands and percentages)

	1961	1971	1976	1979	1982	Percentage Change 1979-1982
Transport and General Workers Union	1,358	1,580	1,930	2,086	1,633	-21.7
Amalgamated Union of Engineering Workers	1,062	1,195	1,421	1,510	1,242	-17.7
National Union of General and Municipal Workers	786	822	916	967	825	-14.7
National and Local Government Officers Association (a)	-	-	683	753	726	- 3.6
National Union of Public Employes	210	395	651	692	702	+ 1.4
Union of Shop, Distributive and Allied Workers	351	319	413	470	417	-11.3
Association of Scientific, Technical and Managerial Staffs (b)	-	220	396	491	410	-16.5
National Union of Mineworkers	675	417(d)	371	372	370	- 0.5
National Union of Teachers (a)	-	-	294	291	260	-10.7
Confederation of Health Service Employees	58	87	201	213	232	+ 8.9
Royal College of Nursing (c)	-	-	-	162	223	+37.7
Civil and Public Services Association	143	185(d)	231	224	199	-11.2
National Union of Railwaymen	317	195	178	170	150	-11.8
Iron and Steel Trades Confederation	125	133(d)	117	110	95	-13.6

a) Owing to changes in the structure of the union comparable data are not available for years prior to 1974.
b) Owing to changes in the structure of the union comparable data are not available for years prior to 1968.
c) Only became a trade union in 1977: comparable data are not available for prior years.
d) Figure relates to 1970.

Source: Ibid. p.164.

such a body is the Transport and General Workers'
Union, which now covers a wide variety of occupations although it started off as a labourers'
union. The Amalgamated Union of Engineering
Workers (AUEW) and the EETPU (which represents
electricians and plumbers), on the other hand,
began as craft unions and now increasingly resemble
general unions in their make-up. Within these
large trade unions, covering both general and
skilled workers, there are sub-groups and sections
for white-collar workers. This hetereogeneity
clearly compounds the complexities of representation and negotiation.(6)

Trade unions, like all highly-structured
institutions, fall prey to the difficulties that
beset other similar organisations. Thus over the
last decades, there has been a loss of authority
away from the centre to the periphery, with a
consequent growth in the influence and activity of
shop stewards and work groups at factory level.
This phenomenon has been reinforced by the existence of several unions operating within one
industry, often within one factory or plant. It is
not surprising that the consequent complexity and
competitiveness within and between trade unions
should be better understood and manipulated by shop
stewards at local level, than by full-time union
officers outside the workplace. In some cases, it
has provided the opportunity for the more radical
members of extreme left-wing factions to exploit
the resultant confusion to compete for influence on
the shop floor.

The picture of the trade union movement in
secular decline is now manifest for all to see.
The process has accelerated since 1979 as manufacturing continued to decline and unemployment began
to rise. In addition, the unions have lost much of
the political influence they seemed able to wield
in the 1960s and 1970s, partly because of the
aforementioned developments, but also because of
the determination of the Conservative Government
under Mrs Thatcher to remove the impression that
the country could not be governed without the
active participation of the trade unions in policy-
making. The unions, it is sometimes said, have
been 'thrown out of Downing Street into Trafalgar
Square', where impotent mass demonstrations,
violent clashes with the police, slogan-shouting
and banner-waving, replace the hard bargaining over
'beer and sandwiches' with senior cabinet ministers

273

and their officials in government departments and inside Number 10 itself.

The course of recent British history suggests, however, that the formal and explicit involvement of central government in industrial and commercial life has given the trade union movement a potentially significant leverage on power despite the decline in influence discussed earlier. The government is the direct employer of civil servants and the paymaster of public services such as the National Health Service and education. The nationalised industries are formally independent of day-to-day government incursion, but who can doubt that major and far-reaching decisions about their activities are made by the government, sometimes at the highest level? Indeed, the policy of British Coal during the miners' strike, and the fate of those corporations destined for privatisation in line with the policies of the Thatcher Administration, are but recent examples.

However much unemployment and structural changes in the economy may have diminished trade union membership, the labour movement still represents a large and key element in British society; the flaws in its internal organisation have not impaired the movement's ability to fight and bludgeon opposition to what it deems to be its central concerns. Governments of whatever shade or opinion are obliged to undertake some long-term or forward planning of the economy. It is widely accepted that ordinary Members of Parliament, be they supporters of the party in power or of the opposition, are woefully short of the facilities to mount an efficient scrutiny of the massive legislation that this entails. The power to initiate and innovate in many important aspects of public life is removed from Parliament and now resides in the civil service and/or the organisations that represent employers and workers. In this context, the trade union movement represents a reservoir of expertise to be acknowledged and used if legislation is ever to be effective.

Tripartite Economic Planning

The opportunity for trade unions and employers to play a leading role along with government in the formulation of economic policy arose in the 1960s and 1970s. During this period, governments seeking to maintain full employment at a time of long-term rising inflation, were forced to concede the need for economic planning. Such planning had not existed since the war and was now not readily accepted by business or by labour. In the context of the early 1960s, when high expectations were being frustrated by policies designed to do little more than hold incomes back, efforts to secure the co-operation of the trade unions were virtually doomed to failure.

The official forum for what became known as the 'New Corporatism' - the partnership between government, employers and workers - was the National Economic Development Council (NEDC), which was set up in March 1962 by the then Chancellor of the Exchequer, Selwyn Lloyd. 'Neddy', as it is colloquially known, was to be chaired by the Chancellor, with other ministers in attendance. Its membership included representatives of both management and the trade unions. However, from the beginning, having a minister in the chair has meant that planning forecasts have not been a matter for negotiation between the various interests. Instead, under all governments of whatever persuasion, such issues have been reserved for ministerial determination with room only for nominal consultation between the interested parties.(7)

The Conservatives' conversion to economic planning caused a dilemma for the trade unions and especially for the TUC. As the representative body of the trade union movement, the Trades Union Congress was not designed to play an active role in planning or managing the economy. It had been successful in pursuing its traditional concerns with the pay and conditions of working people to the extent of gaining direct access to government. However, it could not afford to be seen to be sharing responsibility for Conservative Government policies. The TUC had vigorously opposed the Selwyn Lloyd 'pay pause' of 1961, which it saw as a prelude to far worse things to come. Moreover, any serious attempt by the government to engage in economic planning was bound to be seen as restricting the right to free collective bargaining. Hence, it was reliably reported that the TUC's agreement to join the NEDC was secured only in return for an undertaking by the Chancellor to relax the 'pay pause'.(8)

The TUC could not oppose the idea of planning in principle, however, although many left-wing trade unionists still argued that they should have

275

nothing to do with Conservative planning. The
unions also insisted that wages policy should be
excluded from the NEDC's terms of reference and
this remained the case until Labour came to power
in 1964. Subsequently, the Minister for Economic
Affairs, George Brown, was able to use the Council
to secure an agreement on the question of prices
and incomes policy known as the Statement of
Intent.(9)

Prices and Incomes policy, however, was not
made in the NEDC. Under Labour, the voluntary
policy of 1965 was reinforced by legal sanctions
and changes in policy were made by the government
without any consultation with the members of the
NEDC. The combination of policies pursued by the
government from 1966 onwards made the trade unions
feel they were being victimised and their reaction
was to lead to the pay explosion of the 1970s.
This, in turn, aroused the resentment of the
employers who also lost faith in the idea of an
incomes policy. The 'New Corporatism' foundered in
large part because it was based upon a tripartite
arrangement between the government, the employers
and the trade unions, in which each party had
agreed to play its part. But there was no provision for legally-binding agreements subject to the
adjudication of an independent scrutinising body.
For the government could not surrender its ultimate
control over the determination of public policy to
any outside agency, certainly not in so vital an
area as the management of the country's economy.
(10)

Nevertheless, the inability of the trade union
movement to strike a bargain with the Wilson
Government in which it could have accepted an
incomes policy 'as a definite price of social
progress' was more than just a missed opportunity.
The unions were forced into an oppositional role
more by their own structural and organisational
weaknesses, than by their resistance to government
policies designed to restrain their demands.

Ostensibly, the Trades Union Congress appears
a powerful organisation in that it purports to
represent a major part of organised labour arranged
in a wide variety of occupations. But, ultimately,
Congress's strength as an instrument of opposition
relies on its ability to control and impose its
decisions on its constitutent members. The movement is dominated by a handful of large trade
unions whose traditions are rooted firmly and

historically in the specific skills of their
members. This domination is manifest in the
membership of the TUC's most important committees
and councils. It constitutes a challenge to the
separate identity of Congress as an independent
centre of decision-making and makes more problematic the TUC's overriding function: to sustain a
consistency between the demands of the constituent
members and the external socio-economic environment.

The eminent American historian, Barbara
Tuchman, in seeking to discover why 'governing
institutions' persist in pursuing policies contrary
to their own interests, asks the following
question: 'Why in recent times have British trade
unions in a lunatic spectacle seemed periodically
bent on dragging their country toward paralysis,
apparently under the impression that they are
separate from the whole?'(11) Is this just the
'March of Folly' or, for example, in rejecting
Labour's 'Social Contract' were the trade unions
'hoping for a more decisive advance toward the
socialist commonwealth'?(12)

The answer seems to lie neither in mindless
folly nor in a shift to the left among British
trade unionists, although, since the 1960s, the
Left has been more prominent in the Labour Party.
Rather it derives from the harsh realities of
British economic life.

Relations with the Labour Party

The close historical ties between the trade union
movement and the Labour Party have been marred by
decades of economic crisis and consequent conflict
between government and the unions. Furthermore,
since 1945, both sections of the labour movement
have sought to widen their membership. The TUC was
compelled to attract into its ranks the fast-
growing white-collar unions and to present itself
as a powerful pressure group with all political
parties. The Labour Party in order to gain power
also had to broaden its appeal beyond its traditional working-class base. These considerations
inevitably gave rise to sharp conflicts between the
TUC and the Labour Government over incomes policies
(in 1950 as well as in the 1960s) and attempts to
reform industrial relations through legislation in
1969.

In opposition, however, the Labour Party could

be more supportive of the trade unions and the two wings of the movement were reconciled against the Conservative Government of Mr Heath and the Industrial Relations Act of 1971. Indeed, the drafting of legislation to repeal the Act was a joint venture of the party and the trade unions combining in one committee. In December 1970, a TUC-Labour Party Liaison Committee was set up, initially to provide a forum for joint consultation between the political and industrial wings of the labour movement. Subsequently, it was to provide the institutional framework for the development of the so-called 'Social Contract', for which the repeal of the Conservatives' industrial relations legislation was a major pre-requisite on the return of a Labour Government to office. Thus opposition to the Tory legislation not only united the TUC internally (the only disagreements centred upon the nature and intensity of such opposition), but externally it strengthened relations with the Labour Party.(13)

The Social Contract was central to this new relationship. It was to be a strategy both to overcome immediate crises and to plan for future legislation for a 'coherent economic and social strategy, one designed to overcome the nation's grave economic problems and to provide for co-operation between the trade unions and government'. It was essentially a voluntary agreement between the Labour Party and the trade unions encompassing a number of specific policies ranging from the repeal of Conservative Acts of Parliament to plans for the redistribution of income and wealth. Above all, it was an 'oppositional alliance' between the two wings of the labour movement against Conservative policies.

Implicit in the strategy was a critique of statutory pay policies and a commitment to free collective bargaining. From the mid-1960s through to the beginning of the 1970s, the trade unions disputed the role of law in reforming industrial relations with both Conservative and Labour Governments. The Social Contract was in the nature of a peace-pact between Labour and the unions combining against the intended comprehensive reform of trade union life by the Tories. It was an 'ideal' programme, an abstraction from reality not rooted in the economic situation of the day. However, it was a significant pointer to changes in the policies of the two wings of the labour movement.

The central role of the TUC in the new relationship had been asserted with the outspoken and forceful support of the leadership of the more important unions, particularly Jack Jones of the Transport and General Workers (TGWU). Away from the responsibilities of office and their counter-vailing pressures, the Labour Party in opposition could afford to be sensitive and pliant towards the trade unions. Thus the leadership of the TUC, through its membership of the Liaison Committee, had 'unprecedented access to Labour Party policy-making prior to the 1974 General Elections that excluded employers' organisations and any other interested pressure groups'. Such access to what was seen as the future influential leadership of a Labour Government, and an avoidance on the part of the latter of explicit statements regarding its intentions in such areas as wage bargaining, engendered both high aspirations within the TUC leadership and expectations that bi-partite decision-making would continue in the future.

Indeed, the General Election of February 1974 was fought by the Tories around the constitutional issue of the proper relationship between the government and the unions. 'Who Governs Britain?' was the theme of their campaign. In reply, the Labour Party was able to claim that it had the support of the trade unions for 'an agreed pro-gramme of economic and social policy' - viz. a Social Contract.

Against the background of severe industrial disruption sparked off by a miners' strike and the government's decision to institute a three-day working week to conserve energy supplies, Labour returned to office after the February 1974 elec-tions. However, the new enhanced relationship with the trade unions had to be carried out in the context of a growing international economic reces-sion, exacerbated, if not triggered by, the oil price explosion and increasing crisis in the British economy. The 1975 Budget had to take into account a decline in industrial production and investment, rising unemployment and depreciating sterling. It was, therefore, deflationary and restrictive, the opposite of the trade unions' previous expecatations. Inevitably, with inflation rising rapidly, the role of wages and free collec-tive bargaining was once more on the agenda.

The TUC acknowledged that there had been a marked lack of observance of voluntary pay

279

guidelines and that inflation and unemployment threatened the implementation of the entire Social Contract. In mid-June 1975, following an over-whelming 'Yes' vote in a referendum held to confirm British membership of the EEC, Prime Minister Harold Wilson felt strong enough to remove Tony Benn from his post as Secretary of State for Industry. Primarily, this was because Benn had been a powerful advocate of British withdrawal from the Common Market, but his departure was all the more significant because he had been an ardent supporter of trade union power and government control over private industry.

Shortly after this, the Wilson Government gave notice that it intended to pursue a firm policy on prices and incomes and a 'voluntary' pay policy was incorporated into a Government White Paper with the acquiescence of the TUC. The TUC was fearful of the imposition of a statutory policy and its reper-cussions, especially on the low-paid. The close relationship enshrined in the Social Contract meant that the leadership of the TUC was prepared to accept an involvement in and responsibility for the pay policy. At the 1975 Congress, the leadership argued for a marked rank-and-file commitment to the policies and decisions of the TUC and for the wages policy in particular to be seen in the wider context of the other provisions of the Social Contract. In the event, the Congress endorsed the General Council's policy on the Social Contract including its guidelines on pay constraint.

Less than a year later, under the threat of a huge sterling crisis, the TUC leadership again acquiesced in a further new pay policy. By this time, James Callaghan had succeeded to the Premier-ship and he announced in early May that although he would consult with the TUC on issues of public expenditure and price controls, they were not negotiable as part of a pay deal. The years 1976 and 1977 were marked by retrenchment in capital investment programmes and deflationary budgets by the Labour Government in response, it was alleged, to the price being asked for the renewal of credit arrangements by the US Treasury and the Inter-national Monetary Fund. The TUC argued for con-tinued co-operation with the government, but many public sector unions took unilateral action outside the TUC. Those unions representing civil servants, health, education and local government workers claimed to be fighting on behalf of the whole trade

union movement, not merely for their own sectional
interests, thus presenting a challenge to what was
seen as rather weak criticism of their actions by
the General Council of the TUC.

By 1977, trade union leaders were facing
growing rank-and-file pressure to end any form of
wage restraint and in that year the annual conference of the Transport and General Workers' Union
demanded a return to free collective bargaining.
Against the advice of Jack Jones who was attending
his last Conference as General Secretary, the
delegates voted against a further round of pay
policy. This marked the end of a two-year period
when the TUC had exerted an 'unprecedented degree
of influence over the pay bargaining of affiliated
unions'. The traditional weakness of the TUC in
advocating policies at a national level was again
seen to lie in the insistence of its constituent
members on asserting their autonomy whenever they
believed it to be necessary and expedient to do so.

The state of the economy apart, there were
other more fundamental reasons for the failure of
the Social Contract. There had been a marked
decline in party allegiance, especially among erstwhile Labour stalwarts in the trade union movement,
and a shift from seeing union membership as an end
in itself towards a more instrumental view of trade
unionism. The 'embourgeoisement' thesis of the
late 1950s and early 1960s sought to explain the
electoral success of the Conservative Party in
terms of the rise of the so-called 'affluent
worker'. Full employment, high incomes, rising
standards of living and, above all, high expectations of continuing economic advancement, it was
argued, meant that the Conservative Party could now
be said to represent the interests of working
people in the same way as it had always represented
those of the middle classes. At a superficial
level, the thesis was intended to explain the
decline of the electoral fortunes of the Labour
Party and so, when Labour won all but one of the
next five general elections, the thesis was widely
adjudged to be false.

The effects of affluence on working-class
political behaviour were examined in a famous study
by the sociologists Goldthorpe and Lockwood.(14)
Their findings, including the withdrawal of
allegiance from national unions in favour of
localism, were a foretaste of trends which in the
later 1960s were to be held responsible for

'chaotic pay differentials' and extensive wages drift. Indeed, the Donovan Commission deplored 'the tendency of extreme decentralisation and self-government to degenerate into indecision and anarchy'.(15) The Commission attempted to argue that there was nothing novel in the localism of the 1960s. It had existed before the First World War, it was claimed, but was replaced by a nationally cohesive sense of working-class solidarity under the impact of the mass unemployment of the inter-war years. The reversion to fragmentation was the result of multi-unionism and full employment.(16)

In a later study, Goldthorpe has maintained that it is among white-collar workers that there is ambivalence toward collective action and a lack of class cohesiveness.(17) Among manual workers 'not only is the commitment to trade unionism undiminished, but collective action on this basis is becoming an increasingly potent force'.(18) Much of this it seems, is expressed through collective bargaining over wages and conditions of service. Moreover, Goldthorpe argues, the trade union movement as a whole has shown itself capable of impressive defensive action such as that which it mounted in opposition to the Labour Government's White Paper, 'In Place of Strife' in 1969 and the Conservative Government's Industrial Relations Act of 1971.

What is interesting about both of these examples, however, is that trade union opposition to any attempt to regulate their activities, whether in order to meet the exigencies of government economic planning or to restrict the impact of restrictive practices on industrial relations, was the same. Labour Governments, regardless of their Party's special relationship with the trade unions, could expect no better reception for their policies than that accorded to the legislative proposals of the Conservatives. For so long as the trade union movement continued to represent the interests of the majority of its members who were still manual workers, it was indeed just able to take collective action. Once that manual majority had disappeared, effective opposition, even of a defensive kind, was no longer credible.

Relations with the Conservative Government

The new white-collar majority, then, is said to lack a sense of class solidarity as well as automatic allegiance to the Labour Party. Harold Wilson

282

seemed to acknowledge this when in the General Elections of 1964 and 1966, he aimed the party's campaign successfully beyond traditional class lines by calling for a new society forged by the 'White Heat of New Technology'. Young executives, technocrats, white-collar workers and their families were to give Labour its first real taste of power since the immediate post-war period. However, these were also to be among the most disillusioned by the failure of successive governments, including Edward Heath's Conservative administration of 1970-74, to manage the economy with policies that did not involve the compulsory control of incomes. Among this category of voters resentment increased after 1974 when Labour introduced incomes policies designed to protect the lower-paid from the effects of continuing high inflation but which also eroded pay differentials. This led to a revival of the pay disputes and strikes of the early 1970s and culminated with the election of Mrs Thatcher after the 'Winter of Discontent' of 1978-9. The most attractive aspect of the Conservatives' 1979 election campaign, it has been suggested, was their leader's rejection of any idea of an incomes policy.

The rejection of incomes policies in favour of monetarist measures for controlling inflation and the concomitant rise of large-scale unemployment placed the trade union movement in firm opposition to the Thatcher government. For its part, however, the government was able to expose the impotence of this opposition. There was, primarily, the Conservatives' landslide victory in the General Election of 1983, in which Labour suffered its most serious reverse in over 50 years. Subsequently, the government was able to weather and overcome the year-long miners' strike. It had successfully implemented its, albeit limited, trade union legislation. Arguably, its most significant achievement in this respect was the law enforcing union ballots. The disarray within the TUC over government funding for unions to ballot their members was a clear indication of the movement's inability to maintain a united front against what many of its members regarded as an unwarranted intrusion into their domestic affairs.

The trade union movement, it was now clear, was most effective in both furthering the interests of its members and in its oppositional role when there was full employment, when governments sought

283

its co-operation in managing the economy and when the movement could rely on traditional working-class solidarity. The return of high unemployment, the refusal of Mrs Thatcher's government to involve the trade unions in its economic policy-making in return for their co-operation, and the decline of class solidarity have exposed the impotence of trade union opposition.

Moreover, the trade union movement is no longer able to function so effectively as an interest group, even when it is defending some cherished values. Trade union opposition to the proposed abolition of the State Earnings Related Pensions Scheme (SERPS) illustrates their dilemma. Younger, white-collar workers, many of whom are covered by their employers' own occupational pension schemes, or who have made private provision for their old age, are unlikely to be concerned. On the other hand, it is an issue of considerable significance for the now minority of manual workers in more traditional low-paid employment. Similarly, there is the trade unions' opposition to government plans for the privatisation of state-owned enterprises. In some cases, such as the public utilities, opposition to privatisation is widespread among the workforce. Elsewhere, the workers involved are more prepared to come to terms with a transfer of ownership. Among the public at large, on the other hand, majority opinion has long regarded nationalised industries as over-manned, high-cost and high-priced state monopolies. They are usually compared unfavourably with the more efficient and competitive private sector.

Thus only the most pessimistic conclusions emerge from the discussion of the issues raised at the beginning of this chapter. The impact of economic and social change on the trade union movement has been severe. The unions have been reduced to struggling to defend the level of welfare provision for an increasingly ageing society and a large, and possibly permament, army of unemployed.

The 'New Unionism'

However, the trade unions should not be written off as the archeological remains of Britain's industrial past. As the numbers and influence of the manual workers decline and the white-collar membership increases, there might occur a regeneration of the trade union movement. This could manifest itself in a number of ways. White-collar workers already regard trade unionism as a useful and legitimate way of pursuing their interests. A major growth has taken place in recent decades of unions covering such areas as banking and insurance. The teaching profession is heavily unionised, as is the civil service. Groups employed in the essential public services like firemen, prison officers and the nursing profession, to name but a few, are not only unionised, but have demonstrated their militancy as well.

Unlike the unions in the past, which campaigned for improved conditions and pay, the members of 'new unionism' are motivated, at least in part, by frustrated expectations. Conscious of their key role in society as well as in the economy, they either command new technological skills, or provide an essential public service, or, increasingly, they are members of recognised professions like teaching and nursing. As such, they believe they are fully entitled to a standard of living commensurate with their occupational status.

Such unions are likely to be much more effective in participating in pressure group politics. Their education and training would provide them with the appropriate skills to project their case. Many would be able to appeal with equal effect to both policy-makers and public opinion since they would be able to claim that they are campaigning not solely on their own behalf, but also on behalf of the essential public service that they provide, like education, health and security. Potentially, then, they could be highly effective groups that transcend the usual divide between interest and value and, consequently, constitute a more potent opposition to government than the trade unions of the past.

The white-collar workers' lack of class cohesiveness in the traditional sense and their instrumental view of politics need not mean that they will constitute less of a political opposition. It is probably true that for many of them their trade unionism is based on 'the rejection of class and on the espousal of the market'.(19) However, they are likely to be concerned with other values arising out of their expectations of continuously improving standards of living. Concern for the environment and the general quality of life, education, health, provision for old age, leisure and, most likely, reform of the fiscal system to suit their own particular circumstances, are among the many issues on behalf of which they will unite to campaign.

However, their lack of class cohesion, whatever that meant in the past, might make it difficult, if not impossible, for them to unite to form a common, coherent opposition to legislative interference in industrial affairs by governments. Already, strong differences exist over the issue of government-funded strike ballots. Some unions welcome this, others regard it as an intrusion in their own internal affairs. There are disagreements over the recruitment of members and disputes about demarcation between different trades and occupations. It has been suggested that such differences have less to do with philosophy and ideology than with manning levels and new technologies.

Meantime, however, the emergence of such a new, vibrant and politically active opposition lies somewhere in the future. For the present, it must be concluded that as a political opposition the movement is at best weak and for the most part impotent. The trade unions have traditionally participated in the political process in Britain as interest groups rather than as an opposition that was seeking to transform the political system. Paradoxically, this has meant that they have been most effective in securing their goals when they have been encouraged, as they were for a while in the 1960s and 1970s, to participate more directly and intimately in the policy-making process. Then, in principle at least, they could always bargain for some advantage in return for their support for any particular government policy. The transformation of the British working class, the decline of traditional industries and their workforces, and the rise of the new white-collar unions, have meant that the movement as a whole, and the TUC as its representative body in particular, is less coherent, less cohesive and less able to represent itself to government as an effective political opposition.

Notes

1. For a fuller discussion of this view of opposition see G. Ionescu and I. de Madariaga, Opposition, (Pelican Books, Harmondsworth, 1972) pp.9-19.
2. See D. Capitanchik and P. Williams, 'Pressure Groups and U.K. Defence' in European Military Institutions - A Reconnaisance, (HMSO, Edinburgh, 1971), pp.149-61.
3. A. Flanders, 'What are Trade Unions For?' in W. McCarthy, (ed.) Trade Unions, Penguin Modern Management Readings, (Penguin Books, Harmondsworth, 1972). p.17.
4. Quoted in N. Robertson and K.I. Sams (eds), British Trade Unionism, (Blackwell, Oxford, 1972), vol. 1, p.42.
5. See D. Bell, The Coming of Post-Industrial Society, (Penguin Books, Harmondsworth, 1976).
6. Royal Commission on Trade Unions and Employers' Associations 1965-68, (Donovan Commission Report), Cmnd. 3623, (HMSO, London, 1968).
7. A. Jones, The New Inflation, (Penguin Books, Harmondsworth, 1973), p.62.
8. Ibid., p.51.
9. Ibid., p.63.
10. Ibid., p.62.
11. B.W. Tuchman, The March of Folly, (Sphere Books, London, 1985), p.3.
12. S.H. Beer, Britain Against Itself, (Faber & Faber, London, 1982), p.152.
13. This discussion of the relations between the trade unions and the Labour party in the early 1970s, leading to the agreement on the Social Contract, is based upon the excellent account in I. Clark et al., Trade Unions, National Politics and Economic Management, A Comparative Study of the TUC and the DGB. (Anglo-German Foundation for the Study of Industrial Society, London, 1980).
14. See J.H. Goldthorpe et al., The Affluent Worker Series, 1968-69, (Cambridge UP, Cambridge, 1968, 1969).
15. Royal Commission on Trade Unions and Employers' Associations, p.33.
16. Ibid. Ch. III.
17. J.H. Goldthorpe, Social Mobility and Class Structure in Modern Britain, (Clarendon Press, Oxford, 1980).

18. Ibid., p.271.
19. P. Bassett, 'End of the Decent Brotherhood',
    New Statesman, 28 February 1986, pp.10-12.

11.   THE WRONG RIGHT IN FRANCE

Michalina Vaughan

The subject is an elusive one.   The extreme Right,
the extra-parliamentary Right, the right-wing opposition - or the extreme extra-parliamentary right-
wing opposition?   Either reading could be justified
in the light of contemporary evidence.   It can be
argued   that   three overlapping,   but   analytically
distinct,   categories exist and that the   relationships obtaining between them require investigation,
if only to ascertain whether they are necessary or
contingent.   When the whole of the Right is   in
opposition,   neither   political extremism   nor   the
lack/rejection of parliamentary representation need
reflect   discrepant   value   systems   rather   than
diverging   tactics.   If opposition is a continuum,
differences   in its midst may be of   degree   rather
than   kind.   Yet,   throughout   the history of   the
Fifth   Republic until the 1981   presidential   election, the extreme Right has been consistently anti-
Gaullist.   Relegated to the political wilderness in
the   aftermath of the Vichy regime,   it gained   new
momentum with the loss of Algeria.   At both stages,
sentences   passed   upon   leaders deprived them   of
civic   rights,   thus driving this   opposition   into
extra-parliamentary channels.   A focus on   the
second   reading would therefore highlight the   continuity of a distinct tradition and would construe
the French Right as split by lasting divisions into
different species.   Either way,   it would be a case
of   discussing les droites rather   than   la droite.
However,   the   approach which   stresses   analytical
distinctions   may lead to a recognition of solidarity   on the right of the political   spectrum   while
the obverse one,   concerned with historical persistence, casts doubts upon its durability or even its
credibility.   The former, without denying the exis-

289

tence of multiple trends, posits that they may coalesce when confronting a common challenge, i.e. when in opposition. The latter emphasises the differentia specifica rather than the single genus: extremism is presented as intrinsically and lastingly divisive. As it singles out groups which are either unintentionally or deliberately outside the scope of parliamentary politics, it raises the issue of connections between extra- and anti-parliamentarianism. Hence it calls for greater specificity in defining parameters.

Perhaps to acknowledge this need for definitional clarification amounts in a way to accepting a right-wing perspective. 'Tout discours de droite commence par des définitions' ('Any right-wing speech begins with definitions').(1) Yet extremism is always an evaluative rather than merely a descriptive term. The issue is not only where, but how demarcation lines should be drawn. Any decision about labelling is necessarily both complex and provisional, since to locate extremist groups on the political spectrum entails assumptions about the stability of their make-up and pursuits. In fact, membership fluctuates, while the political activities in which dissenters engage range from those conventionally held to be legitimate to those which are legitimised by ideological considerations. Not only is there a whole range of gradations in militancy, but the continuum is not static, since over time groups dissolve and reform, drawing on a common pool of members and a common fund of ideas. Hence a pattern of intense in-fighting and correlatively short life-expectancy. Consequently most groups remain confined to political marginality. Only a few achieve spells of notoriety by gaining media recognition. Even fewer make a sufficient impact on public opinion to become parties with a stable following on a nation-wide basis. Though their platform is anti-parliamentarian, they are no longer bound to remain extra-parliamentarian.

Whether such incorporation into the mainstream of public life can actually induce a shift towards a more 'responsible', i.e. less extreme, stance, is a moot point. It would be reassuring in terms of systemic stability if a measure of success achieved through officially endorsed channels brought about correlative concessions to the established value system. As a matter of fact, history, particularly that of Western Europe in the inter-war period,

does not encourage optimism in this respect. It
has shown that employing the means made available
in a democracy for gaining power does not necessarily entail any commitment to a congruent set of
values. Extremism need neither remain located on
the fringes of politics nor limit its appeal to
small minorities. The temptation to assume that it
thrives away from the limelight, but shrivels in
the anterooms of notoriety and vanishes in the
corridors of power should be strenuously resisted.
Indeed, it is founded upon the erroneous hypothesis
that a high degree of congruence must exist between
the ends sought and the methods used for their
implementation. Such a view does not allow for
deliberate deceit, justified on Machiavellian
grounds, or for the self-deception involved in
considering exclusively the immediate targets,
regardless of long-term objectives. Whether by
erecting expediency into a value or merely by
relying on it as a prop, a complementarity can be
engineered between intrinsically incompatible ends
and means. Extremism thus appears to be a function
of the readiness to adopt a wide variety of
methods, ranging from the most unorthodox to the
highly conventional, in order to promote a particular ideology. It is distinguished by the determination to fall back on any means whatsoever for
the furtherance of specific ends rather than by the
intrinsic features of these aims. In other words,
it is a function of ruthlessness in advocating and,
if need be, using tough methods of action - and
this in turn is related to steadfastness in endorsing a belief system rather than to the actual
beliefs held.
   Nevertheless one specific conviction, compatible with diverse political ideologies, fosters
extremism: it is the lack of trust in constitutional channels and particularly in elected representatives. Direct action becomes justified by the
perceived unavailability of alternatives for effec-
ting change. This stance, represented both on the
far left and the far right of the political
spectrum, challenges equally the myths on which
consensus rests in Western democracies and the
ground rules which structure the functioning of
their institutions. To cast doubt about the extent
to which political pluralism actually reflects
societal forces, i.e. about the representativeness
of parliamentary assemblies and the effectiveness
of formal democracy, is to opt out of the system.

Thus the relationship between extremism and anti-parliamentarianism seems to be unambiguous. In fact, it is rooted in culturally specific assumptions which render comparisons between different countries highly misleading. Since equating parliamentary institutions with democratic rule is central to the Anglo-American tradition, it seems tempting to generalise from this precedent, despite the fact that it has never become wholly assimilated in the Catholic countries of continental Europe. Originating in England, reinterpreted in the United States and later adopted in the 'old' dominions, the legacy of the Westminster Parliament (not necessarily linked with any allegiance to the Crown) may have proved eminently versatile in the overseas territories settled or at least dominated by emigrants from the British Isles. It has not been easy to transplant to other lands, since cultural remoteness counteracted geographical proximity. France is a case in point.

Although the English pattern of parliamentary democracy was periodically upheld as a remedy for institutional instability or even as a panacea, this remained a party slogan rather than a widely accepted or even a fully understood formula. In the nineteenth century this ideal became clearly identified with the vested socio-economic interests, whose spokesmen dominated the political scene during the July Monarchy, influenced the evolution of the Second Empire towards liberalism and - somewhat half-heartedly - helped establish the Third Republic. Reliance on parliamentarianism à l'anglaise, allied to economic liberalism and to social conservatism, became the platform of a somewhat loose but lasting formation described by René Rémond in his classical study as orléanist.(2) Both the persistence - under various labels - of this trend within the French Right and its shifting position in relation to the centre of the political spectrum contributed to the stability of republican institutions until the Second World War. But they also helped to strengthen the link between parliamentarian politics and the structure of privilege. Not only was this a lasting feature of the system, it was a bitterly and frequently denounced one. Such attacks on the socio-economic bias of the regime were an integral part of right-wing oppositional strategies and their extremist overtones, unmistakably present in the discourse of Action Française, acquired additional shrillness in the

1930s.

A paradox rooted in the history of the French Right is that it contributed to the establishment of parliamentary rule, yet that it contained persistent strains of anti parliamentarianism, expressed mainly, though not exclusively, outside the elected assemblies. They derived either from a nostalgia for legitimacy based on heredity or from a trust in strong leadership incarnating national sovereignty and hallowed by popular assent through plebiscite. Both these legacies - the legitimist and the bonapartist - claimed to embody patriotism, dissociating the nation from the regime, rejecting universalism and asserting ethnicity. Thus they borrowed some concepts which had been central to the philosophical armoury of the Revolution - in particular, national sovereignty. 'Nation est, en matière politique, un mot voyageur' ('In politics, nation is a term which travels far').(3) When it became part, after 1870, of the ideology of right-wing opposition, it acquired counter-revolutionary overtones but retained its potential for mass mobilisation and for the justification of direct action. The accretion of Jacobin, populist and nationalist elements - either mediated through bonapartism or aided by revulsion against the excesses of bourgeois liberalism - imparted a new radicalism to the right from the 1880s onwards. It is on these grounds that Sternhell describes it as 'pré-fascist',(4) stressing its acceptance of violence against liberal democracy and bourgeois capitalism. While arguing that this droite contestataire, though at times openly tempted to extremes, retained a conservative bias, even throughout the militancy of the Ligues in the 1930s, Rémond assents to its fascisant bias. Yet to him what is significant is that the extremism remained largely symbolic. 'Le mélange de contes-tation et de conservation ne se fait pas à parties égales', ('The mixture of protest and conservatism is not made up of equal parts').(5) Hence a fiasco; 'plus de bruit que de mal, plus d'air que de suffrages', (More noise than harm, more hot air than votes').(6) Of course, nothing fails like failure - yet it remains questionable whether a lower dose of conservatism in the ideological mix would have significantly affected the outcome of confrontations and whether it would have definitely made it possible to consider this extremist Right as fascist. Be that as it may, the connection between extremism and anti-parliamentarianism is long-standing and clearly established, even if its exponents did not always merit and seldom claimed the label of fascist (any more than that of bonapartist). One feature which this radical Right certainly shared with fascism - though it was not a necessary component of bonapartism - was the basic hostility to liberal principles both in the political and the economic spheres. It was on those very principles that the republican regime rested: hence the contrast between the disaffection and dissent of some droites and the accommodation of others.

Understandable in the light of past history, this divide no longer seemed to matter, when the Right as a whole was perceived as compromised by collaborationism and implicated in the collapse of the Vichy regime. The only alternative to a complete withdrawal from the political scene was the adoption of protective covering. This could only consist in stressing the 'midde of the road', centrist or, in Rémond's terminology, orléanist stance. In point of fact, it was not a freely available choice, to the extent that enforced or outwardly voluntary exile and the loss of civic rights by court decree made inroads in the potential leadership. Whether literally emigrating or remaining alienated, but insignificant, as émigrés de l'intérieur, a whole generation of prominent right-wingers was eliminated from the arena. For those who remained, the process of regaining ground, i.e. credibility and votes, lasted over a decade, by which time they were actually commanding majorities in Parliament and acknowledging their true allegiance. In fact, the whole history of the Fourth Republic was that of the Right's recovery, aided by the resurgence of nationalism which decolonisation prompted. The stigma of collaboration was lifted as the defence of empire became essential to the glissement à droite, to the growing appeal and enhanced impact of the Right. When the balance of power shifted on the national scene, the corresponding evolution within the Right was a displacement towards extremism, fuelled by resentment about the loss of Algeria. Coming out of the post-war political wilderness was almost immediately followed by the spontaneous emergence and the legal sanctioning of wildness among the supporters of the Right - the rebirth of extremism.

The refusal of decolonisation - which ushered in the collapse of the Fourth Republic - was a

watershed in the alienation of the extreme Right as
well as in the establishment of a right-wing ruling
majority. Perhaps its impact can only be compared
to that of Revolution, with the pieds noirs, forced
out of Algeria, and the colonels (not all of whom
were forced out of the army) becoming the counterparts of the ultras on their return from emigra-
tion. Equally estranged from French society as
those predecessors and equally unprepared to
compromise with the new power structure, they were
much better equipped to engage in insurrectionary
tactics, due to their military training. After the
collapse of OAS (Organisation de l'Armée Secrète),
which perpetuated the Algerian war in mainland
France into the 1960s, a new proliferation of
extremist right-wing groups began. It was initiated by former army cadres toughened and politicised in Indochina and Algeria, and by hard-core
Catholics, whose total rejection of modernity
toughened and politicised them. The intellectual
stimulation was supplied by former supporters of
Action Française; thus a repudiation of modern
values was blended with an espousal of modern techniques. Nationalism, anti-parliamentarianism and
anti-materialism: these slogans of the droite
contestataire re-emerged, along with an equal
readiness to engage in strong-arm tactics. Ultra-
cisme was thus reborn from its own ashes, with
Ordre Nouveau and Occident as its main exponents.
Once again their supporters' brand of violent
protest (e.g. the anti-immigrant riots initiated by
ON in the summer of 1973) turned them into outlaws.
As the Right was becoming established over a long
period in its new role of quasi-immovable majority,
the right-wing extremists were reduced to a choice
between illegality and insignificance.

The Return of de Gaulle

The two processes, though apparently contradictory,
were in fact inextricably related. The regaining
of electoral appeal could only be achieved by
reclaiming the middle ground, by identifying with
traditional values of moderation and common sense,
by negating the relevance of the Right/Left dichotomy. The personality and career of Monsieur Pinay
illustrated the success of this strategy. The less
contrived it appeared, the more successful it
became. But its limitations were obvious. Its
impact was greatest where its message was most

drastically watered down. Whether such dilutions were deliberately deceitful, i.e. devised to achieve power by recovering respectability, or whether they reflected a genuine change of ideology remained an open issue. The true believers - those who were determined to remain faithful to some version of the origin of philosophy - were least prepared to give the benefit of the doubt to the most credible upholders of centrism. They were bound to distrust Pinay - precisely to the extent that he appeared trustworthy to the proverbial man in the street. By the same token, de Gaulle seemed eminently credible: his family background connected him with the legitimist Right, his own past included a spell of commitment to Action Française, his former political record under the Fourth Republic witnessed to a temperamental unwillingness to compromise. Consequently the traditional Right had grounds for trusting him, though his harsh treatment of Pétain in particular, and of collaborationists in general, gained him some lasting enemies. Still, he belonged to the inbred, self-contained universe of the career army and he could rely on its cohesiveness to enlist support for a policy which he left undefined. In the famous speech in which de Gaulle affirmed that he understood the mood of his listeners while he addressed the members of officers' messes, he was certainly believed - and also misunderstood. The extent to which he actually meant to mislead is by now irrelevant, except to biographers. The ease with which he did shows that the solidarity derived from a similar background and a common training proved extremely (excessively?) effective.

The return of de Gaulle to power and the advent of the Fifth Republic were thus aided, if not actually caused, by a number of assumptions which enabled the Right to shed - or, more accurately, to shelve - its Pétainist hangover. These were soon revealed as false under the new regime. Consequently the rallying of the Right in its entirety proved short-lived. The supporters of Algérie Française underwent a traumatic experience which they were unwilling or unable to transcend. Hence they claimed the legitimacy of rebellion (le droit d'insurrection). Though Rémond ascribes this trend to the bonapartist/boulangist tradition, it was clearly related to the philosophy of Action Française. Whichever way its progeny is defined, its repudiation of the political establishment

conformed to a pattern set under the Third Republic. The multiple strains coexisting within the
right (les droites), after having coalesced over a
short period of time, reverted to being not only
distinct, but actually antagonistic. The condemnation of the ruling moderates by the alienated
extremists reproduced the stance of Action
Française, with a similar emphasis on traditional
religious and social values and a comparable rejection of both capitalism and socialism. Yet the
opposition was more extreme precisely to the extent
that the ruling faction was less moderate. The
incestuousness of the initial relationship contributed to the bitterness of the feud once de
Gaulle's Algerian policy was revealed. Had initial
expectations been lower, the sense of betrayal
would not have been equally sharp and the ultimate
hostility would not have been the same. Conceivably the misunderstanding might have been avoided,
had there been either greater integrity or keener
judgement on either side. Instead a pattern of
mutual bad faith was set which had a lasting impact
on the composition of the Gaullist majority and on
the presentation of Gaullism as a rallying point
from which only extremists - of the right as well
as of the left - were excluded.

In the 1950s, the extreme Right moved from the
conventional authoritarian nationalism of nostalgic
Pétainists to a more sophisticated version of neo-
fascism, which emphasised the need to protect
Western European civilisation against the twin
threats of Marxism and liberalism. The lesson of
the colonial wars was that Russian communism and
American capitalism were objective allies in
furthering the dismantlement of empires and in
imposing a new balance of power on a worldwide
basis. By becoming an accessory to this enterprise, de Gaulle was a traitor not only to his
country, but to Europe, and the use of violence
against him was thus legitimate. The same argument
applied to the political class of the Fifth
Republic against whom the use of guerrilla tactics
was justified, since it betrayed those very values
with which the Right claimed to be most concerned.

In February 1963, in the Petit Clamart trial
following an attempt on de Gaulle's life, the
accused, Alain Bougrenet de la Tocnaye, expressed
the ultra stance in every particular. He invoked
the right to insurrection against unworthy rulers,
rejected both capitalism and Marxism as materialist

297

ideologies which had already failed, and literally
called for a plague on both their houses. He was
equally scathing about the short-sightedness of the
privileged bourgeoisie droitière and about the
apathy of the masses (le peuple anesthésié).(7)
The repudiation of the ruling right by the
extremist right was most concisely and forcible
expressed by another self-appointed executioner,
Jean-Marie Bastien-Thiry: 'Nous n'appartenons pas à
cette droite qui est non seulement la plus bête,
mais la plus lâche du monde et qui a fait faillite'
('We don't belong to this right which is not only
the most stupid, but the most cowardly in the
world, and which is bankrupt').(8) The main themes
of the Nouvelle Droite - condemnation of the traditional Right for lack of brains and lack of guts,
denunciation of its total failure - are already
expressed. Yet there is an overwhelmingly important difference: the commitment to Christian
values, the justification of the Right to rebel by
reference to Aquinas, and the denunciation of
social injustice contrast sharply with the subsequent assertion of paganism and of ethics founded
on ruthlessness. From neo-Pétainism to neo-
fascism, the transition was negotiated in the
1960s, but was only perceived by public opinion at
the end of the 1970s.

The Nouvelle Droite

The way this evolution occurred can be illustrated
by the history of Jeune Nation, an extremist group
founded in November 1954, by the activist Pierre
Sidos. Suspected of responsibility for a bomb
outrage in the National Assembly in February 1958,
it was dissolved by decree in May of that year.
Some of its members pursued their activities in a
half-clandestine way under the OAS umbrella.(9)
Even before it had gone underground, the movement
had been taken over by a new leadership in 1956,
when a team headed by Dominique Venner brought
about an update in its ideology. The same group
re-emerged in January 1966 as a legal party, the
Mouvement Nationaliste du Progrès, which explicitly
repudiated the Christian tradition of the
Right.(10) The shift towards a more modern image
was accompanied by an attempt to 'come out of the
cold' and actually to compete for votes. The MNP
set out a Rassemblement Européen de la Liberté, in
order to present candidates to the legislative

elections of Spring 1967, in which it did not gain
a single seat. The shift out of clandestinity into
legitimate political activity seemed to be a
complete failure.
   However, the lesson was not wasted. While
some groupuscules remained committed to strong-arm
tactics and gravitated to the fringe of the underworld, the intellectual elite of the extreme Right
moved up-market. As the prospect of success
through orthodox political channels seemed to
remain remote, an alternative strategy of 'intellectual rearmament' was devised in easy stages
throughout the 1960s. Though its institutionalisation through the setting up of the GRECE (Groupe-
ment de recherches et d'études pour la civilisation
européenne) dated back to 1968/9, (11) another ten
years elapsed before the new Right was actually
discovered by the press. Revealed as worthy of
notice in the heyday of the mode rétro, it owed its
sudden notoriety to the media, but its spokesmen
denounced an alleged conspiracy of silence which
delayed this disclosure deliberately. Even if
there was some media resistance to the message of
the Nouvelle Droite, it certainly gave way to a
blaze of publicity when the time seemed opportune.
In the 1970s there was a much greater receptiveness
of the general public to right-wing views. This
was in part a backlash after the troubles of 1968,
in part because - after de Gaulle's withdrawal from
active politics - Gaullism was no longer perceived
as a rallying point, but shifted further towards
the centre and beyond. Furthermore, the extent to
which officialdom endorsed anti-egalitarian and
anti-universalist themes paved the way for a
greater acceptability of the ND's discourse. At
the same time as this was made to appear less
extreme by the evolution of the ruling majority,
its content gained in persuasiveness by a greater
emphasis on scientificity and the replacement of
crude nationalism by European culturalism.(12) In
keeping with this new-found detachment, the advocacy of subtle methods, such as indoctrination and
infiltration, and the repudiation of strong-arm
tactics confirmed the new-found respectable, almost
academic image of the Nouvelle Droite. The transition from messy politics to metapolitics had been
successfully, if slowly, negotiated.
   For all that, the new Right was not novel and
the continuity of its personnel, as well as of its
main leitmotivs (in substance, though not neces-

sarily in form) with those of the extreme Right in
the 1950s, is fully documented.(13) From the
outset, the sense of belonging to an elite had been
a central feature of revolutionary nationalism.
Increasingly, the awareness that guerrilla tactics
could not prevail within French society was visited
upon right-wing extremists as de Gaulle's Republic
became more firmly established. As an alternative,
the attempt to gain a foothold in Parliament did
not pay off either. The deliberate embracement of
extra-parliamentary opposition was a means of
claiming cultural leadership without being put to
the test of seeking popular support (whose validity
as a source of legitimacy was systematically
challenged anyway). Meanwhile the condemnation of
strong-arm tactics as ineffectual and vulgar
removed the stigma of being involved with - let
alone of encouraging - unlawful behaviour. It made
the ideological contamination of decision-making
circles that much easier while the Right was in
power, and helped the ND's dissociation from its
fate after the 1981 elections sound credible. As a
société de pensée, irreducible to a political formation, the GRECE simply could not fail - whereas
the bodies which had predated it had shown that
they could not succeed.

Learning from its own mistakes, blurring its
antecedents, borrowing freely from its arch-
enemies' arsenal (e.g. by drawing upon Gramsci's
works), the extremist Right managed to acquire a
new image. It proved at once challenging - as a
harbinger of global changes, and reassuring - as a
break-away from the crude activism with which neo-
fascism used to be associated. The political
conjuncture was favourable and its interpretation
was skilful: as a result, the new Right achieved
its immediate targets. It was in the news, it was
taken seriously, it was having an intellectual and
hence - according to its own terminology - a meta-
political impact. The issue is not really whether
its message was either original or accurate. To
the extent that it stressed the Christian/human-
ist/Marxist symbiosis, it was clearly reminiscent
of the fascist and national-socialist discourse
about Judaeo-Christian values. That the analysis
was derivative from such sources invites a verdict
of guilt by association. However, the credibility
attaching to it was not necessarily undermined by
its origins, especially as they were not readily
admitted.

By definition and through choice, the audience
of the new Right was a small though influential
one. However, the inter-personal connections
established through the Club de l'Horloge between
Giscardians and the ND (though apparently fluctuat
ing and, after 1980, on the wane) ceased to be of
paramount importance when the ruling majority
changed. No longer were the glossy publications of
the new Right (Eléments, Nouvelle Ecole, Etudes
et Recherches) a major, if almost always unacknow-
ledged, background of governmental rhetoric.
Admittedly they were able to claim that the defeat
of the former's majority in 1981 and the victory of
the Left confirmed the validity of their own
political diagnoses. The shift of votes was
allegedly made possible by the cultural power of
the Left over the educational system and the media,
as well as by the powerlessness of the moderate
Right - unable to struggle against the ascendancy
of an egalitarian ideology in which its own members
are enmeshed. Though the fall of the moderate
Right from power was thus dismissed as a predictable fluctuation, it had important implications for
the ND. As of 1981, its 'culturalist', extra-
parliamentary stance ceased to be fashionable,
because it was no longer an illustration of successful entryism, but merely a somewhat petulant
condemnation of all French political parties. Yet
the task of making a number of extremist themes
appear vindicated by the findings of modern science
- what might be described as the laundering of neo-
fascism - had already been performed smoothly and
effectively by then. In addition, a number of
activists with a past had acquired a new image as
controversial, but noteworthy, intellectuals. An
analogy may be drawn with Action Française, its
blatant indifference to (or rather contempt for)
organised politics and its demands for intellectual
reform as a pre-requisite for global social change.
For all the differences between the two ideologies,
particularly in respect of established religion
(since the anti-Christian bias of the ND contrasts
with the instrumental view Maurras took of the
Catholic Church), they may be alleged to have
served a similar purpose. Although the consequence
was largely unintended, Action Française helped
create a climate of opinion in which the Ligues
were acceptable in the 1930s and the Nouvelle
Droite rendered the same service to the fringe
parties of the extreme Right in search of popular

support half a century later.

The Front National

As the new Right waned, the extremist right-wing
opposition adopted a more conventional stance,
pursuing electoral strategies, which in the case of
Le Pen's Front National proved strikingly successful in the mid-1980s. The appeal of its propaganda
was enhanced by the veneer of sophistication
derived to a great extent from the literature of
the ND: similar themes treated in more direct,
populist, style. However, it was mainly due to
deep-seated emotions, aroused by a sense of threat
and insecurity which had grown since the late
1970s. The setting up of Légitime Défense in 1978,
of Sécurité et Liberté in 1979 and the bulldozing
of an immigrants' home at Vitry, in the communist-
dominated suburban belt, in 1980, were all symptomatic of a moral panic accompanied by growing
xenophobia. In a period of recession and rising
unemployment, such negative attitudes were necessarily exacerbated, as the contribution of an
imported labour force to prosperity could no longer
be stressed by politicians, planners or employers.
The presence of minority groups whose members are
highly visible and culturally resistant to assimil-
ation, such as North Africans, elicits racism and
chauvinism as predictable responses, especially
among an ageing population. In areas of high immigrant concentration, which are also those where
housing and employment problems are most acute,
these are spontaneous reactions to perceived
dangers both for individuals and for the community.
At the individual level, there is the fear generated by petty crime and the resentment of keener
competition for scarce resources. Within the
community, there is the antagonism caused by the
existence of ghettos in its midst and by the
spreading of rumours about demands on the resources
of the Welfare State. Such responses to the threat
of social change within a decaying economic and
physical environment are understandable. They are
also eminently exploitable by the Right in opposition and, due to the adversarial style of French
politics, they have been persistently exploited
since 1981. The typical claim is that the
interests of the indigenous population are not
being served by a Socialist government and that,
for ideological reasons, there is insufficient

concern for law and order on the part of the
authorities. It is rooted in the contention that
both patriotism and the ability to rule belong on
one side of the political spectrum: hence that the
country is endangered when the Left is in power.
The common denominator of the Right is therefore to capitalise on the fears of the electorate
and, in so doing, to stimulate them. 'Aujourd'hui
est de droite un homme dont le réflexe est de se
sentir menacé par les autres, c'est a dire par les
immigrés, par les femmes, par les enfants et
généralement par tout ce qui lui est étranger'
'(Today the man on the right is the one whose
reflex it is to feel threatened by others, by
immigrants, by women, by children, and generally by
all that is alien to him').(14) To increase such
latent fears, to prove them legitimate and to focus
them more specifically on designated targets (e.g.
young Muslim males) has been the strategy of the
Right in opposition. This has in fact linked up
with propaganda used whilst it was still in power,
particularly after the implementation of more
restrictive laws on immigration.(15) Appeals to
the 'natural instincts' of the common man for self-
preservation and for the protection of his territory ceased to be perceived as extremist. The
Nouvelle Droite, by clothing widespread prejudices
in unemotional language and endowing them with the
prestige of scientific corroboration, had prepared
the ground. Themes which it brought back into
intellectual arguments served the purposes of
parliamentary politics. To the extent that they
were shared by the parties which had formed the
ruling majority until 1981, and by those which had
developed in opposition to the Fifth Republic, in
direct descent from extremist groupuscules, the
divide between these became blurred. The trivial-
isation of gladiatorial and racist discourse by the
ND and its qualified adoption by the Right as a
whole thus contributed to bringing the Front
National into the mainstream of politics. After
1981 there was overlap between the political platforms of all the opposition parties, with a greater
readiness on the extreme right to play the populist
game for all it is worth. In the person of Le Pen,
it found a performer of considerable skill and real
charisma. The fact that his message is devoid of
any originality confirms its apparent grounding in
common sense and contradicts any accusations of
extremism.

The Nietzschean ring in condemning all ideologies which pander to the weak is unmistakable in the writings of the new Right, whether they condemn Christianity as 'the bolshevism of Antiquity'(16) or deny that any society based on welfare could ever produce happiness.(17) The style is much less complex, but the morality is the same when Le Pen attacks policies of reverse discrimination as antisocial:(18)

> En privilégiant, en favorisant par trop tous les faibles dans tous les domaines, on affaiblit le corps social en général. On fait exactement l'inverse de ce que font les éleveurs de chiens et de chevaux. Je ne suis pas hostile à ce qu'on soulage les malheurs, par exemple les handicapes, mais on aboutit maintenant presque a une promotion de l'handicapé. (By granting privileges to the weak, by favouring them excessively in all respects, one weakens the social body as a whole. One does the very opposite of what dog and horse breeders do. I am not against relief for misfortune, e.g. for the handicapped, but nowadays one arrives almost at promotion for the handicapped.)

The reference to breeding is symptomatic of the extent to which rather loose concepts of natural selection have been incorporated into the conventional wisdom. In a number of guises, ranging from ethology to sociobiology, neo-Darwinism has certainly been popularised through the media, prompted mainly by the Nouvelle Droite. Its main exponents have kept the debate going, harnessing selected scientific findings to support their own (pessimistic) view of human nature and of the social world. Yet they have persistently denied that they endorsed any form of biological determinism, (19) since this would contradict their overriding concern for the originality of culture and their belief in the creativeness of exceptional individuals.(20) Even if one accepts these disclaimers, the fact remains that the ND advocates genetic engineering as a means for mankind to transcend the dichotomy of nature and culture by fitting innate endowment to cultural aspirations. Whether the new Right stands convicted of biologism or not hardly matters in comparison with the much more serious

indictment of having buttressed the view that
science supports the enforcement of a particular
moral code. By the time such tenets are reinterpreted into popular language, as they have been by
the Front National, they amount to an unqualified
support for the standards of animal breeders in
human societies. The finer points about culture
are blurred away or, rather, more or less explicitly reinterpreted in terms of an unbridgeable gap
between groups endowed with different physical
attributes, i.e. in terms of race. The analogy of
'dogs and horses' not only suggests that defective
specimens - such as the handicapped - ought not to
have been bred and that compassion for them should
be kept within strict limits, exclusive of any
'promotion'. It also hints at the need to keep
thoroughbreds uncontaminated by miscegenation. The
argument whereby science and common sense coincide
in vindicating racist attitudes contributed power-
fully to the conversion of policies formerly held
by public opinion to be extremist into merely
rightist ones. Since the ND was influential in
furthering this process, it contributed to the
electoral successes of Le Pen and his party since
1983. Despite its aloofness from mundane politics,
it did actually supply the NF with an enhanced
credibility - a kind of respectability by association.
    Undoubtedly the main thrust of Le Pen's rheto-
ric is directed against the dilution of French
identity through immigration: 'une invasion qui se
fait par osmose, par perfusion permanente' ('an
invasion carried out by osmosis, by permanent blood
transfusion').(21) For all the connotations of
this threat to the 'blood', i.e. to racial purity,
Le Pen denies that this is a racist statement.
According to him, it was divinely ordained that a
plurality of peoples, with their own physical and
cultural attributes, should coexist. Therefore
their distinctiveness must be preserved. It is a
positive duty to defend the cultural patrimony
threatened by alien accretions. While this traditional concern of the Right was related by the
Nouvelle Droite to universal interests ('... c'est
la pluralité de l'humanité qui fait sa richesse')
('it is the plural nature of mankind which represents its wealth'),(22) it is once again expressed
in terms of specific rights by the Front National.
The right to protect one's land and one's home, the
right to remain within one's family, the right to

associate with friends rather than strangers, the
right to choose one's guests and to stop them
moving in for good - all these analogies have an
obvious demagogic appeal. However, they are more
than mere rhetorical devices, since they illustrate
the adoption of concentric circles, so that the
acceptance of relatives, friends and neighbours,
i.e. European, Western, Christian peoples, is
accompanied by the rejection of 'unwelcome'
strangers, alien by blood and culture, i.e. immigrants from overseas. In an interview on television (Antenne Deux, 13 February 1984), Le Pen
explained his views on proximity and trust in these
terms:(23)

> J'aime mieux mes filles que mes cousines,
> mes cousines que mes voisines, mes voisines
> que les inconnus, et les inconnus que des
> ennemis.' (I like my daughters better than my
> cousins, my cousins better than my neigh-
> bours, my neighbours better than strangers
> and strangers than enemies.)

Leaving aside the emotive connotations of the
female gender used for those who are nearest and
dearest (the 'daughters' who must be protected) and
the male for those who may or actually threaten
them ('inconnus' and 'ennemis'), and the underlying
hint at fears of miscegenation, the message is
unambiguous. Without any reference to sociobiology, a threat to territorial integrity and to
the preservation of a gene-pool is being denounced.
Thus biological considerations are never very far
from the core of the NF's propaganda, but they
remain linked to assertions of cultural superior-
ity. For instance, the legacy of colonialism - so
important to the rebirth of the extremist Right in
the 1950s - is again proudly claimed. According to
Le Pen, 'le solde est globalement positif' ('the
balance sheet is positive over all').(24) As a
colonial power, France brought both material and
non-material benefits, roads, irrigation, the use
of mineral resources and new crops (e.g. vineyards
to Algeria), as well as literacy, improved health
and enhanced morality. Whether these innovations
were welcome to the indigenous populations (the
original inhabitants of those particular houses) is
not questioned. All cultures may have been originally equal, but some have become more equal than
others.

By contrast with such acknowledgement of the
benefits dispensed to former colonies, there is
sharp condemnation of the harm done to the metropo-
lis by the immigrants from those areas. Admittedly
it is a 'peaceful invasion', but in the long run it
will have the same effect as the hordes of the past
which fought only when denied 'bread, wine and
women'.(25) Analogies from the natural world are
borrowed freely to emphasise the perniciousness of
this process.(26)

> Il existe une araignée qui pond ses oeufs
> dans le corps de sa proie insensibilisée;
> c'est la situation actuelle de notre pays:
> non seulement nous sommes l'objet d'une
> véritable invasion, mais nous l'encourag-
> eons. (There is a spider which lays its
> eggs in the body of its desensitised prey;
> this is the current situation of our
> country: not only are we subjected to a real
> invasion, but we encourage it.)

Committed to the emotionalism of insect imagery and
uninhibited by mixed metaphors, Le Pen goes on to
liken the destructiveness of immigrants to (27)

> la marabunta ... la marche des colonnes de
> fourmis géantes dans la forêt vierge qui
> balaient tout ce qu'elles trouvent. (the
> marabunta ... the march of columns of giant
> ants in the virgin forest which sweep away
> anything they find.)

To remedy the harm done to employment, social
security, law and order, housing, education and,
above all, to French identity, twenty-six specific
provisions restricting the rights of foreign labour
and of their children in relation to all social
benefits, to residence permits and to naturalisa-
tion are put forward as a FN programme. There
would also be financial penalties for their
employers, to implement the principle of 'national
preference', systematically favouring the indigenous population, defined by descent rather than just
by birth in France.

It is worth noting how these differ from the
proposals of the main right-wing parties. About
the social rights of foreign workers, the UDF has
been reticent, while the RPR expressed the intention to restrict additional family allowances,

particularly the 'third child premium', to French
nationals. Chirac has also expressed the view that
unemployed foreigners should be expelled. Both the
UDF and the RPR favour tighter controls on requests
for asylum and the expelling of illegal immigrants,
as well as delinquent aliens, by administrative
decision. In addition, the RPR favours the random
identity checks on the streets, abolished by the
Socialists in power. However, neither party
challenges the automatic renewal of 10-year residence permits, to whose existence the FN objects.
On nationality, the Right as a whole opposes its
unconditional acquisition by all children of immigrant workers, whether at birth or at 18 years of
age for those born in France. But Le Pen goes
further in asking for recent naturalisations to be
reviewed and, in some cases, rescinded. Indeed, he
has argued that his twenty-six points are not
exhaustive and that tougher policies might be put
forward.(28) Clearly an escalation occurs: the
Right, and the RPR in particular, adopting a more
restrictive stance towards the minorities, in
order not to be overtaken by the Front on an electorally sensitive issue, while Le Pen's rhetoric
becomes more inflammatory, if only to retain his
audience.

This process gained momentum, as the scores of
the Front National in the Euro-elections of 1984,
(29) and in a number of municipal/local elections
since, have shown that it can command sufficient
support from voters to become a parliamentary
opposition. Though its candidates have been kept
out in the past by the electoral system (two-
rounds, first past the post), introduced by de
Gaulle to discourage party proliferation, they are
unlikely to be aided by a form of proportional
representation which favours the large political
formations. Therefore the FN would need to rely on
pacts with right-wing parties, whereas the RPR and
the UDF are committed, by their agreement of 10
April 1985 (Accord pour gouverner) 'to govern
together and only together'.(30) To Le Pen, this
stance provided confirmation of his theory whereby
the parliamentary Right in opposition remains - as
it was in power - afflicted by 'creeping social
democracy'. His main theme - denunciation of la
bande à quatre (the group of four) - harps on the
complicity between the mainstream parties of the
left and of the right. The Gaullists and the
Giscardians are implicated - just as the Socialists

and the Communists - in the decline of moral
standards, the growth of state powers and the
inflow of immigrants, which are the three main
evils besetting France. It is the last which has
the greatest electoral appeal in a period of widespread xenophobia, when attempts to discredit Le
Pen by recalling his unsavoury past in Algeria have
proved totally fruitless.(31) By contrast, the
first - clearly derived from a commitment to integr-
alist Catholicism (32) - appears to carry least
weight with NF voters. The link between extreme-
right values, such as hierarchy, respect for the
family and condemnation of sexual deviations, on
the one hand, and Christian morality, on the other,
may be recurrently stressed by Le Pen himself. It
no longer appears to matter to his sympathisers,
who - being both younger and more often male than
the electorate of the two main parties of the Right
(33) - are consequently less influenced by
religious beliefs.(34) The attacks on state
encroachments upon individual rights derive from
the Poujadist strand in French politics,(35) but
seem to contradict the demands for tighter policing
and a stronger judiciary. In fact, they amount to a
condemnation of the socio-economic functions under-
taken under the Fourth and Fifth Republics and to
correlative demands for the resumption of traditional controls to restore law and order. The
'more personal, more presidential state',(36)
advocated by Le Pen, would be more repressive - and
the NF has made it clear at which groups the
repression would be aimed. From sanctions against
homosexuals to the curbing of unions and to the
expelling of immigrants, extreme means are advocated.

All these are negative/repressive policies,
with which the Front is clearly identified by
public opinion, but the constructive aspects of its
message are rather more difficult to define. Some
belong to the legacy of Poujade, focusing on tax
reductions and the liberalisation of the economy.
Hence a definite appeal to the self-employed, shopkeepers, tradesmen and managers, as well as to
office workers, all of which groups tend to favour
cuts in welfare benefits and decreased taxation.
However, contrary to the anti-capitalist bias of
the Poujadist rhetoric, Le Pen appears to endorse
the need for big business to sustain the development of advanced technology on which future prosperity rests. Perhaps as a result, it is among

farmers that the FN receives least support.(37) In
all probability, their reluctance is merely due to
a lower exposure to immigrant groups.   Ultimately
the assessment of the <u>Front</u>'s programme, as well as
of its electoral chances, seems to revolve around
the centrality of two main themes: anti-immigration
and pro-security.   The remainder is both presented
and perceived as make-weight.

It is not only socialism that is about priorities. Whether those which Le Pen advances will
prove acceptable to a significant section of the
electorate depends on two main variables: the
pervasiveness of fear and the persistence of his
own charisma. It is conceivable that both attained
a peak at the time of the Euro-elections when
approximately 10 per cent of the electorate voted
for the NF and another 10 per cent described themselves as sympathisers.   Thereafter two counter-
vailing effects set in.   Firstly, the anti-racist
organisation set up campaigns which emphasised the
extremist content of Le Pen's message and thus
incited the main parties of the Right to dissociate
themselves from him.   Secondly, the leader himself
- though he was the main asset of his party -
became a liability by indulging in behaviour likely
to alienate voters.   That a supporter of integrist
Catholicism should be involved in a divorce procedure is bad enough.   That a life-long anti-
Communist should be receiving subsidies from
Eastern Europe for political campaigning (38) might
be described as even more damaging. The penalty of
relying on the personal appeal of a talented,
unorthodox individual to generate support is that
the vagaries of his private behaviour may undermine
the popularity gained by his public performance.
Though personality characteristics and ideological
tenets are both relevant to the success achieved by
the <u>Front National</u>, their respective contributions
are almost impossible to assess, since - in Le
Pen's campaigns - they have become inextricably
intertwined.

The factors which have contributed to this
success may yet turn counterproductive.   Le Pen's
personality has its rogue effects.   Although the
<u>Front National</u> negotiated the transition from
<u>droite musclée</u> (strong-arm right) to opposition
party intent on a parliamentary future, its leader
does not appear to be negotiating the transition
from media personality to statesman.   At the risk
of alienating his middle-class electorate, he has

not relinquished his flamboyant - not to say out-
rageous - behaviour patterns. On occasions, particularly on television interviews, he has watered
down his rhetoric. However, its acceptability to a
sizeable section of the public has been a function
of responses to the economic crisis rather than to
a dilution of the Front's message. The assumption
that such responses would be more extreme under
Socialist rule appears reasonable.   Nevertheless
the key to the NF's promotion to a political force
must be sought in the issue of immigration. Negative reactions to the minorities have been accentu-
ated by the recession and, to a lesser extent, by
the advent of the Left to power. Yet they pre-
existed both phenomena and account for the increasing responsiveness of certain age groups (mainly
the younger from 18-24 years old) as well as some
socio-occupational categories.   As racism becomes
more widespread in society, it paves the way for
the   acceptance of extremist groups by public
opinion and may even result in turning them into
nationally significant parties.   The issue remains
open whether this increment of credibility actually
amounts to an accretion of respectability.   Electorally successful extremism (whether of the right
or of the left) is, by definition, politically
acceptable - but does this make it less morally
obnoxious?

The Wrong Right

In a sense, the problem is more acute on the right
of the political spectrum, since in France the Left
has as from 1789 claimed a privileged ethical
stance.   By corollary, it has been an intrinsic
part of the evolutionary legacy of successive
republics that rightist parties should always be
open to the challenge of being intrinsically
illegitimate. Initially the whole of the Right was
beyond the pale, out of the institutionalised
political game.   Later some sections acquired a
measure of legitimacy by adopting a moderate
stance. The concept of the 'wrong Right' is therefore deep-rooted in French history, but has shifted
over time from embracing a totality to covering
only those who rejected the standards on which
consensus rested. Even abiding by the conventions
of parliamentary democracy under the Third Republic
did not necessarily suffice for such acceptance
into the regular political game. The question was

always asked of parties on the right: 'Vous
acceptez la République, mais acceptez-vous la
Révolution?' (You accept the Republic, but do you
accept the Revolution?').(39) To demarcate itself
from a disaffected minority on its fringe, mainly
characterised by its unyielding commitment to the
Catholic Church, the moderate Right emphasised that
its opposition was not to the system, but to
extremism as such.

This stress on centrism in electoral and
parliamentary strategies meant negating that the
basic right/left dichotomy, crucial to the history
of French politics, retained any contemporary
significance. Alain denounced such attempts to
relegate the fundamental ideological cleavage into
the past as characteristic of a rightist stance,
masquerading as centrist:(40)

> When I am asked whether the cleavage between
> right-wing and left-wing parties, right-wing
> and left-wing men, still has a meaning, the
> first idea that occurs to me is that the man
> who asks the question is certainly not a man
> of the left.

Yet the drift to the right experienced by republican parties has been such that the author of this
diagnosis, Alain, is now held to be a conservative.
To show that labelling alters over time is to
relativise the divide, to opt for the nominalism
advocated by the Nouvelle Droite. It is also,
however, to acknowledge the historical fact that a
number of conflicting traditions (authoritarian
versus liberal, conservative versus revolutionary,
archaic versus modernist) have always coexisted on
the right.(41)

Among them, extremism appears to have been a
matter of temperament on the part of leaders and of
circumstance helping recruit the rank-and-file.
Its main themes have been the condemnation of the
moderate Right, as in the days of Action Française,
and the repudiation of institutionalised political
channels, either through complete withdrawal or
through the adoption of alternative - rougher -
tactics. Until the Second World War, the wrong
Right was clearly demarcated by its methods rather
than its objectives. After the Liberation, the
whole of the right was deemed unacceptable; only
through a persistent denial of true allegiances
could parliamentary ground be regained under the

Fourth Republic. As soon as the moderate Right was in power, a wrong Right was re-emerging, focused on the issue of colonialism (which had actually been a tenet of centrist republican policies). The collapse of the OAS led to a proliferation of groupuscules,(42) all of which rejected legality and most of whose activities centred on the South-East, an area of pieds-noirs settlement of Italianate political style, i.e. of established links between politicians and organised crime. This remains the heart-land of the wrong Right - the main catchment area of the Front National, with ramifications in Lyons and, of course, in Paris.

A recurring pattern within the established Right, whether in power or in parliamentary opposition, is the condemnation of a 'wrong', unacceptable Right, more extreme, generally more violent, but occasionally (the exception rather than the rule) more sophisticated, i.e. more intellectualised and less in tune with popular aspirations. The Nouvelle Droite illustrated the latter, the Front National is exemplifying the former type. The more capable it appears of gaining a foothold in parliamentary politics, the more determined the right-wing opposition becomes to demarcate itself from what it now denounces as an extremist threat. In 1984, RPR opinion was still summarised by a Paris MP who was resigned to coexistence with the FN; ('Il faut vivre avec Le Pen comme on vit avec son mal') ('One must live with Le Pen as one lives with one's affliction').(43) A product of expediency rather than principle, distantiation followed the unexpected upsurge in Le Pen's and his party's credibility in the electoral stakes.(44) The wrong Right has become one which costs votes by voicing explicitly the ideas which the Nouvelle Droite legitimated through the media, which the moderate Right took on board, albeit half-heartedly, while in power, and with which it dared not fully identify in opposition. It is still extra-parliamentarian and certainly rejects the extremist image in an attempt to identify with grass-roots common sense. Benefiting from the backlash which followed the short honeymoon period of the Socialist majority and from the radicalisation of the whole opposition, the Front National has gained credibility, at least in the short run.

Tempting though it might be to speculate about medium-term prospects, there is an acute shortage of hard data from which to extrapolate. Neither

Euro-elections nor local ones are reliable predic-
tors of the voters' behaviour when it comes to the
serious business of choosing deputies and hence the
country's future government. Both may be construed
as trial runs, but they are more akin to a release
of pent-up emotions. To the extent that the
opposition serves expressive ends, they are useful
by letting extremist parties perform a function of
tension management (45) (the relatively harmless
enactment of destructive fantasies, e.g. about
sending all immigrants 'back where they came
from'). They also give warnings to major parties
and, in inducing them to alter their platforms in
order to regain stray voters, they may actually do
lasting harm. In the last instance, the extremists
are more likely to contaminate the moderates than
to win significant shares of power. Their victory
may be a symbolic one, when voters realise that the
main function of the opposition is an instrumental
one - as the source of an alternative government -
and behave accordingly.

Except for the interlude of the Vichy regime,
which only defeat made possible, the wrong Right
has been perennially in opposition and, at best, on
the fringe of legality. Yet its existence has
profoundly affected the evolution of the Right as a
whole, by providing a pull towards reactionary
populism and a correlative push away from the
centre. In its new incarnation, it adopts conventional means for the pursuit of unchanged ends. It
is the persistence of the ends rather than the
modification of the means that gives cause for
concern.

Notes

1. V. Carofiglio and C. Fernandes, 'Les aventures de la droite française et les avatars de Gramsci' in Troisième Colloque International de Lexicologie Politique, (St. Cloud, 1984), pp.39ff.
2. R. Rémond, La Droite en France de 1815 à nos jours, (Aubier, Paris, 1954).
3. C. Nicolet, L'idée républicaine en France (1789-1924), (Gallimard, Paris, 1982), p.16.
4. Z. Sternhell, La Droite révolutionnaire (1855-1914), (Seuil, Paris, 1978).
5. R. Rémond, Les droites en France, (Aubier, Paris, 1982), p.205.
6. Ibid.
7. R. Rémond, La droite en France de la Restauration à la 5ème République, (Aubier, Paris, 1963), pp.369ff.
8. Ibid.
9. F. Duprat, Les mouvements d'extrême droite en France depuis 1944, (Albatros, Paris, 1972), pp.56ff.
10. H. Coston, Dictionnaire de la Politique Française, (Coston, Paris, 1967), pp.566ff.
11. P.A. Taguieff, 'La stratégie culturelle de la Nouvelle Droite en France (1968-1983)' in R. Badinter et al., Vous avez dit Fascismes? (Montalba, Paris, 1984), pp.20ff.
12. R. Rémond, 'La Nouvelle Droite' in P. Bacot and C. Journes, Les nouvelles idéologies, (Presses Universitaires, Lyons, 1982), p.20ff.
13. M. Vaughan, 'Nouvelle Droite: cultural power and political influence' in D.S. Bell (ed.), Contemporary French Political Parties, (Croom Helm, London, 1982), pp.52ff.
14. J.M. Domenach, 'Des Transferts' in J.P. Apparu (ed.), La Droite Aujourd'hui, (A. Michel, Paris, 1979), p.66.
15. R. Dulong and J. Leon, 'L'insécurité est-elle de droite?' in Troisième Colloque, pp.127ff.
16. P. Vial (ed.), Pour une Renaissance Culturelle, (Copernic, Paris, 1979), p.208.
17. Ibid., p.49.
18. J.M. Le Pen, 'Le Front National' in Apparu, La Droite Aujourd'hui, pp.175ff.
19. Vial, Pour une Renaissance Culturelle, p.36.
20. A. de Benoist, Les idées à l'Endroit, (Copernic, Paris, 1977), p.22.
21. J. Marcilly, Le Pen sans bandau, (Grancher, Paris, 1984), p.190.

22. de Benoist, Les Idées à l'Endroit, p.154.
23. J.P. Honoré, 'Définir et Désigner: le Francais, l'Immigré dans le Front National' in Troisième Colloque.
24. Le Pen quoted by Marcilly, Le Pen sans bandeau, p.193.
25. Ibid., p.190.
26. Speech by Le Pen at Front National's study day on immigration, 24 September 1985 in Paris, cited by R. Dole, 'La campagne de M. Le Pen sere axée sur l'immigration', Le Monde, 24 September 1985.
27. Ibid.
28. Le Monde, 13 November 1985.
29. In the second European election, held on 17 June 1984, the NF gained 10.95 per cent of votes cast, gaining 10 seats out of 81, and thus matching the performance of the Communist Party. The score of the joint list presented by the RPR and the UDR (i.e. the Right as distinguished from the extreme Right) was 43.02 per cent. B. Plenel and A. Rollat, L'Effet Le Pen, (Le Monde, Paris, 1984), p.243.
30. Le Monde, 11 April 1985.
31. Le Pen, as an MP, joined the army in Algeria where he served from September 1956 to May 1957, (Plenet and Rollat, L'Effet Le Pen, pp.225ff) and he is alleged to have tortured prisoners (Le Monde 15 February 1985). According to a Harris survey of 21 February 1985, 43 per cent of respondents believed that, if these accusations were justified, they would not disqualify him from holding public office, 40 per cent believed they would and 17 per cent did not know.
32. 'Je crois que Monseigneur Lefèbvre fait un peu ce que je tente de faire en politique' ('I believe that Bishop Lefèbvre is doing a little what I am trying to do in politics'), Le Pen quoted by Marcilly, Le Pen sans bandeau, p.106.
33. Le Monde, 17 October 1985.
34. According to the Harris survey of February 1985, 53 per cent of NF voters favour abortion on demand, as against 40 per cent of RPR and 31 per cent of UDF voters (the average response being 49 per cent).
35. Le Pen was elected as MP in January 1956 on a Poujadist ticket (having had no previous

political activities except in the Law Faculty
Students Union in Paris, of which he became
chairman and where he proved a - literally -
violent anti-marxist).

36. O. Todd, 'Expériences' in Apparu, La Droite
    Aujourd'hui, pp.242ff.
37. Le Monde, 17 October 1985.
38. The Sunday Times, 29 December 1985.
39. Rémond, La Droite en France de la Restauration
    à la 5ème République, p.184.
40. R. Girardet, 'D'innombrables etrangetés' in
    Apparu, La Droite Aujourd'hui, pp.75ff.
41. Rémond, La Droite en France de la Restauration
    à la 5ème République, p.321.
42. Armée contre révolutionnaire, later renamed
    Armée du Christ-Roi, Fédération d'action
    nationale et européenne, renamed Faisceaux
    nationalistes européens; Ordre et Justice
    Nouvelle; Club Charles Martel; Groupe Delta;
    Honneur de la Police; Groupe Nationaliste
    Révolutionnaire.
43. Le Monde, 2 March 1985.
44. Le Monde, 22 October 1985.
45. J. Remy, 'Il n'y a plue de valeurs', L'Express
    25-31 October 1985, pp.59-60, shows that
    attitudes to the minorities are the main
    divide between right and left.

12. THE TRANSFORMATION OF EXTRA-PARLIAMENTARY OPPOSITION IN WEST GERMANY, AND THE PEACE MOVEMENT

Eva Kolinsky

Parliamentary opposition has been called the 'step-child' of political research.(1) By comparison, extra-parliamentary opposition has suffered near-neglect. The attention it did receive has tended to grind an axe and oscillate between rejection and adulation.(2) Extra-parliamentary politics were branded as a danger to the stability of parliamentary democracy;(3) or they were hailed as the one dynamic component in an ossified party system, a badly needed corrective of parliamentary and party-based practices.(4) The peace movement as the largest of the new political movements in the 1980s attracted both evaluations. One side expected a new orientation of defence policies and defence alliances and the other feared a collapse of the security consensus and the military bulwark against the East.(5) These controversies alone would suggest that the political role of extra-parliamentary opposition in West Germany needs further clarification. There are others. New cleavage lines in society have been linked with support for extra-parliamentary opposition. The very existence of such opposition seems to point to a change in the political equilibrium of parliamentary and extra-parliamentary politics.(6) Catch-all parties - Volksparteien - appear to lose some of their capacity to articulate varied political positions and integrate a broad electorate. Instead, extra-parliamentary movements and small parties may be destined to introduce new issues into the political process.(7) The theory of a transformation of politics with a newly important role for extra-parliamentary forces has been based on a comparative analysis of

318

Western democracies. It can highlight the impact of socio-economic modernisation processes on party preferences and political participation in advanced industrial societies, but does not address itself to some specifically German problems pertaining to the role of parliamentary and extra-parliamentary opposition.

Although both types of opposition have existed since parliaments began to function in the nineteenth century, Germany did not develop a tradition of balanced opposition.(8) Parliamentary opposition could not gain legitimacy in a political culture where parliament itself was questioned or rejected. Extra-parliamentary forces were prone to advocate an abolition of parliament and the political system itself. Post-war democracy was not able to build on a tradition of extra-parliamentary politics which would advocate change without advocating abolition.(9) For extra-parliamentary opposition in West Germany to play the innovative role ascribed to new political movements in advanced industrial democracies, would presume that it has overcome this anti-system legacy. Our analysis in this chapter would suggest that extra-parliamentary opposition has to some extent been transformed from a challenge to the parameters of politics into a catalyst of party reorientation and political change. This transformation has remained incomplete because strong currents of extra-parliamentary opposition are still indebted to the kind of fundamentalism which opposition adopted in a pre-democratic or anti-democratic German past.

The Parameters of Extra-Parliamentary Politics

German parliamentary tradition is too patchy to be explained by the classical model of opposition as a shadow government whose task it is to formulate alternative policies. Neither parliament nor opposition enjoyed the political status on which this model is based. In Imperial Germany, parliament was in opposition to the government; in the Weimar Republic, opposition within parliament denigrated it, and the president wielded the power of appointing a government without parliamentary consent; what was left of parliament under National Socialism was used as a propaganda platform for government policies; in the Federal Republic, finally, the traditions of federalism, of working parliaments and coalition governments combined to generate an 'integrated opposition'(10), with opposition, above all, a co-government. Sharing the consensus about the parameters of the political system, parliamentary opposition has been seen and has seen itself as exercising control through co-operation.(11)

With the legitimacy of parliament and of parliamentary opposition doubtful, extra-parliamentary movements and associations were deemed more effective means of articulating interests and pursuing political aims than parties and parliamentary channels. The weakness of the parliamentary tradition in Germany produced a volatile extra-parliamentary sector. In Wilhelmine Germany, for instance, interest group politics with direct access to government and civil service all but obliterated the role of political parties as mouthpieces for societal concerns. A host of associations and movements outside the party structure articulated the ideologies of the day. Often, these ideologies were not in opposition to the political goals of the government, but a curious reinforcement. The Navy League is a prime example of this. Here, the German middle class attempted to demonstrate its endorsement of German militarism, which was equated with social standing and aristocratic values. Efforts to endear themselves to the ruling classes are evident even among more overtly oppositional groups. The German pacifists who campaigned against the militaristic political culture and against the use of war for political means expected the Emperor himself to become the advocate of disarmament and of peace in the world.(12) By contrast, other extra-parliamentary forces turned to political anarchism to pursue the same aims. Both modes of extra-parliamentary opposition, servility towards the powers-that-be and the policy of violent confrontation, can be seen as products of a political culture in which opposition of any kind was criminalised as a danger to the state.

In the Weimar Republic, it proved impossible to make organised interests accountable to parliament, to make parliament acceptable to the elites, or to integrate political radicalisms and factions into parliamentary politics. The anti-democratic fervour of opposition inside parliament became visible as a mobilisation of paramilitary forces from the left and the right at the eve of the National Socialist seizure of power. Both sides

claimed that political change could emanate only
from extra-parliamentary action and would culminate
in the abolition of parliamentary democracy.(13)
    In the Federal Republic, political stabilisa-
tion changed the role and the potential impact of
extra-parliamentary opposition. The twin forces of
economic prosperity and socio-economic mobility
helped to create and to consolidate a consensus in
society about the democratic institutional framework. The modification of traditional cleavage
lines such as social class or ideological partisanship corresponded to the emergence of broadly
based, integrative parties, and the parliamentarisation of opposition.(14) The distrust of political democracy, which extra-parliamentary opposition
could mobilise in the Weimar years, had decreased
in scale and changed in nature. Disaffected
groups, who considered themselves socially disin-
herited or politically alienated, remained marginal. From the outset, the Federal Republic won
the political loyalty of old and new elites; socio-
economic and political dislocations after 1945
produced some disaffected groups - refugees,
demoted National Socialists, protagonists of
Socialist reconstruction and possibly the vast
numbers who lost their homes and possessions. Yet,
the early political history of the Federal Republic
is the history of their economic integration, and
the reduction of extra-parliamentary opposition to
partisan factions on the left or right. This
extra-parliamentary opposition had not shed its
anti-system fundamentalism, but it had abandoned
its propensity to use violence. For the founder
generation of the Federal Republic, the memory of
the violence inflicted by the National Socialists
in the name of their ideology discredited it as a
means of opposition.(15)

Towards a Transformation of Extra-Parliamentary Opposition

In the 1950s extra-parliamentary opposition was
reduced to the political fringes. In the 1960s, it
mobilised new political support and found a new
place in political life. In the founding years of
West German democracy, politicians and political
researchers were preoccupied with the stability of
democratic institutions. Once the initial fears
had subsided that the splintered politics of Weimar
might continue, the democratic fabric of the new

321

political institutions themselves was found wanting. After nearly two decades of a CDU/CSU-led government, parliamentary politics seemed stale and not open enough towards the people.(16) Established political parties and parliamentary proceedings were perceived as unduly remote from day-to-day concerns and lacking in transparency.(17) Clear differences seemed to have dissipated between parties or between government, parliament and opposition.(18) A cartel of political parties with Bundestag representation, a 'one-party state' seemed set to administer the constitution and consolidate their own dominant positions in politics rather than developing the democratic fabric of life throughout German society.(19) Political observers detected a 'crisis of legitimacy' which separated established politics from society and the spread of political opinion.(20) The coalition government of the two main parties, CDU/CSU and SPD, seemed to confirm that a party cartel had been arranged, since parliamentary opposition itself was reduced to a faction unable to operate as an effective opposition.

Although electoral support for established parties and party concentration remained high, the ability of parties to initiate political change or to respond to issues and demands which were not laid down in their programmes was questioned. One of the remedies was seen in democratising political institutions and decision-making processes. Another remedy seemed to lie at the extra-parliamentary level: opposition here would voice new demands and generate the innovation which established politics could not or would not yield. Extra-parliamentary opposition should expose the deficiencies of political practice or articulate new issues and policies through action groups or mass mobilising campaigns.(21) Although the precise role of extra-parliamentary opposition remained unclear, it was widely credited with a new legitimacy as an agent of political innovation and possibly as a catalyst of political reorientation in parliament and parties.

The new salience of extra-parliamentary opposition as a topic of academic evaluation and as a socio-political factor can be explained as a response to the prescribed consensus of West German politics and more specifically to the Grand Coalition from 1966-9. In a broader perspective, it marks the entry of a new generation into West

German politics: the children of post-war democracy
and affluence for whom the established parties had
lost some of their persuasiveness; whose interest
in political participation was not readily satisfied by party membership or coming out to vote;
whose 'idealist' values gave rise to New Politics.
(22)

The transformation of extra-parliamentary
opposition from partisan commitments to abolish
'the system' to acting as a catalyst of socio-
political change through political parties and
parliaments, fits into a broader context of
de-alignment where the integrative capacity of
political parties has weakened in electoral terms
and as conveyor belts between parliamentary
politics and public concerns.

Partisanship and Popular Support

In the founding years of the Federal Republic, the
boundaries between parliamentary and extra-parliamentary opposition were fluid. The SPD whose
expectations of shaping the political order of
post-war Germany were quashed when it found itself
in opposition, pressed for new elections and looked
for support to the considerable reservoir of
political disaffection and disagreement with post-
war conditions and the course of German politics.
The issue of rearmament in particular had aroused
widespread objections which led to mass demonstrations, an attempt at a referendum, and selective
strike action.(23) With different reasons in
detail, West German Communists and former Nazis met
in their refusal to accept rearmament - one side
stating it would revive German militarism, the
other it would mock it. Pacifist groupings in the
Christian churches insisted that Germany should not
take up arms after having inflicted such mass
destruction in the past. The trade union movement
combined fears of a resurgence of German militarism
with concerns that military expenditure would make
'social rearmament', improvements of wages and
living standards which had not even been attempted
after 1945, impossible.(24)

While the SPD was careful to avoid direct
support for any extra-parliamentary activities -
not least because the Communist Party and affiliated groups were prominent at the extra-parliamentary level - it drew on the rearmament issue to
consolidate its political representation. This

proved effective in a number of early <u>Land</u> elections but failed where it mattered, at the federal level.(25) Some of the reasons can be found in the ambivalent opposition strategy pursued by the SPD. Others relate to the opposition potential in German society at the time.

West Germans were slow to approve of rearmament. Until the mid-1950s, a majority stated they were not willing to take up arms to defend their country. There was also little enthusiasm for the military role within an international alliance - first the European Defence Community, then NATO - which was carved out in negotiations between the Western powers and the new German state. But there was also little enthusiasm for other aspects of political reconstruction: the Basic Law, parliament, party pluralism, for instance.(26) It would be wrong to assume that a majority of West Germans were in opposition to political democracy, or were anti-democratic. Rather, they took little interest in decisions which seemed to be made by those at the top, without regard for the wishes of the people. The same indifference can account in part for the broad reluctance to endorse rearmament. Within this extra-parliamentary opposition, only a partisan minority aimed at altering the course of politics in a specific direction. The majority just wanted to get on with their day-to-day affairs. As living conditions stabilised and the Adenauer Government acquired credibility, much of that opposition potential against rearmament was incorporated into the CDU/CSU vote. Once the Bundestag had approved of NATO membership, residual reservations disappeared and public acceptance of the West German army and the defence alliance rose to nearly 80 per cent.(27)

The extra-parliamentary/parliamentary opposition against rearmament in the 1950s collapsed as the socio-political conditions improved. It also collapsed because the apparent unease about rearmament in West German society at the time sprang from many different sources and did not translate into acceptance for the goals of opposition.

From Ideologies to Issues

In 1958, when the Bundestag was called upon to decide whether to equip the new German army with atomic weapons, the SPD made a half-hearted attempt at starting an extra-parliamentary anti-nuclear

campaign, <u>Kampf dem Atomtod</u>. It could draw on
public fears of nuclear destruction which had been
stoked earlier when a group of Nobel Prize winners
appealed to politicians and public to heed the
dangers and ban nuclear weapons.(28) Although the
SPD soon abandoned the new movement, the German
Trade Union Federation remained affiliated and gave
financial backing. Within months, however, the
mobilising potential against nuclear weapons waned;
steady support came only from remnants of the far
left who sought a new organisational base after the
Communist Party (KPD) had been banned in 1956. The
Easter March Movement, modelled on the Aldermaston
marches, followed in 1961 without backing from
either SPD or trade unions. Lack of public
interest and the marginality of the partisan left
hastened the demise of anti-nuclear protests.(29)

The limitations of ideological mobilisation
also became apparent on the extreme right. Since
the Constitutional Court had banned the Socialist
Reichs Party in 1952, any leanings to right
extremism, which may have been in the German population, found less and less party political expression and were the domain of a handful of publishing
houses and political associations. When the
National Democratic Party (NPD) competed for votes
in the mid-1960s, about half its support originated
from a committed clientele. The other half was
transient, a protest vote against economic uncertainties or against the closely knit party consensus, often without a clear awareness among NPD
voters which ideology the party of their choice
advocated.(30)

The Student Movement, which proclaimed itself
as the only substantive opposition in a society
where opposition seemed to have disappeared from
parliamentary politics, also exemplifies the
diffusion of commitment and partisanship. Although
student organisations on the far left constituted
the core of the movement, and selected the themes
for demonstrations and the targets for direct
actions, such as the offices of Springer newspapers
in 1968, most of the followers were less specific
in their commitment. Their participation arose
from a mixture of outrage at the treatment meted
out to demonstrators by the authorities, police,
and often by-standers, and by a desire for innovation and change of the conditions inside the
universities and in society at large. The structure of authority and the teaching programmes in

universities did not appear to have kept pace with increased student numbers or with technological change and modernisation processes in the employment sector. Unease that academic training bore little relevance to future occupations and might not secure the leadership roles German academics had come to expect, contributed to the oppositional potential among students. Many viewed German society as a 'CDU state' where a democratic constitution was interpreted in a restrictive way, and where personal liberties and personal participation in social and political affairs had remained underdeveloped.(31)

Although extra-parliamentary opposition at the time was confined to a segment within the student population, it was hailed by the activists as mass mobilisation and as the beginning of a revolutionary transformation. As the political rhetoric rehearsed Marxist and Socialist ideas more assertively, erstwhile followers sought less partisan outlets for their political aspirations. Between 1969 and 1972, the SPD incorporated many as voters and as members into the mainstream of politics. Specific ideological aims appear to have been less significant in forging this link between extra-parliamentary opposition and SPD than its perceived role as the party of political innovation.(32) The endorsement of violence as a means of political protest and the commitment of a faction to terrorism hastened the shift towards the SPD and the collapse of the activist core into rival small parties endorsing rival Communist orthodoxies.

In their search for a formula to transform the political system, the old and the new Left in West Germany tend to generalise opposition from a focus on specific issues to a more fundamental challenge of the political order. Too partisan to master parliamentary representation, the splintered Left has travelled on the footplate of the New Politics in the 1970s and 1980s.

Extra-Parliamentary Opposition and New Politics

The comparative study of political behaviour in Western democracies has pinpointed economic conditions and social environments as powerful agents of political socialisation. The prosperity and the relative improvement in living standards enjoyed in many post-war societies formed the backdrop for a change of values from materialism to post-material-

ism.(33) Young people and especially the well
educated were the first to emphasise personal
happiness, self-fulfilment or the quality of life
where their parents may have prioritised economic
security, price stability or law and order. A 1980
survey showed that 44 per cent of West Germans with
education to A-level and beyond could be classified
as post-materialists; so could 18 per cent of those
with education up to O-level and 5 per cent with
just basic schooling.(34) Since the early 1970s,
members of all generations have absorbed some post-
materialist values, making 'mixed types' numerically the largest group in West German society.

In political terms, post-materialism has been
visible as concern for a range of new issues, most
prominent among them environmental protection.
From a quaint preoccupation of nature-loving fuddy-
duddies, environmental protection soared to the top
of priority listings in opinion polls. It relegated traditional front runners such as assured
economic stability or secure employment to lower
ranks.(35)

In the 1980s, concerns about employment prospects have again toppled environmentalism from its
primacy. The wheel has, however, not turned full
circle. Post-materialist issues have remained a
salient feature of West German social and political
life despite the experience that unemployment at
around 10 per cent has become endemic and that
efforts to counterbalance the effects of recession
have lost some of the grip they appeared to possess
in the 1960s.

Environmentalism became an issue of extra-
parliamentary opposition in the early 1970s when it
was perceived as an urgent problem which seemed to
be neglected by the political parties. Public
confidence in the ability of political parties to
combat environmental destruction was low.(36)
Instead, citizens' initiatives were credited with
being most effective. As action groups intent on
influencing political decision-makers, administrators, planners, they were channels of political
participation and opposition. The era of private
virtues, of minding one's own business and letting
the state and the politicians get on with governing
the country, had receded. West Germans were more
prepared than ever before to participate at the
political level. In the 1970s, party membership
doubled from 2 per cent to 4 per cent; about 15 per
cent of West German adults may join a political

party at some point in their lives. Informal
participation takes precedence over more formalised
organisational structures. Between 60 and 87 per
cent appear willing to join an action group in
their neighbourhood should the need arise; nine in
ten would sign a petition, six in ten take part in
an authorised demonstration.(37) Political participation may include non-conventional actions such
as demonstrations and petitions but it does not
extend to an endorsement of violence for political
ends. Just 1.3 per cent would be prepared to
endorse damage to property; 0.6 per cent would
condone the use of violence against people.(38)
The willingness to resort to violence has been
somewhat higher among the young and educated than
in society as a whole.

Most people who have joined a citizens'
initiative appear to have been motivated by a
specific issue or problem. This does not apply
fully to West Germans who have been identified as
'pure post-materialists'. They are also motivated
by a more general sense of dissatisfaction, not
merely by their interest in a specific issue.(39)
This ambiguity of political intentions has led to a
diversity of political action within the citizens'
initiatives. On the one hand, they intended to
reverse policy decisions by producing expert
reports which could also be submitted as evidence
in relevant court cases; on the other hand, mass
demonstrations were to draw public attention to
their causes and the social ills they had singled
out for attack. Environmentalism contains diverse
strands of opposition: an action group movement
concerned with the preservation of members' immediate environments; a campaign against nuclear
power stations, which rejected the uses of nuclear
energy as a danger to the survival of society and
mankind as a whole; and the peace movement which
used similar arguments to refute nuclear weapons.
Issues of this wider extra-parliamentary opposition
have become virtually interchangeable. Those who
oppose nuclear power also oppose the primacy of
economic growth in policy-making, the additional
runway at Frankfurt airport and favour the regime
in Nicaragua and the West German squatters movement.(40)

Extra-parliamentary opposition in contemporary
German democracy has also been moulded by the
integrative capacity of parliamentary parties.
While the diffuse political and social orientations

of Volksparteien have been singled out as unable to respond to a changed salience of issues, leaving new political room for small parties and extra-parliamentary groups, the West German parties have proved flexible enough to respond to some of the new issues.

Environmentalism has crossed the boundaries between extra-parliamentary and parliamentary politics. A study of middle-level functionaries showed to what extent environmental concerns have penetrated all political parties.(41) More importantly, parties across the political spectrum have developed environmental policies. In 1970, the SPD/FDP Government launched a major legislative programme to curb· pollution. In the face of counter-pressures from industry and the parliamentary opposition at the time, only fragments of the original design resulted in legislation.(42) Since then, issues such as the destruction of German forests by acid rain (former domains of action-group opposition) have become issues of mainstream politics, parliamentary debate and legislation even under the CDU/CSU-led government.

While they could not incorporate a possible dissatisfaction with the political environment as a whole which may have inspired environmentalism as extra-parliamentary opposition, parties addressed themselves to specific aspects and offered specific policies or legislative measures. This responsiveness has been called a 'chopping-up of issues', Objektzerstückelung, intended to deflate further-reaching changes.(43) One could, however, also argue that the accommodation of environmental issues by West German parties has confirmed their integrative capacity. In relation to their environmental policies, extra-parliamentary opposition has acted as a catalyst of political innovation.

This party political articulation reduced the gap between the perceived urgency of environmental protection and the ability of political parties to cope with it. At this point, the environmentalist movement adopted a radicalised position, concentrating on protest demonstrations and obstructions of nuclear power plants. In the beginning, residents in the vicinity of designated sites and environmentalist campaigners co-operated. Soon, anti-nuclear demonstrations became general statements of opposition against government policies and the system which generated them; they lost the

backing of the local people who would be directly
affected by the controversial developments which
gave rise to the demonstrations.

Anti-nuclear demonstrators came from all over
the Federal Republic. The political mix of this
extra-parliamentary opposition was as impenetrable
as the geographical. Neo-Nazis, Communists,
adherents of the New Left and remnants of the
citizens' initiative movement all made their
diverse gestures of protest. Frequent clashes with
police and a willingness among some demonstrators
to use violence meant that extra-parliamentary
oppposition had resumed an abolitionist stance. It
also meant that any apprehension in the German
population about the accelerated development of
nuclear energy production would not be translated
into support for an extra-parliamentary opposition
which had cancelled too much of the socio-political
consensus.

Between Parliamentarisation and Confrontation

Conditions to articulate opposition through new
political parties which could do better than fester
as extra-parliamentary factions, have not been
favourable in West Germany. The combined forces of
party integration and electoral hurdles reduced the
party diversity of the early 1950s and gave the
established three a monopoly in the Bundestag and
near-monopoly in Land parliaments. New parties
either took a partisan position on the left or
right, or focused on a specific issue which few
voters found politically relevant. Although many
West Germans do not, in principle, object to new
parties, few would change their preferences. In
1980, for instance, one in three were in favour of
founding a new party; about half that number
thought they might vote for such a party.(44)
Partisan parties to the right of the CDU/CSU or on
the Socialist left fared worst, while issue-related
parties were regarded more positively. Of the two
choices offered, a tax party and an ecology party,
the former attracted more support in principle
while fewer people thought they might vote for it
(3 per cent); the ecology party seemed both more
controversial and more capable of finding an
elctorate (5 per cent).

Attempts at organising a political party in
opposition to the existing tax system and modelled
on the Danish Glistrup party, remained unrewarded

since the FDP was already established as the party
with a specific commitment to tax issues and the
self-employed.(45) The dividing line between a new
party able to break through the <u>cordon sanitaire</u> of
the 5 per cent clause and one which cannot, appears
to be if the issue has already been taken up by
existing parties with parliamentary representation,
or whether it is largely extra-parliamentary at the
time of articulation. The Greens could build on
the extra-parliamentary salience of environmentalism, on the political movements around this issue,
and on the political de-alignment among adherents
of new values and New Politics. Despite the
party's name, and despite vilifications in the
early days that the narrow theme of nature conservation could not possibly sustain a political party
and the range of policies required in the contemporary world,(46) environmentalism was but one of
several core issues to transpose extra-parliamentary to parliamentary opposition.

When the Green Party was founded, 90 per cent
of the West German adult population saw environmental protection as a priority issue; 30 per cent
thought none of the parties had effective policies
in this area. For 88 per cent energy supply ranked
among the top issues; for 38 per cent established
parties seemed unable to offer acceptable solu-
tions. The gap between perceived urgency and
scepticism as to the efficacy of political parties
widened when the ability of parties to put post-
materialist principles into practice was assessed.
(47)

Environmentalism alone had limited potential
as the core issue for a new political party.
Although scepticism did exist, so did confidence in
the ability of the established parties to develop
successful environmental policies. Such confidence
was higher at the threshold of the 1980s than ten
years before. Other issues of extra-parliamentary
opposition, and in particular post-materialist
expectations that economic and social life should
be guided by new priorities, spearheaded the party
de-alignment and created political elbow room for
the Greens to gain parliamentary representation.

New Politics is but one of the parameters to
define the scope for the new party. With the SPD
in government and unable to retain its electoral
dominance among the young and educated, the Greens
could break into the most disaffected and politically mobile segment of the electorate. The return

of the SPD into opposition in 1982 was confirmed by
the 1983 federal elections. It has altered the
opposition role for the new party before it could
even begin to play it. Since CDU/CSU and Greens
occupy opposite poles on the political spectrum as
far as policy expectations of their followers are
concerned, SPD and Greens have become competing
oppositions.(48) In the past, the integrative
capacity of larger parties in opposition has tended
to undermine the smaller ones and generate a
concentrated opposition on the left or the right
respectively. Electoral analyses have revealed
that Green voters regard themselves as closer to
the SPD than to any other West German party. In
the 1985 Land elections in North-Rhine Westfalia,
the largest of the Länder, comprising one-third of
the West German population, the Greens failed to
win parliamentary seats while the SPD won an
overall majority. In opposition, the SPD seems to
have recouped some of the integrative capacity it
had lost while in government. The Greens, on the
other hand, may have been able to translate the New
Politics into parliamentary representation, but
they also won protest votes poised against the
established parties rather than for the Greens.(49)
Here, the integrative capacity of the SPD in
opposition could prove as fatal to the Greens as
that of the CDU/CSU had done to the NPD.

Small parties have tended to adopt more
radical positions than their larger competitors in
order to retain distinctiveness in parliament and
to prove that theirs is a vital role in politics.
The radicalised poise of the Greens also reflected
the claim that the party maintained more immediate
links with extra-parliamentary opposition and
initiatives than traditional party organisations
would permit. While the legitimacy of political
action in representative democracies tends to rest
on the ability of parties to articulate the will of
the voters, the Greens located the source of their
legitimacy at the level of extra-parliamentary
action. Their parliamentary opposition has borne
the marks of this ambiguity, with members of
parliament obliged or eager to demonstrate that
they were part and parcel of the grass roots and
fully involved in extra-parliamentary activities in
addition to their parliamentary ones.(50)

Parliamentarisation has blunted some of the
confrontational elements in Green opposition.
Members of parliament have tended to adopt a more

co-operative stance towards other parties, and rate the significance of parliamentary representation higher than perpetual contacts with the party membership or party organisation.(51) Increasingly, parliamentary parties have initiated Green politics, and determined the image of the party in West German politics and in public. The decision to enter a coalition with the SPD in Hesse in 1985 underpins the transition from confrontational to parliamentary politics. The ambiguity of an extra-parliamentary and parliamentary focus has shifted to an ambiguity of opposition inside or outside government.

Policy Perceptions and the Peace Movement

The geo-political situation of West Germany at the frontier of the Western Alliance with the Eastern bloc has not been conducive to opposition in the broad area of defence policies. The consensus among political parties seemed to be so tightly knit that Kirchheimer referred to it as a major indicator of 'vanishing opposition'.(52) Although the ideological fringes never ceased to agitate against West Germany's place in the Western alliance, their message carried little weight. Since the 1950s, about one in three West Germans have declared their preference for neutralism (53) but these remained largely private views without discernible political repercussions.

The emergence in 1980 of the West German peace movement and its ability to stage some of the largest mass demonstrations in German political history, at one time involving over one million people, point to a new volatility of defence issues, and a discrepancy between policy articulation and policy perceptions in contemporary societies.

While Western defence policies seemed to be prescribed by a military domination of the Eastern bloc and threats of war emanating from it, there was little scope for reorientation or opposition. West Germans responded by accepting the institutional framework of the Western defence system, and by locating the major source of threat in the East.(54) With Ostpolitik, detente and disarmament negotiations, defence policies gained a new flexibility - not so much in tangible negotiated results but in public perceptions that they could be regarded as products of deliberate political

decisions for which both sides were accountable.
Fears of war decreased from 46 per cent in 1961 to
24 per cent in 1983,(55) as did fears of the Warsaw
Pact alliance, and a majority of West Germans saw
the two military blocs as equally strong. More
than half blamed both superpowers for the arms race
and thought both were determined to impose their
military goals on smaller countries.(56)

All surveys of public opinion are tenuous: the
interpretation of questions may vary between social
groups, and may be moulded by personal or political
contexts. In the field of defence policy, certain-
ties are even more elusive. Policy decisions are
less transparent here than in other policy domains,
with the decision processes in West Germany being
particularly obscure.(57) Agreement with the
institutional framework or the priorities of
defence policy is, for example, frequently voiced,
while respondents have little or no factual knowledge about them.(58)

As soon as questions articulate strategic
details about how military defence would be conducted, agreement with defence policies in West
Germany tends to decline. Nuclear weapons in particular have been eyed with caution. The willingness to defend one's country dropped from over 60
per cent to 15 per cent if defence meant nuclear
defence. A five-country comparison conducted in
1983 showed that West Germans were more afraid of
nuclear weapons (55 per cent) than their Western
European neighbours (39-42 per cent), or the Ameri-
cans (52 per cent).(59)

Two currents of policy perception in West
Germany facilitated the rise of the peace movement:
the widespread anxieties about nuclear destruction,
and the preference for negotiations as the major
policy device in the defence sector. The issues
merged in the NATO decision of December 1979 to
station additional nuclear warheads, cruise and
Pershing medium-range missiles, in the Federal
Republic and other NATO countries if the disarmament talks in Geneva should end without agreement.
The so-called twin-track decision did not tally
with West German sentiments. Only 3 per cent
accepted that negotiations should be discontinued
and missiles deployed; 25 per cent favoured deployment while negotiations continued and 72 per cent
opted for continued negotiations and against
deployment.(60)

As an extra-parliamentary opposition against

the deployment of nuclear missiles in line with the
NATO decision, the peace movement could draw on
these reservations. Between 1981 and 1983,
explicit support for the movement rose from 21 to
34 per cent; (61) some 48 per cent declared that
the movement was necessary, i.e. fulfilled a function not otherwise covered in the political process
(62); in 1983, 58 per cent expressed sympathies for
the peace movement, i.e. for its aims but not
necessarily for the extra-parliamentary channels it
chose to pursue them.(63) Actual support has been
low by comparison. Estimates range from 4 to 8 per
cent of West Germans aged 16 or over in 1983; about
half of these could be expected to take an active
part.(64)

Explanations of the socio-political origins of
the peace movement have tended to see it as a
cohesive force. It has been argued that for the
young generation concepts such as 'peace' or
'freedom' are no longer tied to the personal
experience of National Socialism, the Cold War, or
building a democracy, and may have lost much of
their relevance for them.(65) Others have been
more positive and explained the peace movement as a
direct articulation of post-materialism.(66) In
this perspective, the peace movement and other
extra-parliamentary oppositions have to be seen as
constituent components of political life in contemporary societies for years to come. A similar view
is taken when clusters of new values such as 'world
peace', 'human rights', 'social justice' are corre-
lated with support for the peace movement which
becomes the political expression of value orientations among certain sectors of the young and educated.(67) In their eagerness to explain new
social movements as inevitable - whether to blame
them for political instability and ungovernability
or, conversely, to hail them as political innova-
tors - the theoreticians of the peace movement have
overlooked its political and social heterogeneity,
and its transformation as extra-parliamentary
opposition.

Parliamentarisation or Confrontation?

In November 1980, a gathering of academics, clergy,
spokesmen for the Greens, the citizens' initiative
movement, pacifist groupings on the left, and some
Communist factions called on the government 'to
withdraw their consent to station cruise and

Pershing missiles'.(68) Named after the town where it was formulated, the Krefeld Appeal marked the official birth of the peace movement. Within weeks, 300,000 signatures were collected; by 1985, the organisers claimed to have secured between 3 and 5 million. From a petition, the appeal had changed to a presumed prebiscite.(69)

Between October 1981, when the first mass rally was staged, and November 1983, when the federal parliament debated and endorsed missile deployment, the peace movement attempted to swing public opinion through demonstrations, innovative protests and publicity against the missiles.(70) To halt deployment has to be seen as the key issue to hold the movement and its diverse political components together. To that extent, the peace movement has been a single-issue extra-parliamentary opposition, determined to make a parliamentary impact.

By the time parliament decided on the issue, however, the 1983 elections had reversed the majorities and removed all chance of a vote against deployment. The election result had, in any case, given a parliamentary voice to objections against deployment. The Greens regarded themselves as the parliamentary wing of the peace movement, and the SPD had incorporated an anti-missile stance in its opposition programme.(71) The trade union movement, which had stood aloof and warned members not to get involved with the peace movement, gave a cautious welcome to joint actions in the summer of 1983. Speaking out publicly against the proposed missiles, the Deutsche Gewerkschaftsbund also refuted calls by some activists that a general strike should be called to halt deployment.(72)

By the autumn of 1983, the distinction between extra-parliamentary and parliamentary opposition, between movement and established politics had all but disappeared. In order to retain an extra-parliamentary presence for the peace issue, a consultative referendum was organised in June 1984 to coincide with the European elections and to make a direct approach to voters at or near official polling stations. Although 150,000 helpers were mobilised - presumably the active core of the movement at the time - the result showed that only 10 per cent of the West German electorate continued to oppose the missiles.(73) Even these 4.5 million no-votes could no longer be translated into extra-parliamentary commitments. Attempts at mass

336

rallies have since failed. Obstructions at missile sites, and at manoeuvres and military installations have taken their place. The divisions were already apparent when a Peace List fought the European elections and subsequently the Land elections in North-Rhine Westfalia. The Communist and pacifist Left had quickly regrouped in an attempt to win votes on the 'peace' ticket, but also in open antagonism to the Green Party. A handful of terrorist attacks against military, in particular American, personnel also fit the tendency towards a splintered radicalisation of the peace movement.

The parliamentarisation of the peace movement exacerbated its political discongruities. The Krefeld Appeal already had two faces: a moderate version against deployment which was publicised through the media and distributed as a broadsheet to invite signatures; and the full version which blamed the arms race on the USA and condoned any Soviet build-up of weapons as a pardonable response.

A similar dichotomy of political orientations and intentions characterised the movement itself. Groups of the Communist and pacifist Left played a prominent role as co-ordinators, and as the organisational backbone at local and regional level. At 1 per cent, party preferences for the far Left among self-professed supporters of the peace movement have been much lower than its influence at extra-parliamentary level.(74) The significance of the peace movement as a focal point for action of the partisan opposition on the left is much bigger than the significance of that opposition for the peace movement. The socio-political support which made 'peace' as an issue of opposition from the pacifist corner on the left into the rallying cry of a broadly based political movement came from people who shared the consensus about the parameters of politics: from voters of the established parties and from within the Christian churches.

The Protestant Churches in particular played a vital role. Protestantism had entered the post-war era with a strong pacifist wing, the Confessing Church, which had opposed the Nazi state-church and spearheaded resistance. In the early opposition against rearmament, Protestant clergy played a major part.(75) Although a German army and military service were accepted in the late 1950s, the formula 'service for peace with or without arms' preserved a niche for conscientious objectors.(76)

Christian pacifism enjoyed a spectacular revival when about 100,000 young Christians demonstrated at the Day of the Church in 1981 under the motto: 'Create peace without Arms'. The Protestant Church embraced the new topic in a moderate call for disarmament:(77)

> The church has to contribute more than hitherto to make everybody aware of the fact that avoiding war by a policy of nuclear deterrence and military balance has to be seen as a provisional position which is hard to bear and which entails the high risk of leading to war rather than preventing it.

The Reformed Churches went even further in their opposition to established defence priorities:(78)

> Where the state turns to means of mass destruction, where it senselessly piles up offensive weapons and weapons of eradication and revenge, where the state considers in its military and political plans the definite annihilation of the enemy and of enemy societies, where the state even risks in its calculations self-destruction through the use of atomic weapons, where the state already accepts the starvation to death of infinite numbers of people to pay for such weapons, in this situation, the Church has to utter an unconditional 'no', a 'no' without any 'yes'.

Between 1981 and 1983, the peace movement could draw on Christian pacifism; the splintered radicalisation which was to follow induced Christian groups to pursue their concerns with 'peace' in regional and local settings, and under their own auspices. By December 1984, formal ties between the organisational core of the peace movement and Christian groups had been severed.(79)

A second pillar of popular support also collapsed when the Association of Citizens' Initiatives (BBU) turned again to ecological themes after the pledge had been broken to keep demonstrations peaceful. BBU policy had always been to co-operate as broadly as possible and involve representatives of the established parties, the SPD and the trade unions in particular, in public manifestations of extra-parliamentary opposition. The parliamentari-

sation of the peace movement removed the need for a
separate movement after 1983. That Jo Leinen, the
chairman of the BBU at the height of the peace
movement, and a fervent spokesman for co-operation
with the SPD, became a minister in the newly elected SPD government in the Saar region, hastened the
reorientation of the BBU from 'peace' to ecology.
(80)

The organisational core which remained committed to the peace movement resumed various ideological orthodoxies. Issues which had been components
of opposition now became sole concerns. Demands
for a change of policies had given way to demands
for a change of the parameters of politics themselves: a rejection of the NATO alliance, of
American involvement in Western Europe and especially in West Germany. Demands for a neutralist
Germany, whose national and international status
should be newly defined, led to demands to redraw
the political map and create a united Germany. An
alliance of extra-parliamentary oppositions from
the left and the right used fears of nuclear
destruction to claim that political salvation could
emanate from German soil: for the left this would
mean a demilitarised, nuclear-free country in the
centre of Europe; for the right, the united German
nation would once again become a protagonist in
world affairs.(81) The astounding alliance of
extremes points to a new fundamentalism of opposition whose ideological zeal blurs ideological
distinctions: 'What sense can it make today to
speak of right or left or of centre if the mass
grave is already in view of us all?'(82) A dramatised fear of nuclear destruction has been used to
question the legitimacy of the political process
and its institutional framework, which does not
even have to be criticised to be condemned.

The conspicuous politics of partisan groups
tend to obscure the degree of consensus which has
characterised the peace movement as extra-parliamentary opposition. Most followers and sympathisers were drawn from the electorates of the
three established parties, CDU/CSU, SPD and FDP.
While over 90 per cent of the Green voters also
expressed support for the peace movement, the
correlation cannot be reversed: among supporters of
the peace movement, party preferences were frequently expressed for the SPD, followed by the
CDU/CSU, the Greens and finally the FDP.(83) Among
SPD voters, 64 per cent endorsed the peace movement

in 1981 when the party still kept a distance, 83 per cent did so in 1983 when the SPD had incorporated demands against deployment. About half the CDU/CSU voters and three in four FDP voters approved of the peace movement. Activists have tended to adopt more partisan positions on the left or the right than adherents or sympathisers. (84)

As an extra-parliamentary opposition with mass support, the peace movement was dependent on those West Germans who did not perceive their commitment as conflicting with their electoral allegiance. Research into political orientations of young people has shown that new issues of opposition or political commitment are unlikely to change party preferences and normally exist alongside them.(85) Applied to the peace movement this would indicate that the majority of its supporters used extra-parliamentary channels of opposition in addition to the established party structure, not in confrontation with it. The parliamentarisation of opposition and this consensus go hand in hand. As an extra-parliamentary opposition alongside parliaments and parties, the peace movement has been able to function as a catalyst of policy innovation within them.

Conclusion

In the 1950s, extra-parliamentary opposition sought confrontation from a variety of vantage points, and was cold-shouldered by parliamentary politics. While challenges from the left and the right to the parameters of politics have persisted in West Germany, their impact has been limited. They gained prominence, however, in the organisational core of some issue-based movements such as the peace movement, where remnants of anti-system politics were influential at a time when they enjoyed little explicit support elsewhere in society. Since the 1960s, the overall role of extra-parliamentary opposition itself has changed from partisan confrontation to political criticism. The twin factors of increased political participation and the salience of issues not accommodated by the major parties, made extra-parliamentary opposition an additional tier of political innovation. A new linkage between parliamentary and extra-parliamentary politics meant that the environmentalist movement and the peace movement could generate policy adjustments among the West German parliamentary parties. They also facilitated the entry of a new party, the Greens, into parliamentary politics.

The transformation of extra-parliamentary opposition to a catalyst of change is not confined to West Germany. In advanced industrial societies party identifications have become fluid, more people are interested in politics and interested also in taking an active part, and conventional forms of participation exist side-by-side with non-conventional ones. Political action outside parties and parliaments reflects a new political mobility. If catch-all parties should indeed be too inflexible to articulate new issues and concerns, they would lose some of their functions to extra-parliamentary opposition, in particular the function to voice societal concerns at the political level. In the Federal Republic, this does not appear to be the case. West German political parties have shown a considerable degree of flexibility in incorporating issues of opposition, although they tended to react only after new issues had emerged as focal points of mass concern in extra-parliamentary movements or new political parties. The integrative capacity of West German catch-all parties would indicate that extra-parliamentary oppositions act as transient, short-lived agents of policy transformation. The overlap of political support for established parties and extra-parliamentary opposition in the case of the peace movement underlines the function of the latter as a catalyst of socio-political change.

At extra-parliamentary level, substantive pockets of partisan opposition have remained and continue to question the legitimacy of the institutional parameters of politics and society. This Weimar-style fundamentalism has been prominent among activists and organisers and points to an ambiguity of extra-parliamentary opposition. A transformation whereby extra-parliamentary politics would make parliamentary politics more responsive to new issues has not reached the confrontationist core of extra-parliamentary activities and movements in West Germany. The transformation of extra-parliamentary opposition has begun, but has yet to become an indigenous part of contemporary political culture.

Notes

1. Hans Gerd Schumann (ed.), Die Rolle der Opposition in der Bundesrepublik, (Wissenschaftliche Buchgesellschaft, Darmstadt, 1976), p.3. Also Michael Hereth, Die parlamentarische Opposition in der Bundesrepublik, (Olzog, Munich, 1969).
2. For a summary account see Hannah Vogt, Parlamentarische und ausserparlamentarische Opposition, (Leske, Opladen, 1972); also in Schumann, Die Rolle der Opposition, pp.309-90.
3. E.g. Gerd Langguth, Protestbewegung. Entwicklung. Niedergang. Renaissance. Die Neue Linke seit 1968, (Wissenschaft und Politik, Cologne, 1983). Werner Kaltefleiter and Robert L. Pfaltzgraff (eds), The Peace Movements in Europe and America, (Croom Helm, London, 1985).
4. E.g. Karl-Werner Brand (ed.), Neue soziale Bewegungen in Westeuropa und den USA, (Campus, Frankfurt/M, 1985); Hans-Joachim Raschke, Soziale Bewegungen. Eine historischsystematischer Grundriss, (Campus, Frankfurt/M, 1985).
5. For a sceptical view of the peace movement, see the contributions on West Germany in Walter Laqueur and Robert Hunter (eds), European Peace Movements and the Future of the Western Alliance, (Transaction Books, New Brunswick NJ, 1985); for the opposite view Klaus Gerosa (ed.), Grosse Schritte wagen - über die Zukunft der Friedensbewegung, (List, Munich, 1984); Lorenz Knorr, Geschichte der Friedensbewegung in der Bundesrepublik Deutschland, (Pahl Rugenstein, Cologne, 1983); Wolfgang Prosinger, Lasst uns in Frieden. Porträt einer Bewegung, (Rowohlt, Hamburg, 1982); Reiner Steinweg (ed.), Die neue Friedensbewegung. Analysen aus der Friedensforschung, (Suhrkamp, Frankfurt/M, 1982).
6. E.g. Jens Albers, 'Modernisierung, neue Spannungslinien and politische Chancen der Grünen', Politische Vierteljahresschrift 26 (1985), pp.211-26. Joachim Raschke, 'Soziale Konflikte und Parteiensystem in der Bundesrepublik', Aus Politik und Zeitgeschichte, vol. 49, (1985), pp.22-39.
7. Scott C. Flanagan and Russell Dalton, 'Parties Under Stress: Realignment and Dealignment in

Advanced Industrial Societies', <u>West European Politics</u>, vol. 7, no. 1, (January 1984), pp.7-23.

8. In addition to the excellent collection of papers in Schumann, <u>Die Rolle der Opposition</u>, see Waldemar Besson, 'Regierung und Opposition in der deutschen Politik', <u>Politische Vierteljahresschrift</u> 3, (1962), pp.225ff; Dieter Grosser, 'Die Opposition in Deutschland' in G. Doeker and W. Steffani (eds), <u>Pluralismus. Festschrift für Ernst Fränkel</u>, (Hoffmann & Campe, Hamburg, 1973), pp.515ff; Gerhard Lewenberg, 'The patterns of political opposition in Germany' in H.S. Commayer et al. (eds), <u>Festschrift für Karl Löwenstein</u>, (Mohr, Tübingen, 1971); Margit Grubmüller, <u>Die Opposition im politischen Prozess</u>, (Voegel, Munich, 1972); Heinrich Oberreuter (ed.), <u>Parlamentarische Opposition. Ein internationaler Vergleich</u>, (Hoffmann & Campe, Hamburg, 1975).

9. The problem of opposition is discussed from different perspectives by Ralf Dahrendorf, <u>Society and Democracy in Germany</u>, (Weidenfeld & Nicolson, London, 1969); Martin and Sylvia Greiffenhagen, <u>Ein schwieriges Vaterland. Zur Politischen Kultur Deutschlands</u>, (List, Munich, 1979), pp.34-152; also Karl Dietrich Bracher, 'Politische Institutionen in Krisenzeiten' <u>Vierteljahreschefte für Zeitgeschichte</u>, vol. 33, no. 1, (1985), pp.1-27.

10. Eva Kolinsky, <u>Parties, Opposition and Society in West Germany</u>, (Croom Helm, London, 1984), p.6.

11. For detailed analyses of opposition and political consensus see Manfred Friedrich, 'Opposition im Deutschen Bundestag', <u>Zeitschrift für Parlamentsfragen</u> 3 (1973), pp.392ff; Peter Hübner and Uwe Thaysen, 'Opposition im Bundestag und in Schleswig Holstein', <u>Zeitschrift für Parlamentsfragen</u> 1 (1970), pp.44ff; W. Kralewski and K. Neunreither, <u>Oppositionelles Verhalten im ersten Deutschen Bundestag 1949-1953</u>, (Westdeutscher Verlag, Cologne/Opladen, 1963); Dolf Sternberger, 'Opposition des Parlaments und parlamentarische Opposition' in Schumann, <u>Die Rolle der Opposition</u>, pp.66-87; Hans Joachim Veen, <u>Opposition im Bundestag. Ihre</u>

Funktionen, institutionellen Handlungsbedingungen und das Verhalten der CDU/CSU
Fraktion in der 6. Wahlperiode, (Bundeszentrale für Politische Bildung, Bonn, 1976).

12. Wilfried Eisenbeiss, Die bürgerliche
Friedensbewegung in Deutschland während des
Ersten Weltkrieges, Lang, Frankfurt/M, 1980),
pp.62-3; also Peter Brock, Pacifism in Europe
to 1914, Princeton UP, Princeton NJ, 1972);
Roger Chickering, Imperial Germany and a World
Without War. The Peace Movement and German
Society 1892-1914, (Princeton UP, Princeton
NJ, 1975); also Wolfgang Mommsen and Gerhard
Hirschfeld (eds), Social Protest, Violence and
Terror in 19th and 20th Century Europe,
(Macmillan and Berg, London, 1982).

13. For a case study see Eve Rosenhaft, 'Working-
Class Life and Working-Class Politics:
Communists, Nazis and the State in the Battle
for the Streets, Berlin 1928-1932' in Richard
Bessell and Edgar Feuchtwanger (eds), Social
Change and Political Development in the Weimar
Republic, (Croom Helm, London, 1981),
pp.207ff.

14. See Gordon Smith, Democracy in Western
Germany, 2nd edn., (Heinemann, London, 1982);
also Gordon Smith, 'The German Volkspartei and
the Career of the Catch-All Concept' in
Herbert Döring and Gordon Smith (eds), Party
Government and Political Culture, (Macmillan,
London, 1982), pp.59ff. Also Klaus von Beyme,
Political Parties in Western Democracies,
(Gower, Aldershot, 1985).

15. Wolfgang Mommsen, 'Non-Legal Violence and
Terrorism in Industrial Societies: An
Historical Analysis' in Mommsen and
Hirschfeld, Social Protest, Violence and
Terror, p.384.

16. Gerhard Loewenberg, Parliament in the German
Political System, (Cornell UP, Ithaca NY,
1967), p.434.

17. Winfried Steffani (ed.), Parlamentarismus ohne
Transparenz, (Westdeutscher Verlag, Opladen,
1971).

18. Manfred Friedrich, 'Opposition ohne Alternative' in Kurt Kluxen (ed.), Parlamentarismus,
(Kiepenheuer & Witsch, Cologne/Berlin, 1969),
pp.425ff; Otto Kirchheimer, 'Wandlungen der
politischen Opposition', ibid. pp.410ff;
Roland Roth (ed.), Parlamentarisches Ritual

und Politische Alternativen, (Campus,
Frankfurt/M, 1980).

19. E.g. Wolf-Dieter Narr (ed.), Auf dem Wege zum
     Einparteienstaat, (Westdeutscher Verlag,
     Opladen, 1977); Manfred Rowold, Im Schatten
     der Macht. Zur Oppositionsrolle der nicht-
     etablierten Parteien, (Droste, Düsseldorf,
     1974).

20. Jürgen Dittberner and Rolf Ebbighausen (eds),
     Das Parteiensystem in der Legitimationskrise,
     (Westdeutscher Verlag, Opladen, 1973). Also
     PVS Sonderheft, 'Legitimationsprobleme
     politischer Herrschaft', 1976.

21. For the first view see Jürgen Habermas,
     'Einleitung' in Habermas (ed.), Stichworte
     zur 'Geistigen Situation der Zeit' 1.Band:
     Nation und Republik, (Suhrkamp, Frankfurt/M,
     1979), pp.24ff; for the second view see Bernd
     Guggenberger, Bürgerinitiativen in der
     Parteiendemokratie, (Kohlhammer, Stuttgart,
     1980).

22. Wilhelm P. Bürklin, Grüne Politik,
     (Westdeutscher Verlag, Opladen, 1984),
     pp.94ff.

23. Fritz Krause, Antimilitaristische Opposition
     in der Bundesrepublik Deutschland, (Fischer,
     Frankfurt/M, 1971). Hans Karl Rupp, Ausser-
     parlamentarische Opposition in der Ära
     Adenauer, (Pahl Rugenstein, Cologne, 1980)
     (2nd edn.).

24. Klaus von Schubert, Wiederbewaffnung und
     Westintegration. Die innere Auseinandersetzung
     um die militärische und aussenpolitische
     Orientierung der Bundesrepublik 1950-1952,
     (Deutsche Verlagsanstalt, Stuttgart, 1970);
     also Eva Kolinsky, 'Democracy and Opposition
     in West Germany Rearmament and Nuclear
     Weapons in the Fifties' in Contemporary German
     Studies, Occasional Papers No. 1, (University
     of Strathclyde, 1985), pp.17-38.

25. Detailed analyses in Joachim Hütter, SPD und
     nationale Sicherheit. Internationale und
     innenpolitische Determinanten des Wandels der
     sozialdemokratischen Sicherheitspolitik 1959-
     1961, (Hain, Meisenheim, 1975); Udo F. Löwke,
     Die SPD und die Wehrfrage 1949-1955, (Neue
     Gesellschaft, Bonn/Bad Godesberg, 1976);
     Lothar Wilker, Die Sicherheitspolitik der SPD
     1956-1961. Zwischen Wiedervereinigungspolitik
     und Bündnisorientierung, (Neue Gesellschaft,

Bonn/Bad Godesberg, 1977). In a broader context: Norbert Toennies, Der Weg zu den Waffen. Die Geschichte der deutschen Wiederbewaffnung 1949-1957, (Markus, Cologne, 1957); Gerhard Wettig, Entmilitarisierung und Wiederbewaffnung in Deutschland 1943-1955, (List, Munich, 1967).

26. Data in Anna J. Merritt and Richard L. Merrit (eds), Public Opinion in Semi-Sovereign Germany. The HICOG Surveys 1949-1955, (University of Illinois Press, 1980); David P. Conradt, The German Polity, (Longman, London, 1978), pp.44ff; also Lewis J. Edinger, Politics in Germany. Attitudes and Processes, (Little, Brown & Co., Boston, 1968).

27. Hans Rattinger, 'The Federal Republic: Much Ado About (Almost) Nothing' in Gregory Flynn and Hans Rattinger (eds), The Public and Atlantic Defense, (Croom Helm, London, 1985), pp.129 and 143.

28. Peter Graf von Kielmannseck, 'The German Peace Movement's Origins and Aims' in Laqueur and Hunter, European Peace Movements, pp.320-1. Manifestos collected in Anton-Andreas Guha, Die Nachrüstung - Der Holocaust Europas, (Dreisam Verlag, Freiburg, 1981).

29. Karl A. Otto, Vom Ostermarsch zur APO. Geschichte der ausserparlamentarischen Opposition in der Bundesrepublik, 1960-1970, (Campus, Frankfurt/M/New York, 1977). Also Rupp Ausserparlamentarische Opposition.

30. John Nagle, The National Democratic Party. Right Radicalism in the Federal Republic of Germany, (Univ. of California Press, Berkeley, 1970), p.124. Also Kurt P. Tauber, Beyond Eagle and Swastika 2 vols. (Wesleyan UP, Middletown, 1967); an overview in Kolinsky, Parties, Opposition and Society in West Germany, pp.253-91.

31. Gert Schäfer and Carl Nedelmann, (eds), Der CDU Staat. Analysen zur Verfassungswirklichkeit der Bundesrepublik, (Suhrkamp, Frankfurt/M, 1967), (vol. 1). For a critique of the Student Movement see Margherita von Brentano, 'Privilegierter Protest? Chancen und Gefahren der studentischen Oppositionsbewegung' in Schumann, Die Rolle der Opposition, pp.348-57.

32. Bürklin, Grüne Politik, p.169.

33. For recent studies relating to West Germany

see Helner Meulemann, 'Säkularisierung und
Politik. Wertewandel und Wertstruktur in der
Bundesrepublik Deutschland', Politische
Vierteljahresschrift 26 (1985), pp.29-51;
Manfred G. Schmidt, 'Demokratie,
Wohlfahrtsstaat und neue soziale Bewegungen',
Aus Politik und Zeitgeschichte 11 (1984),
pp.3-14; Ronald Inglehart, 'Traditionelle
politische Trennungslinien und die Entwicklung
der neuen Politik in westlichen Gesellschaf-
ten' Politische Vierteljahresschrift 24
(1983), pp.139-65.

34. Hans-Michael Mohr and Wolfgang Glatzer,
'Werte, persönliche Konflikte,
Unzufriedenheit' in Wolfgang Glatzer and
Wolfgang Zapf (eds), Lebensqualität in der
Bundesrepublik. Objektive Lebensbedingungen
und subjektives Wohlbefinden, (Campus,
Frankfurt/New York, 1984), p.223.

35. Ibid., p.227; Bürklin Grüne Politik also
includes data of the 'Eurobarometer' surveys.

36. 'Spiegel Umfrage zur politischen Situation im
Wahljahr 1980', parts IV and V, Der Spiegel 26
May 1980, esp. p.73; and Der Spiegel 2 June
1980, pp.48ff.

37. Wolfgang Lorig, 'Protestverhalten und neue
soziale Bewegungen' in Gegenwartskunde 2
(1984), p.165.

38. Sinus Institut/Bundesministerium für Jugend,
Familie und Gesundheit (eds), Die
verunsicherte Generation, (Leske, Opladen,
1983), pp.55 and 105.

39. Hans Michael Mohr, 'Politische und soziale
Beteiligung' in Glatzer and Zapf,
Lebensqualität, pp.161ff.

40. Karl-Heinz Reuband, 'Politisches Selbstverständnis und Wertorientierungen von Anhängern
der Friedensbewegung', Zeitschrift für
Parlamentsfragen 1 (1985), pp.25-45; also
Werner Harenberg, 'Sicherer Platz links von
der SPD? Die Wähler der Grüner in den Daten
der Demoskopie' in Jörg R. Mettke (ed.),
Die Grünen. Regierungspartner von morgen?,
(Rowohlt, Hamburg, 1982), pp.36-50.

41. Hermann Schmitt et al., 'Etablierte und Grüne.
Zur Verankerung der ökologischen Bewegung in
den Parteiorganisationen von SPD, FDP, CDU und
CSU', Zeitschrift für Parlamentsfragen 4
(1981), pp.516-40.

42. Klaus-Georg Wey, Umweltpolitik in Deutschland,

(Westdeutscher Verlag, Opladen, 1982), pp.207ff.

43. Brigitta Nedelmann, 'Handlungsspielraum politischer Organisationen' in Rudolf Wildenmann (ed.) Sozialwissenschaftliches Jahrbuch 4 (1975), pp.94ff.

44. Manfred Küchler, 'Staats-, Parteien- oder Politikverdrossenheit?' in Joachim Raschke (ed.), Bürger und Parteien. Ansichten und Analysen einer schwierigen Beziehung, (Westdeutscher Verlag, Opladen, 1982), p.50.

45. For an analysis of aims see Detlef Murphy et al., Protest. Grüne, Bunte und Steuerrebellen. Ursachen und Perspektiven, (Rowohlt, Hamburg, 1979), pp.69ff.

46. E.g. Henning Günther, 'Die politische Natur. Die "Grünen" im deutschen Parteienspektrum', Die politische Meinung 181 (1980), pp.5-25; Die Grünen. Geschichte, Programm und Politik. Report compiled by the CDU head office in Bonn, dated 6 October 1982 (mimeo).

47. Gustav Schmidtchen, Was den Deutschen heilig ist, (Goldmann, Munich, 1979), p.149; 69% felt humanitarian concerns should rank higher than economic ones; 47% had no confidence that the established parties would address themselves to this issue; 65% saw an equitable distribution of wealth as a priority; 45% had no confidence in the parties to accomplish it.

48. Hans Joachim Veen, 'Wer wählt grün?', Aus Politik und Zeitgeschichte, 35-36 (1984), p.9; also Deutsche Shell (ed.), Jugend 81, (Leske, Opladen, 1982) shows that orientations and attitudes of young people with party preferences for the Greens and the CDU/CSU are clearly different, with FDP and SPD occupying a middle ground.

49. Ursula Feist et al., 'Die politischen Einstellungen von Arbeitslosen', Aus Politik und Zeitgeschichte 45 (1984), pp.3-17.

50. At the Green party congress in December 1985, the only item which all delegates could agree on was to participate in a demonstration against a nuclear reprocessing plant; buses were chartered to take the Greens to the site; this move underlines the unifying role of extra-parliamentary actions within the party. See The Times, 14 December 1985; Das Parlament, 21/28 December 1985, p.13.

51. Eva Kolinsky, 'The Greens in Germany:

Prospects of a Small Party', Parliamentary
Affairs 37 (Autumn 1984), pp.434-47.
52. Otto Kirchheimer, 'Germany: The Vanishing
Opposition' in Robert A. Dahl (ed.) Political
Oppositions in Western Democracies, (Yale UP,
New Haven, Conn., 1968) (3rd edn) pp.237-59.
53. Bertold Meyer, 'Neutralistische Traümereien?
Öffentliche Meinung, Frieden und Friedensbewegung' in Steinweg, Die Neue Friedensbewegung, p.115.
54. Rattinger, 'The Federal Republic: Much Ado
about (Almost) Nothing', p.108-10.
55. Ibid., pp.112 and 114.
56. Sicherheitspolitik - Bündnispolitik -
Friedensbewegung. (Study of SINUS Instituts
for Friedrich Ebert Stiftung, Bonn, 1983),
(mimeo), pp.14 and 41.
57. There is a vast literature on defence policy;
for policy perceptions see esp. Helga
Haftendorn, 'Aussen- und sicherheitspolitische
Entscheidungssysteme: Bundesrepublik
Deutschland', Aus Politik und Zeitgeschichte
43 (1983), pp.3-15; Daniel Frey,
'Friedenssicherung durch Gewaltverzicht',
Aus Politik und Zeitgeschichte 15/16 (1983),
pp.3-23.
58. Volker Rittberger, 'Europäische Sicherheit und
Neubewertung der Kernwaffen', Aus Politik und
Zeitgeschichte 15 (1984), pp.16-17. The
surveys were conducted in 1977 and 1980.
59. Survey conducted in December 1983 by the
Atlantic Institute for International Affairs,
published in Die Zeit 16 December 1983, p.8;
the survey material collected by Rattinger
'Federal Republic' also shows the variability
of opinions on defence strategies and
policies.
60. Rattinger, 'Federal Republic', p.163.
61. Der Spiegel 35 (1983), p.28.
62. Rattinger, 'Federal Republic', p.159.
63. Reuband, Politisches Selbstverständnis, p.37.
64. Data from Sicherheitspolitik- Bündnispolitik-
Friedensbewegung, p.71; 'Stern Umfrage: Angst
vor den Raketen' in Stern 43, 20 October 1983;
Frantfurter Allgemeine Zeitung, 26 February
1985.
65. Günter Schmid, 'Zur Soziologie der Friedensbewegung', Aus Politik und Zeitgeschichte 24
(1982), p.21.
66. Ronald Inglehart, 'Generational Change and the

Future of the Atlantic Alliance', Politische
Studien 16 (1984), pp.525-35; also Manfred
Küchler, 'Friedensbewegung in der Bundes-
republik - Alter Pazifismus oder neue soziale
Bewegung?' in J.W. Falter et al. (eds),
Politische Willensbildung und Interessenver-
mittlung, (Westdeutscher Verlag, Opladen,
1984), pp.328-37.

67. Reuband, Politisches Selbstverständnis,
pp.39-40; also Helmut Fogt and Pavel Uttitz,
'Die Wähler der Grünen', Zeitschrift für
Parlamentsfragen 2 (1982), pp.215ff.

68. Dieter Lattmann (ed.), Krefeld Initiative.
Der Atomtod bedroht und alle - Keine
Atomraketen in Europe, (Bonn, 1982; mimeo),
p.1.

69. See Innere Sicherheit 68, 12 August 1983,
pp.12ff; Innere Sicherheit 71, 27 February
1984, pp.5ff. In 1985, the American SDI
initiative has become the major issue of the
activist core of the Peace Movement, and the
subject of a mass petition. See Innere
Sicherheit 6/85, 20 December 1985, pp.3-4.

70. Karl Heinz Reuband, 'Die "Volksbefragungs-
kampagne" der Friedensbewegung: Neue
Aktionsformen des Protests und ihr
Mobilisierungspotential', Zeitschrift für
Parlamentsfragen 2 (1985), p.204.

71. See Willie Paterson and Douglas Webber,
Chapter 5 in this volume.

72. Statement by the DGB chairman Ernst Breit, 7
June, 1983, Gewerkschaftliche Umschau, 4,
(July-September 1983), p.4; and DGB Informa-
tionsdienst, 7 July 1983; also Stellungnahme
des DGB zur Friedensbewegung und Sicherheitspolitik. Decision by the DGB executive of 5
July 1983, DGB archive Ref. no. ID 13, pp.4-5.

73. Reuband, 'Die Volksbefragungskampagne', p.217.
In Bavaria, the Land government organised a
referendum on the same day which proposed to
insert a commitment to environmental protection in the Bavarian constitution.

74. Sicherheitspolitik-Bündnispolitik-Friedens-
bewegung, p.71.

75. Joyce Marie Mushaben, 'Cycles of Peace Protest
in West Germany', West European Politics vol.
8, no. 1, (January 1985), pp.24-40. Also Hans
A. Pestalozzi et al. (eds) Frieden in Deutschland. Die Friedensbewegung, (Goldmann, Munich,
1982); also Hans-Jürgen Benedict, 'Ziviler

Ungehorsam gegen Atomraketen', Frankfurter
Hefte, Special Issue 'Friedensbewegung: geht
es weiter?' vol. 30, no. 1, (January 1984),
pp.10-21.

76. Jürgen Plöhn, 'Die Denkschriften der
Evangelischen Kirche in Deutschland',
Aus Politik und Zeitgeschichte 2 (1985),
pp.7-9.

77. Frankfurter Rundschau, 5 November 1981.

78. Frankfurter Rundschau, 21 August 1982.

79. Evangelical Students Association, Press
Release, 16 December 1984. Also 'Die
Beschlüsse des Koordinierungsausschusses der
Friedensbewegung im Wortlaut', Unsere Zeit, 21
December 1984.

80. Since March 1985, the BBU has published a new
membership journal, BBU Magazin, which highlights various aspects of environmentalism and
'resistance' against nuclear power stations,
but no longer refers to the missile issue.
Also interview with Gerd Billen, BBU office in
Bonn, 23 March 1985. The environmental
pressure group Bund für Natur- und
Umweltschutz has displaced the BBU; the
present reorientation is an attempt to recover
some of the lost ground and restore contacts
with environmental groups over issues such as
vivisection or pollution in everyday life; at
the same time, SDI has come to the foreground
as a BBU topic.

81. Herbert Ammon and Peter Brandt, 'The Relevance
of the German Question for Peace in Europe' in
Rudolf Steinke and Michael Vale (eds),
'Germany Debates Defence', Special Issue of
International Journal of Politics (Spring/
Summer 1983), pp.83-96. Critically Sigrid
Meuschel, 'Für Menschheit und Volk. Kritik
fundamentaler und nationaler Aspekte in der
deutschen Friedensbewegung' in Wolf Schäfer,
Neue soziale Bewegungen. Konservativer
Aufbruch im bunten Gewand?, (Fischer, Frank-
furt/M, 1983), pp.37-46; also Wilfried von
Bredow, Aus Politik und Zeitgeschichte 24
(1982) and a reply by Michael Stübel, Aus
Politik und Zeitgeschichte 3/4 (1984).

82. Wolfgang Venohr (ed.), Die deutsche Einheit
kommt bestimmt, (Lübbe, Bergisch Gladbach,
1982), p.13.

83. Ferdinand Müller-Rommel, 'New Social Movements
and Smaller Parties: A Comparative Perspec-

tive', West European Politics vo. 8, no. 1,
(January 1985), p.44.
84. Ibid., p.51; also 'Angst vor den Raketen' in
Der Stern 43, (1983).
85. Klaus Allerbeck, 'Systemverständnis und
gesellschaftliche Leitbilder von
Jugendlichen', Aus Politik und Zeitgeschichte
50 (1984), p.25.

13 NON-PARLIAMENTARY OPPOSITION IN ITALY: THE NEW SOCIAL MOVEMENTS

Grant Amyot

The character of the opposition within any political system cannot be explained or even described without reference to the nature of the government, including the party system, its ideological basis, and the socio-economic foundation on which it rests. This is a particularly important admonition in the case of non-parliamentary opposition, for most of the explanations of the new social movements, such as feminism, the ecological movement, and the peace movement, have not been sensitive to these factors and to the national differences to which they give rise. For Inglehart, for instance, these movements are primarily the result of the spread of 'post-materialist' values in affluent Western societies where immediate material needs have been satisfied.(1) Offe, on the other hand, sees them as the defensive reaction of those threatened by the encroachment of the state and the economic system on previously private spheres of life.(2) Like Offe, Habermas lays stress on the dissolution of traditional value-systems as a precondition for the emergence of the new social movements, and notes that the need to combat the crisis-tendencies of modern capitalism has forced the state to open to discussion issues whose solution was previously taken for granted, because they were regulated by these traditional value-systems. (3) None of these theories leaves much space for consideration of the governments and party systems the new movements are facing; furthermore, as we shall see, they are inaccurate in important respects even as descriptive accounts of the new social movements.

In the Italian case, the new social movements have gained much of their impact and support from the contrast between the relative backwardness of many of the social and political conditions, including the persistence of the Christian Democratic regime since 1947, and the rapidity of the modernisation of the country in the last thirty-five years. As a result of a form of 'combined and uneven development', movements such as the feminists, who are fighting against the quasi-feudal subordination of women in traditional Italian society, were among the most powerful in the Western world. On the other hand, these new groups face a strong, well-entrenched party system with deep roots in traditional sub-cultures and considerable capacity to respond to new issues, although the legislative and bureaucratic processes have a limited ability to implement new policies. Furthermore, the rapid changes of the 1950s and 1960s also gave rise to one of the strongest working-class movements in Western Europe, a movement which tended to relegate other concerns to a secondary position. Therefore, while we would have expected the socio-economic conditions of Italy by themselves to produce very strong non-parliamentary opposition in the 1970s and 1980s, the absorptive capacity of the political system, coupled with the exceptional importance of class politics for much of the period, meant that in fact the new social movements were weaker than in many other European countries.

The Italian political system in the post-war period can best be characterised as a 'regime' dominated by the Christian Democratic Party, which has been the largest and most powerful member of the governing coalition without interruption since 1945. Thus Italy is not a typical two-party or two-bloc system, with alternation in government by relatively moderate 'catch-all' parties,(4) nor one with a plurality of 'pillars', or traditional sub-cultures,(5) coalescing at the top to form an administration. The nearest cousins of the DC regime are those of the Japanese Liberal Democrats and the Indian Congress. All three countries have economic and social structures which are less mature than those of most capitalist democracies: in particular, the petty bourgeoisie is relatively numerous and politically significant. It is this social stratum which provides the characteristic basis of a 'regime party'. The self-employed are linked to the ruling party not simply by personalised clientelistic ties, as Zuckerman implies,(6) but also by general measures benefiting entire categories.(7) In Italy, the most important and costly of these has been the toleration of tax evasion by this group.

Of course, the petty bourgeoisie are only one of the DC's bases of support. It can still rely on the votes of the majority of practising Catholics, and on the traditional Catholic sub-culture, though this link has become somewhat weaker over time. Its 'occupation' of the state, including the various enterprises and other bodies controlled by the state, has been instrumental in securing the enduring support of other important categories. Particularly in the South, patronage has been freely used to generate votes for the DC. And, last but not least, the simple fear of a left-wing government, which in the past often took the form of a rather hysterical anti-Communism, has served as a powerful cement for the DC's bloc of followers. The party has attracted a large, generically conservative 'opinion' vote from middle-class voters who are neither religious nor the beneficiaries of governmental favours.

In spite of the role of Catholicism and anti-Communism in ensuring the continued dominance of the Christian Democrats, it would be an exaggeration to say that the party exercises 'hegemony' in the Gramscian sense.(8) Neither of these ideologies provides a widely shared philosophy of life which links the masses to the regime: the former because it is held by only a minority, the latter because it is too incomplete and inchoate to provide a set of positive values. Rather, the DC primarily uses 'corruption/fraud', which Gramsci says is employed when the ruling class cannot exercise hegemony yet is not strong enough to govern purely by force.(9) None the less, the party has often felt the constraint of Catholic values in its policy decisions, for it cannot afford to lose the Catholic fraction of its electorate.

A corollary of a 'regime party' such as the DC is a party of permanent opposition, in this case the Italian Communist Party. The PCI's oppositional status, broken only by the brief and unhappy experiment with governments of 'national solidarity' (1976-9), has meant that the most progressive forces in Italy have had only a muted voice in government, through the Socialist Party and some left-wing currents in the DC and the other coalition partners. Such immobilism at the parliamentary level is, at first glance, a powerful stimulus to non-parliamentary forms of opposition.

Furthermore, the DC regime depends on many elements which are directly opposed to the new social movements; hence, it is extremely unlikely to be sympathetic to their demands. The ecologists, for example, have called for the closure of the 'historic centres' of major cities to automobile traffic. This proposal is opposed by the shopkeepers in these areas, who are afraid that they will have fewer customers if traffic is stopped. And the DC is especially sensitive to the interests of petty-bourgeois groups such as the shopkeepers. Again, ecologists have requested the requisitioning of unused apartments (including those held for speculative purposes and vacation homes) in order to stem the rash of illegal building that is eating up the open spaces around Rome and other cities. However, the owners of the unused apartments are primarily small investors and members of the same petty bourgeoisie that is a major source of DC strength.

Not only the material interests of its supporters made the DC unresponsive to the demands of the new social movements. Its ideological commitments also limited its freedom of action. Its ties to the Church made it inevitable that it would oppose the demands of the women's movement, particularly on issues like divorce and abortion. (It was not, however, responsible for collecting the signatures that led to the two referenda that sought to reverse the laws introducing divorce and legalising abortion; nor did it campaign as actively against the latter as against the former.) And the importance of anti-Communism as a cohesive factor in its bloc of support meant that it was bound, in the last analysis, to follow a strongly pro-American course in defence and foreign policy. Hence the DC readily agreed to the installation of the cruise and Pershing missiles on Italian soil after the United States requested it.

The DC system of power was quite functional to the 'regime of accumulation'(10) which characterised the Italian economy during the economic miracle of the 1950s and the early 1960s. Italy's growth in this phase was based chiefly on the production of consumer durables for the export market. Hence it did not require strong domestic demand for economic health; on the contrary, Italian industry wanted to keep wage rates low in

356

order to maintain its price advantage in the world market. This 'labour-repressive'(11) system was possible only if the largest working-class party was relegated to opposition. It involved a failure to pursue Keynesian demand-management policies or to develop a modern welfare state, two traits of a domestic-centred economy relying on high wages and a buoyant home market to feed economic growth.

By the mid-1960s, however, such a purely labour-repressive system was no longer viable. Economic growth had created new social and economic problems which required a higher level of state intervention and of welfare-state provision. Moreover, with the absorption of the most employable of the pool of surplus labourers present in the early 1950s, unemployment fell and the trade unions began to gain strength in the factories. In the long run, the economic miracle led to the extraordinary labour militancy of the 1969-73 period, during which the unions were greatly strengthened both in numbers and organisationally.(12) As a result, they began to broaden their horizons beyond the factory and sought to negotiate with the government on social and economic policy as well; class conflict became one of the central foci of Italian politics in the 1970s, even more than it had been in the past.

Modernisation

The wave of modernisation, brought on by economic growth, reached a high point in the movement of 1968, which began as a student protest but became a veritable 'cultural revolution', a far-reaching critique of all established values and institutions. In the process, it attacked the traditional sub-cultures, particularly the Catholic, on which the major parties were in part based. In the long run, this freed large numbers of citizens who would otherwise have entered or remained within the ambit of the established parties. Instead, they became available for mobilisation by new social movements. This modernising wave had a differential impact on the different regions of the country. Rapid demographic and industrial growth took place in the North-West, while many rural areas of the country were being depopulated. In some areas of the Centre and North-East, a more balanced form of growth, based on smaller enterprises often located in small towns, was possible, while the cities of

357

the South experienced population growth with little accompanying economic development. The pressures on social services that resulted differed in the different zones of the country, as did other signi- ficant socio-economic factors, such as the female labour-force participation rate, which contributed to the growth of the new social movements. Simi- larly, changes in political attitudes and the availability of large numbers of people for mobil- isation were unevenly distributed over the country. Barbagli and Corbetta identified three main zones:(13) the provincial capitals of the North- West, where the movement of 1968 and its successors had their epicentre; an intermediate zone, compris- ing the Northern and Central countryside and towns with high working-class conflictuality, and the other provincial capitals, where the movement had an impact but later and in a less radical form than in the first zone; and, finally, the rest of the country, where the movement was felt only very weakly. They noted that the PCI's greatest organisational and electoral growth from 1968 to 1976 occurred in the second zone, confirming their view that the Communists benefited from a movement which they did not originate and which they never supported wholeheartedly. Broadly speaking, the territorial bases of the post-1976 'new' social movements have been similar to those of the slightly earlier cycle of activism: it is the most modern areas of the country which have given rise to these new forms of political involvement.

While the country experienced these major social and economic changes which marked the trans- ition to a mature capitalist economy based on the expansion of domestic consumer demand, the politi- cal system failed to keep pace. In the early 1960s, the Socialist party was taken into the governing coalition in an attempt to respond to the new conditions and at the same time divide and eventually tame the working-class movement. The PSI, however, was quickly integrated into the system of patronage presided over by the Christian Democrats, and the reforms that did result amounted to only a partial and stunted version of a modern, advanced welfare state. The privileged positions of the DC's major clienteles were not attacked in any way; in fact, they were strengthened. Unlike France, Italy saw no movements of protest by the petty bourgeoisie in this period. A typical reform of the centre-left coalition (DC, PSI and allies) was the generous extension of pension benefits approved in 1969: it satisfied the demands of the unions while at the same time providing higher payments to the petty bourgeoisie as well and opening up greater opportunities for corruption to the Christian Democrats, who could now confer even more valuable favours on those able-bodied workers for whom they secured disability pensions. Therefore, the backward features of society and the state against which the new movements rose up persisted into the 1970s and 1980s.

The evident distortions that this disjunction between socio-economic conditions and the political system produced, and the relative closure of the DC regime to the demands of the feminists, the ecologists, the peace activists, and similar movements, prescribed the political manifestations of these movements. They also depended on certain characteristics of the party system, as well as the role of the working class in the polity.

The Party System

The Italian party system remains very strongly rooted in society. Both the Catholic and the Marxist sub-cultures date from before 1900, when the masses of the population were first mobilised politically. The two parties with the longest pedigrees, the Liberals and the Republicans, belong to the smaller lay liberal sub-culture. The post-1945 Cold War only reinforced these traditional attachments. While the strength and importance of traditional value systems is in part an obstacle to the parties' acceptance of the themes of the new movements (e.g. in the case of the DC and the women's movement), these inherited values count for less today as they are being eroded by modernisation; the PCI is not as inhibited today by its traditional commitments to the conventional family, to industrial growth, and to the USSR as it once was. But while the values have been revised and criticised, the parties' organisational strength and resources remain largely intact.

In Italy, the parties organise, rather than simply aggregate, a good part of those interests which, in other advanced democracies, are organised more or less autonomously, and many organisations which on the surface appear independent are in fact closely linked to a party. Furthermore, the parties, particularly the PCI, pursue a 'policy of

359

presence' which leads them to attempt to occupy any new issue fields with their own organisations.

Because of this strong implantation of the party system in civil society, it is not easy to identify any Italian social movements which have no links with the system. Either the parties and their mass organisations are the major part of the movement (e.g. the peace movement), or, at a minimum, the militants of the movement owe their political formation to the parties and continue to see the parties and parliament as their principal point of reference (e.g. the feminist movement).

While they offer relatively little space for the growth of new movements because of their roots in society, the parties also preclude their expansion because of the relative flexibility and openness of the party system. The type of proportional representation used for the election of the Chamber of Deputies creates only a relatively low barrier to entry for small parties: groups with as little as 1.1 per cent of the national vote have secured seats, as the Radical Party did in 1976.(14) Moreover, the stability of the Italian electorate, itself a product of the robust sub-culture bases of the party system, means that even small shifts in votes between parties are perceived as highly significant. Therefore, the existing parties have a strong incentive to pay attention to the demands of new movements as far as possible, in order to secure marginal electoral gains or, alternatively, to prevent losses. The Radical electorate, for example, was strenuously courted by the Socialists during the 1976-9 parliament, as they sought to aggregate opponents of a potential grand coalition of Communists and Christian Democrats.

The Communist Party, as the principal opposition party, deserves special attention here. Unlike the German Social Democrats, for instance, the PCI has not held national office since 1947, and can therefore present itself with a relatively untarnished image to the new social movements. On the other hand, it has often showed little sympathy to non-parliamentary opposition movements. Its attitude to the student movement of 1968 was at best ambivalent.(15) While it was pursuing the goal of an 'historic compromise' with the Catholic bloc from 1972 to 1980, it was unwilling to exacerbate tension with the DC by strongly backing feminist demands for divorce and abortion. When it was supporting the Andreotti Government of 'non-

non-confidence' in Parliament, it was itself the prime target of a wave of student agitation in the Spring of 1977. In the controversy over the installation of the Euromissiles, it was unwilling to adopt radical positions for fear of alienating the Socialist Party, which it now saw as a future coalition partner. More than its formal ideology or the ingrained attitudes of its members, the Party was inhibited from supporting many new movements by these strategic and tactical considerations and also by interests which it itself represented: for example, workers in polluting industries and armaments factories.

In the 1980s, however, the PCI began to demonstrate a much more open attitude to social movements and political groups outside itself. In the 1983 election, for example, space was made on the Party's lists for candidates of the Party of Proletarian Unity, composed of Communists excluded from the PCI in 1969 who had been branded as 'fascists' when they first ran for Parliament in 1972. Overtures were made to women, ecologists, and (something unthinkable only a decade earlier) the homosexual movement.(16) This opening was encouraged by the left wing of the party gathered around Pietro Ingrao, which was able to exercise greater influence in the fluid situation after the abandonment of the historic-compromise strategy.

The relative permeability of the PCI to the ideas and interests of the new movements meant that they had great difficulty building strong autonomous organisations. Moreover, the whole party system is sufficiently open to new demands to produce policy outputs which, while not satisfying these demands, serve to demobilise the movements behind them. A case in point is the liberal abortion law passed by Parliament in 1978 with the votes of the lay parties (PCI, PSI, PSDI, PLI, PRI, Radicals and Proletarian Democracy) over the DC's opposition. While the state has proved unable to provide access to legal abortions in all regions of the country, the law nevertheless contributed to the demobilisation of Italian feminism.

The trade unions came to play a role somewhat analogous to that of the parties in the 1970s, when they emerged as major political actors. Not only did they occupy the political scene with their own agenda, their organisational strength allowed them to concern themselves with other issues, such as peace and disarmament, in much the same way that the parties themselves did, though on a smaller scale. Even when they were weakened by recession in the 1980s, the unions were still powerful enough to make class issues, such as the revision of the cost-of-living escalator, the central focus of national politics by tenaciously defending the ground they had previously won.

A survey of the most salient of the new social movements in Italy - feminism, the peace movement, and the environmental movement - will illustrate the interaction of the factors we have outlined. We shall begin with a discussion of the Radical Party, which was the first group to champion many of the 'new' issues.

A Precursor: The Radical Party

One of the first groupings to take up the new issues as its principal focus was a party founded in 1956, the Radical Party. The Radicals were Liberals and Republicans who were unable to accept their parties' continued governmental coalition with the Christian Democrats; the most salient point of their programme was anti-clericalism. The party remained on the margin of politics until 1967, when it was revitalised under the leadership of Marco Pannella. The Radicals then became the most vigorous supporters of all the new causes, from divorce to abortion to civil liberties, including the environmental and peace movements. They first entered Parliament in 1976 with 1.1 per cent of the popular vote and four seats; in 1979, they achieved their greatest electoral success with 3.5 per cent of the vote and eighteen seats in the Chamber; in 1983, the party urged citizens not to vote, but none the less received 2.2 per cent of the vote and eleven seats.

While the Radical Party is sui generis, it has roots in the established party system, and it eventually decided to participate in elections. The theme of anti-clericalism also marks it as a product of the traditional cleavages that created the Italian party system. However, it is opposed not only to Church domination in politics and private life, but to all large, bureaucratic institutions: the military, the parties, the state. The Radicals' ideological roots are in classical liberalism; their ideal is a democratic system in which individuals are free to engage in open, unconditioned discussion. They therefore have

waged an unflagging polemic against the established
parties, labelled the 'partitocrazia' or the
'Palace'. Their main targets have been long-
standing grievances (e.g. the abortion law, the
military), which they perceive as anachronistic in
modern Italy.

In their social composition, the Radicals are
overwhelmingly middle-class. At the party's 30th
Congress (Rome, October 1984), 71 per cent of the
active membership whose occupations were reported
were professional or white-collar workers;(17) in
1979, 74 per cent of the active congressional
delegates whose occupations were known belonged to
the same categories. At the 1979 congress, 74 per
cent of the delegates were under 35 years old and
60 per cent of them lived in cities of more than
150,000 inhabitants;(18) they thus fitted admirably
Inglehart's description of the 'post-industrial
citizens' who form the basis of the new movements.

On the other hand, the Radical Party is not a
mass movement: at the 30th Congress, total membership was reported as only 3,335,(19) whereas the
party had garnered 811,000 votes in the general
election the previous year, a ratio of one member
for every 243 voters. By contrast, the PCI's ratio
of members to voters was approximately 1:7. The
Radical Party is a small group of dedicated
activists which is able to influence a large
segment of public opinion by the use of the mass
media, modern publicity techniques, and spectacular
imaginative actions such as Pannella's hunger
strikes. Because of its size, it offers its
members opportunities for frequent participation in
decision-making, but in practice it is dominated
most of the time by the personality of Pannella.
The parliamentary group also wields dispropor-
tionate influence because it commands the resources
provided by membership in the Chamber, which are
extremely significant in a party with such a
fragile extra-parliamentary structure. Above all,
Pannella and the other deputies are in a position
to command media attention, the most important form
of communication utilised by the party. (The party
also owns networks of television and radio
stations, which are devoted almost entirely to
political broadcasts of various sorts.)

The Radical Party is most accurately
characterised as a small vanguard of modernisation;
it has won its greatest successes when it has
attacked outdated laws and institutions.

The Feminist Movement

The Italian feminist movement has been without doubt one of the most vital and influential in the industrial world: at its highest point of political mobilisation, it was able to wrest the most liberal abortion law in Western Europe from an originally unwilling parliament. The campaign for abortion reform involved several massive demonstrations and was the culmination of several years' intensive organisation of feminist collectives in schools, universities, and neighbourhoods. While the movement has been less obviously active in politics since its victory on the abortion issue, feminism remains a major current force in Italian society which exerts pressure through many different channels.(20)

The particular character of Italian feminism can be accounted for only by the rapidity of the social and economic changes of the past two decades. These changes opened up the possibility of new roles for women, as education, contraception, and job opportunities became increasingly available. An acute conflict developed between these new roles and women's traditional one in the home. This conflict was most intensely felt by female students, forced to make choices between a career and a conventional marriage.(21) A part of the movement's radicalism can be explained by the very backwardness of Italian women's situation before 1970, characterised by, among other things, low rates of participation in the modern labour force and a criminal code which still defined abortion as a 'crime against the race'.

Another factor that was vital to the feminist movement's growth was the extra-parliamentary Left, where it first took shape and its militants first acquired organisational skills and self-confidence. Most of the early feminist collectives formed within the extra-parliamentary groups in the early 1970s, notably Il Manifesto and its successor, the Party of Proletarian Unity (PdUP). From 1972 on, they adopted increasingly independent positions but the line of filiation to the extra-parliamenrary Left and through it to the working-class movement is clear.

Furthermore, while the movement relied on extra-parliamentary pressure to achieve its goals, rejecting the idea of a women's party or even of official support for one of the left parties, it was crucially tied to and dependent on the official political system. For example, the 1976 election seriously divided and weakened the movement at a key moment in the mobilisation around abortion.(22) Some favoured whole-hearted support for one or other of the parties; others advocated keeping a distance from 'male' modes of political action. And the institutional target provided by the abortion campaign was essential to the movement's cohesion, so much so that it became dispersed into many forms of activity, some of them more cultural and personal than directly political, after the passage of the new law.

The women's movement is typical of the Italian new social movements in that it was a modernising attack on outdated values and structures. The intervention of the state in family relations largely followed, rather than preceded, the rise of feminism.(23) It was the feminist movement, rather than the state, that 'thematised' new issues, such as the family, sexuality, and reproduction. One reason for its loss of momentum in the late 1970s was the response of the state, which, through a series of reforms, was able to undermine some of the movement's bases.(24) For example, the legal-isation of abortion eliminated the clinics set up and controlled by the movement to circumvent the old abortion law. Another law (no. 405 of 1975) had already set up official counselling centres which also supplanted the structures of the move-ment. And in 1976-7, the regional governments established women's consultative committees (consulte femminili) which gave heavy weight to the parties, the unions, and the traditional women's organisations. These policies did not deflect the most radical feminists from their goals, but they did divide and decompose the movement, forcing it to adopt longer-term strategies for women's libera-tion.

The Peace Movement

It has been commonplace to observe that the Italian peace movement of the 1980s has been weaker than those of other European countries, particularly Germany and Great Britain. From one point of view this may seem paradoxical, since the Italian demon-strations for disarmament were generally larger than any but those in Germany (e.g. 300-500,000 demonstrators in Rome as against 150-200,000 in

365

London on 24 October 1981; over 500,000 in Rome as against 250,000 in London on 22 October 1983).(25) Nevertheless, these figures do not give an accurate picture of the strength of the peace movement as such: they would have been much lower if major components of the traditional party system, and especially the PCI and its youth organisation, had not supported the demonstrations and brought their members out. This fact illustrates the most salient point about the Italian movement: while it undoubtedly mobilised many people, especially the young, with no previous political involvement, its politics were dominated by the PCI and the other parties and groups that supported it, so that it is difficult to speak of an autonomous peace movement at all.

The PCI found the peace movement created problems as well as opportunities for it. It did not call it into being, and was surprised by the extent of the support for the demonstration of 24 October 1981, which signalled the beginning of the most recent cycle of initiatives. The Communists were opposed to Italian withdrawal from NATO and to unilateral Italian disarmament; they also wanted to maintain good relations with the Socialists, whom they saw as potential coalition partners at least until the formation of the Craxi Government in the summer of 1983. On the immediate issue which gave the peace movement many of its slogans and its vital intermediate objective, the scheduled installation of American cruise missiles at Comiso in Sicily, the PCI temporised: it advocated the suspension of the construction of the missile base until the results of the Geneva disarmament talks were known, but refused to oppose the missiles on Italian soil regardless of the course of the negotiations. It argued that an agreement to reduce both the number of Soviet SS-20s and the number of cruise and Pershing missiles in the European theatre would be the preferred solution.

Other groups were not so hesitant: Proletarian Democracy (DP), a small party including many former members of the student and extra-parliamentary left, advocated withdrawal from NATO and opposition to civilian nuclear power as well. The Radical Party claimed a long history of activism not only on nuclear disarmament but also on other anti-militarist themes. It opposed the Italian military establishment and criticised the amount of money spent on defence in Italy, attacking the PCI's failure to do battle in Parliament on the defence budget. In the 1970s, before the peace movement became a major force, the Radicals organised anti-militarist marches through the north-eastern regions where the concentration of Italian military units is greatest. They linked arms expenditure and arms exports to the famines in the Third World. They also pioneered the campaign for conscientious objection, and proposed a referendum on the abolition of military tribunals. While they supported the peace camp founded at Comiso, they realised that once the PCI threw its weight and organisational resources into the peace movement they could not hope to hegemonise it. They therefore became increasingly critical of the new peace struggles; for the Radicals, their objectives were too generic and in general tended to favour the Soviet position. As an alternative to the demonstrations of 22 October 1983, the Radicals attempted to send some of their members to Prague to demonstrate for human rights and against nuclear weapons.(26)

As a result of the conflicts within and between the various peace committees, no permanent autonomous peace movement such as the British Campaign for Nuclear Disarmament was formed; an assembly of local peace committees held in January 1983 foundered amid accusations that the parties had 'hijacked' it.(27) The movement also engaged in an 'obsessive search' for union support.(28)

While the peace movement was largely hegemon-ised by the Communist presence, the PCI was not totally dominant; its position may be described as one of 'conditioned hegemony'. Furthermore, the party itself and the unions were in turn influenced by the peace movement. In early 1983, many PCI provincial congresses debated motions calling for Italy's withdrawal from NATO. The unions were made more aware of issues such as the need to reconvert the arms industry. And the Young Communist Federation (FGCI) moved closer to the peace movement than the party itself, advocating Italy's exit from NATO in conjunction with the withdrawal of one nation from the Warsaw Pact. This openness demonstrates the capacity of the parties, especially the PCI, to take account of the new demands put forward by the mass movements. It was purchased at a price. On 2 June 1985, for example, the Communist Mayor of Rome stood on the reviewing stand during the military parade marking the national holiday; nearby, FGCI members accompanied by at least one PCI deputy were

demonstrating against the parade and military
expenditure. The Young Communists were roundly
criticised by some Party members who were committed
to the party's traditional line of support for the
'democratic armed forces',(29)
        As in most of Western Europe, the Italian
peace movement lost momentum once the Pershing and
cruise missiles were in fact installed. This fact
suggests that it was among other things a response
to objective circumstances of international politics and, in the Italian case, an imitation of
international trends, more than a product of value
shifts or the dissolution of traditional values.

The Ecological Movement

The ecological movement illustrates, like the
feminist movement, the modernising character of the
new social movements in Italy. At the same time,
its history demonstrates almost as clearly as that
of the peace movement the pervasive influence of
the parties even in the newest political phenomena.
        In many of its battles, the ecological move-
ment is attempting to combat the distortions and
inadequacies resulting from the persisting backwardness of the Italian state and Italian society,
in order to bring Italy up to the level of ameni-
ties and public services typical of other advanced
capitalist countries. For example, two of the
major themes on which the 'Green List' campaigned
and won two seats on the Rome city council in May
1985 were the control of downtown traffic and the
enforcement of laws against illegal building. One
of the leading figures of the green movement, the
Roman judge Gianfranco Amendola, has initiated a
campaign for the enforcement of the by-laws against
noise pollution. The Radical Ecological Association (ARE) is fighting against the practice of
closing hospital wards for several weeks in the
summer during the staff's vacation(!). Most of
these are acute problems in Italy, as even the
temporary visitor can attest, results of the
failure of the Italian state to provide the framework of regulation and intervention found in most
of the rest of Europe and North America. This
failure is not generic inefficiency, but is due to
the fact that important interests, above all those
of segments of the petty bourgeoisie, are opposed
to a more modern level of service and intervention:
downtown shopkeepers fear the closing of the

historic centres to traffic; owners of small
factories and workshops do not want the expense of
controlling noise or moving away from residential
areas. Illegal building is engaged in not only by
small entrepreneurs but by many workers; it is an
indictment of the state's inability to remedy the
private sector's failure to provide adequate
housing, one of the most basic requirements of a
modern industrial population.

In spite of the gravity of these environmental
issues, there is as yet no Green Party in Italy.
This can be attributed to the persistent strength
and absorptive capacity of the existing parties.
Only in the 1985 regional and local elections did
Green Lists appear on a large scale, and these were
lists of candidates presented by coalitions of
various organisations, not the expression of a
party. The principal components of the green movement are (i) the Lega Ambiente (Environment League)
of the Italian Recreational and Cultural Association (ARCI), a PCI-sponsored mass organisation;
(ii) the Radicals, or rather a segment of them,
organised in the ARE and the Italian branch of the
Friends of the Earth; (iii) the autonomous environmentalist groups, or 'green greens', particularly
strong in the North-East and Trentino-Alto Adige.
The formation of the Green Lists in 1985 was such a
difficult process that in the end two lists (one
sponsored by the Radical Party, one by the other
environmentalist forces) were presented in
Piedmont. The lists in the other regions were
diverse: some of them (e.g. in Abruzzo) were direct
emanations of the Radical Party and its leadership,
and did not have the support of the Lega Ambiente.
While the relative success of the Green Lists (an
average of 1.7 per cent of the popular vote) has
forced the ecological movement to consider the
question of the formation of a party, most of the
activists are opposed to such a move because they
retain strong ties with existing parties, for the
most part the PCI and the Radicals.

Conclusion

The foregoing survey has highlighted the overriding
importance of the political structure and the level
of class conflict in explaining the relative weakness of the new social movements in Italy. At the
same time, it has shown that the more sociological
accounts of these movements not only lack explana-

369

tory power but do not fully fit the facts either.

Offe views the new social movements as primarily responses to external 'provocations': the invasion by the state or the economic system of spheres of life that were formerly private and taken for granted as 'natural'. With the economic crisis of the 1970s, he argues, people's identification with their economic roles has been weakened. At the same time, traditional values and ideologies have been dissolved by the corrosive action of liberal scepticism. As these two bases for self-identification and aggregation have lost their hold, people have fallen back on more basic ascriptive identities, such as gender, language, and territory. The new movements are in part defensive and conservative, to the extent that they want to preserve an existing state of affairs from intervention (e.g. the ecological movement).

Habermas's account, while similar in many respects to Offe's, lays particular stress on the point that the dissolution of traditional value systems is accelerated by the expansion of state activity in response to economic crisis tendencies in advanced capitalism. The state is forced, in entering new fields, to 'thematise' i.e. open for public discussion questions that were previously not discussed because their solution was taken for granted (e.g. child-rearing). This thematisation undermines the inherited motivation systems, such as family privatism, that according to Habermas provide legitimation for the state.

In the Italian case, however, it does not seem that the new movements are defensive or responses to the 'thematisation' of new issues by the state. Rather, they have generally initiated discussion of questions the state would later take up and attempt to resolve through limited reforms; this is certainly the case with the Radicals, the feminists, and the greens, the three movements with more genuine autonomy which we have discussed. Often the grievances they vented were against long-standing problems (e.g. the abortion law) rather than fresh actions by the state. Moreover, they were in many cases protesting at the state's inaction, as in the case of noise pollution, rather than the growth of its activities. All this suggests that the new movements were leading the drive to modernise Italian society, in opposition to a DC regime tied to many retrograde interests, rather than conducting a protest against modernity.

According to Inglehart, the new social movements reflect the fact that widespread affluence
has satisfied the material needs of the majority of
the citizens of the advanced democracies, permit-
ting them to give priority to other values, such as
participation or environmental protection, that may
enter into conflict with the imperatives of
economic growth. The new middle class are the chief
bearers of the new post-materialist values because
of their level of education and relative economic
security. The younger members of this group, in
particular, tend to reject materialism because of
their generational experiences, such as the student
movement of the later 1960s and early 1970s, and
because they did not live through either the
Depression or the Second World War.

The composition of the new social movements
does correspond fairly well to Inglehart's account.
However, it is almost inevitable, especially in
Italy where the cultural distance between elite and
masses is still large, that virtually any movement
will be led by middle-class intellectuals. What is
perhaps surprising is the small size of the active
cadre in some of the movements and the dominant
role played by some leaders in them. (The Radical
Party is the best illustration of both of these
trends in the new movements, but they are evident
to a lesser degree in the others as well.) These
facts contradict Inglehart's contention that the
post-industrial citizens want participatory, mass-
based forms of political activity. Moreover, it is
a mistake to underrate the external, objective
causes of these movements. Feminism and nuclear
disarmament are not supplementary 'life-style'
issues that people may wish to take up when their
material needs have been satisfied: feminism is
rooted in women's role in the economy, while the
peace movement is responding to a threat to the
most basic 'need' of all - life itself.

This study of non-parliamentary opposition in
Italy has shown the crucial importance of the
political system, including the parties and their
ideological positions, in explaining its strength
and character. In Italy, the decline of the traditional sub-cultures and ideologies, principally
Marxism and Catholicism, will weaken the hold of
the established parties on civil society and allow
more room for the development of autonomous social
movements. However, this same 'de-confessionalisa-
tion' of the parties should permit them to be more

371

open to the new themes and perspectives. The principal barrier to the absorption of new movements within the party system will remain the interests which each party already incorporates. While we have laid emphasis on the petty-bourgeois interests that form part of the DC power bloc, the PCI is also, from one point of view, a coalition of interests that includes both the peasants whose fertilisers pollute the Adriatic and the hotel-keepers who wish to see it cleaned up. The same is true of all the other parties. For this reason we can expect that the parties will have difficulty synthesising the new demands with the existing interests, and if they do not engage in some very creative strategic thinking it is likely that the new movements will increasingly seek an autonomous voice both inside and outside Parliament.

Notes

1. Ronald Inglehart, The Silent Revolution (Princeton UP, Princeton NJ, 1977).
2. Claus Offe, Contradictions of the Welfare State, (MIT Press, Cambridge, Mass., 1984), esp. pp.189-90 and 292-5.
3. Jürgen Habermas, Legitimation Crisis, (Beacon, Boston, 1975).
4. See Otto Kirchheimer, 'The Transformation of the Western European Party System', in J. La Palombara and M. Weiner (eds), Political Parties and Political Development, (Princeton UP, Princeton NJ, 1966).
5. See A. Lijphart, Democracy in Plural Societies: A Comparative Exploration, (Yale UP, New Haven, Conn., 1977).
6. Alan Zuckerman, The Politics of Faction: Christian Democratic Rule in Italy, (Yale UP, New Haven, Conn., 1979).
7. Cf. Suzanne Berger, 'The Uses of the Traditional Sector in Italy: Why Declining Classes Survive', in Frank Bechhofer and Brian Elliott (eds), The Petite Bourgeoisie: Comparative Studies of the Uneasy Stratum, (Macmillan, London, 1981).
8. See Antonio Gramsci, Selections from the Prison Notebooks, ed. Quintin Hoare and G. Nowell Smith, (Lawrence and Wishart, London, 1971).
9. Ibid., p.80 n.
10. See Alain Lipietz, The Globalisation of the General Crisis of Fordism, Occasional Paper, Kingston, Ontario, 1984. This paper provides a good summary in English of the theses of the 'regulation school', who are responsible for popularising the concept of Fordism and that of 'regime of accumulation'.
11. See Michele Salvati, 'The Impasse of Italian Capitalism', New Left Review, 76, (November-December 1971).
12. See Peter Lange and Maurizio Vanicelli, Unions, Crisis, and Change, (Allen & Unwin, London, 1982).
13. Maurizio Barbagli and Piergiorgio Corbetta, 'Partito e movimento: aspetti e rinnovamento del PCI', Inchiesta, VIII (January-February 1978), esp. pp.14-20.
14. A good outline of the electoral system in English is by Doug Wertman Italy at the Polls:

The Parliamentary Elections of 1976, (American Enterprise Institute, Washington DC, 1977), pp.44-51.
15. See Grant Amyot, The Italian Communist Party: The Crisis of the Popular Front Strategy, (Croom Helm, London, 1981), pp.173-7 and Chap. 12.
16. See L'Unita, 25 June 1983.
17. '30° Congresso del Partito Radicale, Relazione del Tesoriere Francesco Rutelli e Bilancio del P.R. 1983-84', Rome, 31 October 1984.
18. Piero Ignazi, 'I radicali dal 1976 al 1979: Tre ricerche a confronto' in Argomenti radicali, 16 (June-October 1980).
19. '30° Congresso'. The annual dues were set at 130,000 lire (c.US$70).
20. See Anna Rita Calabro and Laura Grasso, (eds), Dal movimento femminista al femminismo diffuso, (Franco Angeli, Milan, 1985).
21. See Yasmine Ergas, 'Femminismo e crisi de sistema. Il percorso politico delle donne attraverso gli anni settanta', Rassegna italiana di sociologia, XXI, (October-December 1980) and 'Femminismo e giovani', Inchiesta, 54, (November-December 1981).
22. Biancamaria Frabotta, 'Preface' in Giuletta Ascoli et al., La parola electtorale. Viaggio nell'universo politico maschile, (Edizioni dell donne, Rome, 1976), p.9.
23. Ergas, 'Femminismo e crisi de sistema'.
24. Ergas, 'Femminismo e crisi di sistema' and 'Allargamento della cittadinanza e governo del conflitto: le politiche sociali negli anni settanta in Italia', Stato e mercato, 6 (December 1982).
25. Giovanni Lodi, Uniti e diversi. Le mobilitazioni per la pace nell'Italia degli anni '80, (Edizioni Unicopli, Milan, 1984).
26 Ibid., p.78.
27. Il Manifesto, 29 January 1983.
28. F. Crucianelli, 'Questo sindacato fa proprio rabbia', Il Manifesto, 1 June 1982.
29. See L'Unita, 4 June 1985, for some of the polemic generated by this episode.

SELECT BIBLIOGRAPHY

Alba, V. Transition in Spain: From Franco to
    Democracy (Transaction Books, New Brunswick,
    NJ, 1978)
Albers, J. 'Modernisierung, neue Spannungslinien
    und politische Chancen der Grünen', Politische
    Vierteljahresschrift 26, (1985), pp.211-26.
Alt, J. et al. 'Angels in Plastic: The Liberal
    Surge in 1974', Political Studies vol. 25, 3
    pp.343-68.
Amsden, J. Collective Bargaining and Class Conflict
    in Spain, (Weidenfeld & Nicolson, London,
    1972).
Amyot, G. The Italian Communist Party: The Crisis
    of the Popular Front Strategy, (Croom Helm,
    London, 1981).
Andeweg R.B. Dutch Voters Adrift. On Explanations
    of Electoral Change, (Leiden University Press,
    Leiden, 1982).
——— et al., 'Government Formation' in R. Griffith
    (ed.), The Economy and Politics of the Nether-
    lands since 1945, (Nijhoff, The Hague, 1980).
Apparu, J-P. (ed.) La Droite Aujourd'hui, (Michel,
    Paris, 1979).
Arango, R. The Spanish Political System: Franco's
    Legacy, (Westview Press, Boulder, 1978).
Ashkenazi, A. Reformpartei und Aussenpolitik: Die
    Aussenpolitik der SPD, (Wissenschaft und
    Politik, Cologne, 1968).
Aydelotte, W.O. (ed.) The History of Parliamentary
    Behaviour, (Princeton University Press,
    Princeton, NJ, 1977).
Bacot, P. and Journès. C. Les nouvelles idéologies,
    (Presses universitaires, Lyons, 1982).
Badinter R. et al. Vous avez dit Fascismes?,
    (Montalba, Paris, 1984).

Bakvis, H. Catholic Power in the Netherlands,
    (McGill University Press, Montreal, 1981).
Bar, A. 'The Emerging Spanish Party System: Is
    There a Model?', West European Politics, vol.
    7, no. 4 (1984), pp.128-55.
Barnes, I. 'The Pedigree of GRECE', Patterns of
    Prejudice, vol. 14, nos. 3/4, (1980).
Barnes, S. 'Italy: Oppositions on Left, Right and
    Centre' in R.A. Dahl, (ed.) Political Opposi-
    tions in Western Democracies, (Yale University
    Press, New Haven, Conn., 1966).
—— Kaase, M. et al., Political Action: Mass
    Participation in Five Western Countries,
    (Sage, London, 1979).
Beer, S.H. Modern British Politics, (Faber & Faber,
    London, 1965).
—— Britain Against Itself, (Faber & Faber,
    London, 1982).
Bell, D. The Coming of Post-Industrial Society,
    (Penguin, Harmondsworth, 1976).
Bell. D.S. (ed.), Contemporary French Political
    Parties, (Croom Helm, London, 1982).
—— (ed.), Democratic Politics in Spain, (Pinter,
    London, 1983).
Bell, D.S. and Criddle, B. The French Socialist
    Party, (Oxford University Press, Oxford,
    1984).
Belloni, F.P. and Beller, D.C. (eds) Faction
    Politics. Political Parties and Factionalism
    in Comparative Perspective, (Clio Press,
    Oxford, 1978).
Benoist, A. de Vu de Droite, (Copernic, Paris,
    1977).
—— Les idées à l'endroit, (Hallier, Paris, 1979).
Berrington, H. (ed.) Change in British Politics,
    (Cass, London, 1984).
Besson, W. 'Regierung und Opposition in der
    deutschen Politik' Politische Vierteljahres-
    schrift 3, (1962)
Beyme, K. von 'Elite Input and Policy Output: The
    Case of Germany' in M. Czudnowski (ed.) Does
    Who Governs Matter?, (Northern Illinois
    University Press, DeKalb, 1982).
—— 'Governments, Parliaments and the Structure of
    Power in Political Parties' in H. Daalder and
    P. Mair (eds), Western European Party Systems.
    Continuity and Change, (Sage, London, 1983).
—— The Political System of the Federal Republic
    of Germany, (Gower, Aldershot, 1983).
—— Political Parties in Western Democracies.

(Gower, Aldershot, 1985).
Bickerich, W. (ed.) SPD und Grüne: Das neue
    Bündnis? (Rowohlt, Reinbek, 1985).
Billig, M. L'internationale raciste. De la psycho-
    logie à la 'science des races', (Maspero,
    Paris, 1981).
Birch, A. The British System of Government 4th edn
    (Allen & Unwin, London, 1980).
Birnbaum, P. et al. Réinventer le parlement,
    (Flammarion, Paris, 1977).
Blondel J. Comparative Legislatures, (Prentice
    Hall, Englewood Cliffs, NJ, 1973).
Bogdanor, V. Multi-Party Politics and the Consti-
    tution, (Cambridge University Press, London,
    1983).
—— (ed.) Coalition Government in Western Europe,
    (Policy Studies Institute and Heinemann,
    London, 1983).
—— and Butler, D. (eds) Democracy and Elections,
    (Cambridge University Press, London, 1983).
Bourgeois, C. (ed.) El PC Español, Italiano Y.
    Francés Cara al Poder, (Cambio 16, Madrid,
    1977).
Boy, D. et al 1981: Les élections de l'alternance,
    (FNSP, Paris, 1986).
Bracher, K-D. 'Politische Institutionen in
    Krisenzeiten' Vierteljahreshefte für
    Zeitgeschichte, vol. 33, no. 1, (1985).
Bradley, I. Breaking the Mould?, (Martin Robertson,
    Oxford, 1981).
Brand, J. The National Movement in Scotland,
    (Routledge & Kegan Paul, London, 1978).
Brand, K.W. et al. Aufbruch in eine andere
    Gesellschaft: Neue soziale Bewegungen in der
    Bundesrepublik, (Campus, Frankfurt/M, 1983).
—— (ed.) Neue soziale Bewegungen in Westeurope
    und den USA, (Campus, Frankfurt/M, 1985).
Brunn, J. (ed.) La Nouvelle Droite, (Oswald, Paris,
    1979).
Budge, I. and Farlie, D.J. Explaining and Predic-
    ting Elections. Issue Effects and Party
    Strategies in Twenty-Three Democracies, (Allen
    & Unwin, London, 1983).
Bürklin, W. 'The German Greens: The Post-Industrial
    Non-established and the Party System', Inter-
    national Political Science Review, vol. 6,
    no. 4, (1984).
—— Grüne Politik, (Westdeutscher Verlag, Opladen,
    1984).
Bustelo, F. et al. Partido Socialista Obrero

Español, (Avance, Barcelona, 1976).

Caciagli, M. 'Spain: Parties and the Party Regime in Transition' in G. Pridham (ed.) 'The New Mediterranean Democracies: Regime Transition in Spain, Greece and Portugal'. Special issue West European Politics, vol. 7, no. 2, (1984), pp.84-98.

Capdeceille, J. et al. France de gauche, vote à droite, (FNSP, Paris, 1981).

Carr, R. and Fusi, J.P. Spain. Dictatorship to Democracy, (Allen & Unwin, London, 1979).

Carrillo, S. Hacia un Socialismo en Libertad, (Cenit, Madrid, 1977).

—— Eurocommunismo y Estado, (Grijalbo, Barcelona, 1977).

Cazzola, Franco 'Consenso e opposizione nel Parliamento Italieno: il ruolo del PCI dalla I alla IV legislature', Rivista Italiana di Scienza Politica (January 1972).

—— Governo e Opposizione nel Parliamento Italiano, (Giuffre, Milan, 1974).

Cerny, P. and Schain, M. (eds) Socialism, the State and Public Policy in France, (Methuen, New York, 1985).

Charlot, J. The Gaullist Phenomenon, (Allen & Unwin, London, 1971).

Cherot, J.-Y. Le Comportement parlementaire, (Economica, Paris, 1984).

Clark, J. et al. Trade Unions, National Politics and Economic Management, (The Anglo-German Foundation, London, 1980).

Club de l'Horloge Socialisme et Fascisme: une même famille?, (Michel, Paris, 1984).

Colliard, J.-C. Les régimes parlementaires contemporains, (Presses de la fondation nationale des sciences politique, Paris, 1978).

Coston, H. Dictionnaire de la Politique française, (Paris, 1967).

Coverdale, J. The Political Transformation of Spain after Franco, (Praeger, New York, 1979).

Craig, F.W.S. British Electoral Facts, (Parliamentary Research Services, Chichester, 1981).

Crewe, T. et al. 'Partisan Dealignment in Britain 1964-1974', British Journal of Political Science, vol. 7, (1977), pp.129-90.

—— and Denver D. (eds) Electoral Change in Western Democracies, (Croom Helm, Beckenham, 1985).

Da Silva, M. 'Modernisation and Ethnic Conflict:

the case of the Basques', Comparative-Poli-
tics, vol. 7, no. 2, (1975), pp.227-52.
Daalder, H. 'Opposition in a Segmented Society' in
R.A. Dahl (ed.) Political Oppositions in
Western Democracies (Yale University Press,
New Haven, Conn., 1966).
—— 'Exteme P.R. - The Dutch Experience' in S.E.
Finer (ed.) Adversary Politics and Electoral
Reform, (Wigram, London, 1975).
—— and Mair P. Western European Party Systems:
Continuity and Change, (Sage, London, 1983).
Dahl, R.A. (ed.) Political Oppositions in Western
Democracies, (Yale University Press, New
Haven, Conn., 1966).
—— (ed.) Regimes and Oppositions, (Yale
University Press, New Haven, Conn., 1974).
Dahrendorf, R. Society and Democracy in Germany,
(Weidenfeld & Nicolson, London, 1969).
—— Law and Order, (The Hamlyn Trust/Stevens &
Sons, London, 1985).
Dalton, R., Flanagan, S. and Beck, P. (eds)
Electoral Change in Advanced Industrial Socie-
ties: Realignment or Dealignment, (Princeton
University Press, Princeton, NJ, 1984).
De Baecque, F. Qui gouverne la France?, (PUF,
Paris, 1976).
De Estéban, I. et al. Los partidos politicos en la
España actual, (Planeta, Barcelona, 1982).
Debré, J-L. La constitution de la V République
(PUF, Paris, 1975).
Denver, D. 'The SPD-Liberal Alliance: The End of
the Two-party System?' in Berrington, H. (ed.)
Change in British Politics, (Cass, London,
1984), pp.75-102.
Di Palma, G. Surviving without Governing: the
Italian Parties in Parliament, (University of
California Press, Berkeley, 1977).
—— Political Syncretism in Italy: historical
coalition strategies and the present crisis.
(University of California Press, Berkeley,
1978).
Dittberner, J. and Ebbighausen, R. (eds) Das
Parteiensystem in der Legitimationskrise,
(Westdeutscher Verlag, Opladen, 1973).
Döring, H. and Smith, G. (eds) Party Government and
Political Culture in Western Germany,
(Macmillan, London, 1982).
Downs, A. An Economic Theory of Democracy,, (Harper
& Row, New York, 1957).
Duelo, G. Diccionario de Grupos, Fuerzas y

Partidos Politicas Españoles, (La Gaya
    Ciencia, Barcelona, 1977).
Duhamel, O. La gauche et la V république, (PUF,
    Paris, 1980).
Duprat, F. Les mouvements de'extrême droite en
    France depuis 1944, (Paris, 1972).
Dutter, L. 'The Netherlands as Plural Society',
    Comparative Political Studies, (1978)
Duverger, M. La démocratie sans le peuple, (Seuil,
    Paris, 1967).
—— Les partis politiques, (Colin, Paris, 1976),
    (9th edn).
—— Echec au roi, (Albin Michel, Paris, 1978).
—— Le système politique français, (PUP, Paris,
    1985).
Ebermann, T. and Trampert, R. Die Zukunft der
    Grünen. Ein realistisches Konzept für eine
    radikale Partei, (Konkret Verlag, Hamburg,
    1984).
Epstein, L.D. Political Parties in Western Demo-
    cracies, (Pall Mall, London, 1980), (2nd edn).
Equipo, J. (ed.) La Alternative Socialista del
    PSOE, (Cuardernos para el Dialogo, Madrid,
    1977).
Farneti, P. The Italian Party System 1945-1980,
    (Pinter, London, 1985).
Feist, U. et al. 'Die politischen Einstellungen der
    Arbeitslosen', Aus Politik und Zeitgeschichte,
    vol. 45, (1984).
Finer, S.E. Adversary Politics and Electoral
    Reform, (Wigram, London, 1975).
Flanagan, S. and Dalton R. 'Parties Under Stress:
    Realignment and Dealignment in Advanced Indus-
    trial Societies', West European Politics, vol.
    7, no. 1, (1984), pp.7-23.
Frears, J. Political Parties and Elections in the
    French Fifth Republic, (Hurst, London, 1978).
Freeman, G.P. Immigrant Labor and Radical Conflict
    in Industrial Societies, (Princeton University
    Press, Princeton, NJ, 1979).
Fogt, H. 'Die Mandatsträger der Grünen: Zur
    sozialen und politischen Herkunft der alterna-
    tiven Parteielite', Aus Politik und
    Zeitgeschichte, vol. 11, (1986), pp.16-33.
Friedrich, M. 'Opposition ohne Alternative' in
    K. Kluxen, Parlamentarismus, (Kiepenheuer &
    Witsch, Cologne, 1969).
—— 'Opposition im Deutschen Bundestag',
    Zeitschrift für Parlamentsfragen, vol. 3,
    (1973).

Galli, G. and Prandi, A. Patterns of Political
    Participation in Italy, (Yale University
    Press, New Haven, Conn., 1970).
Gaus, G. Staatserhaltende Opposition oder hat die
    SPD kapituliert?, (Rowohlt, Reinbek, 1966).
Gillespie, P. 'The Clandestine PSOE', Spanish
    Studies, vol. 6, (1984), pp.34-47.
Giscard d'Estaing, Valéry Democratie français
    (Fayard, Paris, 1976).
Gladdish, K. 'Coalition Government and Policy
    Outputs in the Netherlands' in V. Bogdanor
    (ed.), Coalition Government in Western Europe,
    (Heinemann, London, 1983).
—— 'The 1982 Netherland Elections', West European
    Politics, vol. 6, no. 3, (1983).
—— 'The Netherlands' in V. Bogdanor (ed.),
    Representatives of the People? Parliamentarians
    and Constituents in Western Democracies,
    (Gower, Aldershot, 1985).
Goldthorpe, J.H. et al. The Affluent Worker Series,
    1968-1969, (Cambridge University Press,
    Cambridge, 1968-1969).
Griffith, R. (ed.) The Economy and Politics of the
    Netherlands since 1945, (Nijhoff, The Hague,
    1980).
Grillo, R.D. Ideologies and Institutions in Urban
    France. The Representation of Immigrants,
    (Cambridge University Press, London, 1985).
Griotteray, A. Les Immigrés: le choc, (Plon, Paris,
    1984).
Grosser, A. 'France: Nothing but Opposition' in
    R.A. Dahl (ed.) Political Oppositions in
    Western Democracies, (Yale University Press,
    New Haven, Conn., 1966).
Grosser, D. 'Die Opposition in Deutschland' in
    W. Doeker and W. Steffani (eds) Pluralismus.
    Festschrift für Ernst Fränkel, (Hoffman &
    Campe, Hamburg, 1973).
Grubmüller, M. Die Opposition im politischen
    Prozess. (Voegel, Munich, 1972).
Guggenberger, B. Bürgerinitiativen in der
    Parteiendemokratie, (Kohlhammer, Stuttgart,
    1980).
Gunther, R. and Bough R.A. 'Religious Conflict and
    Consensus in Spain: A Tale of Two Constituen-
    cies' World Affairs, vol. 143, no. 4, (1981),
    pp.366-412.
Halsey, A.H. Change in British Society, (Oxford
    University Press, Oxford, 1981).
Harrison, M. Trade Unions and the Labour Party

Since 1945, (Allen & Unwin, London, 1960).
Hattem, M. van, 'The State of the Parties in Parliament. The Labour Party's Second Term in Opposition' The Political Quarterly, (1984), pp.364-8.
Hauss, C. The New Left in France. The Unified Socialist Party, (Greenwood, Westport, Conn., 1978).
Heath, A. et al. How Britain Votes, (Pergamon, Oxford, 1985).
Hereth, M. Die parlamentarische Opposition in der Bundesrepublik, (Olzog, Munich, 1969).
Hine, D. 'Thirty Years of the Italian Republic: Governability and Constitutional Reform', Parliamentary Affairs, (Winter 1981).
Hübner, P. and Thaysen U. 'Opposition im Deutschen Bundestag und in Schleswig Holstein', Zeitschrift für Parlamentsfragen, vol. 1, no. 1, (1970).
Inglehart, R. The Silent Revolution, (Princeton University Press, Prnceton, NJ, 1977).
——— 'Traditionelle Trennungslinien und die Entwicklung der neuen Politik in westlichen Industriegesellschaften', Politische Vierteljahresschrift, vol. 24, (1983).
Ionescu, G. and Madariaga, I. de Opposition. Past and Present of a Political Institution, (Watts, London, 1968).
Ismayr, W. 'Die Grünen im Bundestag: Parlamentarisierung und Basisanbindung', Zeitschrift für Parlamentsfragen, vol. 16, no. 3, (1985), pp.299-321.
Johnson N. In Search of the Constitution, (Methuen, London, 1977).
Johnson, R. The Long March of the French Left, (Macmillan, London, 1981).
July, S. Les années Mitterrand, (Grasset, Paris, 1986).
Kaase, M. 'The Challenge of the "Participatory Revolution" in Pluralist Democracies', International Political Science Review, vol. 5, no. 3, (1984).
Kaltefleiter, W. and Pfaltzgraff, L. (eds) The Peace Movements in Europe and America, (Croom Helm, Beckenham, 1985).
Kavanagh, D. (ed.) The Politics of the Labour Party, (Allen & Unwin, London, 1982).
Kieve, R. 'Pillars of Sand, a Marxist Critique of Consociational Democracy in the Netherlands, Comparative Politics, (1981).

Kirchheimer, O. 'The Waning of Opposition in
    Parliamentary Regimes', Social Research, vol.
    24, no. 2, (1957), pp.127-56.
—— 'The Vanishing Opposition' in R. Dahl (ed.)
    Political Oppositions in Western Democracies,
    (Yale University Press, New Haven, Conn.,
    1966).
—— 'The Transformation of the Western European
    Party System' in J. La Palombara and M. Weiner
    (eds), Political Parties and Political
    Development, (Princeton University Press,
    Princeton, NJ, 1966).
—— 'Wandlungen der politischen Opposition' in K.
    Kluxen, Parlamentarismus, (Kiepenheuer &
    Witsch, Cologne, 1969).
Kogan, D. et al. The Battle for the Labour Party,
    (Fontana, London, 1982).
Kolinsky, E. Parties, Opposition and Society in
    West Germany, (Croom Helm, Beckenham, 1984).
—— 'Democracy and Opposition in West Germany:
    Rearmament and Nuclear Weapons in the
    Fifties', Contemporary German Studies,
    'University of Strathclyde) 1, (1985).
Kolinsky M. and Paterson W.E. (eds), Social and
    Political Movements in Western Europe, (Croom
    Helm, London, 1976).
Kralewski W. and Neunreithor, K. Oppositionelles
    Verhalten im ersten Deutschen Bundestag 1949-
    1953, (Westdeutscher Verlag, Cologne/Opladen,
    1963).
Krause, F. Antimilitaristische Opposition in der
    Bundesrepublik, (Fischer, Frankfurt/M, 1971).
Küchler, M. 'Staats-, Parteien- oder Politik-
    verdrossenheit?' in H-J. Raschke (ed.) Bürger
    und Parteien. Ansichten und Analysen einer
    schwierigen Beziehung, (Westdeutscher Verlag,
    Opladen, 1982).
Küchler M. 'Friedensbewegung in der Bundesrepublik
    - Alter Pazifismus oder neue soziale
    Bewegung?' in J.W. Falter et al. (eds)
    Politische Willensbildung und Interessen-
    vermittlung, (Westdeutscher Verlag, Opladen,
    1984).
Lange P. 'Crisis and Consent, Change and Compro-
    mise: Dilemmas of Italian Communism in the
    1970s' in P. Lange and S. Tarrow (eds), Italy
    in Transition: Conflict and Consequence,
    (Cass, London, 1980).
—— and Vanicelli, M. Unions, Crisis and Change,
    (Allen & Unwin, London, 1982).

Langguth, G. Protestbewegung. Entwicklung, Nieder-
     gang, Renaissance. Die Neue Linke seit 1968,
     (Wissenschaft und Politik, Cologne, 1983).
LaPalombara, J. 'Two Steps Forward, One Step Back:
     the PCI's struggle for legitimacy' in H.R.
     Penniman, (ed.) Italy at the Polls, 1979,
     (American Enterprise Institute, Washington DC,
     1981).
—— and Weiner, M. (eds) Political Parties and
     Political Development, (Princeton University
     Press, Princeton, NJ, 1966).
Laqueur, W. and Hunter, R. (eds) European Peace
     Movements and the Future of the Western
     Alliance, (Transaction Books, New Brunswick,
     NJ, 1985).
Lawson, K. (ed.) Political Parties and Linkage,
     (Yale University Press, New Haven, Conn.,
     1980).
Lees, J.D. and Shaw, M. (eds) Committees in Legis-
     latures. A Comparative Analysis, (Martin
     Robertson, Oxford, 1979).
Lehmbruch, G. Parteienwettbewerb im Bundesstaat,
     (Kohlhammer, Stuttgart, 1976).
Levitas, R. (ed.) The Ideology of the New Right,
     (Blackwell, Oxford, 1985).
Lijphart, A. The Politics of Accommodation, 2nd
     edn, (University of California Press,
     Berkeley, 1975).
—— Democracies: Patterns of Majoritarian and
     Consensus Government in Twenty-One Countries,
     (Yale University Press, New Haven, Conn.,
     1984).
Linz, J.J. 'Opposition in and under an Authori-
     tarian Regime: The Case of Spain' in R.A. Dahl
     (ed.) Regimes and Oppositions, (Yale Univer-
     sity Press, New Haven, Conn., 1974).
—— 'The New Spanish Party System' in R. Rose
     (ed.) Electoral participation. A Comparative
     Analysis, (Sage, Beverley Hills, 1980).
Loewenberg, G. Parliament in the German Political
     System, (Cornell University Press, Ithaca,NY,
     1967).
—— 'The Patterns of Political Opposition in
     Germany' in H.S. Conmayer et al. (eds)
     Festschrift für Karl Löwenstein, (Mohr,
     Tübingen, 1971).
—— and Patterson, S.C. Comparing Legislatures,
     (Little Brown, Boston, 1979).
Lorig, W. 'Protestverhalten und neue soziale
     Bewegungen', Gegenwartskunde, vol. 2, (1984).

Luchaire, F. and Comac G. La constitution de la
  V république, (Economica, Paris, 1980).
MacRae, D. Parliament, Parties and Society in
  France 1946-1958, (Macmillan, London, 1967).
Maguire, M. 'Is There Still Persistence? Electoral
  Change in Western Europe, 1948-1979' in
  H. Daalder and P. Mair (eds) Western European
  Party Systems: Continuity and Change, (Sage,
  London, 1983).
Massot, J. Le présidence de la république en France
  1965-1985, (Documentations françaises, Paris,
  1986).
Maravall, J. Dictatorship and Political Dissent:
  Workers and Students in Franco's Spain,
  (Tavistock, London, 1978).
—— 'Spain, Eurocommunism and Socialism',
  Political Studies, vol. 27, (1979), pp.218-35.
—— 'Political Cleavages in Spain and the 1979
  General Election', Government and Opposition,
  vol. 14, (1979), pp.299-317.
—— La Politica de la Transicion, 1975-1980,
  (Taurus, Madrid, 1981).
Marcilly, J. Le Pen sans bandeau, (Grancher, Paris,
  1984).
Marseille, J. Empire colonial et capitalisme
  français. Histoire d'un divorce, (Michel,
  Paris, 1985).
Martinet, G. Le système Pompidou, (Seuil, Paris,
  1973).
May, T.C. Trade Unions and Pressure Groups, (Heath,
  Farnborough, 1975).
McAllister, I and Rose R. The Nationwide Competi-
  tion for Votes, (Pinter, London, 1984).
McCarthy, W.E.J. (ed.) Trade Unions, (Penguin,
  Harmondsworth, 1972).
McDonough et al. 'The Spanish Public in Political
  Transition', British Journal of Political
  Science, vol. 11, (1981), pp.49-79.
Medhurst, K. The Basques, (Minority Rights Group
  Report 9, London, 1977).
Merkl, P. (ed.) Western European Party Systems,
  (The Free Press, New York, 1980).
Mezey, M.L. Comparative Legislatures, (Duke
  University Press, Durham NC, 1979).
Milnor, J. and Franklin M.N. 'Patterns of Opposi-
  tion Behaviour in Modern Legislatures' in
  Kornberg, A. (ed.) Legislatures in Contem-
  porary Perspective, (McKay, New York, 1973).
Mommsen, W. and Hirschfeld, G. Social Protest,
  Violence and Terror in 19th and 20th Century

Europe, (Macmillan and Berg, London, 1982).
Morodo, R. et al. Los Partidos Políticos en España,
    (Editorial Labor, Barcelona, 1979).
Müller-Rommel, F. 'New Social Movements in Smaller
    Parties: A Comparative Perspective', West
    European Politics, vol. 8, no. 1, (1985).
Mushaben, J.M. 'Cycles of Peace Protest in West
    Germany', West European Politics, vol. 8,
    no. 1, (1985)
Narr, W-D, (ed.) Auf dem Wege zum Einparteienstaat,
    (Westdeutscher Verlag, Opladen, 1977).
Naughtie, J. 'The State of the Parties in
    Parliament: the Alliance', The Political
    Quarterley, (1984), pp.369-74.
Nicolet, C. L'idée republicaine en France 1789-
    1924, (Gallimard, Paris, 1982).
Nienhaus, V. 'Konsensuale Gesetzgebung im Deutschen
    Bundestag: Zahlen und Anmerkungen',
    Zeitschrift für Parlamentsfragen, vol. 16,
    no. 2, (1985), pp.163-9.
Norton, P. Dissension in the House of Commons,
    (Clarendon, Oxford, 1980).
—— The Commons in Perspective, (Martin Robertson,
    Oxford, 1981).
Oberreuter, H. (ed.) Parlamentarische Opposition.
    Ein internationaler Vergleich, (Hoffmann &
    Campe, Hamburg, 1975).
Otto, K.A. Vom Ostermarsch zur APO. Geschichte der
    ausserparlamentarischen Opposition in der
    Bundesrepublik, 1960-1970, (Campus,
    Frankfurt/M, 1977).
Panebianco, A. Modelli di partito, (Il Mulino,
    Bologna, 1982).
Pages, P. Transition in Spain, (Transaction Books,
    New Brunswick, 1978).
Parkin, F. Middle Class Radicalism: The Social
    Bases of the British Campaign for Nuclear
    Disarmament, (Manchester University Press,
    Manchester, 1968).
—— Class, Inequality and Political Order,
    (Paladin, London, 1972).
Pasquino, G. 'From Togliatti to the Compromese
    Storico: a party with a governmental vocation'
    in S. Serfaty and L. Gray (eds) The Italian
    Communist Party: Yesterday, Today and
    Tomorrow, (Aldwych Press, London, 1980).
Paterson, W.E. 'Political Parties and the Making of
    Foreign Policy', Review of International
    Studies, vol. 7, no. 4, (1981), pp.227-37.
—— and Thomas, A. (eds) Social Democratic Parties

in Western Europe, (Croom Helm, London, 1977).

Payne, S.G. (ed.) Politics and Society in XXth Century Spain, (New Viewpoints, New York, 1976).

Pen J M. Le Les Français d'abord, (Lafon, Paris, 1984).

Penniman, H. (ed.) The French National Assembly Elections of 1978, (American Enterprise Institute, New York, 1980).

—— (ed.) Italy at the Polls, 1979, (American Enterprise Institute, Washington, DC, 1981).

—— and Eusebio, M-L. (eds) Spain at the Polls 1977, 1979 and 1982, (Duke University Press, Durham NC, 1985).

Peyrefitte, A. Encore un effort, Monsieur le Président, (J.C. Lattès, Paris, 1985).

Pfister, T. A matignon au temps de l'union de la gauche, (Hachette, Paris, 1985).

Pickles, D. Problems of Contemporary French Politics, (Methuen, London, 1982).

Plenel, E. and Rollat, A. L'Effet Le Pen, (Le Monde, Paris, 1984).

Pestalozzi, H. et al. (eds) Frieden in Deutschland. Die Friedensbewegung, (Goldmann, Munich, 1982).

Pizzorno, A. 'Interests and Parties in Pluralism' in S. Berger (ed.) Organising Interests in Western Europe, (Cambridge University Press, London, 1981).

Pollack, B. 'Spain: From Corporate State to Parliamentary Democracy', Parliamentary Affairs, vol. 31, (1978).

—— 'The 1982 Spanish General Election and Beyond', Parliamentary Affairs, vol. 36, (1983).

Potter, A. 'Opposition with a Capital "O"' in R. Dahl, (ed.) Political Oppositions in Western Democracies, (Yale University Press, New Haven, Conn., 1966).

Poulantzas, N. The Crisis of the Dictatorships: Portugal. Spain, Greece, (New Left Books, London, 1976).

Preston, P. 'The PCE's Long Road to Democracy 1954-1979' in R. Kindersley (ed.) In Search of Eurocommunism, (Macmillan, London, 1981).

—— 'The PCE in the Struggle for Democracy in Spain' in H. Machin (ed.) National Communism in Western Europe, (Methuen, London, 1983).

—— The Triumph of Democracy in Spain, (Methuen,

London, 1986).
—— (ed.) Spain in Crisis: The Evolution and
Decline of the Franco Regime, (Harvester,
Brighton, 1976).
Prevost, G. 'Change and Continuity in the Spanish
Labour Movement', West European Politics, vol.
7, no. 1, (1984).
Pridham, G. 'The Government/Opposition Dimension
and the Development of the Party System in the
1970s. The Reappearance of Conflictual Poli-
tics' in H. Döring and G. Smith (eds) Party
Government and Political Culture in Western
Germany, (Macmillan, London, 1982), pp.130-54.
—— (ed.) Coalitional Behaviour in Theory and
Practice: an inductive model for Western
Europe, (Cambridge University Press,
Cambridge, 1986).
Rama, C.M. Ideología, Regiones y Clases Sociales en
la España Contemporánea, (Jucar, Madrid,
1977).
Ranney, A. (ed.) Britain at the Polls 1983,
(American Enterprise Institute, Washington DC,
1985).
Raschke, H-J. Organisierter Konflikt in westeuro-
päischen Parteien, (Westdeutscher Verlag,
Opladen, 1977).
—— 'Soziale Konflikte und Parteiensystem',
Aus Politik und Zeitgeschichte, vol. 49,
(1984).
—— Soziale Bewegungen. Ein historisch-
systematischer Grundriss, (Campus,
Frankfurt/M, 1985).
Rattinger, H. 'The Federal Republic: Much Ado About
(Almost) Nothing' in G. Flynn and H. Rattinger
(eds) The Public and Atlantic Defense, (Croom
Helm, Beckenham, 1985).
Rémond, R. Les droites en France, (Aubier, Paris,
1982).
Reuband, K-H. 'Politisches Selbstverständnis und
Wertorientierungen von Anhängern der Friedens-
bewegung', Zeitschrift für Parlamentsfragen,
vol. 16, no. 1, (1985).
Robertson, D. Class and the British Electorate,
(Blackwell, Oxford, 1984).
Rollet, A. Les Hommes de l'extrême-droite: Le Pen,
Marie, Ortiz et les autres, (Calmann-Levy,
Paris, 1985).
Rose, R. Politics in England, 4th edn, (Faber &
Faber, London, 1985).
—— and McAllister, I. Voters Begin to Choose,

(Sage, London, 1986).
Roth, R. (ed. Parlamentarisches Ritual und
politische Alternativen, (Campus, Frankfurt/M,
1980).
Roussel, D. Les Cas Le Pen, (Lattes, Paris, 1985).
Rowold, M. Im Schatten der Macht. Zur Oppositions-
rolle der nichtetablierten Parteien, (Droste,
Düsseldorf, 1974).
Rupp, H-K. Ausserparlamentarische Opposition in der
Ära Adenauer, 2nd edn, (Pahl Rugenstein,
Cologne, 1980).
Sani, G. 'The Political Culture of Italy:
Continuity and Change' in G. Almond and S.
Verba, (eds) The Civic Culture Revisited,
(Little Brown, Boston, 1980), pp.273-324.
Sarlvik, B. and Crewe, I. Decade of Dealignment:
The Conservative Victory of 1979 and Electoral
Trends in the 1970s, (Cambridge University
Press, Cambridge, 1983).
Sassoon, D. The Strategy of the Italian Communist
Party: from the Resistance to the Historic
Compromise, (Pinter, London, 1981).
Sartori, G. Parties and Party Systems, (Cambridge
University Press, Cambridge, 1976).
Schäfer, W. Neue soziale Bewegungen. Konservativer
Aufbruch im bunten Gewand?, (Fischer,
Frankfurt/M, 1983).
Schendelen M. van (ed.) Consociationalism, Pillar-
ization and Conflict-Management in the Low
Countries, (Acta Politica XIX, Amsterdam,
January 1984).
Schindler, P. Datenhandbuch zur Geschichte des
Deutschen Bundestages 1949-1982, (Presse- und
Informationszentrum des Deutschen Bundestages,
Bonn, 1983).
Schmid, G. 'Zur Soziologie der Friedensbewegung',
Aus Politik und Zeitgeschichte, vol. 24,
(1982).
Schmidt, M. 'Demokratie, Wohlfahrtsstaat und neue
soziale Bewegungen' Aus Politik und
Zeitgeschichte, vol. 11, (1984).
Schmitt, H. et al. 'Etablierte und Grüne. Zur
Verankerung der ökologischen Bewegung in den
Parteiorganisationen von SPD, FDP, CDU und
CSU', Zeitschrift für Parlamentsfragen, vol.
11, no. 4, (1981).
Scholten, I. 'Does Consociationalism Exist? A
Critique of the Dutch Experience' In R. Rose
(ed.) Electoral Participation, (Sage, London,
1980).

Schubert, K. von Wiederbewaffnung und Westintegra-
tion. Die innere Auseinandersetzung um die
militärische und aussenpolitische Orientierung
der Bundesrepublik 1950-1952, (Deutsche
Verlagsanstalt, Stuttgart, 1970).
Schumann, H-G. (ed.) Die Rolle der Opposition in
der Bundesrepublik, (Wissenschaftliche
Buchgesellschaft, Darmstadt, 1976).
Seidel, G. 'Le fascisme dans les textes de la
Nouvelle Droite', Mots 3, (1981).
Share, D. 'Two Transitions: Democratisation and
the Evolution of the Spanish Socialist Left',
West European Politics, vol. 8, no. 1, (1985).
Shell, K. 'Extra-parliamentary Opposition in Post-
war Germany', Comparative Politics, vol. 2,
no. 4, (1970), pp.3-15.
Smith, G. Politics in Western Europe, 2nd edn,
(Macmillan, London, 1976).
—— Democracy in Western Germany, 2nd edn,
(Heinemann, London, 1982).
Steffani, W. (ed.) Parlamentarismus ohne Trans-
parenz, (Westdeutscher Verlag, Opladen, 1971).
Stephenson, H. Claret and Chips, (Michael Joseph,
London, 1982).
Sternberger, D. 'Opposition des Parlaments und
parlamentarische Opposition' in H-G. Schumann,
(ed.) Die Rolle der Opposition in der Bundes-
republik, (Wiss. Buchgesellschaft, Darmstadt,
1976).
Sternhell, Z. La Droite révolutionnaire en France
(1885-1914), (Seuil, Paris, 1978).
Story, J. 'Spanish Political Parties; before and
after the Elections', Government and Opposi-
tion, 12 (1977), pp.474-93.
—— 'El pacto para la libertad: the Spanish
Communist Party' in P.F. della Torre et al.
(eds) Eurocommunism: Myth or Reality?,
(Penguin, Harmondsworth, 1979), pp.149-88.
Tamburrano, G. Perché solo in Italia No, (Laterza,
Bari, 1983).
Thayssen, U. 'Mehrheitsfindung im Föderalismus:
Thesen zum Konsensualismus der westdeutschen
Politik', Aus Politik und Zeitgeschichte, vol.
35, (1985), pp.3-17.
The Times, Guide to the House of Commons, (Times
Books, London, 1984).
Tosi, S. 'Italy: Anti-system Opposition within the
System', Government and Opposition, (October,
1966).
—— 'Systemkonträre Opposition und Stabilität des

Regierungssystems: oppositionelles Verhalten
in Italien' in H. Oberreuter (ed.) Parliamen-
tarische Opposition. Ein internationaler
Vergleich, (Hoffmann & Campe, Hamburg, 1975).
Touraine, A. L'après-socialisme, (Grasset, Paris,
1980).
Troisième Colloque International de Lexicologie
politique, (Ecole Normale Supérieure de St.
Cloud. 1984).
Vaughan, M. 'Nouvelle Droite: Cultural Power and
Political Influence' in D.S. Bell (ed.)
Contemporary French Political Parties, (Croom
Helm, London, 1982).
Veen, H-J. Opposition im Bundestag. Ihre
Funktionen, institutionellen Handlungs-
bedingungen und das Verhalten der CDU/CSU
Fraktion in der 6. Wahlperiode, (Bundes-
zentrale fur politische Bildung, Bonn, 1976).
—— 'Wer wählt grün?', Aus Politik und
Zeitgeschichte, vol. 35-36, (1984).
Vial, P. Pour une renaissance culturelle: le GRECE
prend la parole, (Copernic, Paris, 1979).
Vis, J. 'Coalition Government in a Constitutional
Monarchy' in V. Bogdanor (ed.), Coalition
Government in Western Europe, (Heinemann,
London, 1983).
Vogt, H. Parlamentarische und ausserparlamen-
tarische Opposition, (Leske, Opladen, 1972).
Wheare, K.C. Legislatures, (Oxford University
Press, London, 1968).
Whiteley, P. The Labour Party in Crisis, (Methuen,
London, 1983).
Wiesendahl, E. Parteien und Demokratie, (Leske,
Opladen, 1980).
Williams, P. 'The Labour Party: The Rise of the
Left' in H. Berrington (ed.) Change in British
Politics, (Cass, London, 1984), pp.26-55.
Wilson, F. French Political Parties under the Fifth
Republic, (Praeger, New York, 1982.
Wilson, F.L. and Wiste, R. 'Party Cohesion in the
French National Assembly 1958-1973', Legisla-
tive Studies Quarterly, (1976), pp.467-90.
Wolinetz, S. 'The Dutch Labour Party' in
W. Paterson and A. Thomas (eds), Social
Democratic Parties in Western Europe, (Croom
Helm, London, 1977).
Wollmann, H. Die Stellung der Parlamentsminder-
heiten in England, der Bundesrepublik Deutsch-
land und Italien, (Nijhoff, The Hague, 1970).
Worcester, R. and Harrop, M. (eds) Political

Communications: The General Election Campaign of 1979, (Allen & Unwin, London, 1982).

Wright, V. The Government and Politics of France, (Hutchinson, London, 1978).

Zeuner, B. 'Parlamentarisierung der Grünen' Prokla, vol. 15, no. 4, (1985), pp.5-22.

Index